AF673123

Wildlife In and Around CORBETT TIGER RESERVE

Rajesh Chaudhary

Vinesh Kumar

NIYOGI BOOKS

Published by
NIYOGI BOOKS
Block D, Building No. 77,
Okhla Industrial Area, Phase I,
New Delhi-110 020, INDIA
Tel: 91-11-26816301, 26818960
Email: niyogibooks@gmail.com
Website: www.niyogibooksindia.com

Editor: K.E. Priyamvada
Design: Shashi Bhushan Prasad
Digital art work: Vinesh Kumar
Sketch work: Suresh Lal

ISBN: 978-81-964053-6-6
Publication: 2023

Printed at Niyogi Offset Pvt. Ltd., New Delhi, India

Lt. Colonel, Edward James Corbett
(25 July 1875–19 April 1955)
Naturalist, Conservationist, Writer, and Philanthrope

'A country's fauna is a sacred trust, and I appeal to you not to betray this trust...

If we do not bestir ourselves now, it will be to our discredit that the fauna of our province was exterminated in our generation and under our very eyes, while we looked on and never raised a finger to prevent it...'

CONTENTS

Interior of Sal forest during springs

डा० समीर सिन्हा भा.व.से.
प्रमुख वन संरक्षक (वन्यजीव) एवं मुख्य वन्यजीव प्रतिपालक
उत्तराखण्ड

Dr. Samir Sinha I.F.S.
PCCF (Wildlife) & Chief Wildlife Warden
Uttarakhand

FOREWORD

Corbett Tiger Reserve (CTR), the Land of Roar, Trumpet and Song is one of India's iconic wilderness areas globally acknowledged for its scenic beauty and assemblage of floral and faunal species. Mainland Asia's first National Park established in 1936 and launch site of Project Tiger on 1st April 1973, Corbett has a long history of scientific wildlife management and many significant conservation milestones to its name. Corbett Tiger Reserve, which today includes the Corbett National Park, the Sonanadi Wildlife Sanctuary and the surrounding Reserve Forests, spreads over 1288.31 sq. km. and has been notified on 26th February 2010 as a Tiger Reserve by the Government of Uttarakhand. It is also a shining example of a region seeped into conservation awareness and respect for nature since times immemorial.

Corbett Tiger Reserve occupies a special place in the hearts of all who hold the cause of conservation dear. Every year, a large number of Indian and international visitors come to soak into the delightful charms that Mother Nature has on offer here. Many are repeat visitors who were introduced to Corbett by their elder generations and take delight in coming here again and again with their younger family and friends. Many also make time to visit nearby areas in the Ramnagar and Terai West Forest Divisions such as Sitabani, Powalgarh Conservation Reserve and Phanto.

Sometimes visitors to Corbett and nearabout are primed for just that one wild experience- the sighting of the tiger, of which over 250 find a home here! While the sight of our national animal is indeed a memory to cherish, it is by far not the only treasure on offer here. The mosaic of tall sal forests along with its associates, riverine forests and grasslands, rivers and lake are home to a complex web of plant and animal life including various rare, threatened and endangered species. Corbett is home to over 700+ species of birds of the over 1300 species reported from India and this also makes it a very special birding destination both for the expert and the budding birder.

This delightful book by Sri Rajesh Chaudhary and Sri Vinesh Kumar is a welcome addition to publications on Corbett Tiger Reserve. As a photographic guide book, it leads the reader through the unique charms of this wonderland, introducing them not only to the natural and historical setting of this place but also to many of its denizens. As a guidebook, it provides handy tips on identification of various species of plants, mammals, reptiles, amphibians, butterflies etc. as also techniques for their photography. Without being too technical or overbearing, it gently guides the reader to better understand and appreciate nature and the web of life. The segments on the life of a Dung Beetle, honey bees and the Termite Mound as a marvel of nature add a special flavour to it.

I am sure this All-in-One Guide will find favour with visitors who wish to make their trip more meaningful. It will also be a useful reference to everyone with an interest in Corbett.

I once again congratulate the authors on their labour of love.

21/4/23

(Dr. Samir Sinha)
PCCF Wildlife and
Chief Wildlife Warden,
Uttarakhand

85, राजपुर रोड, देहरादून – 248001 (उत्तराखण्ड)
ई–मेल : cwlw-forest-uk@nic.in
फोन : 0135-2742884, 0135-2745122
फैक्स : 0135-2745691

85, Rajpur Road, Dehradun - 248001 (Uttarakhand)
Email : cwlw-forest-uk@nic.in
Ph. : 0135-2742884, 0135-2745122
Fax : 0135-2745691

PREFACE

The forests of Corbett Tiger Reserve (CTR) are among 32% of the planet's green areas, which are called 'Virgin Forests' or technically 'Primary Forests'. In the popular sense, primary forests are naturally grown forests that have never been significantly disturbed by human activity since their origin, possibly hundreds, thousands or maybe even millions of years ago. These forests are rich repositories of the earth's biodiversity, harbouring many new species waiting to be discovered. According to the Food and Agriculture Organization, worldwide, the area under primary forests has shrunk by over 80 million hectares since 1990. Creating forest cover by planting trees is not a substitute for primary forests, and as the most intelligent creature of the planet, it is the responsibility of humans to protect this natural heritage.

Leisure outings to places with ample flora and fauna are growing in popularity by leaps and bounds. At CTR, nature is at its fullest glory, and one can bask in the invigorating effect of nature on the mind and body. It is at Corbett Tiger Reserve, where the concept of 'conservation of nature' first originated in the country and got translated into reality. It narrates the success story of conservation of the natural world by the participation of local stakeholders. The flourishing ecotourism here that attracts lakhs of national and international tourists every year has played a key role in the economic development of the surrounding areas and better livelihoods for the local people.

Way back in January 2016, after we had explored the dry-deciduous forest of Ranthambhore Tiger Reserve, we began visiting CTR with the same intention. It would not have taken more than a couple of visits to feel that this forest at the foothills of the Himalayas is full of life. And, there is plenty of nature to observe, to listen, to imbibe, and to photograph. Yet, every safari trip ends in tiger-talks among visitors. Our instant reaction was, to portray less sought after natural treasures of CTR!

Of the several challenges we came across during six years of exploration, getting a night stay permit had been always the toughest job. Safariing for trees, herbs, butterflies, and birds were the most unforgettable events. We repeatedly visited ecotourism zones to collect photographs, and other data on biodiversity of CTR. There may still be a long way to go before a complete account of flora and fauna of CTR is documented. Nevertheless, the book presents flora and fauna that are most likely to be spotted in various ecotourism zones. We wish to apprise the readers that most of the photographs in the book have been clicked in the CTR or its vicinity.

The Covid-19 pandemic delayed the publication of this book. However, the lockdown period facilitated ample discussions with naturalists and experts to improve its content. We are hopeful that our work will augment the experience of those visiting Corbett Tiger Reserve, and offer them an in-depth understanding of this precious natural ecosystem.

Rajesh Chaudhary and Vinesh Kumar

OVERVIEW OF THE BOOK

Scope

This guidebook, while being a photographic 'guidebook', also provides information on several aspects of the natural world. The book has been curated for Corbett Tiger Reserve (CTR) visitors who wish to explore wildlife beyond tigers. To make the content easy to assimilate for beginners or non-biologists, information has been provided in a simple and easy to understand manner. For the very same reason, several technical words have been avoided and replaced with easier and simpler words. The very idea behind this book is to arouse the wildlife enthusiasts' curiosity to learn about nature holistically.

The habitats, plant and animal species are quite similar across the foothills of the Himalayas in the state of Uttarakhand. This book, therefore, can also be a great companion for the visitors who wish to explore such other protected areas in the Himalayan foothills like Rajaji Tiger Reserve.

Sources of Information Used

Years of surveys in ecotourism zones of CTR and its neighbouring forested areas, and invaluable inputs from naturalists who have closely observed the wildlife and vegetation in the area, are the main sources of information provided in the book. In addition, the content has been enhanced by consulting the best books available on the natural world, scientific communications, and authentic online resources. Most of the images presented in the book have been clicked inside the CTR and its neighbouring forests.

Content Arrangement

The main body of the book has three parts, and each part has multiple sections. The first part 'Prelude' offers information on the natural and historical settings of CTR and on the naming and identification of organisms. This part helps in creating a backdrop image of CTR, as well as basic concepts pertaining to scientific naming and identification of plant and animal species.

The second part 'Animals and Plants' provides photographs and identifying features of over 700 species of animals (including mammals, birds, reptiles, amphibians, butterflies, etc.), and plants, which are likely to be sighted in CTR, and its vicinity. This part makes it easy to identify the species seen in the wild, and also offers a glimpse of their natural behaviour.

The third part 'Visiting CTR' provides information such as safari route maps and visuals of each ecotourism zone, and also the places of interest close to CTR. This part could be really useful as a quick reference for the readers who wish to plan a visit to CTR. A list of selected literature that can be consulted for further information has been provided at the end of this book.

Early morning at Dhikala

Denoting Various Animals and Plants

Animals and plants mentioned in the book have been denoted by common English names as their primary names, and by their scientific names (Italics) up to the species level (Binomial name). In cases where common English names were not available, Hindi names, local names or even the first part of their scientific names (Genus) have been used as primary names. Wherever satisfactory identification of organisms is not feasible up to the species level, only the generic name (Genus) has been given as the scientific name.

The mentioned abundance/status of animals and plants in each ecotourism zone is based on the frequency of sighting and not on their actual density in that area. The chance of sighting an animal or plant increases if there is some prior knowledge of their habitat and behaviour.

Maps and Route Maps of Various Ecotourism Zones of the CTR

To make it easy to visualize the natural ambience in the ecotourism zones, a safari route map of each zone has been provided—it is dotted with visuals of the landscapes. Such a presentation is intended to help visitors in selecting the desired ecotourism zone. However, the readers of this guidebook may kindly note that the maps and safari route maps provided herein are indicative only, and the boundaries are approximations. Minor tracks in the ecotourism zones have not been shown in the maps. The Forest Department may temporarily alter or prohibit certain stretches of the safari routes and may also change the entry gate to a particular zone.

Naming Various Habitats

Various types of habitats found in the CTR, and its neighbouring forested areas, have been denoted as follows:

Densely forested areas: ▲ stretches of forest where trees are close to one another and their merging crowns prevent most of the direct sunlight from reaching the ground.

Thinly forested areas: ▲ stretches of forest where trees stand far from one another and most of the area of the forest floor is illuminated by direct sunlight.

Fringes of forest: ▲ the outer edges of forest or a place where the continuity of the forest is broken by grassland, river, scrubs, etc.

Scrub: ▲ a stretch with distantly placed short-statured trees and bushes.

Grassland: ▲ an open stretch with tall or short grasses.

Marshy areas: ▲ low-lying waterlogged areas with grassy vegetation, such as certain areas along rivers and large waterbodies.

Prelude

Natural and Historical Settings

Corbett Tiger Reserve (CTR), containing Corbett National Park, is situated in the foothills of the Himalayas in the state of Uttarakhand. Pristine jungle and grasslands of CTR are home to scores of wild animals. Beautiful meandering rivers and countless springs with pure sparkling water sustain the life. CTR and its flanking forested area lie in 'Terai Arc Landscape'—a landscape with distinctive flora and fauna. In close apposition to the CTR is the small town of Ramnagar and many hamlets of mythological and historical significance.

Bygones

CTR and its vicinity contains places of mythological and historical importance. Remains of the ancient city of Vairatpattan scattered inside CTR, Sitabani Temple, the historical town of Ramnagar, and over 100-year-old Forest Rest House Bungalows built during the colonial period remind us of the past.

PC: SC

Historic carved stones

PC: SC

Sitabani Temple

The Land Sculpture

For the most part, CTR rests in the lap of the Shivalik hills. A major expanse of the reserve is enclosed by ridges and is bisected by a central ridge running from east to west. The slopes of ridges give rise to several small springs (locally called *sot, nullas* or *gadher*). River Ramganga enters the CTR by cutting the ridge from the northern boundary and exits from a cut at Kalagarh at the southern boundary. The average altitude of the reserve increases from the south to the north; the zones close to the southern boundary including Jhirna, Dhela and Pakhro have a lower average altitude than those in the northern parts such as Dhikala, Durgadevi and Sonanadi zones. The highest point of the reserve is about 1,100 m, which is near Kanda in the north. The landscape of the reserve, a blend of cliffs, slopes, gorges, valleys, duns, rivers, springs and a vast reservoir (Ramganga reservoir), is a visual treat for anyone who can appreciate the little gifts of nature. Wide grasslands with hills in the backdrop, herds of grazers, looping rivers, sunlight filtering through dense woods, dramatic sunset and sunrise are some of the beautiful sights seen in CTR.

The Realm of the Himalayas—from Sky-high Snow-clad Peaks to Foothills

The province of the Himalayas consists of parallel mountain ranges: the northern-most and the highest 'Greater Himalayas'; lower 'Middle or Lesser Himalayas', and; the lowest and southern-most 'Outer Himalayas' or 'Shivalik Ranges'. Breathtaking snow-clad peaks of Uttarakhand, such as the mighty *Nanda Devi, Trishul, Chaukhamba,* etc., are a part of the Greater Himalayas. Famous hill stations such as Nainital, Almora and Ranikhet lie in the Middle Himalayas. The hilly terrain one sees to the immediate north of the town of Ramnagar is a part of the Shivalik Ranges. Shivaliks, which form the foothills of Himalayas, are bound on the south by a narrow, levelled terrain called 'Bhabar' composed of gravels and boulders overlain with a thin layer of soil. South of Bhabar lies the marshy strip of 'Terai' area which merges with the 'Great Plains' or the Indo-Gangetic Plains of India.

Within the Shivalik hills, there are flat expanses called *'duns'* or *'doons'* (valley); these represent places where, over millions of years, rivers have unloaded sediments carried by them from the higher reaches. Dehradun and Patlidun (in Dhikala zone) are examples of duns.

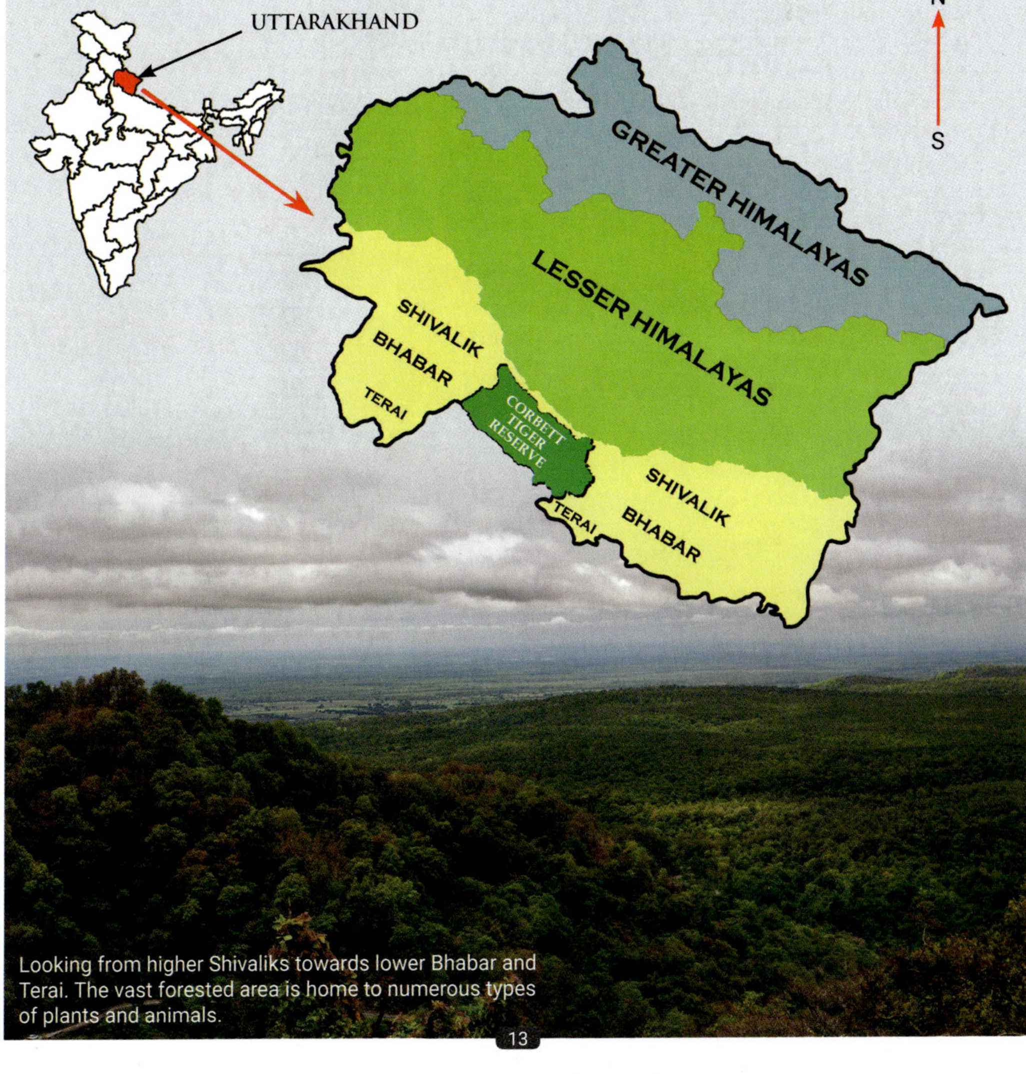

Looking from higher Shivaliks towards lower Bhabar and Terai. The vast forested area is home to numerous types of plants and animals.

Shivaliks—the Favourite Haunt of Animals from Times Immemorial

Shivaliks, with altitude ranging from 600–1,200 m, are made up of loosely packed boulders, pebbles, mud-stones, etc. The face of the Shivalik terrain, as we see today, has evolved over the last 16 million years. Sediment deposition by rivers descending from higher reaches of the Himalayas, movements and uplifting of land, and carving due to erosion by water have together shaped the Shivaliks.

Throughout its evolutionary journey, the Shivaliks harboured a wealth of flora and fauna. The liveable conditions here lured several ancient animals resembling modern-day hippos, horses, cattle, elephants and giraffes from various parts of Africa and Asia. Over the years, the change in climate, however, caused a turnover of the vegetation and the types of animals found here. Early Shivaliks were clothed with dense forests, swamps and lakes (due to the warm and humid conditions), housing crocodiles, turtles, gharials, hippos, rhinos, monkeys, elephants, etc. With the passage of time, the climate grew drier and resulted in the appearance of grasslands which invited grazers.

Terai Arc Landscape

Terai Arc Landscape (TAL) is a strip of land rich in flora and fauna. It is about 800 km long (west to east), 50–60 km wide (north to south), and stretches between River Bagmati in the east and River Yamuna in the west, covering the states of Uttarakhand, Uttar Pradesh and Bihar (along the border of India and Nepal). It is a remnant of a vast area which was once covered with tall grasslands and dense forests. The total area of TAL is 49,500 km^2 of which 30,000 km^2 lie in India. There are many famous protected areas that fall within TAL, including Rajaji Tiger Reserve, Corbett Tiger Reserve and Dudhwa Tiger Reserve in India; and Bardia Wildlife Sanctuary and Chitwan National Park in Nepal. The protected areas in TAL are connected to each other via corridors. These corridors allow easy movement of animals from one protected area to another in search of mates, to establish new territory and for food and water. A few noteworthy animals of TAL include the Greater One-horned Rhinoceros, Asian Elephant, Bengal Tiger, Swamp Deer, Gangetic Dolphin, Marsh Crocodile, Gharial, Hog Deer, Rusty-spotted Cat, Fishing Cat, Leopard Cat and Sarus Crane.

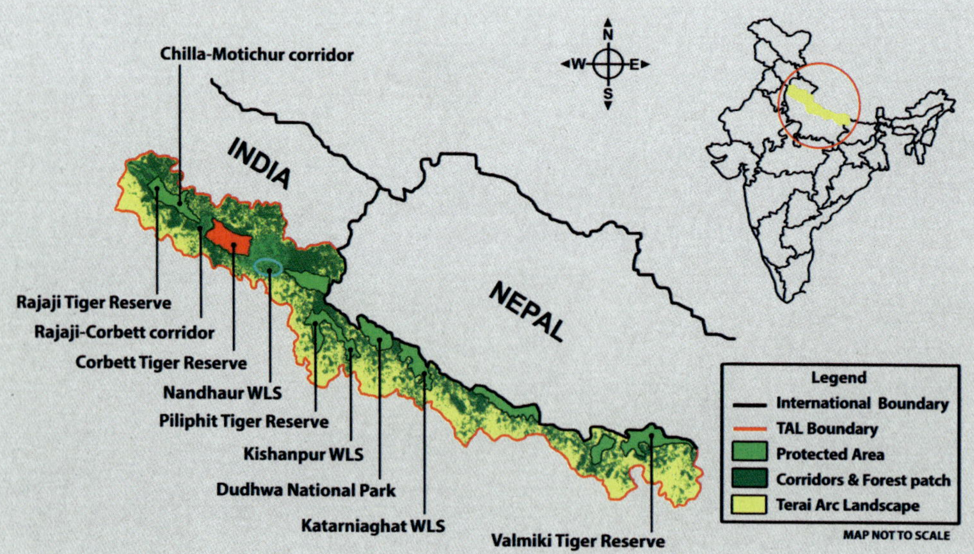

The Terai Arc Landscape

The Plant Life

The undulating terrain of CTR is covered with forested areas, scrubs and grasslands. In these habitats grow scores of trees, shrubs, herbs, climbers, grasses, ferns, mosses, etc. Sal is the most abundant tree in CTR. The interior of dense Sal woods with glances of sprinkles of sunshine is worth witnessing! One also comes across more dense and moist forested areas (composed of mixed varieties of trees) with crisscrossing rills. These moist forested portions have luxuriant green growth of mosses, ferns, climbers, etc. Dense forested areas often merge with stretches having loosely packed trees of mixed varieties. Pure tracts of *Khair* and *Sheesham* trees (Khair-Sisso forest) are seen covering beds of rivers and streams. CTR is dotted with several vast grasslands or *'chaurs'*. These grasslands are often encircled by dense forests. At some places, scrubby areas with distantly placed short and thorny trees, and bushes, allow for a smooth transition from forest to grassland.

A seasonal variation in appearance of vegetation is quite noticeable in CTR. During late winters (December–February), many trees begin to show signs of leaf fall. A majority of trees shed their old leaves in spring and early summer (March–April) and quickly renew. Spring and early summer is also the time when most trees reveal their flowers.

After remaining plain-looking throughout the winters, the herbs and shrubs covering the floor of the forest, and scrubs, begin a display of their gorgeous flowers at the onset of spring till early winters. During spring and summers, flowers of *Bhant, Kamini* and *Kari patta* fill the forest with a bouquet of sweet aromas. During rainy season, the ground has a complete green cover with scattered colourful wild flowers.

Technically, the major forest types seen in CTR and its neighbouring areas have been classified as: Northern Moist Deciduous Forests (Sub-Group 3C), covering most part of the CTR, Northern Tropical Dry Deciduous Forests (Sub-Group 5B) and Himalayan Subtropical Pine Forests (Group 9).

Sal trees in new leaves

Patlidun

Vast flat expanse of Patlidun around Dhikala

Patlidun (local, *patli*: narrow+*dun*: valley) is the name given to the narrow flat expanse along the River Ramganga. The grasslands that one sees around Tourist Complex in Dhikala are a part of Patlidun. During the early 19th century, Patlidun was under cultivation by the *Bhuksas* of Garhwal. Noticing the destruction of the Sal forest due to over-grazing and fire, Henry Ramsay (p.18) put a stop to cultivation in 1861–62 and shifted villagers and cultivators to an alternate place.

Ramganga River

Meandering Ramganga in Patlidun valley

It originates from the slopes of *Dudhatoli Dhar* hills near the town Gairsain (about 150 km from Ramnagar) in the middle Himalayas. As the river advances, it is joined by several smaller springs and rivers. It enters CTR near Durgadevi zone; here, it is joined by the River Mandal. And, as Ramganga meanders through Patlidun, it is joined by two more rivers—Palain and Sonanadi (called so, as gold was extracted from its sand; Hindi: *'sona'* means gold) at Ramganga reservoir near Dhikala. Ramganga exits CTR at Kalagarh where a hydroelectric dam (Kalagarh or Ramganga Dam) was constructed in the year 1974. The vast Ramganga reservoir is a result of obstruction of Ramganga by the dam. Ramganga finally joins the holy Ganga river near Kannauj in the state of Uttar Pradesh. The length of Ramganga from its origin to the final confluence with Ganga is about 596 km.

The Chaurs—Grasslands Among Woods

Chaurs (Local, *'Chaur'*: flat open land) are patches of tall grasslands found at the foothills of the Himalayas. These are usually surrounded by forested areas. Chaurs offer several species of grasses which are excellent food for grazers (deer and elephants). These grasslands are also the habitat for many species of birds and reptiles. The chaurs are managed judiciously by the Forest Department. Unwanted weeds (such as *Lantana*) are removed and the grass is regularly burnt or cut. This practice causes the emergence of fresh sprouts of grass that attract the grazers. Burning also prevents the invasion of chaurs by trees and protects the grasslands from being replaced by the forest.

Spectacular chaurs that lie in ecotourism zones include: Dhikala, Phulai and Khinnanauli chaurs (Dhikala zone), Machan chaur (Bijrani zone), Ringora chaur (Garjia zone) and Laldhang chaur (Dhela and Jhirna zones). Best of these are the chaurs in Dhikala zone (spreading over Patlidun), which are also the showpiece of CTR.

Dhikala chaur

The Animal Life

Undisturbed place to live

Plenty of water to drink

The diversity of habitats in CTR, and year-round availability of food and water ensure a high density of different varieties of herbivores and their predators. Being located at the interface of Gangetic Plains and higher Himalayas, one can also sight in CTR, a few animals characteristic of these two regions. CTR is amongst those forests in India which possess a high density of tigers. The mosaic of grassland and forest along Ramganga river is the favourite congregation point of Asian Elephants. Here, they get all that is needed to sustain—unlimited fodder and water, and mud for cooling their body. CTR attracts a large number of birds and is a paradise for birdwatchers. There are songs and chirps, tweets and flutes all around. All the major rivers of CTR are home to large reptiles such as crocodile and Gharial, fishes, amphibians, and certain mammals such as otters. Not just the large animals, varieties of insects such as butterflies, moths, beetles, bees, dragonflies and damselflies, and spiders are also abundant in CTR and its neighbouring forested areas. The animal life found in CTR and surrounding forested area is typical of Terai Arc Landscape (p.14).

Ample supply of forage

Kosi River

View of Kosi river

This river originates from the *Dharpanidhar* hill located near the famous tourist destination Kausani. While descending from the hills, the river is joined by several small streams; it stems from the Himalayas at 'Kosi Barrage' near Ramnagar and enters the Great Plains. Kosi finally merges with River Ramganga in Rampur district in Uttar Pradesh. The total length of Kosi is 240 km. Kosi, although seemingly gentle in other seasons, carries a large volume of water flowing with great velocity during the monsoon. The violent flow of the river has caused extensive damage to human habitations along its bank.

Tumaria Reservoir

PC: NZ
View of Ramnagar town

It is located on the southern boundary of CTR. The formation of the reservoir is the result of a dam constructed in 1961–62 (and an extension dam constructed in 1969–70). It collects water from the Dhela and Phika rivers. The reservoir is a resort to several species of winter migrant birds and a breeding place for several resident birds.

Ramnagar

This small hamlet in the Nainital district was established by Henry Ramsay in 1850, and was named after him. This scenic Bhabar town at the foothills of Himalayas was an important mart for hill and forest produce, and was the place where large fairs and *Ramlilas* were organised. *Bhotia* traders used to sell wool and borax, brought in from Tibet. Ramnagar was an important part of a pilgrimage route—pilgrims on their way back to the plains from Badrinath used to pass via Ramnagar. The town was connected with Moradabad by railways in 1907. Today this small town still preserves its simplicity and importance, and is the gateway for tourists visiting CTR or seeking weekend leisure in the lap of nature.

Henry Ramsay

Sir Henry Ramsay

Henry Ramsay was the Commissioner of Kumaon from 1856–1884. He was a cousin of Lord Dalhousie, and one of the most prominent administrators of Kumaon during the British period. He came to Kumaon as a British army officer in 1837 and married the daughter of G.T. Lushington—the then Commissioner of Kumaon. Prior to his appointment as the Commissioner, Ramsay also worked as the Assistant Commissioner for a decade-and-a-half (1840–56). One of his most notable contributions was the development of infrastructure such as roads and canals, along with a big boost to education, health and economy, particularly in Bhabar and Terai areas of Kumaon. The town of Ranikhet came up during his tenure, which Lord Mayo (the then Viceroy of India) wished to connect with the railways. Ramsay was the pioneer in forest administration and the first Conservator of Forests in the area.

Ramsay was known as the 'King of Kumaon' to the English and as *'Ramji Sahib'* to the local people. He had friendly relations with locals and could speak Kumaoni language. He loved Kumaon very much, and even after his retirement from the service in 1884, he stayed on in Almora till 1892. It is said that he did not want to leave and cried while leaving Kumaon.

Frederick Walter Champion—The Pioneering Wildlife Photographer of India

Frederick Walter Champion was born in 1893 in Surrey, United Kingdom, in a family of prominent naturalists. Since childhood, he liked exploring his natural surroundings, and developed a passion for wildlife photography. F.W. Champion's initial objects of photography were birds. Compared to today's fast and automatic digital cameras, photographing animals in those days with simple cameras was a frustrating task. At the age of 17, he could photograph a nightjar at its nest—something he had wanted to do since long. Champion was fascinated by the flashlight photographs of wild animals taken by C.G. Schillings, one of the pioneers of flashlight photography of animals.

F.W. Champion

In 1913, F.W. Champion joined the Indian Police, and when World War I broke out, he joined the Indian Army. Subsequently, in 1920s, he joined the Indian Forest Service and took charge of the area which presently houses the Corbett and Rajaji Tiger Reserves. It is here that he entered the Indian forests with his camera. Champion Road and Champion Pool in CTR have been named after him. In 1947, he retired from the service and moved to Africa. In 1955, he settled in Scotland. F.W. Champion passed away in 1970.

F.W. Champion was amongst the earliest persons in India who advocated wildlife conservation at a time when it was a matter of great pride and pleasure to kill wild animals. He did promote the shooting of animals but with a camera and not with a gun.

F.W. Champion was the pioneer of wildlife photography in India—the first person in the country who entered the Indian jungles with a camera to explore wildlife. Photographing animals in the night using flash light and tripwire was his favourite mode of photography. He believed that for animals which are active in the night (such as tigers), daytime images are representative of the half asleep tigers and not of their real, dreadful mood at night.

Hardships notwithstanding, F.W. Champion could obtain magnificent photographs of tigers and other creatures in their completely natural mood. Some of his photographs uncovered the secret moments of animals, which were not possible to observe otherwise.

Present day Corbett National Park and Rajaji National Park were F.W. Champion's studios where he captured spectacular poses of a number of wild animals. Jim Corbett mentions in his book *Man-eaters of Kumaon* that F.W. Champion's work inspired him to photograph tigers.

Modern camera traps are a refined version of the tripwire method used by F.W. Champion some hundred years back. Further, the fact that stripes/patterns can be used to identify the individual tigers (p.44) was first mentioned by F.W. Champion. Today, these two principles are at the heart of the mainstream methods for counting tigers and other cryptic animals.

Portrait of a Tiger by F.W. Champion using tripwire, c. 1926

Photo courtesy: James Champion

Corbett Tiger Reserve Comes into Existence

Since ages, the vast forests of the Himalayan foothills were the property of ruling parties. Forests were exploited for various products such as herbs, resins, dyes, timber and fuel, but on a smaller scale. After defeating the *Gurkhas* in 1815, the British took control over Kumaon and the next few decades saw a reckless cutting of trees due to the increased demand for timber and fuel. The gravity of the problem was realised by a few administrators including Henry Ramsay in the late 1850s. In the subsequent years, with the Forest Act in place, felling of trees was done in a regulated manner. However, the increasing demand of wood for infrastructure development and as a fuel in industries and railways across the country continued to ensure a constant pressure on the pristine forest.

Photo: archival letter and map (above and below), as displayed at Dhikala Tourist Complex

The condition of wildlife was no different. Himalayan foothills and their adjacent areas were known to be home to wild animals such as elephants, tigers, deer, etc., and it had sparse human population. The destruction of forests, expanding agriculture and rising human population exerted pressure on wildlife too. Shooting of big game such as tigers, leopards and deer as recreational activity was popular among the British army officials and civil officers. Animals were also killed for their body parts and meat, and to protect crops from being raided by them.

A few persons including two forest officers E.R. Stevens and E.A. Smythies realised the need to protect the dwindling wildlife and put forth the proposal to establish a sanctuary in 1916 and 1917, which was not entertained by the then Commissioner Percy Wyndham. Later, this idea was pushed by F.W. Champion and Jim Corbett. These conservationists could succeed in convincing Malcolm Hailey, the then Governor of United Provinces, to declare over 300 km^2 area as a sanctuary in 1934 for five years, in which the shooting of animals was prohibited. With the passing of the National Parks Bill, the area was upgraded as a National Park in 1936 and was named Hailey National Park—the first National Park of India.

After its inception, the park saw several conservational events. For a brief period (1952–57), the park bore the name Ramganga National Park. It finally got its present name 'Corbett National Park' in 1957. In the year 1966, the area of the park was increased to 520.8 km^2. In the year 1973, the park became the venue for the launch of Project Tiger.

Today, Corbett National Park, Sonanadi Wildlife Sanctuary and the neighbouring conserved forested areas are clubbed together as 'Corbett Tiger Reserve' with the total protected area of 1,288.31km^2 (core area 821.99 km^2 and buffer 466.32 km^2) spreading over three districts of Uttarakhand, *viz.*, Nainital, Almora (Kumaon Division) and Pauri (Garhwal Division).

Scientific Naming and Identification of Organisms

There is a sense of achievement and satisfaction when the scores of distinct-looking 'life-forms' encountered in the wilderness are also identified. Most likely, one would come across those life-forms or species which have already been described and named in the literature. Identification, naming, and classification of various species, is based on certain rules, agreements and concepts developed by scientists. And, one must be familiar with the basics in order to assign an 'ID' (identity) to various animals and plants sighted.

Basics of Nomenclature and Classification of Species

In the most popular sense, to assign an ID to a life-form means to identify it, preferably up to the species rank.

The millions of distinct life-forms found on the earth need to be named and arranged based on their evolutionary history and relatedness. This is important from a conservation point of view and for other scientific studies. Classification or arrangement of organisms is similar to arranging thousands of books on diverse topics in a library on the basis of their relatedness (e.g. subject wise), so that books on similar topics can be found in one section. Organisms are classified in a hierarchical system; they are grouped on the basis of certain common features (such as appearance). And, individuals within a group which is ranked higher (such as phylum) in the classification system, have fewer features in common than a group ranked lower in the order (such as species).

For instance, scientific classification of the 'Tiger' is as follows:

Phylum: *Chordata* (Includes all the animals with an internal skeletal rod called 'notochord' such as fishes, amphibians, reptiles, birds, and mammals)

Class: *Mammalia* (Includes all the mammals, such as kangaroos, cats, dogs, cattle, bats, whales, deer, etc.)

Order: *Carnivora* (Includes flesh eating mammals, such as cats, dogs, mongooses, bears, otters, etc.)

Family: *Felidae* (Includes all the cats, such as Domestic Cat, Leopard, Tiger, Lion, etc.)

Genus: *Panthera* (Includes large cats, such as Tiger, Lion, Leopard and Jaguar)

Species: *tigris* (Includes all tigers of the world: Bengal Tiger, Sumatran Tiger, Malayan Tiger, Siberian Tiger, Indochinese Tiger and South China Tiger)

Species is the lowest rank in the classification system. All individuals of a given species are similar to each other in most aspects and thus represent one 'life-form'. Individuals from the same species can interbreed and produce fertile offspring, whereas individuals from two different species cannot do so. However, there are a few exceptions to this rule, for example, Golden Jackal and Domestic Dog are two distinct but closely related species that are known to crossbreed and produce fertile cubs.

What is a subspecies?

Individuals of a species living in different geographical areas may differ slightly from each other in appearance; these are called 'Subspecies' or 'Geographical Races'. When two subspecies come in contact with each other they can mate and produce fertile offspring. For instance, the two subspecies of tigers—the one living in India and another in Siberian region—differ slightly in appearance, and when brought in contact with each other can interbreed and produce fertile offspring.

Naming of species:

The scientific name of each species has two words; the first word indicates its 'genus' and the second its 'species'. This is called 'Binomial or Two-part Nomenclature'. Sometimes, a third word is added to indicate the subspecies—'Trinomial or Three-part Nomenclature'. Thus, the genus of Tiger is ***Panthera*** and species ***tigris***, therefore its binomial name is ***Panthera tigris***. The subspecies of Tiger found in India is denoted as '***tigris***' and Siberian subspecies as '***altaica***'. Therefore, the trinomial name of the Indian Tiger is ***Panthera tigris tigris*** and that of the Siberian Tiger is ***Panthera tigris altaica.*** In the present book, organisms have been denoted by their binomial names. As a rule, the scientific names of organisms are always italicized. Also, the first letter of the genus name is always capitalized and that of species is written in small letters.

Identification of Species

One can easily make out tigers and leopards as two different life-forms or species simply by comparing the pattern of colouration on fur, and size and shape of the body. In many other cases the difference between two species, however, is not always clear cut. Take the example of Tawny Pipit and Paddyfield Pipit, these two species of birds look quite alike, and to distinguish them, a careful examination is needed. In several other cases, it is not possible to delineate two individuals seen in the field as two separate species with satisfaction, solely on the basis of external appearance (body colouration pattern, etc.). So, delineation of species simply on the basis of appearance sometimes may lead to errors in identification.

How many species are there on earth today?

According to an estimate, it is expected that there are about 8.7 million species on the earth including 7.77 million species of animals. Over 2 million species have been catalogued so far. In India, about 1,00,000 species of animals and 47,000 species of plants have been recorded.

In practice however, to avoid misidentification, experts do not only rely on matching up of externally visible parts of the body. They also examine other diagnostic features, such as certain body parts which are not visible from outside, and in many cases, behavioural and DNA level comparisons too are used to delineate closely resembling species. Thus, it is not always possible to identify a life-form up to the species rank solely on the basis of external appearance in the field or from photographs.

A photographic field guidebook provides reference images and descriptions of visible diagnostic features of various creatures, with which features of unknown organisms encountered in the field can be compared to assign identity.

Platycorynus **sp. Beetle feeding on** ***Calotropis*** **plant**

Earth May be Heading Towards 'Mass Extinction' of Organisms!

Earth came into existence about 4.5 billion years ago, and till date, about 4 billion species have appeared, flourished, and of them, about 99 percent are extinct. Extinctions happen in two ways–gradual 'background extinction', and catastrophic 'mass extinction'. The former type is a slow ongoing process and is a rather normal affair in nature, the causes of which are non-adaptability to changing climate, eradication by a disease, displacement by competing species, etc. In mass extinctions, the earth loses huge biodiversity in a short geological time period (in geological time scale, 'short' may mean a span of a several thousand years). The major causes of mass extinctions have been widespread volcanic activity and collision of the earth with celestial bodies (and resultant rapid change in the earth's environment).

In the last 500 million years, earth has seen five major mass extinctions. During each of these, the earth lost 75 to 90 percent of the total species that existed before the catastrophe, and thereafter, it took millions of years to recover diversity of life. Mass extinctions have also changed the blueprint of life on the earth, for instance, the fifth mass extinction caused by collision of asteroids with the earth, wiped off all the dinosaurs, and mammals got a chance to rule the earth.

Scientific studies indicate that today, we are entering (or have entered) into the sixth mass extinction. This time, the very cause of devastation is human activities, leading to the loss of wild habitats, toxification of the environment and climate change. The intensity of human induced extinction is such, that the rate of loss of vertebrates (animals with a backbone) in modern times is about hundred times higher than the background rate of extinction. Also, the population of several existing species is shrinking alarmingly. It has been estimated that earth has lost over 900 species of vertebrates since 1,500 CE including 85 mammals, 159 birds, 35 amphibians and 80 species of fishes. Though mass extinctions are not new to the earth and have happened in the past due to non-preventable natural causes, the causes of the present mass extinction (sixth) however are preventable. And, if the trend continues, it may jeopardise the existence of humans too.

'Every time we lose a species we break a life chain which has evolved over 3.5 billion years.'

Jeffrey McNeely, chief scientist at IUCN

IUCN Red List of Threatened Species

The IUCN Red List is the most authentic and globally accepted guide on the status of plant and animal species on the earth. The list is prepared by a group of experts after a rigorous assessment process, and the information can be used to make conservation-related policies. The status of various species in the Red List is classified under nine categories, some of which are:

Extinct:	Beyond reasonable doubt that the last individual has died.
Extinct in the wild:	The species survives only in captivity or outside its past range.
Critically Endangered:	The species is facing an extremely high risk of extinction in the wild.
Endangered:	The species is facing a very high risk of extinction in the wild.
Vulnerable:	The species is facing high risk of extinction in the wild.

Species under any of the three categories—critically endangered, endangered and vulnerable—are considered as 'threatened'. According to IUCN, today, more than 40,000 species are threatened with extinction.

What is Biodiversity and Why Should it be Conserved?

'Nature doesn't need people—people need nature; nature would survive the extinction of the human being and go on just fine, but human culture, human beings, cannot survive without nature...'

Harrison Ford, actor, aviator, environmental activist

Species richness or number of species in a given area can be used as a measure of biodiversity. A forest with greater number of species is said to have higher 'biodiversity' or 'variety of life'. It is generally agreed that we must conserve biodiversity or diversity of life on the earth for the following reasons:

1. The vital services for survival of humans are provided by nature—'Ecosystem services' which include; purification of air, pollination, purification and cleaning of water, detoxification and decomposition of waste, soil fertility, control of floods, fuel, medicine, etc. Humans have been getting all these services almost free of cost. It is the network of interdependence of living components like animals, plants, and microorganisms and their obligatory interactions with nonliving components of earth (soil, water, air, and light) that makes these services possible. If economic evaluation of ecosystem services is done, it may cross billions to trillions of dollars per annum.
2. Nature is also a provider of several intangible needs of humans—knowledge, well-being, aesthetic, cultural and spiritual needs.
3. Ethical and moral reasons—every non-human organism also has moral standing and a right to continued existence in the wild.

'Eventually, we'll realize that if we destroy the ecosystem, we destroy ourselves.'

-Jonas Salk, medical researcher, microbiologist

Carpenter Bee (H: Bhavra)
Xylocopa sp.
Gets it name due to the fact that it makes its nest by drilling holes in the wood

Glossary and Abbreviations

Antelope: Group of animals that have some features similar to cattle, and goats and sheep. Unlike the antlers of deer, the horns of antelope are not extensively branched and do not shed annually.

Barbels (fishes): Whisker-like structure near the mouth in fishes.

Biodiversity: In the simplest form it denotes the collection of all the species (animal, plant and microbes) living in a given area.

Breeding Plumage: The coat of feathers of birds during their breeding period (typically in summers); as soon as the breeding period of a few months is over, the birds acquire a new look (non-breeding plumage or winter plumage) by moulting. Thus, some birds have two different looks during the year. The breeding plumage is usually more colourful and visually appealing than the non-breeding plumage.

Butterfly 'forms': In certain species of butterflies, individuals born from the same parents (or from same batch of eggs), in the same season, have different patterns of wing colouration. For example: females of Common Mormon exist in three 'forms' named; *romulus, stichius* and *cyrus,* differing in wing colouration.

Cap (birds): A patch of distinctly coloured feathers on the head of birds.

Casque: Extended structure above the bills of hornbills.

Cere: Fleshy structure found at the base of the upper half of the bill in some birds.

Crown Stripe (birds): Contrasting lines running from forehead to the back of the head in birds.

Crown (birds): The top portion of the head of birds.

Diurnal Animals: Animals that are primarily active in the day time.

Ecosystem: A collection of organisms (plant, animals, microbes) in an area that interact with each other (or are dependent on each other) and with non-living components and function as a system.

Evolution: A process of gradual change by which over a long period of time (millions of years) the features of organisms change, and organisms with features quite different from ancestors arise.

Eye-ring (birds): Contrasting narrow ring of feathers surrounding the eyes of birds.

Fawn: A young deer.

Fertile: Ability of an organism to produce young ones.

Food Chain: The sequence in which one organism eats another, which is then eaten by another in nature.

Forehead (birds): Small area just above the base of the upper half of the bill in birds.

Forequarter (mammals): The front half of the animal's body, such as front legs, shoulders and surrounding anterior parts.

Frontal Shield: Fleshy looking large area above the upper half of the bill protruding along the forehead in some birds.

Gestation Period: Development period of foetus, between conception and birth.

Head and Body Length: The total length of the animal minus tail length.

Hindquarter (mammals): The hind part of the animal's body, such as hind legs, buttocks and surrounding posterior parts.

Home Range: Most animals do not live a nomadic life but live in a confined area which they know very well, and within which they perform their daily activities.

Infrasonic Sound: Sound waves of the frequencies below the audible range of human ears.

Land Vertebrates: Animals with a backbone living on land. It is a collective term for amphibians, reptiles, birds, and mammals. Fishes are vertebrates but not land vertebrates.

Microorganisms: Organisms which are not visible to unaided eyes such as: bacteria, viruses, protozoa, etc.

National Park: A large ecologically important area, demarcated by a government for conservation of rich flora and fauna, and protection of habitat. No human activity is permitted inside the national park, except for those permitted by the administration. Currently there are over 100 national parks in India.

Nocturnal Animals: Animals that are active at night and asleep/resting during the day.

Non-breeding Plumage: The coat of feathers of birds outside their breeding period.

Opposable Thumb: Thumb which can be positioned opposite to fingers, similar to that found in humans, enabling fingers to grasp objects.

Orbital Ring (birds): Contrasting narrow ring of bare skin surrounding the eyes of birds.

Passage Migrants: Birds which make their appearance in a geographical area only for a few days or weeks in a year. Passage migrants take a halt at CTR while on their way (August to November) to the wintering resort located at some other part of the subcontinent, or on their way back (February to March) to their breeding grounds at the onset of summers.

Plumage: In the most general usage, it refers to the entire feather coat of a bird and pattern of colouration at a given point of time. Some birds have more than one type of plumage in a year. The pattern of colouration of the plumage is the foremost feature used in identification of birds.

Population: A collection or number of organisms of the same species living in the same area at the same time. Individuals of a population can interbreed as they belong to the same species.

Protrusible: A part of the body, capable of being extended.

Pupil: The hole in the centre of eye, that allows light to pass inside the eye and strike the retina.

Resident Birds: Birds that live in a geographical area and can be sighted any time of the year.

Rosettes: Marks on the body of animals, such as those on leopards.

Rump (birds): A small area just above the tail or lower back in birds.

Rut: Period during which, male animals such as stags show behaviour associated with breeding including display, calls, aggression, and seeking access to females.

Scales (reptiles): Thin horny plates derived from the top layer of skin. Large scales such as those on the shell of turtles or crocodiles are called scutes.

Seasonal Forms (butterflies): In certain species of butterflies, individuals born during the wet season (rainy season) have a different pattern of wing colouration and shape than those emerging in the dry season. Seasonal forms have no genetic differences.

Summer Visitors (birds): Birds that migrate into a geographical area during summers. Summer visitors come to CTR for breeding. These begin to arrive at CTR from February onwards, and return by October–November.

Black Triangle Moth
Trigonodes hyppasia

Supercilium (birds): Horizontal streak or stripe above the eyes in birds.

Tail Streamers: Long extensions of tail feathers in some birds.

Taxonomist: A biologist who names and classifies organisms.

Territory: An area (within the home range) over which an animal or groups of animals claim an exclusive right. For some animals, their home range may be identical to their territory.

Tiger Reserve: An area supporting a viable population of tigers; managed according to the guidelines of Project Tiger. Currently, there are over 50 Tiger Reserves in India.

Tines: The pointed ends of the antler of deer.

Vertebrates: Animals with a backbone: fishes, amphibians, reptiles, birds and mammals.

Wattle (birds): A lobe of bare skin growing from the head, usually located near the base of the bill in some birds.

Wildlife Corridor: A strip of generally native vegetation that connects two or more large areas of similar wildlife habitats.

Wildlife Sanctuary: An ecologically important area rich in flora and fauna demarcated by a government for the purpose of conservation. Some restricted human activities such as livestock grazing may be allowed inside the Wildlife Sanctuary area after due permission from the administration. A sanctuary may be upgraded to or merged with national parks. Currently there are over 550 sanctuaries in India.

Wing Bar (birds): A contrasting stripe in the upper part of the wings of some birds.

Winter Visitors (birds): Birds that migrate into a geographical area during winters are called winter visitors. Most of the wintering birds arrive in CTR or surrounding areas during August to November and return during February to May. Winter migrants largely include birds coming in from overseas and from the higher reaches of the Himalayas (Altitudinal winter migrants).

Yearling: An animal that has completed the first year of its life.

Abbreviations

Br: A bird in Breeding Plumage; **CTR:** Corbett Tiger Reserve; **cm:** Centimetre; **dia:** Diameter; **DSF:** Dry Season Form of a butterfly; **F:** Family; **FRH:** Forest Rest House; **gm:** gram; **H:** Hindi name of the species; **kg:** Kilogram; **km:** Kilometre; **km²:** Square Kilometre; **L:** Local name of the species; **m:** Metre; **mtrs:** Metres; **mm:** Millimetre; **NBr:** A bird in Non-breeding Plumage; **PC:** Photo Credit; **sp.:** Used after genus to denote unspecified species of that genus. The organism could not be identified up to the species level. For example '*Panthera* sp.' means unspecified species of genus *Panthera*; **TAL:** Terai Arc Landscape; **WSF:** Wet Season Form of a butterfly; **Zone:** Ecotourism Zones in CTR.

Ramganga reservoir as viewed from Kanda

Animals and Plants

Mammals

The word 'mammal' is derived from Latin, '*mamma*', meaning 'breast'. Mammals are the only animals which have milk-producing glands (mammary glands) to feed and nourish their young ones.

Worldwide, nearly 6,500 species of mammals are known, of which over 420 are found in India. More than 50 species of mammals have been recorded in and around Corbett Tiger Reserve (CTR). This section provides the images and textual information that would help in identifying the 34 species of mammals seen in and around CTR, and provide an insight into their secret life.

Role of Mammals in Nature

Mammals perform several important tasks in nature: 1) plant-eating mammals form a major part of the diet of meat-eating animals, 2) meat-eating mammals keep a check on the population of their prey species, 3) many fruit-eating mammals disperse seeds in the forest, 4) mammals such as squirrels, bats and mice pollinate flowers, 5) burrows of mammals improve water percolation in the ground and cause mixing of soil; burrows also provide shelter for other animals, 6) mammals such as foxes, jackals and hyaenas also function as scavengers that clear the surroundings of animal carcasses by feeding on them, and 7) dung of elephants or other mammals are food and breeding sites for many insects.

Watching Mammals in CTR

One must be aware of the zones and habitat in which the desired mammal is best sighted. The habitat of the sought-after mammal must be thoroughly and patiently scrutinized. The following section provides the zones and habitats where various mammals are best sighted.

Photographing Mammals

Under most conditions, digital compact cameras with 40X zoom or more would be most suitable. For cameras with interchangeable lenses (such as SLR/mirrorless cameras), zoom telephoto lenses with an upper range of 300–500 mm would be suitable. However, to photograph mammals with their habitat or landscape, (large mammals and those quite close to photographers), one may also require wide-angle or ultra wide-angle lenses.

Arrangement of Mammals in the Section

Mammals have been grouped according to their taxonomic '*Orders*':

	Representative members	Order
1.	Monkeys	*Primate*
2.	Tiger, Leopard, Cats, Hyaenas, Civets, Mongooses, Jackals, Bears and Otters	*Carnivora*
3.	Deer, Wild Boar and Blue Bull, Gorals and Serows	*Artiodactyla*
4.	Hares	*Lagomorpha*
5.	Squirrels and Porcupines	*Rodentia*
6.	Bats	*Chiroptera*
7.	Pangolins	*Pholidota*
8.	Elephants	*Proboscidea*

Since many mammals can be easily identified in the field by comparing what one sees with the images, a detailed description of the appearance of animals has not been provided in a number of cases. Wherever necessary, the size of body has been provided as 'body length' which is the combined length of the head and trunk, also called 'Head and Body Length' (HBL).

Naming of Body Parts

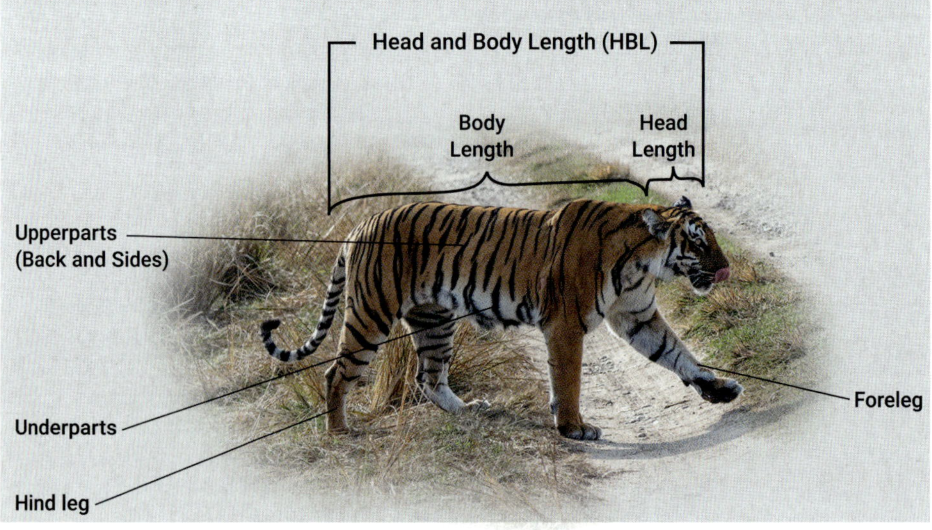

Monkeys (*Primates*)

The word 'Primate' gets its name from Latin, '*primus*', meaning 'first' or 'supreme'. Monkeys, gorillas, chimpanzee, man, are all primates. Several animals of this group are more intelligent than that of other groups. Other distinguishing features of primates include: eyes positioned in a bony case in front of the head, an opposable thumb, presence of nails (not claws) and a shortened snout. Several primates spend most of their time in trees (arboreal life), whereas many others, such as macaques and langurs, enjoy living on trees as well as on the ground.

RHESUS MACAQUE (H: BANDAR)

Macaca mulatta

Pale-brown monkey with an orangish-red tint to hindquarters, and a pinkish face; females have red skin on the rump during the breeding period; newborns are darker than adults. Males have larger canine teeth and are larger in size than females; males weigh 7–10 kg, and females about 5–6 kg. They can live about 27 years in captivity.

Male

Female with Infant

Food: Fruits, young shoots, seeds, roots, insects, crabs, fish and bird eggs.

Breeding: Mates during October–December; gestation period is about 164 days, usually single baby is born at one time, which is taken care of and nourished by the mother.

Behaviour: Lives both on the ground as well as on trees; and if senses the presence of predators nearby, stays on trees; lives in groups (the troop) composed of males and females; the group is ruled by a dominant male and female (pair). Walking with the head held high and erect tail, and shaking the branches, they display their dominance and aggression. Rhesus Macaques groom each other for relaxing, maintaining a healthy relationship among group members and clearing the fur of parasites.

Habitat: Thinly forested areas and fringes of forest.

Can be sighted in: All the zones.

Enemies of monkeys

The Leopard—an expert climber, Tiger, python, crocodile, Yellow-throated Marten and jackal are the main enemies of monkeys. After spotting a Tiger or Leopard, monkeys make alarm calls, jump from one branch to another and in the act, some may accidentally fall down. Even a sudden roar or thunder might cause monkeys to tumble down from the trees.

GRAY LANGUR (H: LANGUR)

Semnopithecus sp.

Gray Langur seen in this area is 'Terai Gray Langur', with the scientific name *'Semnopithecus entellus hector'* (some authorities also denote it as *'Semnopithecus hector'*).

Welcoming the new family member

It has a black face, longer limbs and tail, and a greyish coat that can have a yellowish hue; newborns are pinkish. While walking, it keeps its tail looping forward; males have large canine teeth and are larger than females. It weighs about 9–16 kg and can live about 25 years in captivity.

Food: Their main food includes young shoots, buds, fruits and seeds; they may also consume insects, bird eggs, etc.

Breeding: Mating peaks during July–October; gestation period is about six months. Usually a single young one is born.

Behaviour: Langurs spend time both on the ground as well as on trees. They sleep and feed on the extremities of branches, with their tail hanging downwards that acts as a balancer. They live in groups, each group is led by a dominant male (leader). Birth of a new member takes place under protection of all other females of the group, who also get a chance to hold the infant. An intruding male, that conquers the group by defeating the dominant male, is known to kill the infants sired by the latter.

Habitat: Thinly forested areas and fringes of forest.

Can be sighted in: Commonly in all the zones.

Tiger, Leopard, Cats, Hyaenas, Civets, Mongooses, Jackals, Bears and Otters (*Carnivora*)

These animals feed on meat obtained either by hunting or scavenging (Latin, *'carnivorus'*: flesh eating). Thus, carnivores have dagger-like strong canine teeth which pierce into the flesh of the prey, and blade-like premolar and molar teeth called 'Carnassial' to slice the meat. Their strong jaws and legs, sharp claws and powerful musculature help in overpowering the prey. Most of these animals are fast runners for short distances and also expert climbers. The overall intelligence in carnivores is high, which provides them mental alertness and a coordinated action required for hunting. Carnivores have been divided into several families including, *Felidae* (Cat family)—tigers, leopards, and small cats, etc.; *Ursidae* (Bear family); *Canidae* (Dog family)—foxes, jackals; *Hyaenidae*—hyaenas; *Herpestidae*—mongooses; *Viverridae*—civets, and; *Mustelidae*—martens and otters.

FISHING CAT (H: KHUPYA BAGH)

Prionailurus viverrinus

PC: AG

They are about 80 cm long; distinguishable from Leopard Cat by: larger size, stout built, bulkier appearance, a shorter ringed tail, greyish or greyish-brown fur with spots arranged in rows and cheeks with two small stripes. Its forefeet have partly developed webs. It weighs about 11–15 kg and, can live about 17 years in captivity.

Food: Preys on small animals such as birds, frogs, snakes, snails; can catch fish.

PC: AG

Breeding: Mating-related activities peak in January and February; gestation period is about 60 days. Around 1–4 young ones are born at one time.

Behaviour: Usually active at night; known to lead a solitary life; home range of females about 4–6 km^2 and that of males 4–14 km^2.

Habitat: Swamps, dense vegetation along creeks, marshes, dense forest near water.

Can be sighted in: Possibly in all the zones. There are only few records of this cat from CTR.

PC: AG

JUNGLE CAT (H: JUNGLEE BILLI)

Felis chaus

They are about one-and-a-half times larger than the Domestic Cat. The body is unmarked except for a few faint stripes or rings on the legs and tail; its long ears have tufts of black hair, and there is a white area around the mouth; the body of the kittens has marks for the first few months of their life. Males can weigh about 5–12 kg and females are about 2.5–9 kg. They can live around 15–20 years in captivity.

Food: Jungle Cat preys on small animals such as rats, squirrels, snakes, birds, etc. They can catch and feed on 3–4 rat-like animals per day.

Breeding: They are known to give birth twice a year; gestation period is about 2 months. About 3–5 kittens are born at one time. Kittens are vulnerable to attack by jackals and leopards.

Behaviour: They are primarily nocturnal animals, however, they are also seen hunting in early mornings and evenings in open areas and grasslands. Outside their mating period, jungle cats live a solitary life. They can climb trees and swim; locate prey by the sense of smell and sound. After sensing the presence of their prey located in dense grass cover, they make a sudden leap and land on prey; can take vertical leaps to capture birds.

Habitat: Prefers grasslands and scrubs.

Can be sighted in: All the zones. They usually keep themselves to thickets, therefore, cannot be commonly sighted. To sight Jungle Cat, grasslands of Dhikala and Dhela, and open grassy patches in Bijrani and Jhirna zones can be screened in the early morning and late evening.

PC: HP

PC: DR

Securing her cub

LEOPARD CAT (H: CHEETAH BILI)

Prionailurus bengalensis

PC: DR

This pretty cat looks like a mini Leopard; its size is close to that of the Domestic Cat. Its back, underparts, legs and tail are ornamented with solid large black spots (unlike that of leopards which have rosettes), whereas its face and neck have black stripes and white marks. It weighs about 3–4 kg. Leopard Cat can live up to 15 years in captivity.

Food: Preys on small animals such as rats, squirrels, birds, etc.

Breeding: Usually 3–4 kittens are born at one time, generally during March–May, after a gestation period of 65–70 days. They give birth in tree hollows, under large roots or in rock crevices. Leopard Cat can crossbreed with Domestic Cat.

Behaviour: Leopard Cat is a nocturnal animal; leads a solitary life in its home range. The home range of one male overlaps with one or more females. It is a good climber and can take shelter in hollows of trees as well. They also swim very well.

Habitat: Forests, nearby grasslands and scrubs.

Can be sighted in: All the zones. But since they are strictly nocturnal and shy, they are a rare sight.

PC: SCS

TIGER (H: BAGH)

Panthera tigris

Worldwide, there are six different subspecies of tigers. The one found in the Indian subcontinent is denoted as *'tigris'*, hence, the trinomial name of Indian Tiger is *'Panthera tigris tigris'*, commonly known as the 'Bengal Tiger' or 'Royal Bengal Tiger' or 'Indian Tiger'.

The orangish base of upperparts (back and sides) and white base colour for the underparts (belly) of Tiger is patterned with black stripes. The back of each ear has white spots, which are thought to help the Tiger cubs follow their mother, while moving through tall grasslands. The large round eyes of Tiger has an abundance of rod cells in the retina, making the eyes more sensitive under low light conditions. Tiger is a good swimmer. Males are significantly larger than the females (males weigh 175–260 kg, while the females weigh 100–160 kg). Lifespan of Tiger in captivity can be over 20 years; however, in the wild, tigers can live only upto 12–16 years.

Food: Meat of hunted animals.

Breeding: Tiger may mate at any time of the year; a tigress begins to breed at the age of 3–4 years; gestation period is around 102–108 days, and usually 3 cubs are born at one time; in many cases, not all cubs survive to see their first birth anniversary, they either die of starvation, or get killed by other tigers, natural calamities, disease, etc. On an average, in a well-protected area, roughly one cub is added per tigress per year.

Habitat: Tigers use all kinds of habitats prevalent in CTR.

Can be sighted in: There is a fair chance of sighting tigers in all the zones. They are usually solitary; sometimes a female with her 2–3 cubs or a courting pair can also be seen.

Male

PC: NZ

PC: AM

Good swimmers

Tiger Lives in a Fixed Area—Its 'Home Range'

Urine spray

Claw marking

Tiger leads a solitary life in a fixed area (home range) within which it roams, hunts and mates. Male and female tigers come together only for a while to mate. Males have a larger home range (40–100 km^2) which overlaps with that of two-three female tigers (13–30 km^2). Tigers regularly patrol in their home range and leave evidence of their ownership (or mark the boundary) by spraying scent from their anal gland, depositing excreta and urine (mixed with scent), and scratching tree trunks with their claws. A serious fight may break out against any intruding Tiger, which may end in death or eviction of one of the contenders.

Hunting Strategy

The hunting tactics of tigers include zeroing in on a prey, stalking as close as possible under the vegetation cover, and a final sudden rush towards the prey from behind or from the sides, taking the latter by surprise. After knocking down its prey, tigers usually kill them by strangulation or by breaking their neck. Characteristically, tigers start eating their prey from the rump. Though tigers are excellent hunters, to get a kill they may have to try 10–20 unsuccessful attempts. The highly developed senses of sight, smell and hearing in prey (such as deer), along with the alarm calls they raise upon being suspicious of the presence of tigers around, often foil the hunting attempts.

Taking by surprise

Tiger Food Economy

The amount of meat consumed by a Tiger depends on its age, gender and body size. A full-grown Tiger may require 60–75 deer-sized animals per year to survive, which means one kill every 5–6 days. A tigress raising cubs would require more kills to feed herself and her cubs. To ensure a balance between the amount of energy spent to capture prey and energy gained from feeding, tigers prefer killing large prey (Sambar, Spotted Deer, Nilgai, etc.). Tigers sometimes kill and feed on young elephants too.

Customised to Kill

The body of the Tiger (and that of other cats as well) is specialised for stalking, sudden

An unsuccessful attempt

Hiding the kill among grasses

PC: VB

rush for short distances, leaping, grasping, biting, tearing flesh and digesting flesh. In the forests and tall grasslands, where patches of bright sunlight alternate with shadows, the coat of Tiger with alternating orangish colouration and black stripes helps it to blend well with the surroundings and obscure the body contours. Tigers walk on their toes which bear sharp and curved claws (remain retracted when not in use), and the underside of their feet is cushioned with pads. These features enable tigers to approach their prey stealthily, enhance their capability to run, leap, grasp and seize the prey. The placement of long dagger-shaped canine teeth in the jaws is such that these teeth fully sink into the flesh of prey. Shearing and cutting of flesh and bones is achieved by 'carnassials' or 'flesh-teeth'—modified sharp premolar and molar teeth in upper and lower jaws, capable of scissor-blade-like motion. The rasp-like tongue helps in stripping the skin, fur and feathers of the prey, and also helps in stripping of flesh from the bones.

PC: AM

Tigresses are Extremely Caring Mothers

A tigress gives birth to cubs at a place well hidden from predators or any other disturbances. The cubs, born blind and helpless, are nourished by the mother with her milk for the first couple of months. During this period, the cubs are extremely vulnerable to predators like leopards, jackals, bears and other tigers. While away on a hunt, the mother keeps her cubs hidden in foliage or under the rocks. At about two months of age, the cubs begin to follow their mother to the place where she has hidden the kill. Any suspected predator is confronted with extreme aggression by the mother. As cubs grow, they learn the techniques to kill and tear animals through observation and practice. At the age of 12–18 months, the cubs acquire strong, permanent canine teeth and are capable of killing prey on their own.

Splash time in Ramganga river

PC: AM

Young Tigers Move Away from Parents to Establish Their Own Empire

By the age of 2–2.5 years, cubs can lead an independent life. Now the mother begins to force them to move away from her so that she can mate once again. Young male tigers usually migrate longer distances in search of any unoccupied habitat where they can establish their empire or acquire an area by evicting an aging or ailing male Tiger. Young female tigers generally do not move too far from their mother; they may occupy areas adjacent to their mother's home range by expelling an existing owner, or the mother may shrink her own area to accommodate her daughters.

Shifting her cub to a more secure cradle

PC: RK

Protecting Tigers in India

India is home to about 70 percent of the world's existing Tiger population. In the past centuries, tigers roamed about in India in large numbers; it is said that their number was in several thousands during the 19th century. Alarmed by the declining Tiger population, 'Project Tiger' was launched on 1 April 1973, with the aim to preserve tigers in the country. It has been realised that poaching, shrinkage and disturbance of habitat are the main reasons for the rapid decline in the number of tigers, and these animals can propagate by themselves if provided with adequate space and prey. National Tiger Conservation Authority (NTCA), a statutory body under the Ministry of Environment

Maternal touch

PC: NZ

Forest and Climate Change, through its various conservation activities, ensures protection of tigers in India. Until April 2023, there were 53 Tiger Reserves in India. As of 2022 census, the total number of tigers in India has been estimated to be 3,167 (as per 2018 census, the state of Uttarakhand alone has close to 440 tigers, of which over 250 are expected to be living in the CTR).

Bisected habitat

PC: AM

Human-tiger Conflict

Tigers have learnt to avoid humans, probably out of fear or natural aversion to humans. Thus, under normal circumstances, humans are not considered as prey by tigers. However, a Tiger with inborn physical inability, old age or an injury preventing it from hunting its natural prey can cause a shift in its choice to easy prey—humans and domestic animals. Tigers and leopards killing and feeding on humans have been denoted as 'dangerous to human life'. Humans can also be attacked by tigers during chance encounters (such as in self-defence); these events, however, may not make a Tiger habituated to feeding on humans. A habituated Tiger would avoid feeding on its natural prey, stalk human beings, and feed on the human carcass. NTCA has issued guidelines to declare a Tiger or Leopard 'dangerous to human life' and also laid down a procedure to capture or eliminate them.

One can have a thrilling experience of reading about several infamous human-killing tigers as narrated by the legendary Jim Corbett in his book *'Man-eaters of Kumaon'*.

PC: DR

Tigers often move near human settlements in Ramnagar. Tigers living close to human settlements may lead to human-tiger conflict.

The Infamous Sunderkhal Tiger

A Tiger had terrorised and disrupted the normal lives of the people living between Garjia village and Mohaan, from November 2010 to January 2011. Not one but six humans were killed and eaten near Sunderkhal—a village located near the Garjia Temple along NH-309 in Uttarakhand. The first victim was one of three women who had gone into the forest on 12 November 2010 to bring dry wood and fodder. The body of the victim was found at a distance from the attack site. After an interval of about a week, the Tiger struck again, but this time 5–6 kilometres away (near village Mohaan) from the place where it had killed its first victim. The prey was a woman who had visited the nearby forest for collecting fuel wood. The search team spotted the Tiger near the partially eaten body of the victim. The Tiger, however, managed to escape by leaping away. In the following year, on 11 January, near Garjia village, two *machans* overlooking the partly consumed body of the fourth victim were set up by forest personnel with the hope that the Tiger would be shot when it returns to the kill. The animal turned up but at night, and escaped into the jungle with a gunshot wound. The Tiger made a comeback on 26 January, and killed its last prey—a 25-year-old man who was visiting his relatives. He parked his two-wheeler near Sunderkhal and stepped a few yards towards the forest to relieve himself. Next day, a piece of the man's leg was recovered and it was assumed that the Tiger had eaten the rest of the body. Within a few hours, the Tiger was spotted at the place where the remains of the young man were found. This time, the forest personnel did not take any chances and sprayed bullets on the Tiger. This brought about the end of the most dreadful Tiger that the people living around CTR had ever seen. The Tiger was found to be a male responsible for killing six people within a span of ten weeks.

Slain Sunderkhal Tiger

A royal pair

Male Tigers Tend to Kill Cubs—'Infanticide'

A male Tiger, upon conquering the home range of another Tiger, kills all the cubs fathered by the loser. As a tigress with cubs does not show willingness to mate, by killing her cubs, the victorious male Tiger brings her to readiness to mate. This seemingly cruel act is one of the ways nature works; the victorious male Tiger ensures propagation of its own genes, rather than that of its predecessor.

PC: AM

Cubs

Pattern of Body Stripes—Fingerprints of Tigers

No two tigers have the same pattern of stripes on the body. Thus, stripe pattern is the identifier of an individual Tiger, and this principle is used for counting tigers in the forest. During the counting process, images of tigers are obtained by placing several 'camera-traps' at various locations (such as water-holes, trails, etc.) in the forest. Thereafter, the number of individual tigers can be counted by comparing the pattern of stripes from images. A camera-trap is a compact digital camera which is automatically triggered by body heat and movement of animals close to the camera.

A camera-trap

PC: MS

White, Golden and Black Tigers—a Genetically Mutated Form of the Orange Tiger

The fur of white tigers has a white background with sepia-brown stripes. In golden tigers, the background colouration of fur is pale and stripes are reddish-brown. And, the so-called black tigers are not entirely black; their black stripes are so wide that the orange background of fur is barely visible. All the three tigers with aberrant colouration have been seen in the wild in India. The abnormal colour pattern in tigers is due to a genetic defect (mutation) which affects the production of melanin pigments in the skin (or fur).

Sighting Tigers in CTR
PC: NP
PC: AM
PC: NP

LEOPARD (H: TENDUA)

Panthera pardus

They are smaller than tigers. The pattern of rosette markings on the body is unique to each Leopard and can be used to identify an individual Leopard. Male leopards weigh 45–77 kg and females weigh 30–45 kg. Leopards with an all-black coat and barely visible rosette markings on it ('Black Leopards' or 'Black Panther' or, technically, 'Melanistic Leopard') are genetic variants of the normal spotted leopards and are not a separate species. Like tigers, leopards too have weapons such as large canine teeth, expandable claws and powerful limbs to kill prey. They can live up to 20 years in captivity.

Food: Leopards can hunt down any animal they are able to outrun and overpower (such as small deer, monkeys, rats, porcupines, hares, etc.). By relying on small prey, leopards manage to live alongside tigers in the jungle; each Leopard requires 30–35 small deer-sized animals per year. The method of hunting of leopards is similar to that of tigers. They secure their kill by hiding it in the bushes or placing it high on the trees.

Breeding: Leopards can breed throughout the year. They begin breeding by the age of 3–4 years; gestation period is about 98–105 days. Usually two cubs are born at one time; by the age of 3–4 months, they begin to follow their mother and feed on the kills. By the age of 1.5–2 years, they move away from the mother to begin an independent life.

PC: MV

Behaviour: Much of the behaviour of leopards is similar to that of tigers. Leopards are agile animals and good climbers; they can hunt down langurs by swiftly climbing on trees. Leopards are dominated by tigers and keep themselves away from the sight of the latter; the home range of leopards are not as extensive as those of tigers.

Habitat: Leopards use all the types of habitats prevalent in CTR—forests, grasslands and scrubs.

Can be sighted in: All the zones. Being nocturnal and habituated to keep itself within thickets, the Leopard is sighted less frequently than the Tiger.

SLOTH BEAR (H: REECH)

Melursus ursinus

Piggybacking on mother

PC: SR

It has a 'V'-or 'U'-shaped white mark on the chest. Sloth Bear is equipped for eating ground-dwelling ants, termites and other insects. The curved, long claws on their forefeet act as tools for breaking and digging termite mounds. After tearing the mound, it forcefully sucks up termites through the gap in its upper jaw (gap is formed due to the lack of two of their front teeth); during this action, its extendable upper lip covers the opening of the nose to prevent entry of dust particles. Sloth Bear is a good climber; males weigh around 80–150 kg and females 60–100 kg. They can live up to 40 years in captivity.

PC: DMS

Food: Insects such as ground-dwelling ants, fruits and honey.

Breeding: Sloth Bear is known to mate during May–June; gestation period is 6–7 months, usually 2 cubs are delivered at one time in self-dug dens or natural caves. The mother constantly attends to her cubs for two months, hardly coming out for foraging. While nursing the cubs, she depends on her own body's fat reserves for energy; mothers carry cubs on their back for about 6–9 months, and sometimes do not let them down even when engaged in daily activities such as digging the ground to look for ants. The cubs remain under the care of mother for 1.5–2.5 years after which they lead an independent life.

PC: RB

Behaviour: These are mostly solitary animals and are known to aggressively challenge predators such as tigers. They can climb trees—an ability that helps them in getting honey and fruits. Sloth Bears usually come out just before sunset, remain active in the night and withdraw by morning.

Habitat: Forested areas and scrubs.

Can be sighted in: Jhirna, Dhela and Pakhro zones, but occasionally.

GOLDEN JACKAL (H: GIDAR)

Canis aureus

The subspecies of *'Canis aureus'* found in CTR is considered to be *'indicus'*, and thus, the trinomial name of jackal found here is *'Canis aureus indicus'* the common name of which is 'Indian Jackal'.

PC: AM

Chase

Nearly the size of Common Indian Street Dog; the males weigh around 7.5–10 kg while the females around 6.5–8 kg. The average lifespan is about 14 years in the wild, and over 18 years in captivity.

Food: Jackals consume fruits, small animals such as lizards, snakes, birds, hares, etc. They can hunt down young ones of deer and Nilgai, and scavenge on the kills of tigers and leopards.

Breeding: Golden Jackals mate during February–March; the gestation period is about 63 days; 1–9 pups are born together in secure dens. Provisioning and guarding of the mother and her pups is done by the male as well as by elder brothers and sisters of the pups.

Behaviour: A jackal pair lives in its territory, the boundary of which they mark with the scent of their urine and by howling. Large predators such as tigers, leopards and pythons are the major enemies of jackals.

Habitat: All kinds of habitats found in CTR, such as forests, grasslands and scrubs.

Can be sighted in: Common in all the zones, seen singly or in pairs.

PC: NZ

STRIPED HYAENA (H: LAKKAD BAGGHA)

Hyaena hyaena

Rare photograph near CTR

PC: GR

It is about one-and-a-half times the size of Common Indian Street Dog; its shaggy fur has black stripes and a row of long hair runs from its shoulder to its back; it has a massive head and a strong forequarter; its forelegs are longer than its hind legs; it weighs around 34–38 kg. The lifespan of the Striped Hyaena is about 25 years in captivity.

Food: They feed on leftover carcasses killed by other animals and search for their food by scent. They have strong jaws meant for crushing bones. Hyaena can also kill small animals and livestock.

Breeding: They are known to breed throughout the year; gestation period is around 90–91 days. About 1–4 cubs are born at one time and raised in natural caves, rocky crevices or holes dug by elders. Cubs are taken care of by the mother and other young females.

Behaviour: They become active after sunset and rest in the daytime in caves, fields and under bushes. Home range of male can be over 70 km^2; they use faeces, urine and anal gland secretions to mark their territories. They can make various types of sounds such as cries and laughing chatter.

Habitat: Scrubs, open areas with abundance of ravines, caves and holes.

Can be sighted in: Extremely rare in CTR with only a few records in recent times. Hyaenas were common in Bhabar and Terai area in the early twentieth century.

RED FOX (H: LOMRI)

Vulpes vulpes

Body around 60 cm in length, with long bushy white-tipped tail and reddish coat. It is smaller than the Golden Jackal. It weighs around 5–6 kg and lifespan is about 10 years in the wild.

Food: Small animals such as squirrels, rats, hares, birds, etc.

Breeding: They mate during the end of winters. Their gestation period is about 50 days; 3–12 cubs are born at one time which are taken care of by parents in the den.

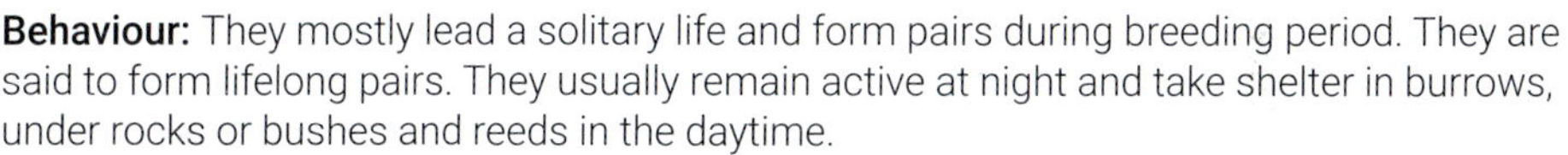

Behaviour: They mostly lead a solitary life and form pairs during breeding period. They are said to form lifelong pairs. They usually remain active at night and take shelter in burrows, under rocks or bushes and reeds in the daytime.

Habitat: Grasslands, shrubs, forested areas and near human habitations.

Can be sighted in: They are occasionally sighted in high reaches near the northern boundary of CTR.

HIMALAYAN PALM CIVET

(L: BIJJU)

Paguma larvata

With a length of about 60 cm, the upperside of the body is brownish to blackish-brown, while the underpart is whitish. It does not have spots or stripes on the body; the unmarked, long and thick tail may be darker at the tip. Its face has a dark area around the eyes and part of the cheeks, and a white band from forehead to nose. It weighs about 3.5–5.0 kg. Lifespan is about 27 years in captivity.

Food: Mainly fruits but can kill and eat small animals too.

Breeding: Breeds once or twice a year; gestation period is about 50 days; 1-4 young ones are born at one time.

Behaviour: Active after sunset through night. In terms of behaviour, they are similar to the Common Palm Civet. When annoyed, they release stinking fluid from anal glands in defence.

Habitat: In forested areas and near human habitations.

Can be sighted in: Possibly all the zones, but being nocturnal, not sighted frequently in daytime.

COMMON PALM CIVET (H: KHATAS)

Paradoxurus hermaphroditus

With a length of around 42–71 cm, it has an elongated body, a long tail and short legs. The face is small and the snout is long; the coat is black to brownish-black. There are dark stripes on the back running from neck to tail, and dark spots on the flanks. There is a white or pale patch below the eyes. This animal can be distinguished from the Yellow-throated Marten which has a yellowish throat and a pale forequarter. Common Palm Civet weighs around 2–5 kg and has a lifespan of about 25 years in captivity.

Food: It feeds on small animals such as birds, rats, snails, eggs and also on fruits. These are known to climb palm trees and steal the sweet juice from pots tapped overnight for making the alcoholic beverage 'toddy'.

Breeding: Breeds throughout the year; gestation period is about 60 days; 3–4 young ones are born at one time, in the shelter of tree holes or under rocks. The young ones are taken care of by the mother.

Behaviour: Its activity usually starts after dusk. During the day, it rests in tree holes and large tree trunks. On sensing danger, it escapes to a safe place. They have a scent gland, the scent of which is used to communicate with other members.

Habitat: In forested areas and near human habitations.

Can be sighted in: Possibly all the zones; being nocturnal, it is usually not sighted in the daytime.

PC: SR

PC: SR

SMALL INDIAN CIVET (H: KASTURI)

Viverricula indica

The length of its body is about 45–63 cm; it is a greyish-brown civet with prominent stripes on the back and rows of spots on flanks; the tail has dark rings. Weighing around 3–4 kg, its lifespan is about 9 years in captivity.

Food: Preys on small animals such as rats, birds, squirrels, but also consumes fruits and roots.

Breeding: They are known to have two breeding seasons in a year; gestation period is about 65 days, 2–5 young ones are born at one time in burrows under rocks or base of trees.

Behaviour: They live a solitary life. Active during nights, they usually seek food on the ground preying on small animals. They are kept in captivity for extraction of scent which is secreted by glands located near genitals.

Habitat: Thinly forested areas, fringes of forest, scrubs and near human habitations. Takes shelter in holes, and under rocks and bushes.

Can be sighted in: Possibly all the zones; since it is nocturnal, it is not usually sighted during daytime.

GREY MONGOOSE (H: NEWALA)

Herpestes edwardsii

It is about 36–45 cm long. The alternating light and dark rings on individual hair gives their coat a grizzled appearance. They take shelter under rocks, holes at the tree base, termite mounds and self-dug burrows. Elongated body, short legs and ears, and prominent claws enable the mongoose to dig and enter burrows. A series of folds in the ears can close ear openings, preventing dust from entering the ears while digging a burrow. Males are larger than the females. They weigh about 1.5 kg, with a lifespan of 7–8 years in captivity.

Food: They prey on small animals such as rats, snakes, lizards, insects, birds, eggs of birds and consume fruits.

Breeding: They breed throughout the year; gestation period is about 60 days. Around 2–4 young ones are born at one time, which are taken care of by the mother alone.

Behaviour: Grey Mongoose can hunt both during the day and night. It stands on its hind legs to screen the vast area for prey. Upon capture, it kills prey by biting; when alarmed, it moves into bushes for safety.

Habitat: Open areas such as scrubs and grasslands.

Can be sighted in: All the zones. To spot a mongoose, one needs to keep looking under bushes and along paths in grasslands and scrubs.

Snake and Mongoose

Mongooses prey on snakes, even on the deadly poisonous ones. *How does the mongoose tackle and protect itself from the poison of snakes?* While fighting a snake, the mongoose protects itself from snake-bite by its extreme agility. Also, mongooses are less sensitive to the venom of certain snakes—their blood has components that can neutralize snake venom, and unlike humans, mongooses are resistant to the effects of the toxins from snakes.

Fire Lines

These are a few feet wide lines that are kept clear of vegetation and inflammable materials such as dry leaves, grass, etc. Fire lines break the continuity of inflammable materials on the forest floor, thus a raging forest fire dies off as it reaches the line and does not progress to the other side of the line. Fire lines are the mainstream method to prevent the spread of forest fires. A forest has a network of fire lines. In fact, many of the safari tracks in CTR also act as fire lines.

Clearing a fire line

Electric Fencing

It is a barrier that the animals avoid crossing. The wires of the fence are connected to an energizer which supplies pulses of low intensity electric current. As the trespasser comes in contact with the electric fence, it receives a short and painful but safe electric shock. It is a psychological barrier—a whole herd of animals (such as deer) can be repelled by the fence if just one of them receives the shock. Other members of the herd, witnessing the reaction of pain to the victim, avoid coming close to the fence.

Tall fencing is a barrier for elephants

YELLOW-THROATED MARTEN (L: CHITROLA)

Martes flavigula

PC: RBP

Its body length is about 45–65 cm. Elongated slender body, long tail, and sharp claws help Yellow-throated Marten to climb and hop on trees with ease. Buffish-brown forequarters, yellow throat, blackish hindquarter, and blackish tail and head—these features help in distinguishing it from the Common Palm Civet. While on the ground, it progresses with galloping movements, keeping its back up and arched. It weighs about 2–3 kg, and can live about 17 years in captivity.

Food: They hunt and feed on small animals such as rats, hares, squirrels, birds and bird eggs, and also eat nectar and fruits. They are also known to hunt down animals larger than their own size, such as monkeys or deer fawn.

Breeding: They are known to breed between February and August. The gestation period is about 220–290 days; around 2–3 young ones are born at one time in dens.

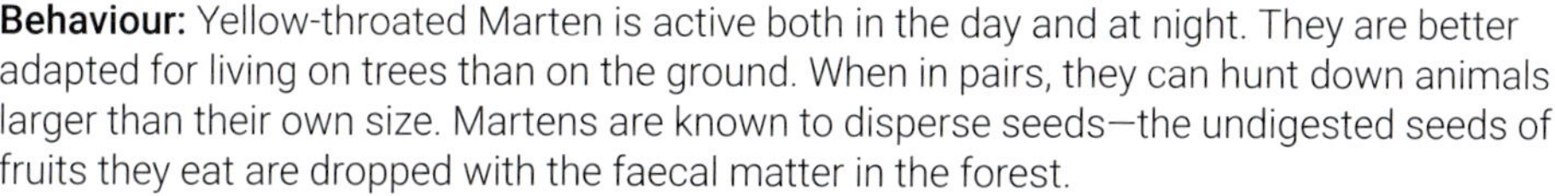

Behaviour: Yellow-throated Marten is active both in the day and at night. They are better adapted for living on trees than on the ground. When in pairs, they can hunt down animals larger than their own size. Martens are known to disperse seeds—the undigested seeds of fruits they eat are dropped with the faecal matter in the forest.

Habitat: Forests and fringes of forest.

Can be sighted in: All the zones. They are fairly common to spot.

PC: HP

Looking for food

PC: NZ

Monkey kill

SMOOTH-COATED OTTER

(H: UDBILAO)

Lutrogale perspicillata

With a length of about 59–75 cm, the smooth sleek pelage is brownish to grey-brown on the upperside and lighter in shade on the underside. Its long fleshy tail flattens towards the tip and its feet are webbed. Weighing about 7–11 kg, it lives about 15–20 years in captivity.

Food: Prefers fish, however, can also eat rats, snakes, crabs, etc.

Breeding: It mates during August–September and November–December. The gestation period is about 62 days. Around 2–5 young ones are born at one time in secure dens on the land.

Behaviour: They are mainly active in the day and hunt in groups. Though well suited to spend time in water, they are equally comfortable on land. Smooth-coated Otters defecate at a common site, which, by tradition, can be used for many years.

Habitat: Rivers, reservoirs and dams.

Can be sighted in: Best in Dhikala zone along Ramganga river at places such as Sambar Road and High Bank, and in Mandal river (Durgadevi zone). The sighting of otters, however, is not very common.

PC: AM

A family

Feeding a cub

Splash in Ramganga river

PC: HP

Otters are Well Suited for Swimming and Hunting Underwater

Otters live and hunt by waterbodies such as lakes, rivers, marshes, etc. They are well adapted to hunt underwater. Their thick water-repellent fur provides them with excellent insulation and thus, they manage to remain in water for a longer time, even in cold water. Their streamlined body, thick muscular tail and paddle-like webbed feet, particularly the longer hind feet, help in propulsion of the body inside water. Their tail assists in swimming. The eyes and nasal openings are placed high on the head, that enable otters to breathe in air and see around, while the rest of the body is submerged. Their ears are smaller and are protected by valves which close the ears while otters are underwater. With the help of long sensitive whiskers, otters can feel the presence of fishes or other prey hidden in rock crevices. Otters can remain submerged in water for several minutes.

Respect Crucial Wildlife Corridors on National Highway-309

PC: AGA

The road heading towards Mohaan from Ramnagar (NH-309 or Old NH-121) marks the eastern limit of CTR. There is a regular movement of animals between CTR and the forest on the other side of the road (managed by the Ramnagar Forest Division). This movement maintains wildlife connectivity between CTR and neighbouring forest, which is essential for the conservation of wildlife. An increase in vehicular traffic, reckless driving and littering particularly with polybags and wrappers along such roads can have serious consequences on wild animals including death of animals in road accidents, ingestion of hazardous plastics, and on-road conflict between man and animal. These consequences, however, can be prevented if the road users:

1. Give respect to animals,
2. drive slowly and don't overspeed in crucial wildlife corridor areas,
3. keep an eye on the road to avoid hitting any small or creeping animal that might be present on the road,
4. remember that the animals have the first right on the area,
5. do not disturb the wild animals seen along the road and maintain adequate distance from them,

PC: AGA

6. do not honk and/or play loud music, and
7. do not litter or throw garbage (plastic bags, bottles, wrappers, glass, etc.) on/along the roads.

Deer, Blue Bull, Wild Boar, Gorals and Serows (*Artiodactyla*)

Ungulates: These are also known as 'hoofed animals' and include horses, cattle, sheep, goats, deer, pigs, rhinoceroses, etc. These animals walk on the tips of their toes, covered with horny hooves. The hoof is a modified form of the nail. In *Artiodactyl* (Greek, *'artios'* meaning 'even-numbered' + *'daktylos'* meaning 'finger') ungulates (deer, sheep, goats, pigs, etc.), it is the third and fourth toes which touch the ground or bear the weight of the animal while the remaining toes are absent or undeveloped. In contrast, *Perissodactyl* (Greek, *'perissos'* meaning 'odd-numbered') ungulates (horses, rhinos and asses, etc.), it is the third toe that is well developed and bears the weight of the animal.

In ungulates, a reduction in the number of toes and walking on toe tips, gives them increased step length and speed of running. These animals, therefore, can run faster and escape swiftly.

Only Artiodactyl ungulates are found in CTR. These belong to families: *Cervidae* (deer family), *Bovidae* (cattle family), and *Suidae* (pig family).

SPOTTED DEER (H: CHITAL)

Axis axis

It is the most common deer in CTR. The older stags have large antlers, a darker coat and a dark band at the snout. Young males have small dagger-shaped or less extensively branched antlers; adult-like antlers grow only after five years of age. Females (weight 45–60 kg) are significantly smaller than males (weight 70–85 kg). They can live about 20–22 years in captivity. In the wild, however, only a few individuals reach 10 years of age.

Food: Grass sprouts emerging right after a spell of rain or cutting or burning of grasslands, leaves, flowers, herbs and fruits.

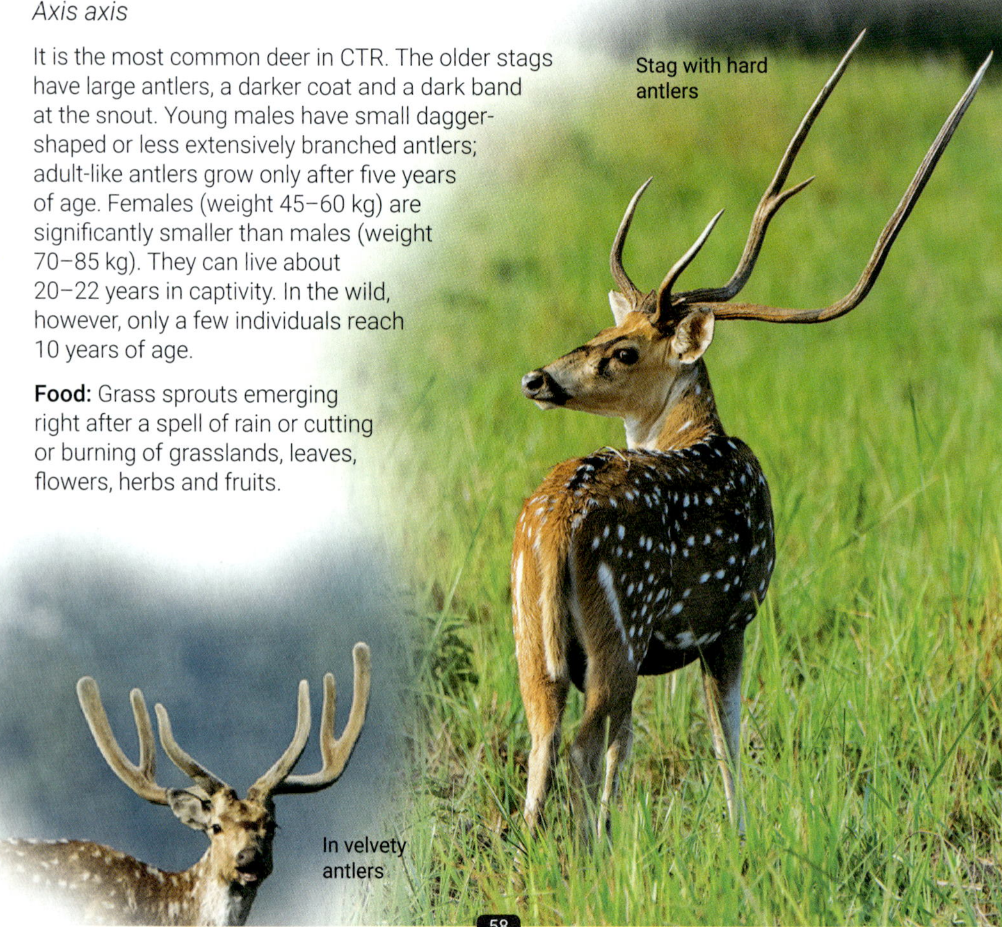

Stag with hard antlers

In velvety antlers

Deadly combat

Breeding: Peak rutting season is June–October; gestation period is 8 months. Usually, one fawn is born at one time. Majority of males shed antlers during November–January and re-grow them (velvet stage) between January–June. During May–August, they get 'mature antlers'.

Behaviour: Alarmed Spotted Deer raises its tail and stomps its forefeet on the ground; it sends out alarm calls (barks) to alert the other members of the herd. They are sometimes seen feeding on leaves and fruits dropped from the trees by langurs. It is a type of association where the deer also get sentinel services of langurs—sitting high on the trees, the langurs can easily spot approaching predators and make alarm calls, which alert the deer.

Habitat: Spotted Deer is seen in both forested areas as well as grasslands; its favourite haunt, however, is near the interface of forest and grassland. In grasslands with plenty of fresh sprouts, Spotted Deer can be seen in large herds.

Boxing fight between does

Can be sighted in: All the zones. CTR is one of the best places to sight this animal. It can be seen in the grasslands and forested areas. Large herds of more than 100 individuals in the grasslands of Dhikala, and Garjia zones make for a picture-perfect scenery.

Fawn

A moment at Dhikala chaur

SAMBAR (H: SAMBAR)

Rusa unicolour

Does in Ramganga river

It is the largest deer of the Indian forests. The mane (long hair near the neck) is prominent in males. The winter coat of Sambar is grey-brown or dark brown; in summers, the coat is chestnut-brown. Older males are darker; stags (weight 225–320 kg) are significantly larger than does (weight 135–225 kg). Their lifespan is about 25 years in captivity; in the wild, however, average life expectancy is about 12 years.

Food: Though it prefers green leaves of a vast variety of herbs and trees, it can consume grass when available in abundance.

Breeding: Peak rutting season is from autumn to spring. Gestation period is 8 months, and usually one fawn is born at one time. Most stags shed their antlers during March–July; stags with mature antlers are seen during December–March.

Behaviour: Sambars are usually sighted in groups of 3–5 individuals. Males typically lead a solitary life; Sambars spend most of the time in forested areas where vision is of little use. Their acute senses of smell and hearing help them attract mates, repel competitors and sense the presence of predators. Their large ears help pick up sound as much as possible. Sambar can walk stealthily even in dense foliage and its dark brown coat conceals it in low-light conditions of forested areas. Once suspicious of danger, it stands still to remain unnoticed and in extreme cases, it stomps the ground with its forefeet and concurrently produces loud 'barks'.

Habitat: It prefers staying in forested areas on slopes of hills; however, Sambar visits rivers and streams for drinking and cooling itself.

Can be sighted in: All the zones; common.

PC: DR

Stag

Fawn

INDIAN MUNTJAC (H: KAKAR)

Muntiacus muntjak

In velvety antlers

A small deer about the size of Common Indian Street Dog. The coat of fawns is spotted. The scent glands on the face are visible as slits on the forehead and slits at the corner of the eyes. Both male and female deer are similar in size; weigh about 20–22 kg. The upper canine teeth in males are larger (tusks) and are sometimes visible from outside. Both antlers and tusks are used as weapons. Indian Muntjac has the lowest number of chromosomes amongst all the mammals—7 in males and 6 in females. Their life expectancy is about 17 years in captivity.

Doe

PC: HP

Food: Fruits, seeds, leaves, buds and grass.

Breeding: Rutting period peaks in the winter months; gestation period is about 6–7 months. Usually one fawn is born at one time. Antlers are shed during summers and re-grown by winters.

Behaviour: Muntjac leads a solitary life. It is a shy animal and swiftly leaps into dense vegetation as it perceives danger; an alert deer produces a loud alarm call which, from a distance, sounds like the bark of a dog. It is also known as 'Barking Deer'.

Habitat: They can be seen in forested areas with dense undergrowth, and sometimes at fringes of forest.

Can be sighted in: All the zones, however, best sighted in Bijrani, Dhikala and Durgadevi zones; common.

Stag

PC: MS

Deer Antlers—Unique Asset

Deer belong to the family *Cervidae*. Several graceful creatures such as Sambar, Chital, Hog Deer, Barking Deer, Reindeer, Moose, etc., all come under the umbrella of deer. Barring a few exceptions, a pair of antlers on the forehead is the most remarkable feature of deer. Antlers differ from horns (found in cattle, goats, sheep, etc.); the former are branched, solid bony projections, from the skull, which are shed annually, while the latter are permanent, unbranched and hollow structures covering a bony core. Moreover, antlers are borne only by male deer, except for reindeers wherein both the sexes possess antlers. Stags (male deer) shed their antlers after the rut or breeding season, and soon new antlers begin to grow. Growing antlers remain covered with hairy skin, giving them a velvety appearance (velvet stage), During this period, extreme care is taken by the stags to avoid any harm to the developing antlers. As the antler attains full growth, blood supply is cut from the base, leading to death of velvety skin, which begins to peel off. Free of velvety skin, the antler appears like a bone and is now hard and mature (hard antler stage). Presence of hard antlers is indicative of deer's breeding period, and they use it for defence and fighting with rival males to possess the hind.

Communication in Deer

Deer have a good sense of sight, hearing and smell—these features keep them aware of predators around them, even when well out of sight. They communicate with each other through various types of vocalisations and gestures (such as emitting barks, raising the tail and stomping their feet when alarmed), and releasing scent from scent glands located on the face and in between the hooves. Deer such as Sambar and Muntjac, which live in forest habitat where vision is of limited use, advertise their presence by their scent. They smear their own scent on tree trunks, rocks, etc., by rubbing their scent glands. The scent can be later sniffed by other members. This way, they can convey their presence in a particular area to other members (mates and competitors) without actually seeing them.

HOG DEER (H: PARA)

Axis porcinus

Its stocky appearance, high-positioned rump relative to forequarters and a hog-like movement suggest its common name. The coat is darker in winters and reddish-brown with pale spotting in summers. Till the age of a few months after birth, the body of fawns is spotted. The males weigh about 40–50 kg and females weigh about 30–40 kg. Hog Deer is closely related to Spotted Deer and the two are known to crossbreed. Their life expectancy is about 20–22 years in captivity.

Food: Hog Deer prefers grass but also consumes herbs and shrubs.

Breeding: Peak rutting season is around September–October; gestation period is 7–8 months. Usually, one fawn is born at a time.

Behaviour: Hog Deer are usually seen in CTR in groups of 2–3 individuals—doe and its young ones, these may be accompanied by a stag. Hog Deer comes out for feeding in the early morning and evening, and takes shelter in tall grasses in the afternoon. When alarmed, it raises its tail, stomps its foot on the ground and makes barking sounds to alert other herd members; to escape, it swiftly rushes into tall grass and moves through grass tunnels while keeping its head low.

Habitat: Tall grasslands along rivers.

Can be sighted in: Possibly all the zones, however, best sighted in Dhikala and Khinnanauli grasslands (Dhikala zone).

Doe

Fawn

PC: SB

Summer coat

Winter coat

PC: MS

PC: MS

Piglets

INDIAN WILD BOAR

(H: JANGALI SUAR)

Sus scrofa

The coat is a mix of grey, black and brown hair. Males (boars) have large tushes (protruding canine teeth), and a row of long stiff hair along their back which is more prominent than that in females (sows); piglets have brownish coat with pale stripes; wild boars have a well-developed sense of smell, however, the senses of sight and hearing are somewhat modest. A fully grown male can weigh over 230 kg. Their life expectancy is about 20 years in captivity.

Sows

Food: Roots, fruits, insects, carrion, and at times small animals (prey) as well.

Breeding: Throughout the year. The gestation period is 4 months, 4–6 piglets are born at one time.

Behaviour: Wild Boars are courageous and determined animals. They are known to resist and fight their predators and fatally injure them (including the Tiger). Males live a solitary life; females are usually seen in small groups and are accompanied by their young ones.

Habitat: Forest, fringes of forest and scrubs.

Can be sighted in: All the zones; common.

PC: MS

Sow

Boar

Cow

BLUE BULL (H: NILGAI)

Boselaphus tragocamelus

The word 'Nilgai' describes the appearance of this animal—*nil* (Hindi) meaning 'blue' and *gai* (Hindi) meaning 'cow'. It is the largest Indian antelope. Adult males (bulls) have an iron-grey coat and a pair of short conical horns. Young males and females (cows) are tawny in colour. Females lack horns. Bulls can weigh 200—270 kg whereas cows weigh 120–220 kg. Their life expectancy is about 20–22 years in captivity, and about 12–13 years in the wild.

Food: Feeds on grasses, herbs, leaves, flowers, pods and fruits.

Breeding: Nilgai can breed throughout the year; gestation period is about 8 months, one or two calves are born at one time.

Behaviour: They are usually seen in groups of 5–10 individuals—females with calves and young males. Nilgai usually returns to the same spot for defecation, which is thought to be a way of communication among group members or marking of territory. Bulls lead a solitary life. Nilgai has well-developed senses of sight and smell. They are good runners and escape by running in a horse-like manner.

Habitat: Prefers scrubs and open areas with distantly placed trees. They usually avoid dense forested areas.

Can be sighted in: Dhela, Jhirna and Pakhro zones.

PC: SM

Bull

Cow

HIMALAYAN BROWN GORAL

(H: GORAL)

Naemorhedus goral

A goat-like animal with a brown coat; it is adapted to climbing and leaping on steep mountain slopes and cliffs; females look similar to males but have thinner horns; weigh about 25–40 kg. Life expectancy is about 17 years in captivity.

Food: Primarily grass.

Breeding: Rutting period during October–December; gestation period is 6–8 months, usually a single calf is born at one time.

Behaviour: These animals are seen in small groups of 3–8 individuals; though males prefer a solitary life, they join a group of females during the rut. An alarmed goral produces a loud 'hiss' and escapes in the nearby forested areas to hide.

Can be often sighted on steep cliffs

Habitat: Prefers grassy and steep mountain slopes and cliffs.

Can be sighted in: All the zones with a hilly terrain, namely; Jhirna, Bijrani, Dhikala, Durgadevi and Sonanadi. One is advised to carefully examine the cliffs along Ramganga, Mandal, Palain and Kosi rivers.

PC: KSS

HIMALAYAN SEROW

(H: SARAO)

Capricornis thar

PC: MN

Its head and body length is 140–170 cm. A goat-like animal, larger in size than the Himalayan Brown Goral, its upperparts and sides are black or blackish brown, and the lower portion of legs are whitish. Ears are large donkey-like, and they have a thick neck. Both the sexes have horns. They weigh 85–140 kg. Their life expectancy is over 18 years in captivity.

Food: Grass, leaves, ferns, moss and lichens.

Breeding: Rutting begins at the end of October; gestation period is about 7 months. Usually, one calf is born at one time.

Behaviour: It usually spends a solitary life; takes shelter in woody gorges and caves, and comes out in the evening and morning for feeding. It can move well on rocky as well as on flat terrain. When alarmed, it moves away with a hissing sound and makes a whistling, scream-like call.

Habitat: Steep hills, rocky places, gorges and gentle slopes of mountain forest.

Can be sighted in: Sighting is extremely rare. However to sight them, a trip to Durgadevi and Sonanadi (Halduparao area) zones is recommended.

PC: RBP

Hares (*Lagomorpha*)

The word 'Lagomorpha' is derived from Greek, *'lagos'* meaning 'a hare' + *'morphe'* meaning 'form' (or hare-like). This group is comprised of hares, rabbits and mouse-hares. These animals have four incisors (front teeth) in the upper jaw—a pair of larger incisors in the front and a smaller pair behind them.

INDIAN HARE

(H: KHARGOSH)

Lepus nigricollis

PC: MS

The subspecies of *'Lepus nigricollis'* found in CTR is *'ruficaudatus'*; thus its trinomial name is *'Lepus nigricollis ruficaudatus'*, commonly known as Rufous-tailed Hare.

It is about 30–50 cm long. The body has a rufous-brown coat which is mixed with black hair on the back. Its longer hind legs help it undertake long leaps to evade predators, and long ears are known to help in controlling body temperature. It weighs about 2–2.5 kg; females are slightly heavier than males. Average life expectancy is about 7 years in captivity.

Food: Mostly grasses. Hares and rabbits eat their excreta (coprophagous) to get the maximum nutrition from food.

Breeding: Throughout the year, with peak during monsoon. Gestation period is about 35 days. Two young ones are born at one time.

Behaviour: Hares become active by night and stay among grass during day time. On spotting a predator (cats, mongooses, etc.), they lie quietly to remain undetected. However, if this said strategy fails, they escape to nearby holes.

Habitat: Grasslands and scrubs.

Can be sighted in: All the zones.

Hares and Rabbits

Hares are different from rabbits in several aspects—they have longer ears than rabbits and give birth in depressions (forms) in the ground that are covered with grass. The hare's young ones are born with open eyes and are coated with fur. Young ones of rabbits, in contrast, are born blind and without fur in holes or burrows.

Squirrels and Porcupines (*Rodents*)

This is the largest group of mammals; worldwide, about 40 percent of all the mammalian species are rodents. Squirrels, rats, mice, porcupines and marmots are all rodents. Most rodents are small animals, porcupines being the largest among them in India. The incisors (front teeth) of the upper and lower jaws of rodents grow continuously and never cease to grow. To prevent the overgrowth of incisors and thus harm to their mouth, these animals regularly grind their teeth against each other and gnaw (Latin, *'rodere'*: gnaw) their teeth against pipes, wood and other material. This serves two purposes: keeps the length of teeth in check and sharpens tooth edges (like a chisel).

FIVE-STRIPED PALM SQUIRREL

(H: GILHERI)

Funambulus pennantii

It has five pale stripes on the body; three middle stripes are longer than the two on the sides. It can live about 3–4 years in captivity.

Food: Nuts, fruits, pods, shoots, buds, nectar and insects.

Breeding: Known to mate in March–April and July–September, one female mates with several males; gestation period is six weeks; 2–3 young ones are born at one time, in nests made with grass, leaves and fibres, on the trees.

Behaviour: Most active during morning and in late afternoon; makes its nest on trees and in tree hollows, which is used for raising young ones and for resting as well.

Habitat: Forested areas, and trees near human habitations.

Can be sighted in: Possibly all the zones, near human habitations, tourist resorts, forest rest-houses, etc.

PC: MS

Flying Squirrels are Not True Fliers!

Flying Squirrels are not true fliers like birds and bats, they can only glide from a higher level of a tree to a lower level. Their patagium (p.70) works like a parachute, enabling them to float in the air and land smoothly. During the glide, the body is steered by altering the position of limbs and thus the orientation of the patagium relative to the body.

RED GIANT FLYING SQUIRREL

(H: GILEHRI)

Petaurista petaurista

It is a large squirrel with body length of about 32–49 cm; the coat is reddish; the long tail with black tip is kept curved at the back. There is a fold of elastic skin along the flanks, the 'patagium' which helps in gliding; it is fixed between the wrist and the ankle and recoils when the squirrel is at rest, and expands as the squirrel stretches its limbs (such as while leaping from one tree to another). It weighs 1.5–2.4 kg, and can live about 11 years in captivity.

Food: Nuts, leaves and fruits.

Breeding: It is known to breed twice a year; gestation period is 45 days; usually one young is born at a time in the nests that are made in tree holes, lined with leaves, fur or other soft material.

Behaviour: They are active during the night and rest in tree holes and branches during the day time. They are excellent gliders—they climb to the top of trees from where they can jump and glide upto 100 mtr and land on the next tree; small cats, owls and martens are among its main predators.

Habitat: Forested areas.

Can be sighted in:
Possibly all the zones excluding Jhirna, Dhela and Pakhro; sighting is rare.

PC: RBP

PC: SR

PC: SC

INDIAN CRESTED PORCUPINE

(H: SAHI)

Hystrix indica

Its 60–90 cm long body is covered with stiff hair—neck and shoulders are topped with a row of bristles, while the back and tail are covered with long spikes (quills). The quills found on the tail are whitish whereas those on the back have alternating black and white rings. Its feet have long claws adapted for burrowing. It weighs about 11–18 kg. Life expectancy is about 27 years in captivity.

Food: Grains, fruits, roots and vegetables. They gnaw at discarded antlers and bones of animals to fulfil the need for calcium (required for quill growth) and also for sharpening of their teeth.

Breeding: Known to breed throughout the year. Gestation period is 90–112 days, 1–3 young ones are born at one time in burrows or dens and both the parents take care of them. The body of the newborn is covered with soft spines.

Behaviour: Porcupines begin their activity after darkness sets in, and rest in caves and in self-dug burrows during the daytime. Their burrows have more than one opening for emergency exits; porcupines have a keen sense of smell.

Habitat: Forest and scrubs, rocky hill sides.

Can be sighted in: Possibly all the zones; however, being nocturnal, it is not commonly seen in the daytime.

Porcupine Quill

The word porcupine comes from Latin, '*porcus*': pig + '*spina*': spine, meaning 'prickly pig'. Its sharp and stiff quills are made of a material similar to our hair, and can be erected by the animal at will. The quill, after coming in contact with the enemy's body, easily dislodges from the body of the porcupine, and remains embedded in the flesh of the enemy. Several microscopic barbs at the tip of the quill anchor it into the flesh and cause severe pain when the predator tries to remove the quill. The lost quill of the porcupine is replaced with another one.

Fighting Strategy of Porcupines

When alarmed or irritated, it erects its body quills and rattles the tail quills. To launch an attack, porcupine keeps its hind-quarters with erected deadly spines towards the predator and rushes backwards to clash its rear with the enemy, planting some of its sharp quills into the latter's body. Tigers and leopards are known to be lethally wounded by the quills which can penetrate deep into their vital organs such as lungs or liver.

PC: MS

Bats (*Chiroptera*)

These mammals are capable of true flight. The word 'Chiroptera' (Greek, *'cheir'*: hand, +*'pteron'*: wing) indicates the structural plan of their wings which are made of a thin skin-like membrane extending from the arms to the ankles (unlike birds in which the wings are composed of a sheet of overlapping feathers). Greatly lengthened fingers support the membrane in a manner similar to how the spokes of an umbrella support the fabric.

Bats have been divided into two subgroups: the larger fruit-eating bats (Megachiropterans) and the insect-eating bats (Microchiropterans) which are usually smaller. Differences in feeding habits of the two groups have led to slight differences in the structural plan of the body and capabilities. One such difference is the way these bats navigate in pitch dark nights. While flying, insect-eating bats can avoid obstacles with extreme precision and locate prey by using their own radar system: they produce ultrasonic sound waves from the voice box/by clicking their tongue, which, after being deflected from the object, are picked up, and amplified by the bat's specially designed ears. In short, these bats can see with their ears! Fruit bats, in contrast, rely more on vision and have an inferior radar system—it could be due to this very reason that fruit bats collide with electric wires more often and get electrocuted.

INDIAN FLYING FOX (H: GADUR)

Pteropus giganteus

It is a large fruit bat which has 20–30 cm long body. With a furry yellowish-brown body, long black snout, and black wings, it weighs about 0.5–0.6 kg. It can live about 30 years in captivity.

Food: Flowers, nectar, leaves, juice extracted from fruits by chewing (remaining fibrous portion of fruit is spat out).

Breeding: Peak mating period is between July–October. Gestation period is about 150 days; usually one young is born at one time, which is fed and carried by its mother. The young one clings tightly to its mother during flight, with the help of claws, and holds one of her teats for grip.

Behaviour: The colony of bats roosts high on the trees during the daytime and leave the roosting site after dusk for feeding. They can cover several kilometres in search of food; these can memorize the location and timing of fruiting of trees; they have a keen sense of smell, which helps them in locating flowers and fruits. While feeding, they also pollinate flowers of several trees such as mango, banana, *Mahua*, figs, etc. They are good at dispersing seeds as the consumed seeds, remain viable in the bat's intestine, and are dropped with faecal matter over the large area they cover while flying.

Habitat: Big trees close to human habitations.

Can be sighted in: Probably in all the zones, however, can be spotted near human habitations in the vicinity of CTR.

FULVOUS FRUIT BAT

(H: CHAMGADAR)

Rousettus leschenaultii

PC: MS

A medium-sized fruit bat with body length ranging from 11–15 cm. It has a yellowish-brown back and greyish front, while the older males have dull-grey flanks. It weighs about 90 gm. It can live about 14 years in captivity.

Food: Similar to that of Indian Flying Fox.

Breeding: Known to mate twice a year. Gestation period is about 125 days; a single baby is born at one time, which is carried by the mother during flight for about two months.

Behaviour: They spend the daytime resting in large groups in caves, tunnels and ruins; they leave at dusk to look for food. Like the Indian Flying Fox, they are known to be good at pollinating flowers and dispersing seeds.

Habitat: Roost in caves, tunnels, etc.

Can be sighted in: Probably in all the zones, however, can be spotted near human habitations in the vicinity of CTR.

GREATER SHORT-NOSED FRUIT BAT

(H: CHAMGADAR)

Cynopterus sphinx

A small bat with body length ranging from 7.6–11.3 cm, it has a brownish body, prominent white margins to the ears and dark wings with pale or whitish fingers. Shoulders, chest and chin of males are rusty brown. They weigh about 50 gm; average life expectancy is about 10 years in captivity.

Food: Similar to the Indian Flying Fox.

Breeding: Known to breed twice a year. Gestation period is 115–125 days. One young is born at one time.

Behaviour: It spends the daytime resting among palm leaves or in tree hollows, singly or in small groups. Like the Indian Flying Fox, it is known to be good at pollinating flowers and dispersing seeds throughout the forest.

Habitat: Roosts on trees in thinly forested areas and fringes of forest, and close to cultivations.

Can be sighted in: Probably all the zones, however, can be spotted near human habitations in the vicinity of CTR.

PC: MS

Fulvous Fruit Bat

Pangolins (*Pholidota*)

Pangolins or scaly anteaters (Greek, '*pholidōtos*': covered with scales), have external armour of overlapping hard scales. The scales are made of a material similar to our hair. These have long toothless snout jaws.

INDIAN PANGOLIN

(H: SILU)

Manis crassicaudata

They are about 60–70 cm long. They feed on ants and termites (thus pangolins are also called 'scaly anteaters'). Their forefeet have long curved claws which help them in digging muddy mounds of termites and ants. To capture ants, pangolins use their long protrusible tongue which is coated with sticky material causing ants to adhere. The grinding role of teeth is compensated by the gut which has a thick muscular wall and also contains small stones—under the strong muscular contraction of the gut, pebbles help in grinding the hard components of food. Pangolins have a highly developed sense of smell. They weigh about 8–16 kg, and can live about 12 years in captivity.

Food: Mainly ants and termites.

Breeding: Known to breed once in a year; gestation period is about 80 days; 1–3 young ones are born at one time in burrows. The newborn has soft scales on the body and is carried by its mother on her back; an alarmed mother curls up to cover the baby.

Behaviour: Usually active at night, and spends the day in self-dug burrows and among boulders. When confronted by a predator, it rolls itself tightly into a ball, hiding its vulnerable underparts beneath the scaly armour. Its rolling habit gives it the name 'pangolin', which is derived from the Malay word '*pengguling*', meaning 'something that rolls up'. Pangolins can climb trees, for which their long and curved claws provide an excellent grip.

Habitat: Forested areas and grasslands.

Can be sighted in: Possibly all the zones; the sighting, however, is extremely rare.

Elephants (*Proboscidea*)

The word 'Proboscidea' is derived from the word '*proboscis*', meaning 'trunk' or the long flexible nose of elephants. Today, wild elephants are confined only to Africa and Asia (including the Indian Subcontinent and South-east Asia). African Bush Elephant (*Loxodonta africana*) is larger than Asian Elephant (*Elephas maximus*). The overall body architecture and behaviour of the elephants from the two continents are however similar. Crossbreeding between the two species of elephants produced a hybrid calf in a zoo in England, which could survive only for a few days. Besides India, Asian Elephants are found in 12 other Asian countries. India harbours over 27,000 elephants in the wild, which is about 60 per cent of the total Asian Elephant population. India has nearly 2,600 captive elephants.

ASIAN ELEPHANT (H: HAATHI)

Elephas maximus

Corbett Tiger Reserve (also Rajaji Tiger Reserve and Dudhwa Tiger Reserve) lies in the north-western range of elephants. This range extends from River Yamuna (Uttarakhand) in the west to Katerniaghat (Uttar Pradesh) in the east, along the Himalayan foothills. In the past, elephants could move unhindered throughout the range, but today man-made barriers such as highways, canals, expanding cities, etc., have fragmented the landscape. In spite of all the challenges, elephants manage to travel from one fragment to another via wildlife corridors. According to 2015 census, CTR harbours over 1,000 elephants of which, close to 240 individuals were counted in Dhikala and nearly 190 in Sarpduli ranges.

A large tusker

PC: MS

Mother and calf

Few Facts and Figures About Jumbos

Weight	Adult Male: 3,500–6,000 kg, Female: 2,000–3,500 kg; Newborn calf: 80–110 kg.
Food and water consumption	Adult: about 150 kg foliage and about 140 litres of water per day; calf: 7.6–9.4 litres of milk per day.
Excreta	Defecating 16–18 times, producing 80 kg dung and 25–53 litres of urine per day, with an average volume of 5.5 litres per urination.
Walking and charging speed	6.5 km/hr which may increase to about 48 km/hr while charging.
Skin thickness	Average 18 mm, back can have a thickness of 30 mm.
Trunk	Fused and elongated upper lip and nose; can carry 300 kg weight and hold about 8.0 litres of water.
Tusks	Elongated upper incisor teeth (front teeth); only male elephants have tusks (hence, called 'tusker'); some male elephants are also without tusks and are called 'makhnas'; females can have thin, small protruding teeth (tushes); tusks can grow up to 3 metres and weigh upto 39 kg; the size of tusks increases with age; it is used as a weapon as well as a tool to remove bark from trees.
Reproduction	Females begin to reproduce at 15–16 years of age; gestation period is 18–22 months; females conceive with a gap of 4–5 years; males mature around 14–15 years of age.
Lifespan	60–70 years.
Swimming	Good swimmer.

Looking for Elephants in CTR

CTR is a great place to sight Asian Elephants in India. Elephants are there in every ecotourism zone. Grasslands, in particular Dhikala chaur, Laldhang chaur (Jhirna zone), grassy Kitchar sot bed (Bijrani zone) and banks of Ramganga river near Sambar Road in Dhikala zone, are a few key places where one can observe elephants. It is not uncommon to come across a group of elephants or a stubborn tusker ahead on your safari path. Occasionally, herds can also be seen crossing National Highway-309 at Ringora, near Sunderkhal and Dhangarhi gate. These points are wildlife corridors through which elephants and other animals move from CTR to the neighbouring Ramnagar Forest Division.

A messed-up foliage, presence of fresh dung and the echoing sound of cracking branches give useful clues about the presence of elephants nearby. Also, to move from one place to another within their home range, elephants have certain preferred paths.

Grassland in Dhikala zone

Day-to-day Life of Elephants

Elephants require a large amount of food to sustain (they are megaherbivores!), therefore, most of the time these can be seen foraging. They move about seasonally in a large but fixed area (few tens to hundreds of square kilometres called home range) in search of food and water. In peak summers, when the sun is up in the sky, the elephants move to shady forested areas for foraging or siesta. Visiting a water point is an important event of each day, where, in addition to quenching their thirst, elephants spray water over the entire body for relief from heat. Dust and mud bathing are other regularly performed activities of elephants.

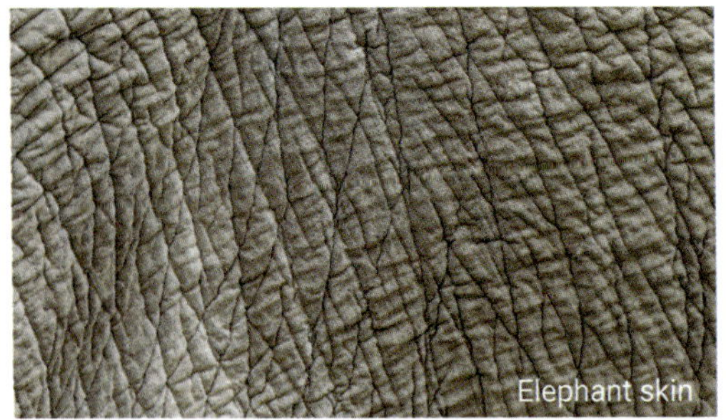

Elephant skin

Time to quench thirst

Why do Elephants Cover their Body with Water, Dust and Mud?

On hotter days, elephants need to shield themselves from solar heat and get rid of the surplus heat generated in their massive body. The process of heat release is less efficient in elephants. They however, have certain unique ways to tackle the situation: their body generates less heat per unit mass and has scanty hair on the skin (which acts as a barrier for exchange of heat). Further, their large fan-like ears are supplied with an extensive network of blood vessels through which a sizable quantity of warm blood flows during hot weather conditions to release excess heat. Fanning of ears further increases the efficiency of heat transfer. Splashing water on the body keeps elephants cool, and a coating of dust and mud (mudbath and dust bath) on the skin shields the body from direct intense solar heat, and offers protection from insects and parasites.

Dust bath

Cooling splash

Elephants are Social, Expressive and Emotional Animals

Elephants live in a joint family of 5–20 individuals—'the herd', the members of which are related to each other as grandmother, mother, aunts, full or half siblings and cousins. A herd is led by the oldest female elephant as she is the repository of social knowledge and experience. After attaining puberty, male elephants disperse away from the family and live a solitary life or in the company of other males. Therefore, a joint family lacks uncles, fathers and adult brothers. Adult males come in contact with herds other than the one in which they were born, to look for a female in heat.

Elephants care for each other in bad times of life: they display sympathy, reassure others in distress and help the injured member or an elephant in trouble. They greet and express joy, love and affection. They feel sorrow and mourn when a member of the herd dies, and visit the remains (such as bones, tusks, etc.) of dead relatives for long.

Musth Elephants

Each year for a few months, an adult male elephant turns more aggressive, tries to dominate other male elephants and shows an increased attraction towards female elephants—he is said to be in *Musth* period. An elephant in musth secretes a foul-smelling fluid descending down his cheek from a gland located midway between eyes and ears. The fluid contains a substance 'Frontalin', the smell of which attracts female elephants. Non-musth elephants keep themselves away from musth elephants to avoid a scuffle. Sub-adult male elephants also experience musth period (they are called *moda musth*). However, their secretion is sweet smelling and has a different chemical composition. Sweet odorous secretion is said to advertise immaturity of younger males and unwillingness to confront mature males to acquire a mate. A fight between two musth males may result in blinding, breaking of tusks, severe wounds or even death.

PC: NZ

In musth

Gentle But Turns the Deadliest When Stressed

Elephants generally do not show aggression in the wild. A herd may change its track or cross the path quickly when there is a confrontation with tourist vehicles. However, bulls during musth period and a herd with young ones may charge vehicles approaching close to them. Elephants are also known to kill humans brutally and damage properties. This shift in the behaviour of elephants could be due to long-term stress owing to human–elephant conflict.

Ramganga river Dhikala zone

Baby Elephant is the Darling of Every Member of the Herd

Birth of a new member is a celebrated event in the herd. The female in labour is surrounded by her relatives for protection and to welcome the newborn. To become self-sufficient, a baby elephant has to learn several essential lessons of life from its elders, and has to practice how to use its iconic organ 'trunk'. It acquires the sense of what is to be eaten by taking a bite of food from the mouth of others, and eats foliage dislodged from the tree by its mother.

It is the responsibility of every member of the herd to provide security to the infant; bring it back when it strays away, push to show the direction of movement, and keep in the middle of the herd or underneath adults in case danger is perceived. Any distress call from the infant draws immediate attention of other members. As evidence of such protective behaviour, one might observe the defensive formation in elephants, where older members align and face the danger keeping the young ones behind them. While crossing a track, one member of the herd often wards off approaching vehicles, making it safe for the other members to move through. The importance of mothers in the life of an elephant is no different from that in humans.

Tele-communication—An Amazing Capability of Elephants to Talk with Their Relatives

Elephants can communicate even if they are miles away or out of sight of each other. They have two systems for long-distance communication: first, by using infrasonic sounds which they can produce (by voice box) and hear (it is beyond the hearing range of humans), and second, by producing seismic waves (vibrations in the ground, such as during earthquakes) that can be sensed by the distant members of the extended family. Using infrasonic sounds and seismic waves in communication has an advantage, as these are less affected by obstacles (such as dense forest) and can travel to distances of several kilometres. Such tele-communication allows herds of elephants, to remain in touch even if they are out the sight of each other in the dense forest.

It is believed that elephants detect arriving seismic signals through their feet and trunk, and can also sense an incoming earthquake well in advance. Further, elephants can sense a rainstorm happening over a hundred kilometres away from them, possibly by sensing the infrasound generated by the rain-system.

PC: AM

Calves under impenetrable security

Elephants' Fear

Elephants are scared of bees and chilli. They retreat after hearing the sound of angry bee buzz or sensing the smell of chilli. These two have been used as tactics to keep raiding elephants away from crop fields.

Animal with Long-term Memory and Intelligence

Elephants are known for their incredible long-term memories. An elephant can recognise its fellow elephants even after decades of separation, and can distinguish voices of about a hundred of its friends and relatives. Moreover, merely by listening to the voices of two ethnic groups, elephants can make out which of the two has threatened them in the past. Elephants can precisely remember the spots/locations of seasonal availability of food and water as well as the routes to access such places across an area spanning several hundred km^2.

Field observations and experiments have unveiled several other extraordinary cerebral capabilities of elephants, such as the imitation of human voice and other sounds, capability to solve problems spontaneously without any hit and trial, and the ability to modify tools to perform a task.

Trunk—a Versatile Organ

Elephants use their trunk to perform a variety of tasks. An elephant may die of starvation and thirst if its trunk is severely damaged. The interior of the trunk has two tubes (nostrils), running along its entire length, which are surrounded by about 60,000 powerful muscles. The trunk is powerful enough to uproot small trees and fracture branches. The function of the trunk, however, is not limited to clasping; it is the organ for smelling, breathing, voice modulation, expressing feelings, and possibly as a sensor for detection of seismic signals.

Checklist of Mammals Seen In and Around CTR

Hedgehogs (*Erinaceomorpha*)

1	Indian Long-eared Hedgehog	*Hemiechinus collaris*

Shrews (*Soricomorpha*)

2	Pygmy White-toothed Shrew	*Suncus etruscus*
3	Asian House Shrew	*Suncus murinus*

Bats (*Chiroptera*)

4	Greater Short-nosed Fruit Bat	*Cynopterus sphinx*
5	Fulvous Fruit Bat	*Rousettus leschenaultii*
6	Indian Flying Fox	*Pteropus giganteus*
7	Great Himalayan Leaf-nosed Bat	*Hipposideros armiger*
8	Least Leaf-nosed Bat	*Hipposideros cineraceus*
9	Hodgson's Bat	*Myotis formosus*
10	Indian Pygmy Pipistrelle	*Pipistrellus mimus*
11	Brown Long-eared Bat	*Plecotus auritus*
12	Asiatic Yellow House Bat	*Scotophilus heathii*
13	Peter's Tube-nosed Bat	*Murina grisea*

Monkeys (*Primate*)

14	Rhesus Macaque	*Macaca mulatta*
15	Gray Langur	*Semnopithecus* sp.

Squirrels, Porcupines, Rats, etc. (*Rodentia*)

16	Five-striped Palm Squirrel	*Funambulus pennantii*
17	Red Giant Flying Squirrel	*Petaurista petaurista*
18	Indian Gerbil	*Tatera indica*
19	Greater Bandicoot Rat	*Bandicota indica*
20	Indian Bush Rat	*Golunda ellioti*
21	Little Indian Field Mouse	*Mus booduga*
22	House Mouse	*Mus musculus*
23	Short-tailed Bandicoot Rat	*Nesokia indica*
24	House Rat	*Rattus rattus*
25	Indian Crested Porcupine	*Hystrix indica*

Hares (*Lagomorpha*)

26	Indian Hare	*Lepus nigricollis*

Pangolins (*Pholidota*)

27	Indian Pangolin	*Manis crassicaudata*

Tiger, Bears, Civets, Jackals, etc. (*Carnivora*)

28	Golden Jackal	*Canis aureus*
29	Red Fox	*Vulpes vulpes*
30	Tiger	*Panthera tigris*
31	Leopard	*Panthera pardus*
32	Striped Hyaena	*Hyaena hyaena*
33	Jungle Cat	*Felis chaus*
34	Leopard Cat	*Prionailurus bengalensis*
35	Fishing Cat	*Prionailurus viverrinus*
36	Rusty-spotted Cat	*Prionailurus rubiginosus*
37	Yellow-throated Marten	*Martes flavigula*
38	Sloth Bear	*Melursus ursinus*
39	Asian Black Bear	*Ursus thibetanus*
40	Masked or Himalayan Palm Civet	*Paguma larvata*
41	Common Palm Civet	*Paradoxurus hermaphroditus*
42	Small Indian Civet	*Viverricula indica*
43	Large Indian Civet	*Viverra zibetha*
44	Grey Mongoose	*Herpestes edwardsii*
45	Smooth-coated Otter	*Lutrogale perspicillata*
46	Eurasian Otter	*Lutra lutra*

Deer, Wild Boar, Blue Bull, etc. (*Artiodactyla*)

47	Indian Wild Pig or Indian Wild Boar	*Sus scrofa*
48	Spotted Deer	*Axis axis*
49	Sambar	*Rusa unicolour*
50	Indian Muntjac	*Muntiacus muntjac*
51	Hog Deer	*Axis porcinus*
52	Blue Bull	*Boselaphus tragocamelus*
53	Himalayan Brown Goral	*Naemorhedus goral*
54	Himalayan Serow	*Capricornis thar*

Elephants (*Proboscidea*)

55	Asian Elephant	*Elephas maximus*

PC: HP

Jungle Cat

Mammals That were Once Seen or Common in CTR and Surrounding Areas

Indian Grey Wolf (*Canis lupus*): Awards were given during the colonial period for the destruction of this animal. It is not sighted in the present times.

Wild Dog (*Cuon alpinus*): These caused extensive destruction to cattle and deer, and awards were given during the colonial period to kill them. There are only scanty records of this animal in the past few decades.

Pygmy Hog (*Porcula salvania*): Occasionally seen in Terai areas south of the present CTR during the colonial period. Its flesh was greatly prized by *Tharu* and *Bhuksa* people who inhabited that area. It is not sighted in the present times.

Four-horned Antelope (*Tetracerus quadricornis*): These were seen occasionally in Sal forests. It is not sighted in the present times.

Swamp Deer (*Rucervus duvaucelii*): Once plenty in swampy areas south of CTR. It is said to be occasionally seen in certain swampy pockets south of CTR.

One-horned Rhinoceros (*Rhinoceros unicornis*): There is a record of sighting of this animal in the eighteenth century from foothills near Kotwar, Pauri Garhwal. It is not seen in the present times.

A peacock train has about 165–170 eyespots (p.92)

Birds

Everyone enjoys watching the animated activities of birds, the repertoire of colours and melodious songs just adds a little extra icing to the cake. Many people pursue 'birdwatching' or 'birding' as their main recreational activity. These hobbyists generate enormous amounts of observational data that has been used for conservation purposes. Birds are also the most common celebrities whom every nature photographer wants to capture with their cameras.

Corbett Tiger Reserve (CTR) is a birder's paradise; more than 500 species of birds of over 1,300 recorded in India can be seen in CTR (about 10,000 species of bird have been recorded worldwide). The diverse habitats found here are home (for resident birds), resorts (for migratory birds) and halt (for passage migrants) for numerous birds. CTR has been recognized among 'Important Bird and Biodiversity Areas' (IBAs) in India—it holds significant numbers of globally threatened species. This section provides photographs with textual identification features of about 330 species of birds seen in and around CTR. Birds that are less likely to be sighted during visits to CTR have not been included.

Role of Birds in Nature

1) Many birds, seeking insects and nectar in flowers, can transfer pollen, thus act as pollinators for plants, 2) birds are important agents of seed dispersal; the undigested seeds of fruits they eat are dropped over a large area, 3) birds feeding on insect pests and small mammals (such as rats) can help in controlling their population, and 4) many birds (such as kites, crows and vultures) function as scavengers—they consume the animal carcasses and speedily remove them from the environment, which otherwise would putrefy and serve as a breeding ground for pathogenic organisms.

Watching Birds In and Around CTR

One can go for birdwatching in the CTR in safari vehicles. Since alighting from the vehicle and walking is prohibited, birdwatching and photographing must be done from the vehicle. Bird populations are not distributed uniformly across the jungle; sometimes, one might not hear even the chirping of birds or may encounter only a few birds in some stretches of the forest. On the other hand, places such as interface of forest and grassland, around streams and on trees laden with fruits (such as fig trees), there is always a higher possibility to find birds of several species. At times in the forested areas, one comes across stretches with several species of birds (including flycatchers, minivets, thrushes, babblers, nuthatches, drongos, tits, warblers) busy foraging on the ground, bushes, tree trunks and high up on the trees. This alliance of birds is called *'Mixed Species Flock'* (p.134).

Birds are choosy about their habitats. Ecotourism zones include varieties of habitats such as woodlands, thin forests, scrubs, grasslands, river banks, marshy areas and reservoirs. Thus, in CTR, one gets the opportunity to watch birds living in diverse habitats. Also, the average altitude in CTR increases from north to south; the northern most part (Durgadevi and Sonanadi zones), being closer to higher reaches of the Himalayas, offers the opportunity to spot a few bird species that are usually sighted at higher altitudes.

There are also a few sites for observing birds (like waders, waterfowls, herons and egrets) outside but close to the boundary of CTR; these sites are 'Tumaria Reservoir' (about 25 km from Ramnagar), banks of Kosi river near 'Garjia Devi Temple', and 'Kosi River Barrage'. One might also enjoy birdwatching on foot, in villages located at the periphery of CTR. It is, however, advised not to enter the forested areas without due permission from the forest department.

Best time of the year for birdwatching in CTR:

February—a period when the number of bird species is the highest (wintering birds have not yet left and those wintering in some other parts of the subcontinent are on their return halt).

March–mid-May—it is the best time for witnessing breeding activities of birds, such as territory marking, courtship display, songs and nest making.

Best time of the day for birdwatching:

Morning and the last couple of hours before sunset.

Scenic Tumaria reservoir

Photographing Birds

Getting the perfect portrait and capturing birds in action is a challenging task. Success depends on the experience and patience of photographers, and how technically advanced their camera is. Many digital compact cameras available these days, that are capable of quick focusing on objects and giving nearly 50X or greater zoom, are quite suitable for photographing birds in all situations. To get good portraits of birds perched within the range of 20–30 m, visitors using cameras with interchangeable lenses would require a lens with a focal length of at least 500 mm.

Identifying Birds

Spotting or locating birds in their natural habitat is the first step in birdwatching and for that, quiet vigil is needed. It is easy to locate birds which are making some kind of sound or movements. However, to spot birds sitting quietly, making less perceptible movements or camouflaging with the surroundings, one needs to scan the area thoroughly. Once a bird has been located, its behaviour (how it forages, flies, walks, perches, the way it moves on trees, etc.) and the habitat in which it is seen, together with its body outline and field marks, help in assigning the identity. Some important field marks include: the size and shape of bill, wings, tail, legs and feet, colour of bill, legs and eyes, and pattern of plumage colouration. In some cases, the song or call of birds also aid in their identification. It is often useful to record the month in which a bird is spotted.

Note that!

1) In many bird species, plumage colouration in breeding and non-breeding adults, in males and females, and juvenile and adult birds is drastically different.

2) The body outline of many bird species may differ in resting and alert postures.

3) Plumage colour reproduction in field guidebooks is only an approximation of the actual colour of the bird seen in the field.

An experienced birder can identify many birds just by a quick look; beginners require frequent field trips to hone their identification skills. In cases where identification in the field is not possible, photographs of birds taken from different angles can be compared with the reference images in various websites or field guidebooks.

The Life of Birds

The life of a bird begins from the egg which is produced in the body of female birds, and gets fertilized when the female birds mate with the male birds. Fertilized eggs are then laid in a secure cradle—'the nest'. Shaping of chick inside the egg begins when parents provide the warmth of their body (Incubation). Chicks emerge from the egg by breaking open the shell with the help of their beaks. In birds such as sparrows and bulbuls, chicks are born helpless; they have scanty or no feathers on the body, closed eyes, and are totally dependent on the parents for food and body warmth. In contrast, chicks of many other birds including fowls are covered with downy feathers and are capable of moving around with parents soon after hatching.

Hatchlings of many birds take a few days to recognize their parents by call and appearance. Chicks gain in weight

Coming into Existence on Earth—the Journey of Birds Through Time

Birds evolved from distant relatives of the dreadful dinosaur *Tyrannosaurus rex* in the Jurassic period (around 165–150 million years ago). The early ancestors of birds gradually evolved bird-like features over several millions of years. The modern look of birds and their diversity seen today is thought to have come about (evolved) after the mass extinction which took place on the earth about 66 million years ago. The cause of this devastation is believed to be a 10-kilometre-wide asteroid which collided with the part of the earth that presently comprises Mexico. The impact led to widespread earthquakes, tsunamis, wildfires, and released large amounts of energy, water, dust and gases which changed the climate. This event wiped out over 80 percent of the entire land-dwellers—such as all the dinosaurs, many early birds and other animals from the face of the earth. However, birds that were not dependent on trees (ground-dwelling), birds that fed on seeds (seeds are hardy enough to survive fire and last for years), and others which were capable of diving, swimming or taking shelter in water and marshlands survived to give rise to over 10,000 species of birds found on present-day earth.

Birds are living Dinosaurs

Arrangement of Birds in the Section

Birds have been clustered according to the 'family' (a rank in classification system) to which they belong. For example, the family '*Anatidae*' includes 'Geese and Ducks' and has been represented as 'Geese and Ducks (*Anatidae*)'.

Each species of birds has been denoted by 'Common English Name' and 'Scientific Name' (in *italics*).

The placement of birds under appropriate families, the arrangement of families, and the common as well as the scientific names of the birds that have been used are largely based on *Grimmett et al. 2011*.

Readers may note that recent taxonomic advancements have led to shifting of birds (particularly from families *sylviidae* and *timaliidae*) from one family to another or put under new families. One may refer to the latest checklist of birds of India in: Praveen J. *et al*. 2016, *Indian BIRDS*, 11:113-170.

To make the text useful to beginners, several technical scientific terms have been avoided and more general or common words have been used instead. It has been assumed that the readers would rely more on images for details of colouration, shape and size of the various body parts of birds. The supporting text provided with each bird species mainly highlights the features which enable distinction between similar looking birds.

Size Guide: For easy visualisation, certain common birds seen in most parts of India have been used as reference for the comparison of approximate size and outline of the bird's body.

Abbreviations: Br= Breeding Plumage; NBr= Nonbreeding Plumage

Reference Birds	Approximate Body Size
Sparrow (House Sparrow, *Passer domesticus*):	15 cm
Bulbul (Red-vented Bulbul, *Pycnonotus cafer*):	20 cm
Myna (Common Myna, *Acridotheres tristis*):	25 cm
Pigeon (Common Pigeon, *Columba livia*):	35 cm
Crow (House Crow, *Corvus splendens*):	40 cm
Parakeet (Rose-ringed Parakeet, *Psittacula krameri*):	42 cm
Domestic Hen (*Gallus* sp.):	45–60 cm
Domestic Duck (*Anas* sp.):	62 cm
Kite (Black Kite, *Milvus migrans*):	65 cm

For a few birds (such as herons, storks, etc.) however, body size is given in centimetres.

exponentially during the first couple of weeks and demand a large amount of nutritious food. Their ever-increasing appetite can be judged in the field, by the extent of begging when parents bring food to the nest. In some birds, only one member of the parental pair performs the duty of raising the young ones (Baya Weaver, buttonquails), and certain parasitic birds (such as cuckoos) get this job done by other bird species.

Growing chicks discard their downy feathers and acquire a new type of feathers. These feathers resemble that of the parents, though the texture (and in some birds the pattern of colouration as well) may differ. At this stage chicks are said to be in juvenile plumage. In some birds, the chicks after independence from parental care, live with parents, while in some others, the chicks disperse away from the parents to begin their adult life.

Smaller birds such as sparrows and woodpeckers can live about 10–13 years, parrots can live for more than 30 years; owls and falcons live for 10–20 years, birds like waterfowls, cranes, herons and storks live for 20–30 years, and albatrosses, flamingos and petrels live for 30–50 years or even more.

Silver-eared Mesia (*Leiothrix argentauris*)—one of the most colourful birds in this region

Feathers—a Unique Asset

Feathers are unique to birds. Depending upon the bird species, there might be 1,000 to over 20,000 feathers on a bird. Feathers are fabricated of a protein called 'Keratin' which is also the building material of claws and scaly covering over legs.

An adult bird has two major types of feathers: those found on wings and tail (flight feathers), and those covering the rest of the body. These two types of feathers are collectively called 'contour feathers' because they give the bird a characteristic outline. Flight feathers have a long, rigid axis which gives off numerous thin filaments along its length on either side. Adjacent filaments on both the sides are tightly hooked with each other, forming continuous stiff blades. The feathers covering the remaining part of the body are soft and the filaments are locked only at the upper part of feathers; the lower unlocked part gives a fluffy appearance.

Found beneath the body feathers are the third kind of feathers—'down feathers': these are fluffy and greatly assist in insulation of the body. Commercially, down feathers from geese are used as insulator in jackets, quilts, sleeping bags and other mountaineering garments. Bristles near the beaks and long feathers forming the crest in some birds are specialized feathers. Feathers of birds undergo wear and tear, and since feathers are dead structures that cannot be repaired, birds lose them at regular intervals, and they are quickly re-grown by a process called 'moulting'.

Body Parts of a Bird

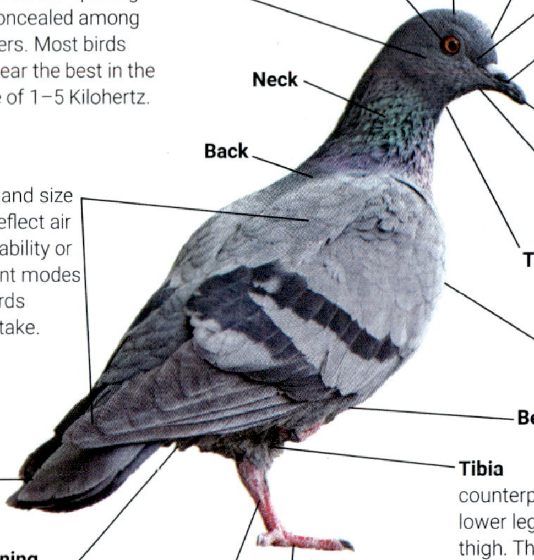

Eyes
birds are known to have the best vision among all the animals.
Crown
Forehead
Nose openings
some birds have a protective flap to keep away debris while feeding on the ground. Birds, in general, have a sense of smell and can make use of it to locate food and nesting burrows.
Ear
birds have no external ears. The ear openings are concealed among feathers. Most birds can hear the best in the range of 1–5 Kilohertz.
Lore
Neck
Back
Wing
the shape and size of wings reflect air manoeuvrability or the different modes of flight birds can undertake.
Chin
Throat
Bill or Beak
it is elongated toothless jaw bones covered with a sheath. The functional utility of bill compensates for the absence of hands. The shape and size of the beaks often indicate the type of food eaten by the bird and methods of obtaining and handling food.
Breast
Belly
Tail
Tibia
counterpart of human lower leg and not the thigh. The part of bird's leg that is the counterpart of the human knee and thigh, is hidden under feathers.
Cloacal opening
cloaca is a common chamber in the body of birds, where genital, intestinal and urinary ducts open. Cloaca opens to the outside through an opening called vent. Birds defecate, urinate and copulate through this opening. In bird's droppings the white pasty material is urine and the darker mass in the centre is faeces.
Toe
counterpart of human digits; birds walk on their toes.
Tarsus
counterpart of human midfoot bones which are fused in birds.

Feathers from Different Parts of the Body of Common Pigeon

Tips of wings
Middle of wings
Tail
Belly
Neck

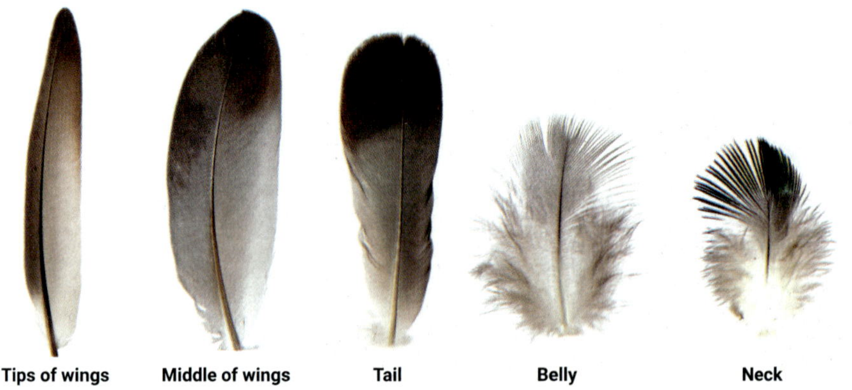

Francolins, Quails, Pheasants and Fowls (*Phasianidae*)

Heavy bodied birds; seen walking on the ground in scrubs, tall grasslands (francolins and quails), thinly forested areas and fringes of forest (Red Jungle Fowl, Kalij Pheasant and Indian Peafowl). These birds feed on seeds, insects, worms, etc., hidden beneath dry leaves and soil. When alarmed, they escape by running or taking flight for short distances and disappearing in dense foliage. In this group of birds, generally males are gorgeously coloured while females are cryptically coloured. Many members of this group are ground nesters and make simple nests under bushes, grass or rock. Young ones are capable of walking and feeding, shortly after hatching. ***These birds can be sighted in all the zones.***

Male

▲

BLACK FRANCOLIN

Francolinus francolinus

Slightly larger than Pigeon. Females lack black colouration on the face and breast, and lack white area below the eyes.

COMMON QUAIL

Coturnix coturnix

Myna-sized or slightly larger. Distinguished from Grey Francolin by its smaller size and by the lack of wavy markings on the underparts.

▼

PC: AC

GREY FRANCOLIN

Francolinus pondicerianus

Slightly larger in size than Pigeon. It has fine barrings on upperparts and underparts.

▼

▲
RED JUNGLEFOWL

Gallus gallus

Same size as the Domestic Hen. Females and chicks with cryptic colourations.

▲
KALIJ PHEASANT

Lophura leucomelanos

Slightly larger than Domestic Hen.

▲
INDIAN PEAFOWL

Pavo cristatus

Males with long colourful train; females lack long train and have greenish neck, whitish belly and brownish upperparts.

The Mystery of the Peafowl Train

The long train of the male Indian Peafowl (Peacock) is basically a bunch of about 200 elongated feathers. As soon as the breeding season is over, the train is shed and re-grown. The train has multicoloured rings (eyespots), which a male bird begins to develop after reaching the age of two years.

Why do peacocks bear such a cumbersome ornamental train? The train serves as an indicator of the quality of males. While the males are engaged in fanning their erect trains (Peacock dance), the peahens scrutinize the trains and choose the males with the best looking trains. Peahens are generally impressed by those peacocks which have longer trains with more eyespots, and hue and iridescence of the blue-green portion of the eyespot. These measurements reviewed by the peahen are linked to the health of male birds; for instance, in spite of carrying a bulky train, the male contender is strong enough to cope with the problems faced in the wild, such as timely escape from predation. Also, the colour and iridescence are the result of proper arrangement of bio-molecules in feathers. A peacock bearing such feathers would be expected to be healthy and sturdy and carrier of a superior set of genes. Therefore, by selecting the best male, the peahens ensure propagation of a superior set of genes for future generations.

Geese and Ducks (*Anatidae*)

These are seen in large, mixed flocks in or near large waterbodies such as rivers, lakes or reservoirs, feeding mainly on aquatic plants by diving, picking from water surface, and by probing the mud and water with their beaks. These birds typically have webbed feet adapted for swimming by paddling. They fly in a characteristic 'V'-formation. Most birds of this group are winter migrants from Russia, Mongolia, China, and Central Asian countries such as Kazakhstan, Turkmenistan, Uzbekistan, etc.

Though birds of this group can be sighted in Ramganga river inside CTR and near Kosi river barrage, the best place, however, to sight these birds is the Tumaria reservoir.

Male

KNOB-BILLED DUCK

Sarkidiornis melanotos

Nearly the size of Domestic Duck or larger. Females similar to males but are smaller and lack a comb.

RUDDY SHELDUCK

Tadorna ferruginea

Nearly the size of Domestic Duck. Breeding males have a distinct dark neck-collar which is less prominent or may be absent in the non-breeding plumage; females lack a neck-collar.

Female

Male

GADWALL

Anas strepera

Smaller than the Domestic Duck. Females have orange sides to dark bill.

Male

Female

Front: female; Rear: male

Front: male; Rear: female

▲
MALLARD

Anas platyrhynchos

Domestic Duck sized. It has blue speculum (arrow). The speculum is white in Gadwall.

▲
EURASIAN WIGEON

Anas penelope

Nearly the size of Domestic Duck. Females with uniform brown head and brownish back.

▲
INDIAN SPOT-BILLED DUCK

Anas poecilorhyncha

Nearly the size of Domestic Duck. Sexes similar, however males have a prominent red mark between the eye and base of the bill.

▲
NORTHERN SHOVELER

Anas clypeata

Nearly the size of Domestic Duck.

NORTHERN PINTAIL ▶

Anas acuta

Nearly the size of Domestic Duck.

COMMON TEAL

Anas crecca

Smaller than Domestic Duck.

FERRUGINOUS DUCK

Aythya nyroca

Slightly smaller than Domestic Duck. Females similar to males but with dark eyes.

TUFTED DUCK

Aythya fuligula

Slightly smaller than Domestic Duck. Females lighter in colouration than males, and with paler flanks.

GARGANEY

Anas querquedula

Smaller than Domestic Duck. Females dull in colouration.

RED-CRESTED POCHARD

Netta rufina

Nearly the size of Domestic Duck.

COMMON MERGANSER

Mergus merganser

Nearly the size of Domestic Duck or larger. Breeding males with dark green whereas females and immature males with chestnut head and neck.

The Flight of a Bird—a Marvel in Itself

The body of birds is customized for flight: they have hollow bones, short intestine, lack urinary bladder and teeth, and eat less bulky and highly nutritious food (seeds, fruits, insects and meat). All these features reduce body weight of birds. Their streamlined bodies covered with smooth, light-weight yet strong feathers help them easily navigate through air. Unlike ours, bird lungs get fresh air during both exhalation and inhalation; also, their large heart and fast heartbeat pump more blood to provide an uninterrupted supply of oxygen to the wing muscles.

The aerodynamics of a bird's flight is complex, however it can be explained in the simplest form by considering two basic natural forces that act on birds when they fly: 'gravitational force' and 'drag force'. The former is their own body weight that pulls them downwards and prevents lift off from the ground or makes it difficult to remain aloft. The latter force is exerted by the air which prevents the flier from moving forward (by pushing backwards). Birds are capable of opposing these restraining forces by virtue of the particular shape of their wings, vigorous flapping of which generates counter forces: 'lift', that opposes gravitational force and 'thrust', that opposes drag force. This, of course, requires a large amount of the bird's energy, and is therefore called 'powered flight'.

The lift and thrust is generated in the following way: as the bird moves through air, the leading ends of the wings deflect air on their upper and lower surfaces. Due to the particular shape of the wings (recall the shape of wings of an airplane!) air flows backwards faster across the upper surface of wings than the lower surface. The difference between the velocities of air passing over the two surfaces creates lower air pressure on the upper surface and higher pressure below the wings, forcing the bird up in the air, i.e., provides lift. Also, while the wings are being flapped, their outer part moves faster and functions as blades of a propeller to generate thrust. Thus, these two forces work together to enable the birds to fly.

Birds are capable of performing a myriad of flight manoeuvres such as diving, climbing, somersaulting, hovering, soaring and taking sharp turns at high speed. These are necessary for mid-air hunting, escape, long-distance migration, food searching, etc. Flight manoeuvres are accomplished by the shape and size of wings, the ratio of the weight of a bird to the surface area of its wings and minor adjustments (such as the extent of stretching and tilting of wings) made during flight. For example, short, narrow and pointed wings of falcons, hawks and swallows enable high speed and manoeuvrability, and broad and fingered wings of vultures, eagles and storks are meant for efficient soaring with limited manoeuvrability.

Force involved in keeping birds afloat

Gliding and Soaring—Energy-saving, Flight Modes in Birds

Sometimes, birds such as vultures, eagles and storks are seen flying effortlessly over a long distance without flapping their stretched wings—this is called gliding (non-powered flight). A gliding bird gradually loses altitude due to gravitational pull. To regain altitude, the bird must begin flapping its wings (powered flight) or shift to 'soaring' mode of flight. During soaring, birds gain altitude not by wing-flapping; instead, they are uplifted by the rising air current. In a type of soaring known as 'thermal soaring', birds get uplifted to a higher altitude while they glide in circles within a column of rising warm air. After achieving a sufficient height, the birds exit the air column and glide in a straight path to cover long distances, again with a loss of altitude. The birds, thereafter, may encounter another column of rising warm air and gain altitude. This way they repeat the soaring-gliding sequence till they reach their final destination, without expending much of the body fuel.

Gliding and soaring require a large wing-span, and therefore, these flight modes are seen in birds such as vultures, eagles, storks, gulls, etc. Vultures can be commonly seen circling in the sky during the day time, scanning vast areas on the ground to locate carcasses.

Hovering: A few birds remain in the air at the same point while vigorously flapping their wings (humming birds have mastered this mode of flight!). This is called hovering. Many birds often choose this mode of flight while foraging. Hovering is tough and quite an energy-demanding process, and is practised only by a few birds.

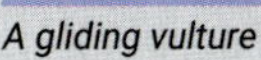

A gliding vulture

A hovering kite

Moulting—Replacement and Renewal of Feathers

Birds periodically shed and regrow all or some of their feathers by the process called moulting. A bird undergoes two types of moulting during its life: one takes place as the birds grow from chick to adult, and the second occurs annually in adult birds. In the former type, growing chicks replace their downy feathers with juvenile feathers, after which the chick is said to possess juvenile plumage. In most birds, juvenile plumage is duller, streaky and cryptic. Juvenile plumage is replaced with adult plumage, after which the growing birds resemble adults. Time taken to attain adult plumage varies among birds—it may take less than a year in some birds to a few years in others. After attaining adult plumage, most birds renew their plumage once a year. However, males of many birds, just before the breeding season, replace some of their feathers (usually non-flight ones) with colourful feathers. At this stage, these birds are said to have 'breeding plumage'. The main purpose of this showy plumage is to impress mates. One might observe a few birds (males of weaver birds, Purple Sunbird, Red Avadavat, etc.) which are colourful during spring and summers, and look dull during the rest of the year. Breeding plumage is retained only for a short period of time, i.e., during the breeding season, since the bright and colourful plumage makes birds more noticeable to predators. Flight is important for the survival of birds, and therefore, many land birds shed their flight feathers in a systematic manner; they moult only a few feathers of wings or tail at any given time.

Birds cannot consciously induce moulting, just as we cannot shed our hair at will. The induction and timing of moulting is controlled by hormones and the internal clock of birds guided by environmental conditions. Moulting serves several purposes: birds can renew their worn-off feathers, some birds get the opportunity to change their look for better camouflage with surroundings and to attract mates during the breeding season.

Breeding (left) and non-breeding (right) plumage forms of Purple Sunbird male

Grebes (*Podicipedidae*)

These are aquatic birds with short tail and legs, and an elongated neck. Their legs are placed at the rear of the body. Grebes can dive and swim underwater to catch their prey, such as fishes and other small aquatic animals. These birds make their nest on water-weeds or floating vegetation.

Grebes can be sighted in the Ramganga river, near Kosi river barrage and Tumaria reservoir.

▲ **LITTLE GREBE**

Tachybaptus ruficollis

Pigeon-sized. Distinguished from Great Crested Grebe by its smaller size and dark crown extending to eyes (arrow).

◀ **GREAT CRESTED GREBE**

Podiceps cristatus

Slightly smaller than Domestic Duck. In breeding plumage it has a tuft of rusty -brown feathers behind the cheek.

Bird Migration—an Annual Marathon Towards the Alternate Resort

Worldwide, over 1,800 species of birds leave their place of residence (place where they were born and where they breed) every year, and migrate to a fixed geographical area. Birds migrate to avoid unliveable seasonal conditions, and when circumstances are favourable, they return and breed. Most birds migrate at the onset of winter (Winter Migrants). In the northern hemisphere, winter migrants often migrate from their residence located in a more northern (and hence, colder) part to a more southern part of the earth, where winters are liveable, covering hundreds to thousands of kilometres (Long Distance Migrants). Also, many birds living at higher altitudes (such as in high reaches of Himalayas) descend to lower altitudes during winters (Altitudinal Winter Migrants), and return with the onset of spring to the higher altitudes to breed. One may witness several winter migrant birds in CTR during October–March.

Winter migration, particularly over long distances, is a well-planned event. Birds can foresee the timing of migration, and accordingly finish all sorts of preparations ahead of the flight marathon. Thus, by the late summers, the birds begin to renew their feathers (moulting), store huge amounts of fat as fuel and increase the size of flight muscles to power their long migratory flight. They take short breaks at stopovers (for rest and refuelling) that have been used over generations.

How do birds navigate in the wide expanse of the sky to reach the same wintering resort precisely every year and return? To find their way, birds need mechanisms equivalent to the clock, calendar, map and compass. The functions of these gadgets are fulfilled by the bird's internal clock system, their ability to gauge direction by taking cues from the position of celestial bodies (such as the sun and stars), and the earth's magnetic field.

High intensity urban lighting can cause disorientation in birds migrating by night, lead them to aggregate around light in a high density, and might also cause their death due to collision with buildings and other structures.

Using Earth's Magnetic Field for Navigation

Birds have the ability to sense the earth's magnetic field and make its use for navigation. The properties of this magnetic field, which varies at different points on the earth, can be sensed by birds to get a cue about the location and direction. Certain protein molecules called 'cryptochromes' in the eyes, and 'magnetite', a magnetic mineral near the beak, are known to sense the properties of the earth's magnetic field.

Flying in 'V'-Formation—a Reflection of Cooperation Among Fliers

A few species of birds are seen flying in 'V'-formations and cluster formations. Clustering in a disordered manner and flying haphazardly in large numbers is supposed to confuse nearby predators. However, the purpose of 'V'-formation, as seen in many large birds while they cover a long distance, has been explained thoroughly in scientific terms. In this type of formation, the flapping of wings by the leading bird produces favourable air vortices behind it; these vortices provide lift to the pursuing bird. In this way, the pursuer can fly even by flapping its wings at a lower frequency. This simply means that the pursuer bird can relax or conserve energy. Thus, in order to take this aerodynamic advantage and optimise air resistance, a group of flying birds must arrange themselves in a 'V'-formation. Since the leader in the formation is at an energetically unfavourable position, birds in the formation take turns being the leading bird.

'V'-formation in a Common Crane flock

Storks (*Ciconiidae*)

These are large-sized birds with long legs, long neck and large bill—which are adaptations for feeding by slow walking in marshes and shallow waters along lakes and rivers. They feed on small aquatic animals, snakes, lizards, etc. Storks have broad wings that allow them an efficient, soaring mode of flight. While flying, storks keep their neck stretched forward. These birds make their nest with coarse sticks and coat the nests with leaves, high on the trees. Helpless chicks are fed by both the parents who bring food and regurgitate it before feeding it to the chicks. ***Storks can be sighted near rivers, streams and dry river beds in all the zones in CTR, and near Kosi river barrage and Tumaria reservoir.***

▲

PAINTED STORK

Mycteria leucocephala

Size about 100 cm. Juvenile birds have a brownish head and neck.

ASIAN OPENBILL

Anastomus oscitans

Size about 70 cm. It has a thick bill with a gap between upper and lower half of the bill.

▼

BLACK STORK

Ciconia nigra

Size about 100 cm. It can be distinguished from the Black-necked Stork by its smaller size, all black upperparts, and reddish bill. A winter migrant from the Russian region, known to cross high mountain ranges of the Hindu Kush and Karakoram for migration.

▼

▲
BLACK-NECKED STORK

Ephippiorhynchus asiaticus

Size about 130 cm. Males similar to females but have brown eyes (yellow in females).

▲
WOOLLY-NECKED STORK

Ciconia episcopus

Size about 75–90 cm. It can be distinguished from Black and Black-necked storks by the woolly appearance of its neck.

Bird Egg—a Chamber Where Life is Fashioned

The function of a bird's egg is similar to that of the womb, where a cluster of few cells develop into an individual. As developing eggs pass through reproductive tract of female birds, they get coated with layers of albumin (egg white), few other layers and finally with a shell-forming material (calcium carbonate). An egg encloses all sorts of raw material required to craft a chick; the albumin and yolk, commonly known as the white and yellow of an egg respectively, are the storehouse of proteins, fats, minerals and vitamins. The hard egg shell serves as a protective coat; it has thousands of micropores through which the developing chick takes in oxygen and flushes out carbon dioxide. The colouration of egg shell varies among different species of birds. It can be pure white, brown, violet, turquoise, reddish or greenish and for many cases, are also adorned with blotches, speckles or streaks.

Though many functions of egg colouration have been indicated, the most plausible explanation is protection from predators. Cryptically coloured or blotched eggs, such as those of lapwings, sandpipers, plovers, etc., laid on bare soil, sand and among pebbles enable better camouflage with the surroundings, and make the eggs unnoticeable to predators.

Cryptic eggs of Red-wattled Lapwing

Ibises and Spoonbills (*Threskiornithidae*)

These are large-sized birds with long legs and a long neck. Ibises have downward curved bills and they forage by slow walking in mud, shallow water and grass. These birds make platform nests with coarse sticks, high on trees. Helpless chicks are fed by both the parents.

Ibises and spoonbills can be best sighted around Tumaria reservoir.

▲

RED-NAPED IBIS

Pseudibis papillosa

Size about 70 cm. It can be differentiated from storks by its curved bill and stockier appearance.

◀

EURASIAN SPOONBILL

Platalea leucorodia

Size about 80 cm. It has a long spoon-shaped bill.

Sensors at Bill Tips—Enabling Birds to Catch Sparsely Visible Prey in Mucky Waters

Birds such as ducks, geese, shorebirds and ibises forage on small creatures submerged under shallow muddy water or on those buried in sand or mud. Foraging birds fish out the out-of-sight prey with the help of their bill. The tip of the bill of these birds has special touch sensors called 'bill tip organs' which allow the birds to detect the presence of prey when the latter come in contact with the bill. Some birds can even sense the prey buried inside wet sand and also well beyond the reach of their bill. In this case, the bird uses its bill to probe the wet sand and push away the water trapped in sand particles. A buried prey obstructs the water being pushed, leading to the generation of pressure in the sand, which is sensed by the bill.

Probing for prey

Herons and Egrets *(Ardeidae)*

These birds form a group of medium to large-sized birds with long legs enabling them to wade. Herons prefer to live close to lakes, ponds and rivers where they feed on aquatic animals. Both herons and egrets retract their head backwards while flying. Though egrets are behaviourally similar to herons, they are white and develop fine, long plumage during the breeding season. Herons and egrets both make their nests with twigs or sticks on trees or reeds.

These birds can be sighted near rivers, streams and dry river beds in all the zones, and near Kosi river barrage and Tumaria reservoir.

▲

STRIATED HERON

Butorides striata

Crow-sized or slightly larger. Adults have a black crown and dark greenish-grey upperparts; juveniles are brownish with prominently streaked underparts.

▲

GREY HERON

Ardea cinerea

Size about 90–100 cm. Juveniles with greyer neck and lack a black patch on the belly, and have darker legs.

▲

INDIAN POND HERON

Ardeola grayii

Slightly larger than a Crow. Breeding adults have a buffish neck and dark reddish-brown back.

PURPLE HERON

Ardea purpurea

Size about 80–90 cm. Juveniles have a brownish hue all over the body.

CATTLE EGRET

Bubulcus ibis

Slightly smaller than a Kite.

GREAT EGRET

Casmerodius albus

Size about 100 cm. Breeding plumage with a spread of long thin plumes on the back, bluish lores and dark bill. Can be distinguished from Intermediate Egret by its larger size, longer bill, and long curved neck, also, the gape line extends beyond the eye (arrow).

INTERMEDIATE EGRET

Mesophoyx intermedia

Size about 65–70 cm. Breeding plumage with black bill and yellowish-green lores; unlike Great Egret, the gape line does not extend beyond the eye.

LITTLE EGRET

Egretta garzetta

Size about 55–65 cm. Breeding plumage with elongated plumes on the back and two plumes extend from the head.

Darters (*Anhingidae*)

These are large-sized aquatic birds with a long slender neck and a pointed bill. These birds are adapted for hunting beneath the surface of water. Their food mainly includes fishes which they hunt by spearing them with their bill and then flipping the catch into the mouth. It makes a platform nest with twigs, on trees close to water.

They can be sighted near Ramganga River, near Kosi river barrage and Tumaria reservoir.

PC: AG

ORIENTAL DARTER

Anhinga melanogaster

Size about 85–100 cm. It can be distinguished from cormorants by the shape of its head, spear-shaped bill, and long 'S'-shaped neck. Swims with half-submerged body with head and neck protruding out of the water in a serpent-like manner, this lends it the name 'Snake Bird'.

To Birds, the World is More Colourful than to Humans

In reality, colours are non-existent; what we perceive as colour is actually the light energy (or electromagnetic waves that by themselves are colourless) sensed by cone cells in the retina of our eyes and transferred to the brain to give a perception of colour. The ability of an animal to distinguish between colours of different objects, and the range of colours, depends upon the types of cones in its retina. Humans have three types of cones, whereas many birds have four types of cones, which enable them to see ultraviolet light as well (which humans cannot see!). Many colour blind people have just two types of cones, and to them the world is not as colourful! The cone cells of birds also have substances which act as colour filters—this feature further improves colour vision. Thus, to a bird, the plumage colouration of its companion may appear different from how we humans perceive it.

Cormorants (*Phalacrocoracidae*)
These medium to large-sized water birds possess a long neck and hooked bill. They forage by submerged swimming, i.e., paddling in water with their feet, in search and pursuit of fishes. Cormorants are seen perched on rocks and trees, with their wings spread out; this is apparently to dry their wings or to soak up some warmth. Unlike darters, cormorants hunt by grabbing the fishes in their hooked bills. These birds make platform nests with twigs, on trees close to water.
These birds can be sighted near major rivers in all the zones, near Kosi river barrage and Tumaria reservoir.

▲

LITTLE CORMORANT

Phalacrocorax niger

Slightly smaller than a Kite. All over black in breeding plumage. Smaller body size, flat top of head distinguishes it from Great Cormorant.

▲

GREAT CORMORANT

Phalacrocorax carbo

Size about 80–100 cm. Non-breeding adult lacks white plumes on throat and head.

Kestrels and Falcons (*Falconidae*)
These form a group of 'Raptors' or 'Birds of Prey' known for their speed of flying; they have narrow and pointed wings, and fly with rapid wing beats. Many of these birds can capture their flying prey (bird or insects) in midair strike, and can kill the prey by damaging their neck through strike impact and biting with a special sharp structure in the beak called 'Tomial tooth'. These are seen in thinly forested areas, scrubs and grasslands. The nest is a collection of twigs and straw on cliff holes or cliff ledges (in case of Common Kestrel and Peregrine Falcon).
These birds can be sighted in all the zones.

COLLARED FALCONET ▶
Microhierax caerulescens
Bulbul-sized. It is one of the smallest birds of prey.

COMMON KESTREL
Falco tinnunculus
Pigeon-sized. Males with grey head and tail; head of females with pale-brownish streak, and tail barred; hovers with rapid beating of wings to scan prey such as lizards, insects, and small birds on the ground.
▼

PEREGRINE FALCON
Falco peregrinus
Slightly larger than a Crow. Juveniles with brownish-black upperparts and streaked underparts. It is known for diving in air with extraordinary speed.
▼

Insecticide DDT—a Threat to Raptors

Dichlorodiphenyltrichloroethane or DDT was initially used by military during World War II to control malaria, bubonic plague, etc. It became available for use in agriculture and for other domestic applications in 1945. Its worldwide use in the subsequent two to three decades was linked to the declining population of many raptors such as the Peregrine Falcon, Osprey, sparrowhawks and eagles in different parts of the world. *How does DDT affect these birds?* DDT is highly persistent in the environment. It enters the body of these predatory birds via the 'food chain'. For instance, Peregrine Falcons pick DDT when they prey on small birds that had eaten DDT-contaminated insects or seeds. Since DDT has the tendency to accumulate in the body of animals, the falcons, over a long period of preying on contaminated birds, accumulate DDT at toxic levels. This level of DDT, however, is not enough to kill the falcons; instead, it adversely affects their ability to form the shell around the eggs, resulting in eggs with thinner shells. Thin shelled eggs are prone to be broken accidentally by parents during incubation, thereby killing the developing baby bird. Since only a few young were hatched to replace the adults that died, the population of Peregrine Falcon declined over time. Currently, though the use of DDT has declined worldwide, it has not yet stopped completely.

Birds' Eye

Birds have the best vision among all animals—a property which is crucial for foraging, swift flight, vigilance, mid-air as well as underwater hunting, and leading a nocturnal life. A few key features that make the birds eye so superior are: 1) larger eyes compared to their body mass for high-resolution vision and light sensitivity, 2) ability to see a broader range of colours, and 3) the presence of a third eyelid (technically called 'nictitating membrane')—a translucent film which (unlike eyelids) moves sideways. This third eyelid functions analogous to goggles, to protect the eyes from being damaged due to dust or other material during flight or while the birds are excavating wood/soil and foraging.

Depending upon the lifestyle, especially the way a bird feeds, several specializations have evolved for birds' eyes. For instance, raptors have a more acute vision required for scanning the surroundings, and tracking and capturing prey. Some birds have a vast field of vision useful in detecting predators while foraging.

Sleeping Exercise of Birds—Shutting Down Half the Brain at a Time

Many birds sleep keeping one of the eyes open, and also only half of their brain is shut down. This mode of sleeping is advantageous for vigilance against predators.

It has been discovered that frigatebirds flying continuously over oceans for several days can sleep on their wings for a short period. These birds sleep by keeping one of their eyes open so that they can keep track of their direction and avoid collision with other birds flying alongside. To prevent falling in the ocean, they fly at higher altitudes and shift from flapping to effortless gliding (floating with air current) mode of flight.

Hawks, Eagles, Harriers, Vultures and Osprey (*Accipitridae*)

These birds form a group of raptors feeding on dead animals or by hunting. They prefer a variety of habitats including forests, vicinity of rivers, scrubs and grasslands. Most of these birds have broad wings and are capable of performing efficient gliding and soaring type of flights. Their nest is a large platform of sticks with slight depression, placed on top of tall trees or cliff ledges.

Many of the above mentioned raptors can be sighted in all the zones; however, to sight most of these, a visit to Dhikala zone is highly recommended.

Raptors

These birds are adapted to kill and eat animals that could well be larger than their own size. However, some of these birds also consume carcasses or dead animals. Kestrels, falcons, hawks, eagles, harriers, ospreys and vultures are categorized as 'Raptors,' or more specifically, 'Diurnal Raptors' because these hunt mainly during the day. This excludes owls which hunt in the night. Raptors have a remarkable eye sight to locate their prey or carcass from a distance; a powerful hooked bill helps them in tearing flesh and sharp curved claws attached to strong legs help in clutching the prey.

BLACK-WINGED KITE ▶

Elanus caeruleus

Pigeon-sized. Seen hovering in grasslands in search of prey; can be distinguished from the male of Hen Harrier which is larger and has no black patch on its shoulders.

BLACK KITE

Milvus migrans

A scavenging raptor with forked tail. Juveniles have prominent pale streaking on the body. ▼

OSPREY ▶

Pandion haliaetus

Kite-sized. Male Osprey is known to impress a female by feeding her fishes. It is seen in winters.

PC: AG

PALLAS'S FISH EAGLE

Haliaeetus leucoryphus

Slightly larger than a Kite. It is seen on river beds or perched on snag trees along rivers.

LESSER FISH EAGLE

Icthyophaga humilis

Kite-sized. Dark greyish-brown head and breast, white belly and thighs, uniform brown tail, and smaller body size help distinguishing it from Pallas's Fish Eagle.

ORIENTAL HONEY-BUZZARD

Pernis ptilorhynchus

Kite-sized. Males have brownish eyes, greyish face, and two black tail bands; females with browner head, yellow eyes and three tail bands; fond of feeding on honey and larvae of bees; scale-like feathers on the face protects it from bee stings while the bird attacks hives.

EGYPTIAN VULTURE

Neophron percnopterus

Slightly larger than a Kite. Juveniles are blackish-brown.

RED-HEADED VULTURE

Sarcogyps calvus

About one-and-half times the size of a Kite. Blackish body, bare red head, neck, legs and feet, and white feathers at the collar distinguish it from all other mentioned vultures; males have pale or white eyes; brown to dark red eyes in females.

HIMALAYAN VULTURE

Gyps himalayensis

About twice the size of a Kite. It has buffish back and ruff, and dark flight feathers; legs and feet pinkish. Juveniles are dark brown with buff streaking.

CINEREOUS VULTURE

Aegypius monachus

About twice the size of a Kite. Blackish vulture, seen in winters; it has pink base to black bill, pinkish feet, and dark face. Adults dark brownish with paler head and ruff; Juveniles are uniformly black.

◀ **WHITE-RUMPED VULTURE**

Gyps bengalensis

About one-and-half times the size of a Kite. It has blackish upperparts, white neck-ruff contrasting with rest of the body, and white rump; juveniles are dark brown with streaking on underparts, and whitish head and neck.

Medicine '*Diclofenac*'—a Cause for the Shrinking Population of Vultures in India

Vultures feed on carcasses of livestock and wild animals. The number of certain species of vultures, namely the White-rumped Vulture, the Indian Vulture and the Slender-billed Vulture, declined rapidly during the mid-1990s. The cause of decline was found to be poisoning from 'Diclofenac'—a medicine widely used to treat livestock. Vultures feeding on carcasses of animals treated with Diclofenac, accumulate the medicine in their body to lethal levels and die of kidney failure. After banning of Diclofenac for veterinary usage in the year 2006, the decline in vulture population has reduced.

Vultures in Dhikala grassland

CRESTED SERPENT EAGLE

Spilornis cheela

Kite-sized. It has white spotting and barring on brownish underparts, white band on the tail and black crest blotched with white. It can be seen in forested areas and fringes of the forest.

Female

Male

◀ EURASIAN MARSH HARRIER

Circus aeruginosus

Slightly smaller than a Kite. Males with brownish back, pale head streaked with brown, grey margins of wings (arrow), and brown streaking on breast and belly; females brown all-over with pale crown and throat. These features are lacking in females of Hen Harrier which has prominently streaked underparts. It is seen gliding in grasslands a few metres above the ground to scan for prey.

Female

◀ HEN HARRIER

Circus cyaneus

Slightly smaller than a Kite. Females (as shown) brownish with streaked underparts; males greyish with black wing tips. Seen gliding a few metres above the ground in grasslands and scrubs.

SHIKRA ▶

Accipiter badius

Pigeon-sized. Females similar to males but upperparts brownish-grey and has yellowish eyes (red in males); seen in thinly forested areas. It can be confused with Common Hawk Cuckoo, however the former has a strong raptor-like hooked bill.

Female

PC: AG

Juvenile

Male

RUFOUS-BELLIED EAGLE

Lophotriorchis kienerii

Nearly the size of a Kite. It has black upperparts, white breast and throat, and rufous belly and thighs streaked with black.

STEPPE EAGLE

Aquila nipalensis

Slightly larger than a Kite. Seen in winters perched on snag trees along rivers; distinguished from Pallas's Fish Eagle by its dark brown head and front, and dark tail.

CHANGEABLE HAWK EAGLE

Nisaetus cirrhatus

Slightly larger than a Kite. Distinguished from Mountain Hawk Eagle by its streaked underparts, (barring confined to thighs and sides only, arrow), and less prominent crest.

MOUNTAIN HAWK EAGLE

Nisaetus nipalensis

Slightly larger than a Kite. It has prominently barred underparts.

Crakes, Coot and Moorhens (*Rallidae*)

These are well adapted to moving through dense reeds and tall grasses, and walking on marshy vegetation. They have long legs and toes, and their body is compressed from the sides. Their food includes insects, parts of plants and aquatic animals. Birds of this group make their nest near water or marsh, with aquatic plant material padded on the ground or on floating vegetation.

Inside CTR, these can be sighted around pools of stagnant water. However, these can be best sighted near the Kosi river barrage and Tumaria reservoir.

PC: AC

▲

RUDDY-BREASTED CRAKE

Porzana fusca

Myna-sized or slightly larger with longer legs and feet. Juveniles lack rusty colouration on underparts.

PC: HP

◀

BROWN CRAKE

Amaurornis akool

Pigeon-sized with longer legs and feet. It has greyish face and underparts, and pinkish legs.

WHITE-BREASTED WATERHEN

Amaurornis phoenicurus

Pigeon-sized with longer legs and feet. Upperparts of juveniles browner.

▼

PURPLE SWAMPHEN

Porphyrio porphyrio

Slightly smaller than a Kite with longer legs and feet. Juveniles duller in colouration.

▼

▲
COMMON MOORHEN

Gallinula chloropus

Pigeon-sized or slightly larger. Non-breeding plumage with duller bill colouration; juvenile brownish.

▲
EURASIAN COOT

Fulica atra

Crow-sized with longer legs and feet. Juveniles with whitish face, throat and breast.

Buttonquails (*Turnicidae*)

These birds are seen in open areas such as grasslands and scrubs. They feed on seeds and small insects, and move by walking to seek cover in grass. In buttonquails, the gender role is reversed—it is the female which displays to attract males, and courts with the chosen one. After laying eggs, she deserts the male who then takes care of the offspring by first incubating the eggs and then feeding and nursing the young ones. ***Buttonquails can be best sighted in the grasslands of the Dhikala zone.***

SMALL BUTTONQUAIL ▶

Turnix sylvaticus

Sparrow-sized. It is heavily marked on upperparts; has a rufous neck, and its underparts are plain orangish-white.

Cranes (*Gruidae*)

Birds with long legs and a long neck; these are efficient fliers and usually fly in 'V-formation'; male and female pair usually lives together for entire life. *These can be best sighted near Tumaria reservoir.*

DEMOISELLE CRANE

Grus virgo

Size about 100 cm. It has a tuft of white feathers behind eyes, and a tuft of black feathers extending over the breast.

COMMON CRANE

Grus grus

Size about 120 cm. Immature birds have brownish upperparts.

Female Birds are Picky About Spouses

It is the inherent tendency of female birds to choose the best males for reproduction so that they can produce healthy offspring. They prefer to mate with those males who are healthy, whose sperms carry good quality genes, and/or who can provide adequate parental care such as making a nest, feeding and protecting the offspring.

How do female birds get a cue as to which of the several males have superior quality of genes and no hidden diseases or artefacts?

Females of several birds, over thousands and millions of years, have evolved somewhat unique and bizarre ways to scrutinize males. In some birds, the female evaluates the male on the basis of whether he can vocalise a particular syllable or sing complex songs. In some others, males are screened on the basis of their elaborate or colourful plumage or other ornaments on their body. In some other instances such as in Osprey, female monitors the rate at which the male provides her with fish during courtship, thereby verifying his ability to provide parental care to offspring; male Baya Weaver birds are tested by their ability to weave nests at a secure location (p.184). It is only after observing the desired features in males, that the female birds are induced to mate.

Thick-knees (*Burhinidae*)

This group includes crow-sized birds with long thick legs. These birds prefer scrubs, open forest, and dry river beds. Their plumage colouration helps them to camouflage with the surroundings. When alarmed, they run away to some other place to conceal themselves. Their nest is a well-camouflaged shallow depression on the ground near bushes, or an exposed nest lined with pebbles on the sandbank. These birds lay blotched eggs perfectly camouflaging with the surroundings.

These can be best sighted in Jhirna, Dhela and Pakhro zones.

Waders

It is a common term for birds which live and forage in areas near waterbodies, (sea shores, marshes, lakes, ponds, etc.). Some waders are also capable of living in drier areas. Many of them have long legs to walk through shallow water and marsh. Some waders are known to possess special organs in their bills that help them in locating prey hidden beneath the ground surface or in shallow muddy waters. Waders include lapwings, plovers, jacanas, thick-knees, sandpipers, stints, snipes, shanks, etc. Several of these birds are winter visitors to CTR.

Waders can best be sighted in Dhela, Jhirna, Bijrani and Dhikala zones. Outside CTR, waders can be seen along Kosi river and Tumaria reservoir.

INDIAN THICK-KNEE ▶

Burhinus indicus

Crow-sized with longer legs; it has brown streaked plumage and greenish-yellow legs.

◀ GREAT THICK-KNEE

Esacus recurvirostris

Slightly smaller than a Kite with longer legs. It has a black stripe behind and above the eyes; bill heavier and slightly up-curved.

Jacanas (*Jacanidae*)

Jacanas are pigeon-sized birds with long thin legs and very long toes. These features help them to walk on the floating vegetation found around lakes, ponds and other waterbodies. These birds make their nest with grass and aquatic weeds, on floating vegetation.

Jacanas can be sighted near Tumaria reservoir.

BRONZE-WINGED JACANA ▶

Metopidius indicus

Pigeon-sized, with longer legs and feet.

◀ **PHEASANT-TAILED JACANA**

Hydrophasianus chirurgus

Pigeon-sized with longer legs and feet. Breeding plumage with extensively long-curved, black tail.

Lapwings and Plovers (*Charadriidae*)
These include birds with a shorter neck and shorter bill. Many lapwings have long, slim legs whereas plovers have a stockier appearance. Both these birds are found in open areas such as grasslands, scrubs and wet areas close to water (rivers and lakes). While foraging, they walk quickly in short spurts, take a pause and pick up prey. Their nest is a depression in sand or mud, or a shingle in open areas; they lay blotched eggs. *Lapwings are sighted in all the zones, except for the Yellow-wattled Lapwing which is primarily seen in Jhirna and Dhela zones. Plovers are best sighted in Dhikala zone, near the Kosi river and Tumaria reservoir.*

▲ **RED-WATTLED LAPWING**

Vanellus indicus

Pigeon-sized with longer legs. Juveniles are duller with a whitish throat.

RIVER LAPWING

Vanellus duvaucelii

Pigeon-sized with longer legs. Seen along rivers.

▼

YELLOW-WATTLED LAPWING

Vanellus malabaricus

Slightly smaller than a Pigeon with longer legs. Juveniles with brown cap and dull yellow wattles.

▼

▲ **LITTLE RINGED PLOVER**

Charadrius dubius

Bulbul-sized. It can be differentiated from a Kentish Plover which has dark legs, lacks an eye-ring and a breast band.

▲ **KENTISH PLOVER**

Charadrius alexandrinus

Bulbul-sized. Seen in winters.

Ibisbill (*Ibidorhynchidae*)
It is seen along streams and rivers, probing for prey with its long curved bill among the pebbles and boulders. Ibisbill is a winter visitor to CTR and spends summers in the higher reaches of the Himalayas (altitudinal migrant). ***It can be best sighted along the Kosi river, near the 'Garjia Temple'.***

IBISBILL ▶

Ibidorhyncha struthersii

Crow-sized with longer legs. Juveniles lack a prominent black face and black breast band.

Stilts (*Recurvirostridae*)
These birds with long slim legs and long beak feed on insects and aquatic animals by slow-walking close to rivers and lakes or by wading in shallow waters. Their nest is a shallow depression in the ground along the dry banks. They lay densely blotched eggs. ***It can be best sighted in Bijrani and Dhikala zones, and also near Kosi river, and Tumaria reservoir.***

BLACK-WINGED STILT ▶

Himantopus himantopus

Crow-sized with longer legs. Juveniles have browner upperparts; seen in winters.

Sandpipers, Snipes, Stints etc. (*Scolopacidae*)

These are wading winter migrants, many of which have a thin and long bill, medium to long legs and cryptic colouration. The length and curvature of bills of birds of this group vary, and are an adaptation to access the hidden prey—for instance, those picking the prey from the ground surface have smaller bills, and those foraging on prey hidden beneath the surface of ground possess long probing bills.

Some of the birds of this group can be sighted in all the zones. These birds, however, can be best sighted along the banks of Ramganga river in Dhikala zone, and near Tumaria reservoir.

▲

COMMON REDSHANK

Tringa totanus

Pigeon-sized, with longer legs. Breeding plumage with heavily streaked neck and underparts.

COMMON GREENSHANK ▶

Tringa nebularia

Pigeon-sized with longer legs. It can be distinguished from the Common Redshank by its larger size, greenish legs, and slightly up-curved long bill.

▲

COMMON SNIPE

Gallinago gallinago

Pigeon-sized with longer legs. It has a stocky appearance, and has a long bill.

COMMON SANDPIPER ▶

Actitis hypoleucos

Larger than a Bulbul. Distinguished from Green Sandpiper by its tail projected beyond wings (red arrow), white area near shoulders, and prominent supercilium (blue arrow).

◀ **GREEN SANDPIPER**

Tringa ochropus

Myna-sized with longer legs. Stockier than shanks; greenish legs, spotted upperparts, and supercilium restricted to the front part of eyes (arrow) aid in the identification of this bird.

▲

TEMMINCK'S STINT

Calidris temminckii

Sparrow-sized. Non-breeding plumage with uniform greyish-brown upperparts; breeding plumage with dark patches on upperparts; it has yellowish legs.

▲

LITTLE STINT

Calidris minuta

Sparrow-sized. Breeding plumage with rufous cast to head, breast and upperparts; non-breeding plumage with greyish-brown upperparts. It has dark legs.

Pratincoles (*Glareolidae*)

These birds have pointed bill, long pointed wings, and short legs. They are seen in groups, along sandy riverbanks or close-by areas. These birds obtain most of the food by capturing their prey in the air. The nests of Pratincoles are merely shallow depressions on the sandbanks.

Pratincoles can be sighted in Dhikala, and Sonanadi zones, and near Tumaria reservoir.

SMALL PRATINCOLE

Glareola lactea

Bulbul-sized. It has a sandy grey body; distinguished from the River Tern which has a long yellow bill.

▼

Gulls and Terns (*Laridae*)

These birds have narrow, long wings and short to moderately long legs. These can be seen near waterbodies, feeding on aquatic animals. Terns are usually smaller than gulls and have slimmer bodies with long pointed wings.

These birds can be best sighted near the Ramganga river in Dhikala zone, and Tumaria reservoir.

PALLAS'S GULL

Ichthyaetus ichthyaetus

Kite-sized. Its larger size, yellow bill with bulging red area near the tip help in distinguishing it from Brown-headed and Black-headed Gulls; seen in winters.

BROWN-HEADED GULL

Chroicocephalus brunnicephalus

Crow-sized. It has a reddish bill and pale-yellow eyes; heads of birds in breeding plumage turn dark brown; seen in winters.

RIVER TERN

Sterna aurantia

Crow-sized with shorter legs. In breeding plumage, it has long tail feathers (lacking in non-breeding plumage) and a black cap (greyish in non-breeding). Captures fishes and other prey from rivers by plunge-diving from air.

Br

BLACK-HEADED GULL

Chroicocephalus ridibundus

Crow-sized. Extensive white area on the tips of wings (visible in flying birds, arrow), and brown eyes help in distinguishing it from similar looking Brown-headed Gull; seen in winters.

WHISKERED TERN

Chlidonias hybrida

Myna-sized. In breeding plumage, it can be distinguished from the similar looking River Tern by absence of long tail feathers and its reddish bill.

Pigeons and Doves (*Columbidae*)
This group includes birds with a compact body, short neck, short legs, and small head. They mainly feed on seeds, fruits and leaves though some of these birds might also eat insects. Their flight is fast, with rapid wing-beats. These birds lay whitish eggs.
Birds of this group can be sighted in all the zones.

COMMON PIGEON
Columba livia
Greyish-blue bird. Common near human habitations.

EURASIAN COLLARED DOVE
Streptopelia decaocto
Pigeon-sized. Distinguished from smaller Red Collared Dove female which has darker upperparts.

ORIENTAL TURTLE DOVE
Streptopelia orientalis
Pigeon-sized. Chequered patch on the sides of neck and rufous wings with scaly appearance help in distinguishing it from Spotted Dove.

LAUGHING DOVE
Streptopelia senegalensis
Slightly smaller than Pigeon. Similar to Red Collared Dove from which it can be distinguished by its brownish-pink head, black speckling on breast, and absence of black collar.

RED COLLARED DOVE
Streptopelia tranquebarica
Myna-sized. Seen in thinly forested, and close by open areas.

Female

Male

▲
SPOTTED DOVE

Streptopelia chinensis

Pigeon-sized. Seen in open areas and thinly forested areas.

ORANGE-BREASTED GREEN PIGEON

Treron bicinctus

Pigeon-sized. Keeps itself to higher parts of trees; males have an orange breast bordered from above with pale violet; females lack orange breast colouration.

▲
PIN-TAILED GREEN PIGEON

Treron apicauda

Pigeon-sized. Keeps itself to higher parts of trees; it has long pointed tail feathers, greenish head, light-blue base of bill. Males have an orangish cast to the breast.

▲
YELLOW-FOOTED GREEN PIGEON

Treron phoenicopterus

Pigeon-sized. Keeps itself to higher parts of trees; has yellow legs, grey cap and belly, greenish-yellow collar and breast, and pale violet shoulder patch.

EMERALD DOVE ▶

Chalcophaps indica

Slightly smaller than Pigeon. Keeps itself to forested areas where it flies at a pace even in dense foliage; occasionally seen on tracks.

Parakeets (*Psittacidae*)
This is a group of greenish birds with a short neck, strong curved upper-half of the bill and usually a long tail. These birds live in flocks and are quite noisy. Parakeets feed on fruits, seeds and other parts of plants. They nest in natural or self-made holes in trees, and lay white eggs. *These birds can be sighted in all the zones.*

Male

PC: MS
Female

Female

SLATY-HEADED PARAKEET

Psittacula himalayana

Parakeet-sized. It has a black stripe around the neck, yellow-tipped greenish tail, and yellow lower half of the bill. Males have a red patch at the shoulders.

ROSE-RINGED PARAKEET

Psittacula krameri

Parakeet-sized. Males have a black stripe around the neck and a pink collar; females lack these features.

Female

Male

PLUM-HEADED PARAKEET

Psittacula cyanocephala

Slightly smaller than a Parakeet. The upper half of the bill is yellow in both the sexes; juveniles have a greenish head.

PC: MV
Male

RED-BREASTED PARAKEET

Psittacula alexandri

Parakeet-sized. It can be distinguished from other mentioned parakeets by its pinkish breast and black forehead. Males with red upper half of the bill; females with all black bill.

Cuckoos, Malkohas and Coucals (*Cuculidae*)

Cuckoos prefer forested areas. During breeding season, males of many cuckoos sing melodious songs and can be specifically identified by listening to their characteristic song. Cuckoos are notorious 'Social Parasites' (lay eggs in the nest of other birds). *Malkohas* are long-tailed birds and prefer forests or areas with small trees and shrubs. *Coucals* prefer shrubs, thinly forested areas, tall grasslands and reeds. Coucals are usually seen close to ground or on low perches. They escape danger/predators by walking or by disappearing into dense vegetation through a powerful short distance flight.

Most of the above mentioned birds can be sighted in all the zones.

COMMON HAWK CUCKOO

Hierococcyx varius

Pigeon-sized. It is known as 'Brainfever bird' due to its repeated call—*brain fever.. brain fever....* which is rendered in Hindi as *Pee kahan... Pee kahan...* giving it the Hindi name *Papiha*. Adult with whitish chin and throat and rufous underparts with faint barrings; juveniles have streaked underparts and browner upperparts. Likely to be confused with Shikra, from which it can be distinguished by the shape of bill (hook shaped in Shikra) and yellow rings around its eyes.

PC: MV

JACOBIN CUCKOO

Clamator jacobinus

Size about 33 cm. Adults with black upperparts, and white underparts; upperparts of juveniles brown. It is seen in summers.

PC: AS

INDIAN CUCKOO

Cuculus micropterus

Pigeon-sized. Females have rufous-grey cast to breast; can be distinguished from Common Hawk Cuckoo by bold black barring on its underparts. Makes a characteristic call—*kuckoo..kuckoo...* in a burst. Seen in summers.

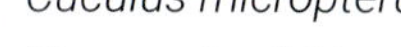

PC: SP

Male

EURASIAN CUCKOO

Cuculus canorus

Pigeon-sized. Distinguished from Indian Cuckoo by narrowly placed barring on underparts, and grey upperparts (some females have rufous upperparts). Makes characteristic call—*Cuckoo.... Cuckoo...* repeated after a short pause. Seen in summers.

PC: SM

PC: SM

Male

Cuckoos—Cheat by Nature

Some birds do not take the pain of making a nest, incubating eggs, and feeding and protecting young ones. Instead, they get these jobs done by other birds. They quietly lay eggs in the nest of other birds (host) and leave all the duties of raising the young ones to the unsuspecting 'foster' parents. These cheats are known as 'Brood Parasites'. Cuckoos and Koel are notorious brood parasites in Asia. Cuckoos keep a close watch on target nests of hosts from nearby trees, and wait till the latter starts laying eggs. The cuckoo then approaches this nest when the host is not around, and replaces a host egg with one of her own. The host, unable to differentiate between her own egg and that of the cuckoo, begins to incubate the entire batch of eggs. After hatching, the emerging chick of the cuckoo, through its exaggerated begging call resembling that of the host's own chicks, stimulates the host to bring more food. The poor host expends a great amount of time and energy to rear the parasite chick and fails to feed her own sufficiently.

Young Common Hawk Cuckoo (left) and foster parent—Jungle Babbler (right)

Hosts are not completely helpless though, they too retaliate: they sound alarm calls whenever they spot cuckoos around their nest, to alert their neighbours and chase away the parasite. Hosts have gradually developed the ability to recognize foreign eggs in their nest and remove them. Cuckoos go further—they resemble the frightening birds of prey (such as hawks) to keep the host away and fine tune the colouration of their eggs to fool the host.

PC: RP

◀ **DRONGO CUCKOO**

Surniculus lugubris

Myna-sized; seen in forested areas. Distinguished from 'drongos' by white markings on its under-tail feathers (arrow) and finer bill.

ASIAN KOEL ▶

Eudynamys scolopaceus

Crow-sized but slimmer. Commonly known as 'Koel' in Hindi. Glossy black male is famous for its melodious song.

GREEN-BILLED MALKOHA

Phaenicophaeus tristis

Size about 38 cm. Greyish-green bird with red patch around eyes; seen in forested areas and fringes of forest; keeps itself to thickets.

SIRKEER MALKOHA

Phaenicophaeus leschenaultii

Size about 40 cm. Brownish bird with stout red bill; juveniles intensely streaked; seen hopping from one branch to another in scrubs and fringes of the forest.

GREATER COUCAL

Centropus sinensis

Slightly larger than a Crow, tail longer. Seen hopping close to high bushy shrubs, and tall grasslands.

PC: VSR

LESSER COUCAL

Centropus bengalensis

Pigeon-sized, tail longer. Non-breeding plumage is dark brown with streaking; in breeding plumage, it is distinguished from the Greater Coucal by its much smaller size, fine pale streaking on back and darker eyes (red in Greater Coucal).

Owls (*Strigidae*)

These are nocturnal birds (some are active in daytime too) with eyes placed on the front of a large round head. They feed on fishes, snakes, lizards, and rat-like animals. Many owls are experts in hunting under low light conditions, locating prey by acoustic cues, and possess sensitive eyes that have a wonderful ability to see in the dark. Soft feathers give them a noise-free flight, thus enabling the owls to take prey by surprise. Most of the owls have brown cryptic colouration, making it difficult to spot them even in daylight. They can, however, be located by their distinctive calls. There is a restriction on the movement of eyes in the eye-sockets of owls; however, owls compensate for it with their amazing ability to rotate their head in all directions. Most owls are seen in forested areas and fringes of forests. The Short-eared Owl, however, is seen in scrubs and open areas. Owls make their nests in natural tree holes, among rocks, and on the trees, using sticks. These birds lay white eggs.

Most of the above-mentioned owls can be spotted in all the zones.

▲

SHORT-EARED OWL

Asio flammeus

Crow-sized. Shorter ear tufts and gross facial features can easily distinguish it from mentioned fish owls, which are also larger.

JUNGLE OWLET ▶

Glaucidium radiatum

Bulbul-sized, tail shorter. It has rufous barrings on the wings (arrow).

PC: SCH

◀ **INDIAN SCOPS OWL**

Otus bakkamoena

Myna-sized. It has long ear tufts that are not prominent when relaxed.

PC: MS

ASIAN BARRED OWLET ▶

Glaucidium cuculoides

Myna-sized. Distinguished from Jungle Owlet by broadly placed barring on the body and absence of rusty colouration on sides of wings (arrow).

SPOTTED OWLET

Athene brama

Bulbul-sized, tail shorter. Distinguished from Jungle Owlet, and Asian Barred Owlet by having spots rather than bars on the head, back and front.

PC: SM

BROWN HAWK OWL

Ninox scutulata

Pigeon-sized. It has a narrow head, brown upperparts and prominent brown streaking on its underparts.

PC: MV

PC: MS

SPOT-BELLIED EAGLE OWL

Bubo nipalensis

Kite-sized. It can be distinguished from Tawny and Brown Fish Owls by its prominent ear tufts; 'V'-shaped marks on the underparts, dark eyes and palish bill.

BROWN FISH OWL

Ketupa zeylonensis

Kite-sized. Distinguished from Tawny Fish Owl by its brown colouration (absence of orange tone), finer streaking on crown, upperparts and underparts (underparts also show faint barring).

PC: NZ

PC: AM

TAWNY FISH OWL

Ketupa flavipes

Kite-sized. It has bold streaking on its pale-brownish body, and whitish area above the beak (forehead).

Owls' Eyes and Ears—Working Together to Hunt in the Dark

Owls undertake their important activities during dusk and night, thanks to their larger eyes, more dilatable pupils (which allow more light to enter the eye) and more rods (light-sensitive cells in eyes) in the retina than day-active birds. Moreover, the positioning of their eyes helps in creating a three-dimensional image, providing an accurate idea about the three dimensional structure of the object.

Owls that hunt almost exclusively at night (dark) have a well-developed hearing system. Ear openings of these owls are covered with specialised feathers of the facial disc—a shallow depression on the face made of feathers. Its function is to amplify and focus sound into ears. Some owls have skin folds around the ears which also function to funnel sound inwards. With these modifications of ears, owls can pick up even very faint sounds. Barn Owls can hunt in pitch dark by tracking prey on the basis of sound produced by the latter. These birds can sense slight differences in the time and intensity with which sound hits the two ears, and thus precisely strike their target.

Hunting by night—Indian Scops Owl with kill (Spotted Dove)

The disc shaped face of a Barn Owl collects and directs sound waves to ear openings placed behind its eyes

Contrary to the popular assumption that owls cannot see in daytime, it is known that they can see equally well, if not better than most of the birds in the daytime. Owls however have limited ability to see colours.

More Hunting Gadgets of Owls

Owls have a few more adaptations which make them perfect hunters. The wings of owls make less or almost no sound when they are flapped, enabling owls to approach their target silently. The reason for this is: the special type of velvety feathers on the surface of wings which make less noise when these rub against each other during flight. Also, the edges of feathers of wings have serrations, this design breaks up turbulent air and muffles the sound generated by air.

Owls can rotate their head far beyond 90 degrees on both sides (left and right). This helps them to turn their head backwards too, and see on all sides without changing position of their body (helping them remain motionless and go unnoticed by their prey).

Nightjars (*Caprimulgidae*)

These are nocturnal and crepuscular (active during dawn and dusk) birds that possess cryptic colouration. Sighted in grasslands, scrubs, thinly forested areas and fringes of forest. They roost on the ground or on trees in daytime, camouflaging well with the surroundings. These birds make no nest and lay blotched, cryptic eggs on bare ground. Additional protection for the eggs is accomplished when the cryptic-coloured parents cover the eggs for incubation. Nightjars are noisy and can be heard with the onset of darkness.

These can be sighted in all the zones.

PC: SSD

▲ **LARGE-TAILED NIGHTJAR**

Caprimulgus macrurus

Nearly the size of a Pigeon, tail longer. It has a prominent white throat, more extensive black and pale patches (arrow) on sides and back than the Savanna Nightjar.

◀ **SAVANNA NIGHTJAR**

Caprimulgus affinis

Myna-sized, tail longer. It has grey-brown upperparts, pale-rufous markings on the wings (arrow) and a broken white throat band. It is smaller in size and less prominently marked than the Large-tailed Nightjar.

Swifts (*Apodidae*)

These are Sparrow to Myna-sized birds with long pointed wings, short bill, and short legs. Seen flying endlessly; some swifts can remain airborne for more than six months! Swifts feed by capturing insects in air and drink by swooping over water. They make cup-shaped or shallow nests with feathers, straw, grass, moss, etc., glued together with saliva, and secured in clefts in cliffs, caves and tree branches. These birds lay white eggs.

Swifts can be sighted in all the zones.

PC: AC

ALPINE SWIFT

Tachymarptis melba

Bulbul-sized. In flight shows white throat and belly, and brown breast band; seen in summers near cliffs and open areas.

LITTLE SWIFT

Apus affinis

Sparrow-sized. It is seen near cliffs and open areas; in flight, it shows a white throat and rump (arrow).

CRESTED TREESWIFT

Hemiprocne coronata

Bulbul-sized. In flight shows a whitish abdomen; males have an orangish area below the eyes.

Hoopoes (*Upupidae*)

These are birds with a long, slightly downward-curved bill and a prominent crest. They usually feed on insects picked from the ground.

It can be sighted in all the zones.

COMMON HOOPOE ▶

Upupa epops

Pigeon-sized. It is seen foraging on the ground in grasslands and scrubs.

Mixed-species Flock—Staying Together is Beneficial

Sometimes, one may come across places in the forest where there are several species of active birds all around—on the ground, in bushes, on tree trunks and in the canopy. Such flocks are associations of birds which forage and roam together in the forest. The benefits of making such an association are protection from predators and locating food. For instance, by foraging in a flock, some birds get sentinel services of other species that are more sensitive to predators and give reliable alarm calls upon spotting a foe. Other advantages of foraging in a flock include improved foraging, for example one member can capture and feed on insects exposed by the activities of other flock members.

Rollers and Dollarbird (*Coraciidae*)

These birds have a large head, a strong bill and short neck; they are seen in thinly forested areas and scrubs. *These birds can be sighted in all the zones.*

INDIAN ROLLER

Coracias benghalensis

Pigeon-sized. It is sighted in tall grasslands and scrubs.

DOLLARBIRD

Eurystomus orientalis

Slightly larger than a Myna. It appears blackish when spotted from a distance.

Kingfishers (*Alcedinidae*)

These birds have a long bill, a large head and short legs. They spend most of their time in surveillance of their surroundings quietly along the banks of rivers, lakes and streams, and swoop down after spotting the prey. Some kingfishers are even more skilled—they hover over water and after locating the prey (a fish), they plunge dive to catch it. Their food also includes snakes, crabs, lizards, etc. They nest in a self-dug tunnel in the mud-banks or earth-banks of rivers and streams, in termite nests and inside holes in the trees. They lay white eggs. *Kingfishers can be sighted in all the zones.*

STORK-BILLED KINGFISHER

Pelargopsis capensis

Pigeon-sized. It has a large red bill, buffish collar and underparts, and bluish-green upperparts.

▲
PIED KINGFISHER

Ceryle rudis

Myna-sized. It has white supercilium (arrow), and black breast bands (two in male, and one in female which is usually broken).

COMMON KINGFISHER

Alcedo atthis

Sparrow-sized. It has greenish-blue upperparts and orangish underparts.
▼

▲
WHITE-THROATED KINGFISHER

Halcyon smyrnensis

Slightly larger than a Myna. It has a white throat and breast, dark brown head and rest of the underparts.

▲
CRESTED KINGFISHER

Megaceryle lugubris

Nearly the size of a Crow. Can be distinguished from Pied Kingfisher by its larger size, prominent crest, spotting on the breast, and absence of supercilium.

Bee-eaters (*Meropidae*)
Greenish to bluish-green birds with fine, slightly downward curved bill. They are sighted in thinly forested areas or in scrubs. Bee-eaters are specialists in catching flying insects—any passing insect is chased and caught in a skilled manner. Bees and wasps are among their preferred food items. They nest in self-dug tunnels in earthen banks, and lay white eggs.
Bee-eaters can be sighted in all the zones.

PC: RBP

▲ **BLUE-BEARDED BEE-EATER**

Nyctyornis athertoni

Nearly the size of a Pigeon, but has a slimmer body. It has light blue feathers in the middle of its throat and breast (beard).

PC: AM

◀ **BLUE-TAILED BEE-EATER**

Merops philippinus

Myna-sized, but with slimmer body. Combination of features such as blue tail and chestnut colouration to throat distinguishes it from all the mentioned bee-eaters.

PC: MS

◀ **GREEN BEE-EATER**

Merops orientalis

Bulbul-sized. Absence of chestnut colouration to its head, and lack of yellow colouration to its throat distinguishes it from Chestnut-headed Bee-eater. Absence of chestnut colouration to its throat and lack of blue colouration to its tail distinguishes it from Blue-tailed Bee-eater.

▲ **CHESTNUT-HEADED BEE-EATER**

Merops leschenaulti

Bulbul-sized. It has a chestnut head and prominently yellow neck, which distinguishes it from all other mentioned bee-eaters.

Hornbills (*Bucerotidae*)

Large birds with a gigantic downward curved bill. They prefer staying on trees; their main diet is fruits (though they may eat small animals). These birds are known to be efficient agents for seed dispersal over a large area of the forest. The flight of many species is a combination of a few rapid wing beats followed by gliding. The noise made during the wing-beat of larger hornbills, such as the Great Hornbill, can be heard from a distance. Hornbills lay eggs in holes located high up on trees. The incubating female seals herself inside the hole using her droppings and mud as plaster, leaving a small hole through which she is fed by the male partner. Once chicks are hatched, the female frees herself after a few days by gently breaking the plaster. Thereafter, the hole is sealed/plastered again from the outside, and both the parents feed the chicks until the latter become independent. *Hornbills can be sighted in all the zones.*

GREAT HORNBILL

Buceros bicornis

Size about 100 cm. Males with red eyes and casque (arrow) black at both the tips; females have whitish eyes, and lack a black area at the tips of the casque. It has a loud hoarse voice that echoes in the jungle.

ORIENTAL PIED HORNBILL

Anthracoceros albirostris

Kite-sized, tail longer. Females have a smaller and less curved casque with no projecting tip, and a black area at the tip of the bill. It produces a loud echoing noise.

INDIAN GREY HORNBILL

Ocyceros birostris

Slightly smaller than a Kite, tail longer. Females similar to males but with a smaller casque (arrow).

Barbets (*Ramphastidae*)

These greenish or bluish birds are usually seen on trees. They prefer feeding on fruits, though they might also consume insects. Barbets make characteristic repetitive calls during the breeding season. Their nest is a self-dug tree hole, and they lay white eggs. ***The Brown-headed, Lineated, Blue-throated and Coppersmith barbets can be sighted in all the zones; the Great Barbet can be best sighted in Dhikala, Durgadevi and Sonanadi (Halduparao) zones.***

GREAT BARBET

Megalaima virens

Pigeon-sized. Combination of features such as large yellow bill, bluish-black head, and red under-tail feathers distinguish it from all mentioned barbets.

COPPERSMITH BARBET ▶

Megalaima haemacephala

Slightly larger than a Sparrow. It has a yellow throat, crimson forehead and upper breast.

BROWN-HEADED BARBET

Megalaima zeylanica

◀ Slightly larger than a Myna. Distinguished from similar looking Lineated Barbet by its reddish-orange bill, extensive orange area of bare skin around the eyes, finer white streaking on head and breast, and white dots on shoulders.

LINEATED BARBET

Megalaima lineata

Slightly larger than a Myna. It is likely to be confused with the similar looking Brown-headed Barbet.

▼

BLUE-THROATED BARBET

Megalaima asiatica

Slightly smaller than a Myna. Distinguished from Coppersmith Barbet by its larger size, blue face and throat, and red hind-crown.

▼

Woodpeckers, Piculets and Wrynecks (*Picidae*)

These birds are usually sighted in forested areas, fringes of forest and forest clearings, clinging to tree trunks. They climb up on vertical trunks and advance on branches with jerky movements. Some of them, however, forage on the ground too. These birds feed on termites, ants and larvae of wood-boring insects. Their nest is a hole in the tree which is self excavated. They lay white eggs.

These birds can be sighted in all the zones. CTR offers the opportunity to sight several species of woodpeckers inhabiting the Himalayas.

Woodpeckers in Action

Woodpeckers climb tree trunks by hopping in an upward direction; two crucial adaptations of their body help them in doing so—1) special grasping feet and 2) stiff tail feathers. The two adaptations work together while climbing—the feet firmly hold the bark and the tail is used as a prop, also it keeps their body off the tree trunk.

A foraging woodpecker picks insects from the bark surface or probes the crevices in the bark for hidden insects by inserting its bill. Its long tongue, the tip of which is barbed and coated with sticky fluid, glues out insects hidden inside even deeper crevices. To access wood-boring insects, woodpeckers tap the tree trunk to locate the hole and then excavate the wood by pecking to extract their prey.

Drumming is another activity of many woodpeckers wherein they rapidly and repetitively pound their bills against the trunk to produce sounds. Males tend to drum more than the females. These sounds which can be heard from a distance, are produced with the intention to defend territory and attract mates. A given species of woodpecker produces a characteristic drumming sound, which can help in its identification.

◀ SPECKLED PICULET

Picumnus innominatus

About the size of a Sparrow. Males have faint orange colouration at the forehead which is lacking in females.

◀ EURASIAN WRYNECK

Jynx torquilla

Bulbul-sized. It has a pale throat with fine barrings, and a long barred tail.

RUFOUS WOODPECKER ▶

Micropternus brachyurus

Myna-sized. Males with reddish hue near eyes (arrow). It nests within the ball shaped nests of ants.

Male

PC: SSD

GREAT SLATY WOODPECKER

Mulleripicus pulverulentus

Slightly larger than a Crow. Males with a red patch close to the bill.

PC: SSD

Female

Female

GREY-CAPPED PYGMY WOODPECKER

Dendrocopos canicapillus

Sparrow-sized. Males with a reddish mark on sides of the crown which may be obscured. Similar to Brown-capped but has a grey crown, darker eyes, and lacks white spotting on the tail.

BROWN-CAPPED PYGMY WOODPECKER

Dendrocopos nanus

Sparrow-sized. Males with a small red mark on the sides of the crown which may be obscured; distinguished from Grey-capped by its browner crown and upperparts, pale-white or grey-white underparts with faint streaking, and white spots on the tail (arrow); eyes are usually pale.

FULVOUS-BREASTED WOODPECKER

Dendrocopos macei

Bulbul-sized. It has faint streaking on buffish underparts; males have a reddish crown which is black in females.

Male

Female

GREY-HEADED WOODPECKER

Picus canus

Pigeon-sized. Males with a red forehead, which is black in females.

PC: AM

Female

PC: AM

Male

▲
LESSER YELLOWNAPE

Picus chlorolophus

Slightly larger than a Myna. Males have a red stripe extending from the base of the bill (faded in some) and red stripe above the eyes; distinguished from Greater Yellownape by its smaller size, presence of barring on underparts, and red and white marks around its bill.

▲
GREATER YELLOWNAPE

Picus flavinucha

Pigeon-sized. It has plain olive-grey sides of the neck and large bill; males have a yellow throat which is reddish-brown in females.

HIMALAYAN GOLDENBACK

Dinopium shorii

Nearly the size of a Pigeon. Males with a red crown which is black (streaked with white) in females.
▼

▲
STREAK-THROATED WOODPECKER

Picus xanthopygaeus

Pigeon-sized. Males with red crown which is black in females; distinguished from Grey-headed Woodpecker by its streaked throat and breast, and white stripe above the eyes.

Male

LESSER GOLDENBACK

Dinopium benghalense

Slightly larger than a Myna. It can be distinguished from Himalayan Goldenback by barred margins of wings (red arrow), and spotting on shoulders (blue arrow).

Female

GREATER GOLDENBACK

Chrysocolaptes lucidus

Pigeon-sized. Males with a red crown which is black (spotted with white) in females; distinguished from other mentioned goldenback woodpeckers by a combination of—white spotting near neck (red arrow), larger bill and split moustachial stripes (blue arrow).

Male

PC: AC

Female

PC: SSD

WHITE-NAPED WOODPECKER

Chrysocolaptes festivus

Slightly smaller than a Pigeon. Large white area on neck and upper-back distinguishes it from other similar looking woodpeckers; females have a yellow crown.

Male

Broadbills (*Eurylaimidae*)
These birds are seen in forested areas, camouflaging well with the foliage. Broadbills feed on insects picked from tree branches. These birds make globular nests high on trees. Their nests can be seen hanging from the tips of tree branches over ravines and streams. *It can be best sighted in Dhikala and Durgadevi zones.*

LONG-TAILED BROADBILL ▶
Psarisomus dalhousiae
Myna-sized, tail longer. Greenish bird with yellow throat and collar, and bluish cap.

Pittas (*Pittidae*)
These short-tailed birds are seen on the ground in forested areas, hopping and flicking fallen dried leaves. Pittas feed on insects, worms, etc. These birds produce whistling vocalizations. The two species of pittas seen in CTR are summer visitors. Pittas make globular or oval nests of grass and dry leaves; the nests are hidden on the ground or on the forked branches of trees. *Pittas can be best sighted in Pakhro, Dhela, Jhirna, Bijrani, Garjia and Dhikala zones.*

HOODED PITTA ▶
Pitta sordida
Slightly smaller than a Myna. Distinguished from Indian Pitta by its dark brown crown, black neck and face.

INDIAN PITTA ▶
Pitta brachyura
Slightly smaller than a Myna. Juveniles duller with scaly pattern on the crown.

Woodshrikes (*Vangidae*)
They are insect eating birds seen on trees. The habitat of the Large Woodshrike is well-wooded areas, whereas the Common Woodshrike prefers thinly forested areas and scrubs. These birds make cup-shaped nests on trees. *Woodshrikes can be best sighted in Pakhro, Dhela, Jhirna, Bijrani, Garjia and Dhikala zones.*

▲
COMMON WOODSHRIKE
Tephrodornis pondicerianus
Bulbul-sized. It can be distinguished from the Large Woodshrike by its smaller size and white supercilium (arrow); juvenile brownish with spotted crown.

◀ **LARGE WOODSHRIKE**
Tephrodornis virgatus
Myna-sized. It has a large bill and whitish throat; females have a paler bill (dark in males), brownish crown and less contrasting black stripe around the eyes than males.

BAR-WINGED FLYCATCHER-SHRIKE ▶
Hemipus picatus
Sparrow-sized. It has a prominent white band across the wings (arrow); females have a brown crown.

Minivets and Cuckooshrikes (*Campephagidae*)
These birds are seen on trees in forested areas and fringes of forest, feeding on insects. Bright colouration and agility of the minivets make them more conspicuous in the forest. The birds of this group make cup-shaped nests with grass and twigs, the nests are covered with cobwebs and secured on trees. *These birds can be sighted in Bijrani, Garjia, Dhikala, Durgadevi and Sonanadi (Halduparao) zones.*

▲
LARGE CUCKOOSHRIKE
Coracina macei
Slightly smaller than a Pigeon. Sexes similar.

BLACK-WINGED CUCKOOSHRIKE

Coracina melaschistos

Myna-sized. Sexes similar but females have faint barring on the belly; distinguished from Large Cuckooshrike by its smaller size, darker body and extensive black colouration on wings.

ROSY MINIVET

Pericrocotus roseus

Bulbul-sized. Pinkish cast to underparts and greyish upperparts distinguishes males from the males of other mentioned minivets; females distinguished from females of other minivets by a combination of greyish forehead and throat, and faint yellow cast to the underparts.

SCARLET MINIVET

Pericrocotus speciosus

Myna-sized, tail longer. Males reddish with two or more red patches on wings (arrow). Females yellowish.

SMALL MINIVET

Pericrocotus cinnamomeus

Bulbul-sized, tail longer. Males with slaty-grey head and orange wash to breast; females with greyish head and pale underparts.

LONG-TAILED MINIVET

Pericrocotus ethologus

Bulbul-sized, tail longer. Males have 'U'-or 'V'-shaped red patch on black wings. Females yellowish, and have less extensive yellow colouration on underparts and forehead than females of Scarlet Minivet.

Ioras (*Aegithinidae*)
These small birds are seen on trees, feeding on insects and worms, in thinly forested areas and fringes of forest. They produce a melodious whistle. Ioras make cup-shaped nests of grass, coated with cobwebs, on trees or bushes, and lay pinkish eggs blotched with purplish-brown. *It can be sighted in all the zones.*

▲
COMMON IORA
Aegithina tiphia
Sparrow-sized. Sexes similar.

Shrikes (*Laniidae*)
The word 'Shrike' means unpleasant calls. These are predatory birds feeding on large insects, small birds, lizards and other small animals. Shrikes have strong legs and feet, and sharp hooked bills with a small tooth -like structure. The first name in the scientific naming *'Lanius'* means 'butcher', reflecting their feeding behaviour as these predatory birds pin their prey onto thorns and spikes. This habit also gives them the name 'Butcher birds'. Shrikes are seen in scrubs and in tall grasslands with scattered bushes. These birds make cup-shaped nests with grass, on trees or bushes. *Shrikes can be sighted in all the zones.*

BAY-BACKED SHRIKE
Lanius vittatus ▶
Bulbul-sized but tail longer. Distinguished from other mentioned shrikes by a combination of its maroonish-brown back, white patch on the wings (arrow) and white rump.

PC: *HP*

LONG-TAILED SHRIKE ▶
Lanius schach
Myna-sized, tail longer. It has a rufous cast to its back.

SOUTHERN GREY SHRIKE ▶
Lanius meridionalis
Myna-sized, tail longer. It has a grey back and head, and whitish underparts.

Drongos (*Dicruridae*)
These are black or blue-black birds with a long forked tail and a strong bill. These are usually seen on trees in forested areas and fringes of forest. They make a wide range of whistling, fluty and harsh calls. Many of these birds can mimic calls of other birds. Drongos feed on large insects and sometimes also on small birds and reptiles. These birds make cup-shaped nests with grass and fibres on trees. ***Drongos can be sighted in all the zones.***

SPANGLED DRONGO ▶

Dicrurus hottentottus

Pigeon-sized, tail longer. Distinguished from other mentioned drongos by a combination of its broader tail twisted at the tip, long downward curved bill, and long hair-like crest.

BLACK DRONGO ▶

Dicrurus macrocercus

Slightly larger than a Myna, tail longer. Forked tail, glossy blackish colouration and tiny white rictal spot (arrow) distinguishes it from other mentioned drongos; juveniles have dark brown body.

◀ LESSER RACKET-TAILED DRONGO

Dicrurus remifer

Myna-sized but slimmer. Distinguished from Greater Racket-tailed by its smaller size, lack of crest, and smaller oval rackets at the end of tail-streamers (arrow); immature birds lack tail-streamers.

PC: RP

PC: DS

◀ GREATER RACKET-TAILED DRONGO

Dicrurus paradiseus

Pigeon-sized, but slimmer. It has a prominent crest, large bill and tail with long tail-streamers; rackets are twisted and longer than that of Lesser Racket-tailed.

ASHY DRONGO ▶

Dicrurus leucophaeus

Slightly larger than a Myna, tail longer. Distinguished from the Black Drongo by its dark greyish body with bluish shine, bright red eyes, and lack of rictal spot; seen in summers.

PC: MS

▲
WHITE-BELLIED DRONGO

Dicrurus caerulescens

Myna-sized, tail longer. Features such as whitish belly and tail, and absence of white rictal spot, help in distinguishing it from Black and Ashy Drongos.

▲
BRONZED DRONGO

Dicrurus aeneus

Myna-sized. It has a shining bluish body; distinguished from the Black Drongo by its smaller size, spangled crown and back, and shallowly forked tail.

Orioles (*Oriolidae*)
These birds are seen on trees in forested areas and fringes of forest. Orioles can be located by their melodious fluty calls. These birds make cup-shaped nests with grass and fibres on trees. ***Orioles can be sighted in all the zones.***

INDIAN GOLDEN ORIOLE ▶

Oriolus kundoo

Myna-sized; has a yellow head and black area around the eyes; females have yellowish-green upperparts and streaked underparts; seen in summers.

▲
BLACK-HOODED ORIOLE

Oriolus xanthornus

Myna-sized bird with a black head, distinguishing it from the Indian Golden Oriole; females have an olive-yellow back.

▲
MAROON ORIOLE

Oriolus traillii

Slightly larger than a Myna. Males with shining maroon underparts and back.

Fantails (*Rhipiduridae*)
These birds are seen on trees and bushes in forested areas and fringes of forest. While moving on branches, they spread their tail feathers (fanning), and make soft vocalizations. Fantails make deep cup-shaped nests with grass, fibres and moss; the nests are coated with spider webs and are placed on tree branches, few metres from the ground.
Fantails can be sighted in all the zones; Yellow-bellied Fantail can be best sighted in the Sonanadi (Halduparao) and Durgadevi zones.

WHITE-THROATED FANTAIL ▶

Rhipidura albicollis

Bulbul-sized. Distinguished from White-browed Fantail by a thin white line above the eyes, white throat, dark underparts, and lack of white spots on shoulders.

YELLOW-BELLIED FANTAIL

Chelidorhynx hypoxanthus

Sparrow-sized. Forehead, area above the eyes and underparts are yellow, distinguishing it from other mentioned fantails.

WHITE-BROWED FANTAIL

Rhipidura aureola

Bulbul-sized. It has a broad white line above the eyes, white belly, and white spots on shoulders.

Paradise Flycatchers and Monarchs (*Monarchidae*)

These birds are seen actively moving, foraging on flying insects in forested areas and fringes of the forest. Their nest is a cup-shaped structure made of fine grass and moss, coated on the outside with cobwebs and egg cases, and secured on trees. These birds lay pale-pink eggs blotched with brown. *These can be sighted in all the zones.*

BLACK-NAPED MONARCH

Hypothymis azurea

Slightly larger than a Sparrow, tail longer.

ASIAN PARADISE-FLYCATCHER

Terpsiphone paradisi

Bulbul-sized, with long tail-streamers in males. Two forms of male birds 'white' and 'rufous' can be seen; females similar to rufous males but have a greyish throat and face and lack tail streamers. It is seen in summers.

Magpies, Treepies and Crows (*Corvidae*)

These birds with strong toes and claws feed on large insects, other small animals, carrion and fruits. Their voice is loud and harsh. *Treepies* and *Magpies* are seen hopping on trees in forested areas and fringes of the forest, they may descend on the ground for feeding. *Crows* can be seen in a variety of habitats including thinly forested areas, fringes of the forest. The nest of this group of birds is made of twigs and sticks on trees, and depending upon the species, they lay lightly coloured or blotched eggs. ***These birds can be sighted in all the zones. House Crow, however, is mostly sighted in and near the Pakhro, Dhela and Jhirna zones.***

RED-BILLED BLUE MAGPIE

Urocissa erythroryncha

Size about 65–70 cm with a long tail. Juveniles have dull upperparts.

COMMON GREEN MAGPIE

Cissa chinensis

Size about 40 cm with a long tail.

RUFOUS TREEPIE

Dendrocitta vagabunda

Size about 50 cm with a long tail.

GREY TREEPIE

Dendrocitta formosae

Size about 40 cm with a long tail. Distinguished from Rufous Treepie by its all black wings with a white patch, and greyish head and underparts.

▲ **LARGE-BILLED CROW**

Corvus macrorhynchos

Slightly larger than a Crow. All-black with a heavier bill which is more curved at the tip.

▲ **HOUSE CROW**

Corvus splendens

Neck and underparts lighter than the back.

Tits (*Paridae*) and Long-tailed Tits (*Aegithalidae*)

The words 'tit' and 'titmouse' mean a small bird. Typically, these agile birds are sparrow-sized or smaller. Tits are seen on trees in forested areas and fringes of the forest. Their main food is insects which they are seen searching in bark crevices, buds and around leaves, in an acrobatic manner. These birds make their nests in tree holes or stone walls, or with a ball of moss and cobwebs placed among bushes.

Tits are best sighted in Dhikala, Durgadevi and Sonanadi (Halduparao) zones.

GREAT TIT ▶

Parus major

Nearly the size of a Sparrow.

▲

GREEN-BACKED TIT

Parus monticolus

Slightly smaller than a Sparrow. It can be distinguished from the Great Tit by its greenish-yellow back, and yellow sides of the breast and belly.

▲

BLACK-THROATED TIT

Aegithalos concinnus

About two-third the size of a Sparrow.

BLACK-LORED TIT ▶

Parus xanthogenys

Slightly smaller than a Sparrow. It has a yellow stripe above the eyes, yellow cheeks and black crest. These features distinguish it from Great and Green-backed Tits.

Swallows and Martins (*Hirundinidae*)

The name 'Martin' is given to the birds with shorter tails, whereas those with longer tails are called 'Swallows'. These birds have a streamlined slender body, long pointed wings and a small flat bill. They are adapted to capture flying insects. These can be spotted in open areas, near rivers or other large waterbodies. They make nests in tree holes and mud banks, or construct cup-shaped structures of mud pellets fixed to cliffs or buildings. Some birds of this group lay plain eggs, while others lay blotched eggs. ***These birds can be sighted in all the zones.***

PLAIN MARTIN

Riparia paludicola

Slightly smaller than a Sparrow.

▼

PC: AC

▲
WIRE-TAILED SWALLOW

Hirundo smithii

Sparrow-sized. It has a rufous crown, plain white underparts and wire-like long tail streamers.

▲
STREAK-THROATED SWALLOW

Petrochelidon fluvicola

Slightly smaller than a Sparrow. Distinguished from other mentioned swallows by its rufous crown and neck, brown streaking on throat, breast and sides of face, and fine white streaking on its back.

▲
RED-RUMPED SWALLOW

Cecropis daurica

Slightly larger than a Sparrow, tail longer. Distinguished from the Barn Swallow by its pale-white streaked underparts, rufous rump and neck.

▲
BARN SWALLOW

Hirundo rustica

Slightly smaller than a Bulbul. It has bluish-black upperparts, a black breast band, and rufous forehead and throat. There is a long tail streamer.

Female Barn Swallows Prefer Males with Long Tail-Streamers

In Barn Swallow, tail-streamers provide manoeuvrability when the bird captures a prey while in flight. The length of streamers in males is more than that required to provide manoeuvrability. The extra length of the streamers is said to impress females who prefer mating with males possessing longer tail-streamers.

Larks (*Alaudidae*)

These sparrow-sized birds with dull, streaked plumage, are seen feeding by running or walking on the ground in grasslands and scrubs, along with pipits which too have similar plumage. Larks are, however, stouter, with a shorter tail, thicker bill, and some larks have crests. Depending upon the species, larks make cup-, dome- or saucer-shaped nests from grass in depressions on the ground, sheltered among tall grass, under bushes, stones, etc. Larks lay blotched eggs. ***Larks can be best sighted in grasslands of Jhirna, Dhela and Dhikala zones.***

BENGAL BUSHLARK

Mirafra assamica

Sparrow-sized. It has a crest, and margins of wings have prominent rusty colouration.

ORIENTAL SKYLARK

Alauda gulgula

Sparrow-sized. It has a prominently streaked body and crest.

ASHY-CROWNED SPARROW LARK

Eremopterix griseus

Sparrow-sized. It has a broader bill.

Stockpiling of Food—Dealing with Period of Food Scarcity

Birds such as tits, nuthatches, crows and jays, hoard food items such as seeds during periods of food abundance to be used after few months when there is shortage. To keep food hidden from stealers, these birds hide food at several locations such as in tree crevices, knotholes, among dead leaves and in the earth. Food hoarding birds have a remarkable capability to remember the location of their cache.

Bulbuls (*Pycnonotidae*)

These noisy birds are seen in forested areas and fringes of forest, on trees, bushes, and sometimes on the ground, feeding on berries, insects, floral buds, etc. Bulbuls make cup-shaped nests of rootlets, grass and fine twigs, and lay blotched eggs. All the bulbuls are of similar size, except for the Black Bulbul which has a Myna-sized body.

Bulbuls can be sighted in all the zones.

HIMALAYAN BULBUL

Pycnonotus leucogenys

Bulbul-sized. It has a prominent crest.

RED-WHISKERED BULBUL

Pycnonotus jocosus

Bulbul-sized. Juveniles have an orangish vent.

ASHY BULBUL

Hemixos flavala

Bulbul-sized.

BLACK-CRESTED BULBUL

Pycnonotus flaviventris

Bulbul-sized.

PC: HP

BLACK BULBUL

Hypsipetes leucocephalus

Myna-sized, but slimmer. It has a slaty-grey body, red bill and legs.

RED-VENTED BULBUL

Pycnonotus cafer

Bulbul-sized. Juveniles browner than the adults.

Prinias, Cisticolas and Tailorbirds (*Cisticolidae*)

The usual haunt of *Prinias* and *Cisticolas* are bushes at the fringes of forests, grasslands and scrubs. *Tailorbirds* are seen in thinly forested areas and fringes of forest. All these birds have a fine bill and feed on insects, spiders and seeds. The nest of these birds is spherical or cup-shaped, made of grass, and hidden in bushes or attached to grass stems. The beautiful nest of tailorbird is made of broad leaves, skilfully stitched together to form a cone filled with soft fibres, cotton, grass, etc.

Many of these birds can be sighted in all the zones, however the best zone to sight them is Dhikala

GREY-BREASTED PRINIA

Prinia hodgsonii

About two-third the size of a Sparrow. Breeding plumage has greyish head, and grey breast band; non-breeding plumage with brownish upperparts and a thin white line above the eyes.

ASHY PRINIA

Prinia socialis

Slightly smaller than a Sparrow, tail longer. Distinguished from other prinias by a combination of its slaty-grey head, neck and back and orangish underparts.

Br

NBr

PLAIN PRINIA

Prinia inornata

Slightly smaller than a Sparrow, tail longer. Breeding adults have black bill, greyish-brown upperparts and whitish underparts; non-breeding adults with pale base at lower half of the bill, and brownish upperparts and pale-brownish underparts.

COMMON TAILORBIRD

Orthotomus sutorius

Slightly smaller than a Sparrow. It has a rufous-brown forehead, greenish-yellow upperparts; breeding males have longer tail feathers; distinguished from mentioned prinias by colouration of upperparts and forehead.

BRISTLED GRASSBIRD

Chaetornis striata

Bulbul-sized. Body size and shape of bill can distinguish this bird from similar looking birds such as larks, pipits and cisticolas which are found alongside in tall grassland.

GOLDEN-HEADED CISTICOLA

Cisticola exilis

About two-third the size of a Sparrow. Breeding males have pale crown and underparts, and streaked upperparts; females and non-breeding males have a streaked crown and back.

ZITTING CISTICOLA

Cisticola juncidis

About two-third the size of a Sparrow. Breeding adults with shorter tail, and rufous rump; non-breeding adults are heavily streaked, with a longer tail.

Annual Calendar of Birds—Doing the Right Activity at the Right Time of the Year

Breeding, moulting and migration are the main annual activities of birds. In many birds, every year, each of these activities is timed in a particular season when conditions are the most favourable. For instance, birds begin displaying breeding-related behaviour (singing, defending territory, acquiring breeding plumage, courtship, nest making, etc.) at the onset of spring, and this continues till the monsoon (breeding season). After completing their duty as parents and as winter approaches, birds replace their bright breeding feathers with dull ones. Also, those going for long winter migratory journeys store huge amounts of fat in their body to fuel their flight.

Precise timing of each of the annual activities is controlled by interplay of hormones, body's time-keeping system, and relative length of day and night (which the brain of birds can measure). Therefore birds can foresee the forthcoming season well in advance and their body can make necessary adjustments. In essence, the arrival of longer days increases the warmth, terminates winters and brings about spring, followed by the rainy season during which there is ample food to nourish the young ones. The internal time-keeping system of birds together with increasing day length keeps the birds informed about the change in the season, and triggers secretion of reproductive hormones to stimulate the necessary biochemical and physiological processes.

Warblers and Allies (*Sylviidae*)

A group of yellowish, greenish-yellow or pale-brown birds; many of these are smaller than the Sparrow, have a shorter tail and a fine small bill. If one sights a bird with these features, moving rapidly in bushes and on branches of trees, it would most likely be a warbler (ruling out female sunbirds, white-eyes, flowerpeckers and munias by the shape of the bill and eye-rings).

Warblers are seen in varieties of habitats such as forested areas, fringes of forests, scrubs, grasslands and reeds, feeding on insects, worms, spiders, berries and seeds. Species of warblers which are commonly seen on trees and bushes in the forest and scrubs have been mentioned here.

Many warblers make round nests of grasses or moss, close to the ground or in the bushes.

These birds can be sighted in all the zones.

◀ **COMMON CHIFFCHAFF**

Phylloscopus collybita

About two-third the size of a Sparrow. Combination of features such as: brownish upperparts, buffish underparts, weak supercilium (arrow), blackish bill and legs, and absence of wing bars, aid in identification of this bird.

▲ **CHESTNUT-HEADED TESIA**

Cettia castaneocoronata

Nearly half the size of a Sparrow, tail shorter. It has a chestnut head and yellow underparts.

LESSER WHITETHROAT ▶

Sylvia curruca

Slightly smaller than a Sparrow. Combination of features such as slaty-grey head, dark area around the eyes, white throat, black bill and legs help in identification of this bird.

▲

PALE-FOOTED BUSH WARBLER

Cettia pallidipes

About two-third the size of a Sparrow. It has whitish underparts and pinkish feet.

▲

BLYTH'S REED WARBLER

Acrocephalus dumetorum

Slightly smaller than a Sparrow. It has a prominent bill and faint supercilium (arrow).

▲

TICKELL'S LEAF WARBLER

Phylloscopus affinis

About two-third the size of a Sparrow. Distinguished from Sulphur-bellied Warbler by a combination of features such as greenish-brown upperparts and lemon-yellow underparts; colour of supercilium is similar to that of the throat.

HUME'S LEAF WARBLER

Phylloscopus humei

About two-third the size of a Sparrow. Greyish upperparts with slight olive cast, two wing bars, dark bill and legs, indistinct crown stripe, help in identification of this bird; upperparts greyer in worn plumage.

▼

▲

SULPHUR-BELLIED WARBLER

Phylloscopus griseolus

About two-third the size of a Sparrow. It has brownish-grey upperparts (absence of greenish cast), buffish underparts; yellowish colouration of supercilium brighter than that of the throat.

LEMON-RUMPED WARBLER

Phylloscopus chloronotus

About two-third the size of a Sparrow. Combination of features such as prominent stripe on the head, lemon-coloured rump, two wing bars (one of which is smaller, and may wear away), eye-stripe (arrow) that hooks near its neck help in identification of this bird.

▼

GREENISH WARBLER ▶

Phylloscopus trochiloides

About two-third the size of a Sparrow. It has whitish underparts, one wing-bar and prominent whitish supercilium. These features help in identification of this warbler.

WHISTLER'S WARBLER ▶

Seicercus whistleri

About two-third the size of a Sparrow. Yellow eye-ring, two black crown stripes which fade out as they reach the forehead, help in identifying this warbler.

PC: AC

GREY-HOODED WARBLER ▶

Phylloscopus xanthoschistos

About two-third the size of a Sparrow. Combination of features such as a grey head with faint crown stripe; grey neck and back; bright yellow underparts, help distinguish it from other mentioned warblers.

Sometimes it is difficult to identify every warbler sighted in the field with certainty, particularly for a beginner. The reasons for this are: close resemblance among the various species of warblers and lack of bold differentiating colours. Further, in many species, wearing away or bleaching of the plumage with time obscures the key identification features of the bird's plumage.

Babblers, Laughingthrushes, Yuhinas and Allies (*Timaliidae*)

Many members of this group of birds are often seen in small groups in bushes and forest undergrowth. They feed on the ground by flipping and tossing fallen leaves with their bills to look for insects and worms. Depending upon the species, these birds make dome-shaped, cup-shaped or globular nests on the ground or in bushes, and lay white, bluish or pinkish eggs with or without blotching.

Laughingthrushes are seen in forested areas; these birds quietly forage on the ground and when alarmed, the congregation begins to make loud screaming, hissing or laughter-like noises. They fly from one tree to the other, wherein one congregation member is followed by another.

Babblers, such as Common Babbler, Tawny-bellied and Yellow-eyed Babblers are seen in tall grasslands and scrubs; others such as the Puff-throated, Rusty-cheeked Scimitar and Black-chinned Babblers are seen in forested areas and fringes of the forest. Many babblers are noisy, though some produce pleasant sounds too.

Yuhinas, *Siva* and *Leiothrix* are seen in bushes and undergrowths in the forest and fringes of the forest.

Though many of these birds can be sighted in all the zones, Dhikala, Durgadevi and Sonanadi (Halduparao) zones are the best places to sight most of them.

BLACK-CHINNED BABBLER

Stachyridopsis pyrrhops

About two-third the size of a Sparrow. It has black lores, chin and middle of the throat.

SCALY-BREASTED WREN BABBLER

Pnoepyga albiventer

About two-third the size of a Sparrow, tailless. Seen in forested areas; has prominent scaly looking underparts.

TAWNY-BELLIED BABBLER

Dumetia hyperythra

Slightly smaller than a Sparrow. Absence of black patch at chin and lores, and rufous cast to body distinguishes it from the Black-chinned Babbler.

RUSTY-CHEEKED SCIMITAR BABBLER

Pomatorhinus erythrogenys

Myna-sized, tail longer. It sings loud *kuee...kip...kuee... kip*...duets from the bushes. ▶

YELLOW-EYED BABBLER

Chrysomma sinense

◀ Bulbul-sized. It has yellow eyes, prominent orangish orbital rings, dark bill, and white throat and breast.

▲

COMMON BABBLER

Turdoides caudata

Slightly smaller than a Myna, tail longer. Distinguished from Jungle Babbler by its smaller size, unstreaked white throat and darker bill.

▲

JUNGLE BABBLER

Turdoides striata

Myna-sized, tail longer. A rather noisy bird.

◀

PUFF-THROATED BABBLER

Pellorneum ruficeps

Sparrow-sized. It produces a melodious whistling sound.

BLUE-WINGED SIVA

Siva cyanouroptera

Sparrow-sized. It has a bluish-grey crown, brown back, and blue wings and tail.

WHISKERED YUHINA

Yuhina flavicollis

Slightly smaller than a Sparrow. It has a forward projecting brownish crest, yellowish collar, black moustachial stripe and white eye-ring.

BLACK-CHINNED YUHINA

Yuhina nigrimenta

About two-third the size of a Sparrow. It has a grey head (lacking forward projecting crest) which distinguishes it from the Whiskered Yuhina.

STREAKED LAUGHINGTHRUSH

Garrulax lineatus

Bulbul-sized. Brownish-grey bird with finely streaked upperparts and underparts; has brown tail with grey area at the tip and rufous area behind its eyes.

RED-BILLED LEIOTHRIX

Leiothrix lutea

Slightly smaller than a Sparrow.

WHITE-THROATED LAUGHINGTHRUSH

Garrulax albogularis

Slightly larger than a Myna, tail longer. Seen in groups of 5–7 individuals or more in densely forested areas; makes varieties of loud sounds such as shrills, laughs, etc.

WHITE-CRESTED LAUGHINGTHRUSH

Garrulax leucolophus

Slightly larger than a Myna, tail longer. Seen in groups of 5–7 individuals or more in densely forested areas, makes laughing sounds, which can be heard from a distance.

White-eyes (*Zosteropidae*)
These are agile birds, seen in flocks of 5–10 or sometimes more than 30 individuals depending upon the availability of food. They forage on insects, fruits and berries, on trees and bushes. They make cup-shaped nests with fibres, and lay bluish eggs.
It can be sighted in all the zones.

▲
ORIENTAL WHITE-EYE
Zosterops palpebrosus
About two-third the size of a Sparrow. It has a prominent white eye-ring.

Dippers (*Cinclidae*)
These have short wings and a short tail; are adapted for feeding under fast running water by hunting small aquatic animals. These birds are seen along streams and rivers, looking for prey hidden among pebbles and rocks. Their dense waterproof plumage keeps them insulated from the chilled mountain river water. They have a stout bill which helps in probing for prey among pebbles and boulders; strong legs provide the dippers a firm hold on the pebbles. The short wings are supplied with strong musculature that allows the wings to be used as flippers while moving under water. The nest of the dipper is a large ball of moss, made along rivers.
It can be best sighted in Durgadevi and Sonanadi (Halduparao) zones.

PC: RP

▲
BROWN DIPPER
Cinclus pallasii
Bulbul-sized bird, tail smaller. Adult brown all-over; juveniles spotted.

Dipper in action
PC: RBP

Nuthatches and Wallcreeper (*Sittidae*)

These birds have an ability to creep on vertical surfaces such as tree trunks, cliffs, rocks or walls. These have a compact body, small tail and long toes with long-curved claws adapted for creeping or clambering on vertical surfaces. Unlike woodpeckers and treecreeper, these birds do not use their tail feathers as prop or support while hopping up on the trunk.

Nuthatches are seen creeping on tree trunks sideways as well as upwards and downwards with jerky hops. They begin from a higher location on the trees and move downwards in a head-first manner—a behaviour unlike other clinging birds like woodpeckers and treecreepers. The nuthatches feed on insects and spiders hiding in the bark, and also feed on seeds. Nuthatches get their name due to the behaviour of breaking nuts by hammering into them with their bill. These birds are known to store seeds and nuts in crevices for future consumption. Nuthatches make their nests in tree holes and lay blotched eggs.

Wallcreepers are seen on rock cliffs, gorges and river beds. They flick their wings while hopping on a vertical surface. They feed on insects or other tiny animals by extracting them from crevices, with a forceps-like bill. Wallcreepers make nests in holes in rocks or crevices.

Wallcreepers and nuthatches can be best sighted in Bijrani, Garjia, Dhikala, Durgadevi and Sonanadi (Halduparao) zones.

VELVET-FRONTED NUTHATCH

Sitta frontalis

About two-third the size of a Sparrow. Males have a black eye stripe (arrow). ▼

▲

WALLCREEPER

Tichodroma muraria

Slightly larger than a Sparrow. It can be identified by crimson area on wings and long downward curved bill; breeding plumage has black throat.

◀

CHESTNUT-BELLIED NUTHATCH

Sitta cinnamoventris

Slightly smaller than a Sparrow. Underparts of males dark reddish-brown; paler in females. Colour of underparts, and eye colour helps in distinguishing it from the Velvet-fronted Nuthatch.

Mynas and Starlings (*Sturnidae*)

These birds are usually seen in open and thinly forested areas (though some birds such as the Jungle Myna may be seen in densely forested areas), in small groups to large noisy flocks. They have stout bills, strong legs, and feed on fruits, insects, seeds, etc. Most of them make their nests in natural tree holes or in holes dug by woodpeckers or barbets, or holes in earth banks. Depending upon the species, these birds lay pale-blue or blue eggs.

These birds can be sighted in all the zones.

JUNGLE MYNA

Acridotheres fuscus ▶

Myna-sized. Lacks bare skin behind its pale eyes, a feature which distinguishes it from Common and Bank Mynas.

ASIAN PIED STARLING

Gracupica contra

Myna-sized. Adults black and white; juveniles browner. ▼

BANK MYNA

Acridotheres ginginianus

◀ Myna-sized. It has a bluish-grey body, reddish-orange bill and legs.

PC: MS

COMMON MYNA

▲

Acridotheres tristis

It has a yellow skin patch behind the eyes, yellow bill and legs, and white patch on its wings.

CHESTNUT-TAILED STARLING

Sturnia malabarica

Bulbul-sized. Seen in summers. ▼

BRAHMINY STARLING

▲

Sturnia pagodarum

Slightly smaller than a Myna. Juveniles browner.

Treecreepers (*Certhiidae*)
These brownish, heavily streaked birds with short legs, long toes and curved claws are adapted for clambering on vertical rough surfaces such as tree bark. These birds are seen creeping on the bark of trees; they use their stiff tail as a prop while climbing. Their usual behaviour is to land at the bottom of the trunk and then to move upwards while foraging. Treecreepers feed on insects, spiders and seeds. These birds make their nests behind loose flaps of bark and inside deep crevices of trees, and lay blotched eggs.
It can be best sighted in Dhikala, Durgadevi and Sonanadi (Halduparao) zones.

▲ **BAR-TAILED TREECREEPER**
Certhia himalayana
About three-fourth the size of a Sparrow. Seen on tree trunks, perfectly camouflaging with the bark; has a long downward curved bill, bars on its tail and pale white underparts.

The Basic Science of a Bird's Colouration

White light or sunlight is a blend of light of all the colours (or wavelengths to be more precise!). Coloured objects or feathers have the property of reflecting just one or few colours and simultaneously suppressing other colours. The reflected colour is perceived as the colour of the object. Feathers of birds (or coloured parts of all other animals) have two fundamental ways to do the above: 1) by pigment-based colouration, and 2) structure based colouration.

In *pigment-based colouration*, certain coloured chemical compounds, 'pigments', are incorporated in the feathers during feather development on the bird's skin. This is analogous to fixing dye in the fabric to get the desired colour of the cloth. In birds, two pigments 'melanin' (responsible for skin tone in humans) and 'carotenoids' (for yellows and reds) are widespread. In *structure based colouration*, certain colourless nano-sized structures made of keratin (feather protein) together with trapped air produce colours. The geometry of these nano-sized structures is such that they can split white light into various colours by the same phenomena responsible for the production of the range of colours in a rainbow (from water droplets), colours seen at times on the surface of computer CDs and the colours on soap bubbles. Usually, bright blues and iridescent colourations are produced by this method.

In many cases, the observed colour of the bird feathers or wings of butterflies (p.235) is produced by complex interactions between the pigment- and structure-based colouration mechanisms.

Thrushes (*Turdidae*)

These form a group of rather cryptic birds, many of which are seen foraging on the ground by flipping or turning over dry leaves to expose hidden insects and worms. These birds prefer densely to thinly forested areas. They make cup-shaped nests of moss and grass, on trees, bushes or in crevices along the banks of streams.

Some of these birds can be sighted in all the zones; however, to sight most of the above-mentioned thrushes, one is recommended to visit Bijrani, Garjia, Dhikala, Durgadevi and Sonanadi (Halduparao) zones.

▲

BLACK-THROATED THRUSH

Turdus atrogularis

Myna-sized. Males have a black throat and breast, females instead have diffuse spots; females can be distinguished from females of Tickell's Thrush by larger size and prominent black spots on the breast; seen in winters.

▲

SCALY THRUSH

Zoothera dauma

Slightly larger than a Myna. Distinguished from Long-billed Thrush by scaly appearance of its plumage, smaller bill and golden sides of wings (arrow); seen in winters close to ground in forested areas.

▲

TICKELL'S THRUSH

Turdus unicolour

Slightly smaller than a Myna. Males bluish-grey all-over except for the belly which is whitish; both the sexes have yellowish bill and legs; black streaking on breast and lighter underparts distinguish females from females of the Grey-winged Blackbird. It is seen in winters.

◀

LONG-BILLED THRUSH

Zoothera monticola

Slightly smaller than a Pigeon. It has a large bill.

BLUE WHISTLING THRUSH

Myophonus caeruleus

Slightly smaller than a Pigeon. Distinguished from Grey-winged Blackbird by the absence of greyish area on its wings; makes a melodious whistling sound.

GREY-WINGED BLACKBIRD

Turdus boulboul

Slightly larger than a Myna. Females brownish. It has an orangish-yellow bill.

ORANGE-HEADED THRUSH

Zoothera citrina

Slightly smaller than a Myna. Females have slight brownish cast on their back. Seen in summers.

Which One to Feed—a Puzzle for the Parent Birds

Studies have indicated that depending upon environmental conditions, parents might either prefer feeding all their hungry chicks, or opt to feed only the healthy chicks, while ignoring the needy ones. For instance, when food is aplenty, parents prefer feeding those chicks which are in worse condition or hungrier. They identify the needy chicks by the intensity with which they beg. However, in many species, when there is scarcity of food, parents prefer feeding healthier chicks. This way, when food is limited, parents manage to raise fewer but healthier chicks.

Scaly-breasted Munia family

Chats, Robins, Flycatchers, Redstarts, Rock Thrushes, Niltavas and allies (*Muscicapidae*)

These are Bulbul to Sparrow-sized birds feeding largely on insects. Many of these birds make cup-shaped nests of moss, grass, hair and wool, or make a nest with pads of grass and rootlets in the crevices of rocks, clefts, earth cuttings, tree holes and beneath bushes.

Flycatchers are seen on bushes and trees, in thinly forested areas and fringes of forest. These birds are well adapted for catching insects in air; they have flat bills suited to capture flying insects. They possess bristles at the base of the bill which are known to protect their eyes from the particles blown towards the eyes when the bird strikes to capture insects. The common practice of many flycatchers is to perch on trees and bushes, catch insects in mid-air or on the ground, and then return to the same perch.

Chats are usually seen on perches close to the ground in grasslands, scrubs and among scattered bushes. These birds drop to the ground from perches and hop to catch insects.

Redstarts, particularly the White-capped and Plumbeous Redstarts, and forktails are seen foraging on the ground close to the streams, rivers and ravines.

Niltavas are seen perched on trees and bushes in forested areas and fringes of forests.

Many birds in this group such as robins, redstarts and flycatchers often cock or vibrate their tail.

Most of the chats, robins, flycatchers, redstarts, rock thrushes and niltavas can be sighted in all the zones; the forktail can be best sighted in Dhikala, Durgadevi and Sonanadi (Halduparao) zones.

Male

WHITE-TAILED RUBYTHROAT

Luscinia pectoralis

Sparrow-sized. Males not to be confused with Rufous-gorgeted Flycatcher which has a black throat; females duller with a white throat and lack a black breast band; seen in winters in bushes, and on ground in open areas and fringes of forest.

Male Female

Male

BLUETHROAT ▶

Luscinia svecica

Sparrow-sized. Males have a blue and rufous patch or band on the throat and breast; females have a band of black spots; seen in winters in bushes and on the ground in open areas.

▲

CHESTNUT-BELLIED ROCK THRUSH

Monticola rufiventris

Myna-sized. Males distinguished from Blue-capped Rock Thrush by their larger size, absence of white patch on the wings, and presence of blue rump (orange in Blue-capped). Seen in rocky forested areas.

Female
Male

BLUE ROCK THRUSH ▶

Monticola solitarius

Bulbul-sized. Males bluish; females with slaty-brown upperparts and scaly underparts; seen in winters, foraging in dry rocky areas, and among boulders along the streams or open places.

Male

BLUE-CAPPED ROCK THRUSH

Monticola cinclorhyncha

Slightly smaller than a Bulbul. Females brownish with scaly underparts; seen in summers in thinly forested areas.

INDIAN ROBIN

Saxicoloides fulicatus

Slightly smaller than a Bulbul. Seen in open areas and scrubs.

WHITE-CAPPED REDSTART

Chaimarrornis leucocephalus

Bulbul-sized. It has a white cap, black face, breast and wings, and rufous underparts.

ORIENTAL MAGPIE ROBIN

Copsychus saularis

Bulbul-sized. Produces variable whistling sounds; seen in thinly forested areas and fringes of forest.

PLUMBEOUS WATER REDSTART

Rhyacornis fuliginosa

Slightly smaller than a Sparrow.

BLACK REDSTART

Phoenicurus ochruros

Sparrow-sized. Females brown and can be confused with Brown Rock Chat which lacks rufous colouration to its tail and under-tail feathers. Seen in winters.

BROWN ROCK CHAT

Cercomela fusca

Slightly larger than a Sparrow. Sexes similar.

SPOTTED FORKTAIL

Enicurus maculatus

Slightly larger than a Myna, tail longer. It has a long forked tail, white spots on its back, white forehead and belly.

COMMON STONECHAT

Saxicola torquatus

Sparrow-sized. Females brownish with streaked upperparts and orange cast to the breast; seen in grasslands and scrubs.

GREY BUSHCHAT

Saxicola ferreus

Sparrow-sized. Females brownish with white throat and prominent palish-grey line above the eyes.

PIED BUSHCHAT

Saxicola caprata

Slightly smaller than a Sparrow. Males with black upperparts and whitish belly.

WHITE-RUMPED SHAMA

Copsychus malabaricus

Myna-sized, tail longer. Produces a melodious song; seen in thinly forested areas and the fringes of forest.

▲
RUFOUS-GORGETED FLYCATCHER

Ficedula strophiata

Slightly smaller than a Sparrow. Females have duller colouration than males.

▲
TAIGA FLYCATCHER

Ficedula albicilla

About three-fourth the size of a Sparrow. Females greyish-brown.

▲
SNOWY-BROWED FLYCATCHER

Ficedula hyperythra

About three-fourth the size of a Sparrow. Females brownish.

▲
RED-BREASTED FLYCATCHER

Ficedula parva

About three-fourth the size of a Sparrow. Males distinguished from males of Taiga Flycatcher by the rufous colouration on throat extending to breast (restricted to throat in Taiga). Lower half of the bill with paler base (black in Taiga). Upperparts of females brownish and underparts whitish; seen in winters.

◀
LITTLE PIED FLYCATCHER

Ficedula westermanni

About three-fourth the size of a Sparrow. Female brownish-grey. Seen in winters.

▲
ULTRAMARINE FLYCATCHER
Ficedula superciliaris

About three-fourth the size of a Sparrow. Males can be distinguished from Slaty-blue Flycatcher by a white line above the eyes; distinguished from Little Pied Flycatcher by absence of a white patch on the wings. Females brownish. Seen in winters.

▲
SLATY-BLUE FLYCATCHER
Ficedula tricolour

Slightly smaller than a Sparrow. Males dark blue with contrasting white throat and underparts, and brown cast to their wings; females brownish. Seen in winters.

▲
TICKELL'S BLUE FLYCATCHER
Cyornis tickelliae

Slightly smaller than a Sparrow. Males and females similar.

▲
BLUE-THROATED BLUE FLYCATCHER
Cyornis rubeculoides

Sparrow-sized; males distinguished from males of Snowy-browed Flycatcher by absence of a white line above the eyes and absence of rusty cast to wings; dark-blue throat distinguishes males of this bird from Tickell's Blue Flycatcher. Females brownish.

◀
GREY-HEADED CANARY FLYCATCHER
Culicicapa ceylonensis

Slightly smaller than a Sparrow.

Bird's Nest—a Tactically and Skillfully Built Secure Nursery

Birds make nests to hold eggs during incubation. The nest also protects eggs and nestlings from bad weather and predators (snakes, monkeys, martens and predatory birds etc.). Depending upon the species of birds, one or both the parents can take part in the construction of the nest. The site, material and design of the nest vary widely among birds. However, closely related birds tend to make their nests on a similar architectural plan, and therefore, by looking at a nest, one can broadly guess its owners.

The site chosen by a bird to make its nest is often close to its food source and well protected from predators. Thus, some birds make nests which are beyond the reach of predators: inside tree holes or other natural holes (parakeets, woodpeckers, mynas, kingfishers, hornbills, owls, bee-eaters, etc.), on high cliffs or high up on trees (eagles, vultures, hawks) or a nest hanging from the tip of a long branch (weavers and broadbills). Other birds make cryptic nests sheltered in bushes, trees, or even inside the ground, and use common, dull-coloured stuff such as grass, dry leaves, moss and twigs as the construction material (fowls, warblers, babblers, thrushes, etc.). A few groups of birds either make no nest and lay eggs directly on the ground or make shallow depressions in the ground for laying eggs (lapwings, terns, plovers). For protection, these birds rely on blotchy patterns on the exterior of the eggs, which perfectly camouflage with the surroundings.

Birds Nest Types

Platform nest (eagle)

Cup nest (white-eye)

Pendant nest (weaver)

Stitched leaves nest (tailor bird)

Tunnel nest (bee-eater)

Mud-pellet nest (swallow/martin)

Hanging ball nest (broadbill)

Nest in a tree-hole (barbet)

Male

Male

VERDITER FLYCATCHER

Eumyias thalassinus

Slightly larger than a Sparrow. Males have more prominent black lores than females.

RUFOUS-BELLIED NILTAVA

Niltava sundara

Slightly smaller than a Bulbul. Females brownish with a white patch on the throat, and blue patch on the sides of the neck.

Male

SMALL NILTAVA

Niltava macgrigoriae

Slightly smaller than a Sparrow. Females brownish with a blue patch on the sides of the neck; males likely to be confused with Slaty-blue Flycatcher, which has a white throat.

Female

Leafbirds (*Chloropseidae*)
These are seen on trees in the fringes of forest and forested areas, camouflaging with the greenery. They feed on fruits, nectar and insects, and make cup-shaped nests on trees.
These birds can be sighted in all the zones.

GOLDEN-FRONTED LEAFBIRD

Chloropsis aurifrons

Bulbul-sized. Distinguished from males of Orange-bellied Leafbird by combination of features such as orange forehead, and tail same colour as the body (bluish in Orange-bellied).

ORANGE-BELLIED LEAFBIRD

Chloropsis hardwickii

Bulbul-sized. Margins of wings and tail bluish in males; females greenish all-over but with a bluish moustachial stripe.

Flowerpeckers (*Dicaeidae*)

These small birds are seen on trees in forested areas where they feed on fruits and nectar, and restlessly move on twigs. These birds make purse-shaped nests and lay white or blotched eggs. ***Flowerpeckers can possibly be sighted in all the zones.***

THICK-BILLED FLOWERPECKER

Dicaeum agile

About two-third the size of a Sparrow. Stout greyish bill, whitish underparts and reddish eyes distinguish it from Pale-billed Flowerpecker.

PALE-BILLED FLOWERPECKER

Dicaeum erythrorhynchos

About half the size of a Sparrow. It has a thick pinkish bill.

A male Crimson Sunbird engaged in impressing its mate

Sunbirds (*Nectariniidae*)

These birds are smaller than the Sparrow, with long and narrow downward curved bills. Sunbirds are seen in bushes and trees, probing flowers with their bill to access nectar. Their long tubular tongue helps in extracting the nectar seated deep inside flowers. While looking for nectar, sunbirds act as pollinating agents: pollen that get stuck to their body are transferred to the other flowers they visit. In this way, sunbirds pollinate plants. Sunbirds also consume small insects that are lodged around flowers and twigs.

Male sunbirds are gorgeously coloured. In some sunbirds, males drop their colourful plumage after breeding season and wear female-like plumage (eclipse plumage). Sunbirds make pear-shaped or oval nests from grass and cobwebs, wrap them with dry leaves, bark, etc., and suspend the nests from twigs. These birds lay plain white to off-white eggs which are faintly speckled with brown.

PC: AM

Purple Sunbird can be sighted in all the zones; Green-tailed Sunbird and Crimson Sunbird can be best sighted in Dhikala, Durgadevi and Sonanadi (Halduparao) zones.

Male (Br)

Female

Male (NBr)

PURPLE SUNBIRD

Cinnyris asiaticus

About two-third the size of a Sparrow. A faint yellowish stripe above eyes and darker area in front of the the eyes distinguish the female of Purple Sunbird from the female of Crimson and Green-tailed Sunbirds.

Male

PC: AC

GREEN-TAILED SUNBIRD

Aethopyga nipalensis

About three-fourth the size of a Sparrow, tail longer. Females distinguished from females of other mentioned sunbirds by a combination of greyish colouration to throat and breast, longer tail, dark bill and absence of a white stripe above the eyes.

Male

Female

CRIMSON SUNBIRD

Aethopyga siparaja

About three-fourth the size of a Sparrow. Females greenish-yellow and have pale-brown lower half of the bill.

Sparrows and Petronias (*Passeridae*)

These are birds with conical bills, adapted for eating seeds. These are seen in groups, on the ground in thinly forested areas, fringes of forest and near human habitations.

These can be seen in all the zones; Russet Sparrow is best sighted in villages near Sonanadi (Halduparao) zone.

Female

Male

RUSSET SPARROW

Passer rutilans

Sparrow-sized. Rusty crown and back, and yellowish underparts distinguish males from males of the House Sparrow; females have rufous colouration near the shoulders.

Female

Male

HOUSE SPARROW

Passer domesticus

Non-breeding males with duller throat and breast. Juveniles similar to females.

CHESTNUT-SHOULDERED PETRONIA

Gymnoris xanthocollis

Sparrow-sized. Males have a chestnut mark on shoulders and yellow patch on throat. Females similar but lack chestnut colouration at the shoulders.

Male

Female

Weavers (*Ploceidae*)
These seed eating, Sparrow-sized birds with conical, stout bills are known for their skill of weaving nests using coarse grass. Weavers are seen in grasslands, scrubs and marshes with scattered trees. Weavers lay white eggs. Male weaver birds develop bright yellow plumage during the breeding season, but they resemble female birds in appearance for the rest of the year.
Weaver birds can be best sighted in Jhirna, Dhela, Pakhro, Bijrani and Dhilkala zones.

▲
BLACK-BREASTED WEAVER

Ploceus benghalensis

Sparrow-sized. Non-breeding males lack a yellow crown and have black blotches on the breast.

◀
BAYA WEAVER

Ploceus philippinus

Sparrow-sized. Females lack yellow colouration on the head; non-breeding males similar to females.

Finches (*Fringillidae*)
These sparrow-like birds are seen foraging on seeds, berries and insects on the ground and on bushes, in open areas and fringes of thinly forested areas. Finches have massive conical bills and strong jaw muscles for cracking seeds, and a well-developed gizzard in the alimentary canal for churning. These birds make cup-shaped nests hidden in vegetation and lay handsomely marked eggs. Finches migrate from the higher reaches of Himalayas to CTR in winters.
Finches can be sighted in all the zones.

YELLOW-BREASTED GREENFINCH

Carduelis spinoides

Sparrow-sized. Females with pale greenish-grey upperparts with faint streaking, and dull yellow underparts.

▼

Baya Weaver's Nest—a Structure Made with the Highest Level of Skill to Attract Mates

The superbly woven weaver bird nests are constructed by the male birds, preferably on high thorny trees and tall date-palms. The retort-shaped nest hangs from the tip of the branch. How the male Baya learns the skill to weave the nest is not well known, but it seems to involve both their instinct and experience.

Once the appropriate site is acquired, male bird begins making the nest with grass. When the nest is only partially built, it is inspected by the female bird, who if impressed by the quality of construction, stays there as the wife. Thereafter, the male completes construction of the remaining portion of the nest. After the female gets engaged in the duty of incubating the eggs, the male begins constructing a new nest to attract a second female Baya.

What criteria are used by the females to ensure the quality of the nest?

Females prefer those nests that are located high on thorny trees and woven with fine fibres. They have reasons for this: 1) a nest made with good quality material would be strong enough to resist a gush of monsoon winds, 2) nests built high on trees would protect the young ones from ground-dwelling predators, and 3) a thorny tree would make it difficult for predators, such as snakes, to creep on branches to access the nest. The long neck of the nest too checks predators from reaching the eggs placed deep inside a chamber in the nest.

Songbirds—Vocalists in the Forest

Singing is the feature of a group of birds known as 'songbirds'. The sound-producing organ in these birds, 'syrinx'—analogous to human voice box, is a complex structure that enables them to produce melody. Air is pushed from the lungs (air sac of birds) into the syrinx, which causes certain structures within the latter to vibrate and produce sound. Usually male birds are singers, and each bird species has its own characteristic song which they have learnt from their elders during childhood. *Why do these birds sing?* The vocalisation, which we humans perceive as a song, is actually a way of birds' communication with other birds of the same species. Main functions of bird song are to attract mates and repel rival males. Female birds identify the most suitable sire by the attributes of the song. A bad song may mean that the singer has low-quality genes or inappropriate development of the neural circuits (required to sing songs) in the brain, or that he is low in the requisite physical strength to produce impressive sounds.

It is a common occurrence that many birds begin chorusing loudly just before sunrise (dawn chorus), and as the light intensity increases, they commence their daily activities such as foraging. *Why do birds chorus just before sunrise?* There are some scientific explanations: since sound propagates with fewer disturbances during dawn, birds can communicate their messages over longer distances; moreover, at dawn, the intensity of light is too low to commence foraging yet adequate to perform social activities. Skilled birders can identify a hidden or distant bird just by listening to its song or calls!

COMMON ROSEFINCH ▶

Carpodacus erythrinus

Sparrow-sized. Males with red colouration to the body; females brownish with faint streaking.

Male

Male

PC: AC

Female or Young Male

Munias and Silverbills (*Estrildidae*)
These seed eating birds are smaller than sparrows, and are seen in flocks in grasslands, scrubs, reeds and bushes. These birds lay white eggs in nests made from grass, and both parents share the duties of raising the young ones.

Munias and silverbills can be best sighted in Dhikala, Bijrani, Garjia, Jhirna, Dhela and Pakhro zones.

▲

INDIAN SILVERBILL

Euodice malabarica

Slightly smaller than a Sparrow. It has plain upperparts.

Female

Male (Br)

▲

RED AVADAVAT

Amandava amandava

About two-third the size of a Sparrow. Non-breeding males similar to females.

SCALY-BREASTED MUNIA

Lonchura punctulata

About three-fourth the size of a Sparrow. Juveniles pale-brownish and may be confused with adult Indian Silverbill which has a dark tail and black margins across the wings.

▼

Wagtails and Pipits (*Motacillidae*)

These are bulbul-sized, slim-bodied birds with thin bills. *Wagtails* are bright and contrastingly coloured; their plumage colouration is a combination of black, grey, white and yellow. They are seen near lakes, rivers and streams, and close-by open areas. *Pipits* have dull cryptic colouration and are seen on the ground in scrubs, grasslands and thinly forested areas (Olive-backed Pipit and Tree Pipit).

Wagtails make their nests from dry grass and roots, placed under stones and bushes; pipits make their nests from grass and roots, on the ground in open areas. Wagtails and pipits lay blotched eggs. Most wagtails and a few pipits swing (wag) their tail up and down.

Similar looking wagtails are easy to identify during their breeding season when plumage colouration (especially that of males) is more distinctive. Most wagtails in this area are passage migrants or winter visitors.

Many pipits lack bold or bright colouration; wearing away or bleaching of plumage with time also obscures many subtle identifying features such as streaks, stripes, fringes, etc. This sometimes makes it difficult to tell apart similar looking pipits, even for an experienced birder. Criteria other than plumage colouration, such as vocalization, beak shape, feet projections, etc., also aid in the identification of pipits. Distinction between male and female pipits based on appearance is not usually possible for many species.

Wagtails and Pipits can be sighted in all the zones.

YELLOW WAGTAIL ▶

Motacilla flava

Bulbul-sized. Breeding males have yellowish-green upperparts (which distinguish it from Citrine Wagtail) and yellow underparts; depending on the race, the head can be black, white, yellow or grey.

◀ GREY WAGTAIL

Motacilla cinerea

Bulbul-sized. It has a longer appearing tail than other wagtails; breeding males have a black throat and yellow underparts; outside breeding season males and females look similar.

CITRINE WAGTAIL

Motacilla citreola

Bulbul-sized. Breeding males distinguished from that of Yellow Wagtail by their yellow head contrasting with black or grey back; non-breeding adults have a yellow line above eyes which turns behind the ear and meets the yellow throat.

WHITE-BROWED WAGTAIL

Motacilla maderaspatensis

Slightly larger than a Bulbul. It has a broad white stripe above the eyes. Sexes similar.

WHITE WAGTAIL

Motacilla alba

Bulbul-sized. Broad white area on the forehead and around the eyes distinguishes it from similar looking White-browed Wagtail. Depending on races, back may be grey or black. Sexes similar.

LONG-BILLED PIPIT

Anthus similis

Bulbul-sized. A combination of features such as larger body than other pipits, larger bill, faintly streaked underparts, and upperparts, may aid in the identification of this pipit.

PADDYFIELD PIPIT

Anthus rufulus

Slightly larger than a Sparrow. A combination of features such as prominently streaked upperparts, rows of streaking on the breast, paler lores (often) may aid in identification of this pipit.

TAWNY PIPIT

Anthus campestris

Slightly larger than a Sparrow. It has faint streaking on upperparts and breast; dark lores and dark moustachial stripes (arrow) may aid in identification of this pipit.

OLIVE-BACKED PIPIT

Anthus hodgsoni

Sparrow-sized. Prominent whitish line above eyes which is buffish in the front; white spot and a black patch behind its eyes (arrow) distinguish it from the similar looking Tree Pipit.

TREE PIPIT

Anthus trivialis

Sparrow-sized. Upperparts pale-brownish, heavily streaked with black.

Buntings (*Emberizidae*)

The shape and size of buntings grossly resembles that of the sparrows, but buntings have slightly longer tails. Buntings are usually seen feeding on the ground in bushy and rocky places in winters. In fresh plumage (during autumn), males of many buntings look duller. However, by the breeding season (in summer), the outer portion of the feathers in males wears away exposing its bright basal portions, bringing the males into their breeding attire with more contrasting plumage colouration. Many buntings seen in this area migrate to CTR from higher reaches of the Himalayas.

Buntings can be best sighted in Bijrani, Dhikala, Durgadevi and Sonanadi (Halduparao) zones.

CHESTNUT-EARED BUNTING

Emberiza fucata

Slightly larger than a Sparrow. It has a chestnut patch behind the eyes, and black streaking on the breast. Sexes similar.

ROCK BUNTING

Emberiza cia

Slightly larger than a Sparrow. Sexes similar but females have duller and less contrasting plumage.

WHITE-CAPPED BUNTING

Emberiza stewarti

Slightly larger than a Sparrow. Black throat and lack of a grey or black stripe on the head distinguishes males from males of the Rock Bunting. Females brownish with faint streaking on the body.

CRESTED BUNTING

Melophus lathami

Slightly larger than a Sparrow. Females brownish with faint streaking and with rufous wings.

Noise and Light Pollution Affect the Singing Behaviour of Birds

Research has indicated that artificial night lights and anthropogenic noise cause male birds to begin their dawn chorus early or sing louder at a higher frequency, in order to counter the effect of the background noise. This altered behaviour, as has been predicted, can affect the process of mate selection and communication among birds (p.117 and p.184).

Checklist of Birds Seen In and Around CTR

Francolins, Quails, etc. (*Phasianidae*)

1	Black Francolin	*Francolinus francolinus*
2	Grey Francolin	*Francolinus pondicerianus*
3	Common Quail	*Coturnix coturnix*
4	Jungle Bush Quail	*Perdicula asiatica*
5	Red Junglefowl	*Gallus gallus*
6	Kalij Pheasant	*Lophura leucomelanos*
7	Indian Peafowl	*Pavo cristatus*

Geese and Ducks (*Anatidae*)

8	Lesser Whistling-duck	*Dendrocygna javanica*
9	Greylag Goose	*Anser anser*
10	Bar-headed Goose	*Anser indicus*
11	Bean Goose	*Anser fabalis*
12	Ruddy Shelduck	*Tadorna ferruginea*
13	Common Shelduck	*Tadorna tadorna*
14	Knob-billed Duck	*Sarkidiornis melanotos*
15	Cotton Pygmy-goose	*Nettapus coromandelianus*
16	Gadwall	*Anas strepera*
17	Eurasian Wigeon	*Anas penelope*
18	Mallard	*Anas platyrhynchos*
19	Indian Spot-billed Duck	*Anas poecilorhyncha*
20	Northern Shoveler	*Anas clypeata*
21	Northern Pintail	*Anas acuta*
22	Garganey	*Anas querquedula*
23	Common Teal	*Anas crecca*
24	Red-crested Pochard	*Netta rufina*
25	Common Pochard	*Aythya farina*
26	Ferruginous Duck	*Aythya nyroca*
27	Tufted Duck	*Aythya fuligula*
28	Common Merganser	*Mergus merganser*

Grebes (*Podicipedidae*)

29	Little Grebe	*Tachybaptus ruficollis*
30	Great Crested	*Podiceps cristatus*
31	Horned Grebe	*Podiceps auritus*

Storks (*Ciconiidae*)

32	Painted Stork	*Mycteria leucocephala*
33	Asian Openbill	*Anastomus oscitans*
34	Black Stork	*Ciconia nigra*
35	Woolly-necked Stork	*Ciconia episcopus*
36	Black-necked Stork	*Ephippiorhynchus asiaticus*

Ibises and Spoonbills (*Threskiornithidae*)

37	Black-headed Ibis	*Threskiornis melanocephalus*
38	Red-naped Ibis	*Pseudibis papillosa*
39	Eurasian Spoonbill	*Platalea leucorodia*

Herons and Egrets (*Ardeidae*)

40	Yellow Bittern	*Ixobrychus sinensis*
41	Cinnamon Bittern	*Ixobrychus cinnamomeus*
42	Striated Heron	*Butorides striata*
43	Black-crowned Night Heron	*Nycticorax nycticorax*
44	Indian Pond Heron	*Ardeola grayii*
45	Grey Heron	*Ardea cinerea*
46	Purple Heron	*Ardea purpurea*
47	Cattle Egret	*Bubulcus ibis*
48	Great Egret	*Casmerodius albus*
49	Intermediate Egret	*Mesophoyx intermedia*
50	Little Egret	*Egretta garzetta*
51	Western Reef Egret	*Egretta gularis*

Darters (*Anhingidae*)

52	Oriental Darter	*Anhinga melanogaster*

Cormorants (*Phalacrocoracidae*)

53	Little Cormorant	*Phalacrocorax niger*
54	Indian Cormorant	*Phalacrocorax fuscicollis*
55	Great Cormorant	*Phalacrocorax carbo*

Kestrels and Falcons (*Falconidae*)

56	Collared Falconet	*Microhierax caerulescens*
57	Common Kestrel	*Falco tinnunculus*
58	Red-necked Falcon	*Falco chicquera*
59	Amur Falcon	*Falco amurensis*
60	Oriental Hobby	*Falco severus*
61	Peregrine Falcon	*Falco peregrinus*

Hawks, Eagles, etc. (*Accipitridae*)

62	Black Baza	*Aviceda leuphotes*
63	Black-winged Kite	*Elanus caeruleus*
64	Black Kite	*Milvus migrans*
65	Brahminy Kite	*Haliastur Indus*
66	Osprey	*Pandion haliaetus*
67	White-tailed Eagle	*Haliaeetus albicilla*
68	Pallas's Fish Eagle	*Haliaeetus leucoryphus*
69	Lesser Fish Eagle	*Ichthyophaga humilis*
70	Oriental Honey-Buzzard	*Pernis ptilorhynchus*
71	Black Eagle	*Ictinaetus malayensis*
72	Lammergeier	*Gypaetus barbatus*
73	Egyptian Vulture	*Neophron percnopterus*
74	White-rumped Vulture	*Gyps bengalensis*

75	Slender-billed Vulture	*Gyps tenuirostris*
76	Himalayan Vulture	*Gyps himalayensis*
77	Griffon Vulture	*Gyps fulvus*
78	Cinereous Vulture	*Aegypius monachus*
79	Red-headed Vulture	*Sarcogyps calvus*
80	Short-toed Snake Eagle	*Circaetus gallicus*
81	Crested Serpent Eagle	*Spilornis cheela*
82	Eurasian Marsh Harrier	*Circus aeruginosus*
83	Pied Harrier	*Circus melanoleucos*
84	Hen Harrier	*Circus cyaneus*
85	Pallid Harrier	*Circus macrourus*
86	Crested Goshawk	*Accipiter trivirgatus*
87	Shikra	*Accipiter badius*
88	Besra	*Accipiter virgatus*
89	Eurasian Sparrowhawk	*Accipiter nisus*
90	Northern Goshawk	*Accipiter gentilis*
91	White-eyed Buzzard	*Butastur teesa*
92	Common Buzzard	*Buteo buteo*
93	Long-legged Buzzard	*Buteo rufinus*
94	Indian Spotted Eagle	*Aquila hastata*
95	Greater Spotted Eagle	*Aquila clanga*
96	Tawny Eagle	*Aquila rapax*
97	Steppe Eagle	*Aquila nipalensis*
98	Eastern Imperial Eagle	*Aquila heliaca*
99	Bonelli's Eagle	*Hieraaetus fasciata*
100	Booted Eagle	*Hieraaetus pennatus*
101	Rufous-bellied Eagle	*Lophotriorchis kienerii*
102	Changeable Hawk Eagle	*Nisaetus cirrhatus*
103	Mountain Hawk Eagle	*Nisaetus nipalensis*

Crakes, Coots and Moorhens (*Rallidae*)

104	Water Rail	*Rallus aquaticus*
105	Baillon's Crake	*Porzana pusilla*
106	Ruddy-breasted Crake	*Porzana fusca*
107	White-breasted Waterhen	*Amaurornis phoenicurus*
108	Brown Crake	*Amaurornis akool*
109	Purple Swamphen	*Porphyrio porphyrio*
110	Common Moorhen	*Gallinula chloropus*
111	Eurasian Coot	*Fulica atra*

Buttonquails (*Turnicidae*)

112	Small Buttonquail	*Turnix sylvaticus*
113	Yellow-legged Buttonquail	*Turnix tanki*
114	Barred Buttonquail	*Turnix suscitator*

Cranes (*Gruidae*)

115	Common Crane	*Grus grus*
116	Sarus Crane	*Grus antigone*
117	Demoiselle Crane	*Grus virgo*

Thick-knees (*Burhinidae*)

118	Indian Thick-knee	*Burhinus indicus*
119	Great Thick-knee	*Esacus recurvirostris*

Lapwings and Plovers (*Charadriidae*)

120	Northern Lapwing	*Vanellus vanellus*
121	River Lapwing	*Vanellus duvaucelii*
122	Yellow-wattled Lapwing	*Vanellus malabaricus*
123	Red-wattled Lapwing	*Vanellus indicus*
124	White-tailed Lapwing	*Vanellus leucurus*
125	Little Ringed Plover	*Charadrius dubius*
126	Kentish Plover	*Charadrius alexandrinus*
127	Lesser Sand Plover	*Charadrius mongolus*

Ibisbill (*Ibidorhynchidae*)

128	Ibisbill	*Ibidorhyncha struthersii*

Stilts and Avocets (*Recurvirostridae*)

129	Black-winged Stilt	*Himantopus himantopus*
130	Pied Avocet	*Recurvirostra avosetta*

Jacanas (*Jacanidae*)

131	Pheasant-tailed Jacana	*Hydrophasianus chirurgus*
132	Bronze-winged Jacana	*Metopidius indicus*

Painted-snipes (*Rostratulidae*)

133	Greater Painted-snipe	*Rostratula benghalensis*

Sandpipers, Snipes, etc. (*Scolopacidae*)

134	Eurasian Woodcock	*Scolopax rusticola*
135	Jack Snipe	*Lymnocryptes minimus*
136	Common Snipe	*Gallinago gallinago*
137	Black-tailed Godwit	*Limosa limosa*
138	Eurasian Curlew	*Numenius arquata*
139	Common Redshank	*Tringa totanus*
140	Marsh Sandpiper	*Tringa stagnatilis*
141	Common Greenshank	*Tringa nebularia*
142	Green Sandpiper	*Tringa ochropus*
143	Wood Sandpiper	*Tringa glareola*
144	Common Sandpiper	*Actitis hypoleucos*
145	Little Stint	*Calidris minuta*
146	Temminck's Stint	*Calidris temminckii*

Pratincoles (*Glareolidae*)

147	Oriental Pratincole	*Glareola maldivarum*
148	Small Pratincole	*Glareola lactea*

Gulls and Terns (*Laridae*)

149	Caspian Gull	*Larus cachinnans*
150	Pallas's Gull	*Ichthyaetus ichthyaetus*
151	Brown-headed Gull	*Chroicocephalus brunnicephalus*

152	Black-headed Gull	*Chroicocephalus ridibundus*
153	Gull-billed Tern	*Gelochelidon nilotica*
154	River Tern	*Sterna aurantia*
155	Whiskered Tern	*Chlidonias hybrida*

Pigeons and Doves (*Columbidae*)

156	Common Pigeon	*Columba livia*
157	Oriental Turtle Dove	*Streptopelia orientalis*
158	Eurasian Collared Dove	*Streptopelia decaocto*
159	Red Collared Dove	*Streptopelia tranquebarica*
160	Spotted Dove	*Streptopelia chinensis*
161	Laughing Dove	*Streptopelia senegalensis*
162	Orange-breasted Green Pigeon	*Treron bicinctus*
163	Yellow-footed Green Pigeon	*Treron phoenicopterus*
164	Pin-tailed Green Pigeon	*Treron apicauda*
165	Wedge-tailed Green Pigeon	*Treron sphenurus*
166	Emerald Dove	*Chalcophaps indica*

Parakeets (*Psittacidae*)

167	Alexandrine Parakeet	*Psittacula eupatria*
168	Rose-ringed Parakeet	*Psittacula krameri*
169	Slaty-headed Parakeet	*Psittacula himalayana*
170	Plum-headed Parakeet	*Psittacula cyanocephala*
171	Red-breasted Parakeet	*Psittacula alexandri*

Cuckoos, Malkohas, etc. (*Cuculidae*)

172	Jacobin Cuckoo	*Clamator jacobinus*
173	Chestnut-winged Cuckoo	*Clamator coromandus*
174	Common Hawk Cuckoo	*Hierococcyx varius*
175	Indian Cuckoo	*Cuculus micropterus*
176	Eurasian Cuckoo	*Cuculus canorus*
177	Himalayan cuckoo	*Cuculus saturatus*
178	Banded Bay Cuckoo	*Cacomantis sonneratii*
179	Grey-bellied Cuckoo	*Cacomantis passerinus*
180	Drongo Cuckoo	*Surniculus lugubris*
181	Asian Koel	*Eudynamys scolopaceus*
182	Green-billed Malkoha	*Phaenicophaeus tristis*
183	Sirkeer Malkoha	*Phaenicophaeus leschenaultii*
184	Greater Coucal	*Centropus sinensis*
185	Lesser Coucal	*Centropus bengalensis*

Barn Owl and Grass Owl (*Tytonidae*)

186	Barn Owl	*Tyto alba*

Owls (*Strigidae*)

187	Short-eared Owl	*Asio flammeus*
188	Mountain Scops Owl	*Otus spilocephalus*
189	Indian Scops Owl	*Otus bakkamoena*
190	Oriental Scops Owl	*Otus sunia*
191	Collared Owlet	*Glaucidium brodiei*
192	Asian Barred Owlet	*Glaucidium cuculoides*
193	Jungle Owlet	*Glaucidium radiatum*
194	Spotted Owlet	*Athene brama*
195	Indian Eagle Owl	*Bubo bengalensis*
196	Spot-bellied Eagle Owl	*Bubo nipalensis*
197	Brown Fish Owl	*Ketupa zeylonensis*
198	Tawny Fish Owl	*Ketupa flavipes*
199	Brown Wood Owl	*Strix leptogrammica*
200	Brown Hawk Owl	*Ninox scutulata*

Nightjars (*Caprimulgidae*)

201	Grey Nightjar	*Caprimulgus jotaka*
202	Large-tailed Nightjar	*Caprimulgus macrurus*
203	Savanna Nightjar	*Caprimulgus affinis*

Swifts (*Apodidae*)

204	Himalayan Swiftlet	*Collocalia brevirostris*
205	White-rumped Spinetail	*Zoonavena sylvatica*
206	Silver-backed Needletail	*Hirundapus cochinchinensis*
207	Alpine Swift	*Tachymarptis melba*
208	Crested Treeswift	*Hemiprocne coronata*
209	Fork-tailed Swift	*Apus pacificus*
210	Little Swift	*Apus affinis*

Hoopoes (*Upupidae*)

211	Common Hoopoe	*Upupa epops*

Rollers (*Coraciidae*)

212	Indian Roller	*Coracias benghalensis*
213	Dollarbird	*Eurystomus orientalis*

Kingfishers (*Alcedinidae*)

214	Stork-billed Kingfisher	*Pelargopsis capensis*
215	White-throated Kingfisher	*Halcyon smyrnensis*
216	Common Kingfisher	*Alcedo atthis*
217	Crested Kingfisher	*Megaceryle lugubris*
218	Pied Kingfisher	*Ceryle rudis*

Bee-eaters (*Meropidae*)

219	Blue-bearded Bee-eater	*Nyctyornis athertoni*
220	Green Bee-eater	*Merops orientalis*
221	Blue-tailed Bee-eater	*Merops philippinus*
222	Chestnut-headed Bee-eater	*Merops leschenaulti*

Hornbills (*Bucerotidae*)

223	Indian Grey Hornbill	*Ocyceros birostris*

224 Oriental Pied Hornbill *Anthracoceros albirostris*

225 Great Hornbill *Buceros bicornis*

Barbets (*Ramphastidae*)

226 Great Barbet *Megalaima virens*

227 Brown-headed Barbet *Megalaima zeylanica*

228 Lineated Barbet *Megalaima lineata*

229 Blue-throated Barbet *Megalaima asiatica*

230 Coppersmith Barbet *Megalaima haemacephala*

Woodpeckers, Piculets and Wrynecks (*Picidae*)

231 Eurasian Wryneck *Jynx torquilla*

232 Speckled Piculet *Picumnus innominatus*

233 Rufous Woodpecker *Micropternus brachyurus*

234 Great Slaty Woodpecker *Mulleripicus pulverulentus*

235 Brown-capped Pygmy Woodpecker *Dendrocopos nanus*

236 Grey-capped Pygmy Woodpecker *Dendrocopos canicapillus*

237 Fulvous-breasted Woodpecker *Dendrocopos macei*

238 Yellow-crowned Woodpecker *Dendrocopos mahrattensis*

239 Lesser Yellownape *Picus chlorolophus*

240 Greater Yellownape *Picus flavinucha*

241 Streak-throated Woodpecker *Picus xanthopygaeus*

242 Scaly-bellied Woodpecker *Picus squamatus*

243 Grey-headed Woodpecker *Picus canus*

244 Himalayan Goldenback *Dinopium shorii*

245 Lesser Goldenback *Dinopium benghalense*

246 Greater Goldenback *Chrysocolaptes lucidus*

247 White-naped Woodpecker *Chrysocolaptes festivus*

Broadbills (*Eurylaimidae*)

248 Long-tailed Broadbill *Psarisomus dalhousiae*

Pittas (*Pittidae*)

249 Hooded Pitta *Pitta sordida*

250 Indian Pitta *Pitta brachyura*

Woodshrikes (*Vangidae*)

251 Large Woodshrike *Tephrodornis virgatus*

252 Common Woodshrike *Tephrodornis pondicerianus*

253 Bar-winged Flycatcher-Shrike *Hemipus picatus*

Woodswallows (*Artamidae*)

254 Ashy Woodswallow *Artamus fuscus*

Minivets (*Campephagidae*)

255 Large Cuckooshrike *Coracina macei*

256 Black-winged Cuckooshrike *Coracina melaschistos*

257 Black-headed Cuckooshrike *Coracina melanoptera*

258 Rosy Minivet *Pericrocotus roseus*

259 Small Minivet *Pericrocotus cinnamomeus*

260 Long-tailed Minivet *Pericrocotus ethologus*

261 Scarlet Minivet *Pericrocotus speciosus*

Ioras (*Aegithinidae*)

262 Common Iora *Aegithina tiphia*

Shrikes (*Laniidae*)

263 Brown Shrike *Lanius cristatus*

264 Isabelline Shrike *Lanius isabellinus*

265 Bay-backed Shrike *Lanius vittatus*

266 Long-tailed Shrike *Lanius schach*

267 Grey-backed Shrike *Lanius tephronotus*

268 Southern Grey Shrike *Lanius meridionalis*

Drongos (*Dicruridae*)

269 Lesser Racket-tailed Drongo *Dicrurus remifer*

270 Greater Racket-tailed Drongo *Dicrurus paradiseus*

271 Spangled Drongo *Dicrurus hottentottus*

272 Black Drongo *Dicrurus macrocercus*

273 Ashy Drongo *Dicrurus leucophaeus*

274 White-bellied Drongo *Dicrurus caerulescens*

275 Bronzed Drongo *Dicrurus aeneus*

276 Crow-billed Drongo *Dicrurus annectans*

Orioles (*Oriolidae*)

277 Indian Golden Oriole *Oriolus kundoo*

278 Black-hooded Oriole *Oriolus xanthornus*

279 Maroon Oriole *Oriolus traillii*

Fantails (*Rhipiduridae*)

280 Yellow-bellied Fantail *Chelidorhynx hypoxanthus*

281 White-throated Fantail *Rhipidura albicollis*

282 White-browed Fantail *Rhipidura aureola*

Paradise Flycatchers (*Monarchidae*)

283 Asian Paradise-flycatcher *Terpsiphone paradisi*

284 Black-naped Monarch *Hypothymis azurea*

Magpies, Treepies, etc. (*Corvidae*)

285 Black-headed Jay *Garrulus lanceolatus*

286 Red-billed Blue Magpie *Urocissa erythrorhyncha*

287 Common Green Magpie *Cissa chinensis*

288 Rufous Treepie *Dendrocitta vagabunda*

289 Grey Treepie *Dendrocitta formosae*

290 Large-billed Crow *Corvus macrorhynchos*

291	House Crow	*Corvus splendens*

Tits (*Paridae*)

292	Great Tit	*Parus major*
293	Green-backed Tit	*Parus monticolus*
294	Black-lored Tit	*Parus xanthogenys*
295	Fire-capped Tit	*Cephalopyrus flammiceps*

Long-tailed Tits (*Aegithalidae*)

296	Black-throated Tit	*Aegithalos concinnus*

Swallows (*Hirundinidae*)

297	Plain Martin	*Riparia paludicola*
298	Eurasian Crag Martin	*Ptyonoprogne rupestris*
299	Dusky Crag Martin	*Ptyonoprogne concolor*
300	Common House Martin	*Delichon urbicum*
301	Nepal House Martin	*Delichon nipalensis*
302	Streak-throated Swallow	*Petrochelidon fluvicola*
303	Wire-tailed Swallow	*Hirundo smithii*
304	Barn Swallow	*Hirundo rustica*
305	Red-rumped Swallow	*Cecropis daurica*

Larks (*Alaudidae*)

306	Bengal Bushlark	*Mirafra assamica*
307	Greater Short-toed Lark	*Calandrella brachydactyla*
308	Sand Lark	*Calandrella raytal*
309	Ashy-crowned Sparrow Lark	*Eremopterix griseus*
310	Crested Lark	*Galerida cristata*
311	Eurasian Skylark	*Alauda arvensis*
312	Oriental Skylark	*Alauda gulgula*

Bulbuls (*Pycnonotidae*)

313	Himalayan Bulbul	*Pycnonotus leucogenys*
314	Black-crested Bulbul	*Pycnonotus flaviventris*
315	Red-whiskered Bulbul	*Pycnonotus jocosus*
316	Red-vented Bulbul	*Pycnonotus cafer*
317	Ashy Bulbul	*Hemixos flavala*
318	Black Bulbul	*Hypsipetes leucocephalus*

Prinias, Cisticolas, etc. (*Cisticolidae*)

319	Striated Prinia	*Prinia criniger*
320	Grey-breasted Prinia	*Prinia hodgsonii*
321	Jungle Prinia	*Prinia sylvatica*
322	Yellow-bellied Prinia	*Prinia flaviventris*
323	Ashy Prinia	*Prinia socialis*
324	Plain Prinia	*Prinia inornata*
325	Zitting Cisticola	*Cisticola juncidis*
326	Golden-headed Cisticola	*Cisticola exilis*
327	Common Tailorbird	*Orthotomus sutorius*
328	Bristled Grassbird	*Chaetornis striata*

Warblers (*Sylviidae*)

329	Pale-footed Bush Warbler	*Cettia pallidipes*
330	Brown-flanked Bush Warbler	*Cettia fortipes*
331	Chestnut-crowned Bush Warbler	*Cettia major*
332	Aberrant Bush Warbler	*Cettia flavolivacea*
333	Grey-sided Bush Warbler	*Cettia brunnifrons*
334	Moustached Warbler	*Acrocephalus melanopogon*
335	Blyth's Reed Warbler	*Acrocephalus dumetorum*
336	Chestnut-headed Tesia	*Cettia castaneocoronata*
337	Grey-bellied Tesia	*Tesia cyaniventer*
338	Common Chiffchaff	*Phylloscopus collybita*
339	Dusky Warbler	*Phylloscopus fuscatus*
340	Smoky Warbler	*Phylloscopus fuligiventer*
341	Tickell's Leaf Warbler	*Phylloscopus affinis*
342	Sulphur-bellied Warbler	*Phylloscopus griseolus*
343	Buff-barred Warbler	*Phylloscopus pulcher*
344	Lemon-rumped Warbler	*Phylloscopus chloronotus*
345	Hume's Leaf Warbler	*Phylloscopus humei*
346	Greenish Warbler	*Phylloscopus trochiloides*
347	Western Crowned Warbler	*Phylloscopus occipitalis*
348	Blyth's Leaf Warbler	*Phylloscopus reguloides*
349	Tytler's Leaf Warbler	*Phylloscopus tytleri*
350	Whistler's Warbler	*Seicercus whistleri*
351	Grey-hooded Warbler	*Phylloscopus xanthoschistos*
352	Lesser Whitethroat	*Sylvia curruca*

Babblers, Laughingthrushes, etc. (*Timaliidae*)

353	Puff-throated Babbler	*Pellorneum ruficeps*
354	Scaly-breasted Wren Babbler	*Pnoepyga albiventer*
355	Nepal Wren Babbler	*Pnoepyga immaculata*
356	Pygmy Wren Babbler	*Pnoepyga pusilla*
357	Chestnut-capped Babbler	*Timalia pileata*
358	Black-chinned Babbler	*Stachyridopsis pyrrhops*
359	Tawny-bellied Babbler	*Dumetia hyperythra*
360	Rusty-cheeked Scimitar Babbler	*Pomatorhinus erythrogenys*
361	White-browed Scimitar Babbler	*Pomatorhinus schisticeps*
362	Streak-breasted Scimitar Babbler	*Pomatorhinus ruficollis*

363	Common Babbler	*Turdoides caudata*
364	Large Grey Babbler	*Turdoides malcolmi*
365	Jungle Babbler	*Turdoides striata*
366	White-throated Laughingthrush	*Garrulax albogularis*
367	White-crested Laughingthrush	*Garrulax leucolophus*
368	Rufous-chinned Laughingthrush	*Garrulax rufogularis*
369	Streaked Laughingthrush	*Garrulax lineatus*
370	Chestnut-crowned Laughingthrush	*Garrulax erythrocephalus*
371	Silver-eared Mesia	*Mesia argentauris*
372	Red-billed Leiothrix	*Leiothrix lutea*
373	Blue-winged Siva	*Siva cyanouroptera*
374	White-browed Shrike Babbler	*Pteruthius flaviscapis*
375	Rufous Sibia	*Malacias capistrata*
376	Whiskered Yuhina	*Yuhina flavicollis*
377	Stripe-throated Yuhina	*Yuhina gularis*
378	Black-chinned Yuhina	*Yuhina nigrimenta*
379	White-bellied Erpornis	*Yuhina zantholeuca*
380	Yellow-eyed Babbler	*Chrysomma sinense*

White-eyes (*Zosteropidae*)

381	Oriental White-eye	*Zosterops palpebrosus*

Dippers (*Cinclidae*)

382	Brown Dipper	*Cinclus pallasii*

Nuthatches and Wallcreeper (*Sittidae*)

383	Chestnut-bellied Nuthatch	*Sitta cinnamoventris*
384	White-tailed Nuthatch	*Sitta himalayensis*
385	Velvet-fronted Nuthatch	*Sitta frontalis*
386	Wallcreeper	*Tichodroma muraria*

Treecreepers (*Certhiidae*)

387	Bar-tailed Treecreeper	*Certhia himalayana*

Mynas and Starlings (*Sturnidae*)

388	Spot-winged Starling	*Saroglossa spiloptera*
389	Common Hill Myna	*Gracula religiosa*
390	Jungle Myna	*Acridotheres fuscus*
391	Bank Myna	*Acridotheres ginginianus*
392	Common Myna	*Acridotheres tristis*
393	Asian Pied Starling	*Gracupica contra*
394	Chestnut-tailed Starling	*Sturnus malabarica*
395	Brahminy Starling	*Sturnus pagodarum*
396	Common Starling	*Sturnus vulgaris*

Thrushes (*Turdidae*)

397	Blue Whistling Thrush	*Myophonus caeruleus*
398	Orange-headed Thrush	*Zoothera citrina*
399	Long-tailed Thrush	*Zoothera dixoni*
400	Scaly Thrush	*Zoothera dauma*
401	Long-billed Thrush	*Zoothera monticola*
402	White-collared Blackbird	*Turdus albocinctus*
403	Grey-winged Blackbird	*Turdus boulboul*
404	Tickell's Thrush	*Turdus unicolor*
405	Black-throated Thrush	*Turdus atrogularis*
406	Purple Cochoa	*Cochoa purpurea*

Chats, Robins, Flycatchers, etc. (*Muscicapidae*)

407	Bluethroat	*Luscinia svecica*
408	Siberian Rubythroat	*Luscinia calliope*
409	White-tailed Rubythroat	*Luscinia pectoralis*
410	Indian Blue Robin	*Luscinia brunnea*
411	Himalayan Bush Robin	*Tarsiger rufilatus*
412	Golden Bush Robin	*Tarsiger chrysaeus*
413	Oriental Magpie Robin	*Copsychus saularis*
414	White-rumped Shama	*Copsychus malabaricus*
415	Indian Robin	*Saxicoloides fulicatus*
416	Blue-capped Redstart	*Phoenicurus coeruleocephalus*
417	Black Redstart	*Phoenicurus ochruros*
418	Plumbeous Water Redstart	*Rhyacornis fuliginosa*
419	White-capped Water Redstart	*Chaimarrornis leucocephalus*
420	Blue-fronted Redstart	*Phoenicurus frontalis*
421	Little Forktail	*Enicurus scouleri*
422	Slaty-backed Forktail	*Enicurus schistaceus*
423	Spotted Forktail	*Enicurus maculatus*
424	Hodgson's Bushchat	*Saxicola insignis*
425	Common Stonechat	*Saxicola torquatus*
426	Pied Bushchat	*Saxicola caprata*
427	Grey Bushchat	*Saxicola ferreus*
428	Isabelline Wheatear	*Oenanthe isabellina*
429	Red-tailed Wheatear	*Oenanthe chrysopygia*
430	Variable Wheatear	*Oenanthe picata*
431	Desert Wheatear	*Oenanthe deserti*
432	Brown Rock Chat	*Cercomela fusca*
433	Blue Rock Thrush	*Monticola solitarius*
434	Blue-capped Rock Thrush	*Monticola cinclorhyncha*
435	Chestnut-bellied Rock Thrush	*Monticola rufiventris*
436	Dark-sided Flycatcher	*Muscicapa sibirica*
437	Asian Brown Flycatcher	*Muscicapa dauurica*

438	Rufous-gorgeted Flycatcher	*Ficedula strophiata*
439	Red-breasted Flycatcher	*Ficedula parva*
440	Taiga Flycatcher	*Ficedula albicilla*
441	Snowy-browed Flycatcher	*Ficedula hyperythra*
442	Little Pied Flycatcher	*Ficedula westermanni*
443	Ultramarine Flycatcher	*Ficedula superciliaris*
444	Slaty-blue Flycatcher	*Ficedula tricolor*
445	Verditer Flycatcher	*Eumyias thalassinus*
446	Tickell's Blue Flycatcher	*Cyornis tickelliae*
447	Blue-throated Blue Flycatcher	*Cyornis rubeculoides*
448	Pale-chinned Flycatcher	*Cyornis poliogenys*
449	Grey-headed Canary Flycatcher	*Culicicapa ceylonensis*
450	Rufous-bellied Niltava	*Niltava sundara*
451	Small Niltava	*Niltava macgrigoriae*

Leafbirds (*Chloropseidae*)

452	Golden-fronted Leafbird	*Chloropsis aurifrons*
453	Orange-bellied Leafbird	*Chloropsis hardwickii*

Flowerpeckers (*Dicaeidae*)

454	Thick-billed Flowerpecker	*Dicaeum agile*
455	Pale-billed Flowerpecker	*Dicaeum erythrorhynchos*

Sunbirds (*Nectariniidae*)

456	Purple Sunbird	*Cinnyris asiaticus*
457	Green-tailed Sunbird	*Aethopyga nipalensis*
458	Black-throated Sunbird	*Aethopyga saturata*
459	Crimson Sunbird	*Aethopyga siparaja*
460	Fire-tailed Sunbird	*Aethopyga ignicauda*

Sparrows and Petronia (*Passeridae*)

461	House Sparrow	*Passer domesticus*
462	Russet Sparrow	*Passer rutilans*
463	Chestnut-shouldered Petronia	*Gymnoris xanthocollis*

Weavers (*Ploceidae*)

464	Black-breasted Weaver	*Ploceus benghalensis*
465	Baya Weaver	*Ploceus philippinus*

Munias and Silverbills (*Estrildidae*)

466	Indian Silverbill	*Euodice malabarica*
467	Red Avadavat	*Amandava amandava*
468	White-rumped Munia	*Lonchura striata*
469	Scaly-breasted Munia	*Lonchura punctulata*
470	Black-headed Munia	*Lonchura malacca*

Wagtails and Pipits (*Motacillidae*)

471	Yellow Wagtail	*Motacilla flava*
472	Citrine Wagtail	*Motacilla citreola*
473	Forest Wagtail	*Dendronanthus indicus*
474	Grey Wagtail	*Motacilla cinerea*
475	White Wagtail	*Motacilla alba*
476	White-browed Wagtail	*Motacilla maderaspatensis*
477	Paddyfield Pipit	*Anthus rufulus*
478	Tawny Pipit	*Anthus campestris*
479	Long-billed Pipit	*Anthus similis*
480	Tree Pipit	*Anthus trivialis*
481	Olive-backed Pipit	*Anthus hodgsoni*
482	Rosy Pipit	*Anthus roseatus*
483	Red-throated Pipit	*Anthus cervinus*
484	Water Pipit	*Anthus spinoletta*

Finches (*Fringillidae*)

485	Common Chaffinch	*Fringilla coelebs*
486	Yellow-breasted Greenfinch	*Carduelis spinoides*
487	European Goldfinch	*Carduelis carduelis*
488	Common Rosefinch	*Carpodacus erythrinus*

Buntings (*Emberizidae*)

489	Crested Bunting	*Melophus lathami*
490	Pine Bunting	*Emberiza leucocephalos*
491	Rock Bunting	*Emberiza cia*
492	White-capped Bunting	*Emberiza stewarti*
493	Grey-necked Bunting	*Emberiza buchanani*
494	Chestnut-eared Bunting	*Emberiza fucata*
495	Little Bunting	*Emberiza pusilla*
496	Red-headed Bunting	*Emberiza bruniceps*

Kalij Pheasant

PC: AM

Some Extraordinary Records by Birds

- **Arctic Tern** *(Sterna paradisaea)*: ***Longest migration distance known.*** It starts its migratory journey from its Arctic breeding ground near the North Pole to reach its wintering ground at the Antarctic near the South Pole and then back. For this return journey, it covers a distance of over 80,000 km, with refuelling halts. Arctic terns are known to live for more than 30 years, so the total distance travelled by one bird in its life time might well be over 2.4 million km (roughly equivalent to three return journeys to the Moon!).
- **Alaskan Bar-tailed Godwit** *(Limosa lapponica baueri)*: ***Longest non-stop flight.*** It starts its migratory journey from Alaska and by flying non-stop over the Pacific Ocean, it reaches its wintering resort in New Zealand, covering more than 11,000 km in about 8 days.
- **Bar Headed Goose** *(Anser indicus)*: ***Highest bird migration.*** It breeds in Central Asia and migrates to India after crossing the higher reaches of the Himalayas. It has an extraordinary ability to fly under severely low atmospheric oxygen levels. While crossing the Himalayas, this bird flies at an altitude of more than 7,000 m where the level of oxygen drops to half of that at the sea level.
- **Common Swift** *(Apus apus)*: ***It can fly non-stop for 10 months.*** Swifts are adapted to an aerial lifestyle wherein they can capture food mid-air.
- **Grey-headed Albatross** *(Thalassarche chrysostoma)*: ***The fastest flying bird***. This bird can fly at a speed of 127 km/h and sustain this speed for more than 8 hours. Golden Eagle (*Aquila chrysaetos*) is also known to attain a similar speed.
- **Peregrine Falcon** *(Falco peregrinus)*: ***Bird with the highest speed during diving***. It can reach speeds of over 380 km/h while diving to hunt for a bird/prey.
- **Bee Hummingbird** *(Mellisuga helenae)*: ***The smallest living bird***. It is found in Cuba. Males measure 2.24 inches in length.
- **Ostrich** *(Struthio camelus)*: ***The largest living bird***. Also, the largest recorded bird egg weighing 2.589 kg was laid by an Ostrich.
- **Vervain Hummingbird** *(Mellisuga minima)*: ***The smallest recorded bird egg*** weighing 0.35 gm (size less than 10 mm). This bird is found in Haiti and Jamaica.

PC: AM

Crested Kingfisher

MONOCLED COBRA
(H: NAG)
Naja kaouthia

Size similar to Spectacled Cobra. It has a 'whitish circle with dark centre' on the rear of its hood.

Reptiles

PC: DR

Reptiles belong to the taxonomic class '*Reptilia*' (Latin, '*repere*': to crawl). The skin of reptiles is covered with a horny layer (such as scales) which protects them from desiccation. Reptiles are cold-blooded animals—their body temperature fluctuates with that of the surroundings. Unlike mammals and birds, the body of a reptile produces less heat, lacks sweat glands and feathers or fur, which are all helpful in regulating the body temperature. Thus, in cold conditions, the body temperature of reptiles drops too low, making them inactive. To maintain body temperature suitable for routine activity, reptiles rely on basking in sunlight, or exposing themselves to hot surfaces.

Reptiles came into existence on earth about 340 million years ago from amphibian-like animals. Reptiles are considered as the 'First True Land Vertebrates' which, unlike their amphibian ancestors, do not depend on water or moisture for reproduction. Their eggs are covered with layers which protect developing young ones from desiccation and shock. Gigantic 'dinosaurs' were reptiles which ruled the earth for more than 150 million years. Modern reptiles represented by turtles, snakes, crocodiles, and Gharial are descendants of ancient reptiles.

Reptiles found in India belong to three Taxonomic orders; *Crocodilia* (Crocodiles and Gharial), *Testudines* (Turtles and Tortoises) and *Squamata* (Snakes and Lizards). Worldwide, over 11,500 species of reptiles are known. As of 2018 data: there are 572 species of reptiles known from India including 3 species of *Crocodilia*, 34 *Testudines* and 535 *Squamata* (231 species of lizards and 304 snakes).

About 55 species of reptiles are known from CTR and neighbouring areas. In the following section, images and features of 31 species of reptiles seen in CTR and its vicinity have been provided to help in their identification.

Role of Reptiles in Nature

Reptiles perform several useful tasks in keeping nature healthy: 1) many species of turtles are known to disperse seeds of fruits they eat, 2) lizards that consume floral nectar also pollinate flowers, 3) several reptiles and their eggs are food for other animals, 4) reptiles control the population of animals on which they feed, and 5) burrows and ditches that reptiles make are also used by other animals as shelters.

CROCODILES AND GHARIAL (*CROCODILIA*)

This taxonomic order gets its name from Greek, *'krokē'*: pebble + *'drilos'*: worm; referring to the behaviour of crocodilians basking on pebbles, or named after their appearance of 'worm of small pebbles'. The body of *Crocodilia* is covered with armour of horny skin and scales, below which, on the upperside of the body lie bony plates making the upper surface tougher. The sense of smell, sight and hearing is well developed in crocodilians. To control their body heat, these animals perform open mouth basking. They lay hard-shelled eggs and bury them in the soil or make nest with soil and vegetation. Parents guard eggs and hatchlings from predators such as jackal, monitor lizards, birds of prey, etc.

Two members of order Crocodilia are found in CTR: Marsh Crocodile and Gharial. These can be best sighted in Dhikala zone along Ramganga river at sites such as; Crocodile Pool, Gorkha Sot, near Gairal FRH, Champion Pool, High Bank and along Ramganga reservoir.

MARSH CROCODILE

(H: MUGGAR MACHH)

Crocodylus palustris

Crocodiles are large reptiles with a flat body and can be distinguished from similar looking gharials by their shorter and broader snout; adults greyish to brownish; juveniles light tan with dark bands on the body. They regulate their body temperature by basking in sunlight and are sometimes seen with their mouth open. The latter behaviour helps them to keep their brain cool by evaporative cooling while the rest of the body heats up. They can grow to a length of 5 m, weigh 450 kg, and can live about 44 years in captivity.

During Diving, Crocodiles Can Hold Their Breath for Several Minutes

Crocodiles breathe air, but can stay submerged under water for over an hour without coming to the surface for breathing. This ability helps crocodiles in killing prey by drowning them. *How do crocodiles manage to stay submerged for so long without breathing or, in other words, how do they manage without reloading their blood with oxygen?* In a bid to conserve oxygen during prolonged diving, the heart rate of a crocodile is reduced to just few beats per minute and oxygen consumption of muscles and other organs is drastically reduced. Further, they can survive underwater even if most of the oxygen in the blood has been used up.

Crocodiles—More at Home in Water Than on Land

Crocodiles are adapted for living in and near water. Some of their amazing capabilities include: remaining afloat in water for a long time without making any movement, sinking silently, walking or lying motionless on the bottom of the water-body, and swimming efficiently. The position of the eyes, ears and nostrils high on the head allows crocodiles to see, smell, breathe and hear, even while the rest of the body is submerged. To prevent entry of water while diving, the nostrils and ears can be closed by flaps. Also, folds on the tongue and at the roof of the mouth, check rushing of water into the stomach and lungs when the mouth is opened under water (such as during encounter with a prey). The webbed hind feet and sideways compressed tail make crocodiles good swimmers.

GHARIAL

(H: GHARIAL)

Gavialis gangeticus

PC: MS

Gharials have a relatively slender body, with a longer and narrower snout than crocodiles; upperside is dark-olive or brownish-olive and underside is whitish; tip of snout is swollen (resembling a 'pot') in males which gives it the name Gharial (Hindi, '*ghara*': a pot); the *ghara* is said to act as a resonator and enhances the volume of sound when males vocalize during breeding period; mainly feeds on fishes but may also eat birds, turtles etc.; can grow to a length of 7 m and weigh 250 kg; longevity about 60 years in captivity.

Monitor Lizards (p. 214) are known to be the major predator of Gharial eggs in CTR

At Champion pool

TURTLES AND TORTOISES (*TESTUDINES*)

A shell enveloping the body is the most distinguishing feature of '*Testudines*' (Latin, '*testa*': shell). The word 'turtle' is used for those that prefer staying in or close to water, and 'tortoise', for land dwellers. Tortoises have sturdy legs for walking on land, lack webbed feet, and have a dome shaped shell. The word 'turtle' however, is also used to include all the turtles, tortoises and terrapins (small freshwater forms).

Turtles breathe in air and have lungs. However, to stay submerged for an extended period of time, some turtles have devised an additional mode of breathing. They gulp water and soak up its oxygen from the mouth and neck region. Some turtles pump water over a pouch located in their cloaca where oxygen is absorbed through a special structure.

Where to Look for Turtles in CTR

Turtles are seen in all the zones. Since most of the time, they remain submerged in water, coated with mud, camouflaged with the surroundings, and move sluggishly, they may go unnoticed. Thus to spot them one needs to screen the areas near the waterholes, stagnant water and rock platform or boulders along the rivers. Sometimes tortoises may be seen crawling near the safari track.

Turtles lack teeth, some however, have razor-like ridges, and others have serrations on their jaws or jaws with hooked tips. These structures serve the purpose of teeth. Turtles have a good sense of vision and smell, but they are not good at hearing.

Turtles living near water eat insects, frogs, fishes, snails, earthworms, aquatic plants, etc., while tortoises eat grass, flowers, fallen fruits and occasionally carcasses and small animals such as frogs, insects, etc.

Depending on the species, turtles can lay between 1–50 eggs, however, marine turtles can lay nearly 150 eggs at one go. After burying the eggs in the soil or sand for incubation, the female departs and does not provide further parental care.

ELONGATED TORTOISE

(H: PARBATI)

Indotestudo elongata

Maximum length of shell about 30 cm; has a yellowish upperside with black blotches, pale head, and heavily scaled legs; prefers living on land and is seen in forested areas; feeds on fallen leaves, flowers and fruits.

PC: SB

GANGES SOFTSHELL TURTLE

(H: KHATAWA)

Nilssonia gangetica

Maximum length of shell about 95 cm; upperside is low and flat, and has olive-green colouration with fine irregular markings; head has oblique black stripes and an elongated fleshy nose. It can be sighted along the rivers.

PC: SB

PC: RBP

INDIAN ROOFED TURTLE

(H: CHANDAN KACHUA)

Pangshura tecta

Maximum length of shell about 25 cm; dark-green upperside with prominent spike-like ridge in the middle; underside reddish-yellow; neck has thin yellow stripes and forelegs with yellow spots. There is a prominent red crescentic mark behind the eyes. They can be seen near stagnant water on logs, boulders and near rivers.

PC: SB

INDIAN TENT TURTLE

(H: PACHERA)

Pangshura tentoria

Maximum length of shell about 30 cm; upperside olive-brown with prominent spike-like ridge in the middle, and underside is reddish-yellow. It differs from Indian Roofed Turtle by the absence of red crescentic mark behind eyes, fewer spots on legs and less prominent stripes on neck. It can be seen basking on rocks in the pools of water along rivers.

TRICARINATE HILL TURTLE
Melanochelys tricarinata

Maximum length of shell about 15 cm; has blackish or dark-olive upperside with three parallel yellowish ridges (keels), and yellowish underside; head and legs are black or grey-black; forelegs have enlarged scales, and feet are half-webbed. They are seen in grassy or thinly forested areas.

PC: SB

INDIAN BLACK TURTLE
(H: KALA KACHUA)
Melanochelys trijuga

Maximum length of shell about 20 cm; has elongated, dark or almost black upperside with three ridges; legs with enlarged scales and fully webbed feet. They can be seen near stagnant water.

INDIAN FLAPSHELL TURTLE
(H: ABHUA)
Lissemys punctata

Maximum length of shell about 35 cm; upperside low and oval with olive colouration and yellow blotches; head dark greenish with large yellow blotches. They can be sighted near rivers, and pools of water.

PC: SC

The Shell of Turtles

The shell has two main parts; the upper 'Carapace' and the lower 'Plastron'. The two remain jointed along the flanks of the animal, making a protective case around the body. The shell is made of bony plates overlain with a thin horny layer or 'scutes'. Soft-shelled turtles lack scutes, and their bony plates (which are thinner) are covered with a layer of skin. The bony plates of turtles are intimately fused with the backbone and ribs. Thus, the animal remains fixed in the shell and cannot creep out of it.

> Turtles are the longest living animals; the oldest living land animal is a Seychelles Giant Tortoise (*Aldabrachelys gigantea*), believed to have been born in 1832, and is presently 190 years old.

The most obvious function of the shell is providing protection—on sensing danger, the animal completely withdraws its flexible head and limbs inside the shell. It requires considerable effort to break or open the shell (even by predators with strong jaws and teeth) to extract the soft body parts of the turtle.

SNAKES AND LIZARDS (*SQUAMATA*)

This taxonomic order '*Squamata*' derives its name from Latin, '*squama*' meaning 'scale'— the bodies of the animals placed in this order are covered with horny scales.

Snakes have an elongated cylindrical body and lack legs (found in some as vestigial), eyelids and opening of ears or eardrum. The two halves of the lower jaws of snakes are loosely attached making the mouth expandable.

Lizards, in contrast, have ear-pits and eardrum, movable eyelids, and most have well-developed legs. The two halves of lower jaws are firmly attached, so the size of the mouth is not expandable.

SNAKES

About three dozen species of snakes have been recorded in and around CTR. The following section provides images and features of about 18 species of snakes which are likely to be seen here. Snakes mentioned in this section possibly can be seen in all the zones in suitable habitats.

Caution!

Snakes are cryptic animals and remain motionless, and thus go unnoticed. Some of the snakes are deadly poisonous, and their bite can be fatal. We do not recommend visitors to enter bushes, go close to piles of wood or straw in order to look for snakes. Always wear high ankle boots, and do not walk without a torch after sunset.

Life of Snakes

Snakes, like other reptiles, are cold-blooded animals and bask in sunlight to keep themselves warm and active. They have preference for specific types of habitats; some spend most of their time on trees, whereas others live near water, among bushes, inside burrows or beneath rocks. Depending on the species, snakes can be active by day or by night or both at day and night. Snakes lack eyelids; however their eyes are covered with a transparent disc-shaped membrane which protects eyes from dirt. All snakes shed their thin outer part of the skin every two to three months by a process called 'moulting', to renew their scales.

Snakes feed on other animals such as rats, mice, lizards, birds, frogs, bats, snails, insects and eggs. Some snakes such as King Cobra are snake-eaters, whereas pythons can kill and eat a deer-sized animal!

About one-fourth of the Indian snake species do not lay eggs; their eggs develop inside the body and they give birth to young ones. The majority however, lay eggs covered with parchment-like shell. Depending on species, snakes may lay from two to over hundred eggs (as in pythons). Emergence of young ones from eggs generally takes about two months. Baby snakes are not assisted by parents and lead an independent life soon after emergence from the egg. The apparatus of producing and injecting venom (venom gland and fangs) is fully functional in newborns.

Lifespan, as known for few species of snakes, can be about 7 to over 30 years.

Why do Snakes Flick Their Tongue?

Snakes flick their tongue to sense their surroundings. During flicking, they sweep their tongue in the air or on objects to collect chemicals. The tongue is then retracted in the mouth, and adhered chemicals are transferred to the special sense organ- 'Vomeronasal organ' located in the roof of the mouth. This way, snakes get information about their immediate surroundings.

BURMESE PYTHON

(H: AJGAR)

Python bivittatus

Maximum length: 6 m; non-venomous; a long and fat snake with triangular head broader than the neck; upperside has large dark-brown blotches having pale-yellow borders; underside of the body is yellowish. Pythons are slow-moving snakes, can climb trees and swim well. They are active at night—heat sensors on snout help them to locate prey in pitch dark conditions. They coil tightly around the body of prey to kill the latter by suffocation and choking of blood circulation. Pythons can live over 30 years in captivity.

Contesting Monitor Lizard and Burmese Python

COMMON TRINKET SNAKE ▶
(H: BHUSHAN SARP)
Coelognathus helena

Maximum length: 1.68 m; non-venomous; slender-bodied snake with large eyes; upperside brownish or olive with two black stripes on the neck, and bands (alternating light and dark) on the front half of the body; hind part has two black stripes running along both sides of the body up to the tail; prefers staying in open areas near forest.

PC: DR

PC: SC

COPPER-HEADED TRINKET SNAKE (H: TAMRA BHUSHAN SARP) ▲
Coelognathus radiatus

Maximum length: 2.3 m; non-venomous; named due to their attractive appearance; has a slender body with large eyes. Upperside is greyish-brown or yellowish-brown, and along the front half of the body, there are four black stripes. There is a black half-ring behind the head and three black lines radiating from the eyes. It prefers open areas close to forest.

INDIAN RAT SNAKE ▶
(H: DHAMAN)
Ptyas mucosa

Maximum length: 3.5 m; non-venomous; slender bodied snake with large eyes; upperside yellowish-brown or olive or pale; body is faintly marked with meshwork of dark lines particularly towards the tail; scales at lips are separated by dark lines. It is a fast snake seen in forest, fringes of forest and scrubs.

PC: VS

COMMON KUKRI SNAKE
(H: KUKRI SANP)
Oligodon arnensis

Maximum length: 0.7 m; non-venomous; has brownish body with black or dark-brown bands; head has three arrow-shaped marks; prefers forested areas.

PC: VS

COMMON BRONZEBACK TREE SNAKE
(H: GOOBRA)
Dendrelaphis tristis

Maximum length: 1.69 m; non-venomous; slender bodied snake with long wire-like tail; upperside is bronze-brown or purplish-brown and underside pale, white or pale-green; when disturbed, displays light-blue colouration on front part of the body; seen in thinly forested areas among bushes and small trees.

PC: DR

COMMON WOLF SNAKE
(H: KAURIALA)
Lycodon aulicus

Maximum length: 0.8 m; non-venomous; gets its name because of large front teeth; has a slender body with head slightly broader than neck; upperside is dark-brown with pale bands; found close to human habitations in piles of stones, roofs, crevices in walls, etc.

PC: DR

BARRED WOLF SNAKE

Lycodon striatus

Maximum length: 0.48 m; non-venomous; slender bodied snake with blackish upperside marked with white or yellowish bands which are not as distinct near the tail; width of head and neck similar.

TWIN-SPOTTED WOLF SNAKE

Lycodon jara

Maximum length: 0.55 m; non-venomous, slender bodied brownish snake; upperside decorated with tiny yellow spots.

Snakes Can Sense Ground Vibration But Cannot Hear Music or Other Sounds!

Humans and most other animals have a sequence of structures inside their ear which pick, amplify and sense sound. The first or outer component in the sequence is the eardrum, which is attached to the next component—a chain of three tiny 'ear-bones'. The other end of the ear-bone chain is connected with the 'internal ear'. Airborne sound waves strike and cause the eardrum and the attached tiny ear-bones to vibrate. On the other side, vibrating ear-bones set fluid in the internal ear in motion, which activates sensors. The activated sensors translate motion of the fluid into electric current, which is carried to the brain via nerves giving the sensation of hearing a sound. Snakes have fully formed internal ears but no eardrum. Their ear-bone is connected to the lower jaw, which snakes keep in contact with the ground. This arrangement enables snakes to pick up vibrations coming through the ground with the help of the jaw, and transfer to the internal ear via the ear-bone. Thus, snakes can sense a walking person or prey coming close to them, very well.

Snakes however, cannot hear sounds like music or other airborne sounds as humans do. In some cases, very low-frequency airborne sounds hitting their skull can be transferred to internal ears giving snakes some sense of hearing.

BUFF STRIPED KEELBACK ▶
(H: HURVA)
Amphiesma stolatum

Maximum length: 0.8 m; non-venomous; slender-bodied snake, with upperside greyish or greenish-grey; two yellow or buff stripes run from neck to tail; front half of the body has dark bands; found in the vicinity of water and grasslands.

CHECKERED KEELBACK ▶
(H: PANI KA SANP)
Xenochrophis piscator

Maximum length:1.7 m; non-venomous; upperside olive-green with checkered appearance, and black stripes running from eyes to upper lips; found in rivers, ponds, marshes and nearby areas.

COMMON CAT SNAKE ▶
(H: VIDAL SARP)
Boiga trigonata

Maximum length: 1.25 m; mildly venomous; gets its name because of large eyes with cat-like pupils; has a long and thin body compressed from the sides and triangular head; eyes are larger with a vertical pupil; upperside of body is brownish with dark zigzag markings; head has pale 'Y' shaped mark; it is active at night. Its mild venom can paralyze small prey such as rats, mice, birds and lizards.

FORSTEN'S CAT SNAKE

Boiga forsteni

Maximum length: 2.3 m; mildly venomous; two colour forms can be seen—some with reddish-brown and others with greyish-brown body; has bands on the body; head triangular; eyes large with vertical slit (pupil); lives in tree hollows and seen in forested areas and nearby fields.

PC: DR

COMMON KRAIT

(H: KARAYAT)

Bungarus caeruleus

Maximum length: 1.75 m; venomous; upperside is black or dark-brown with narrow white bands (arranged in pairs), which in the front part of the body are replaced with white spots; active at night. The venom of krait is toxic to the nervous system and causes paralysis of muscles and respiratory failure.

PC: VS

Snake Venom

PC: DR

Venom is produced in specialized glands called 'Venom gland' located in the mouth of snakes. In venomous snakes such as cobras, krait and vipers, venom from the glands is delivered outside via sharp and hollow teeth—'fangs', positioned in the front of the upper jaw. Venom is a cocktail of several types of enzymes, proteins and peptides. For the venom to show its toxic effect, it must be injected deep under the skin of the victim. From the site of injection, venom enters the blood vessels and is transported to internal organs. Once inside the body, the components of venom specifically damage the functions of certain crucial molecules.

Non-venomous snakes have milder venom, and their fangs are not suitable to inject adequate amount of venom to kill larger animals or humans. Their bite, however, may cause local swelling, bleeding and pain.

Snakes are predators and the system of producing and injecting venom has evolved as a tool for rapid immobilization of prey and self-defence.

KING COBRA (H: NAGRAJ) ▶

Ophiophagus hannah

Maximum length: 5.85 m; venomous; upperside usually grey-black or olive-brown with white or yellowish bands; hood longer and narrower than Spectacled Cobra; found in forests and close-by areas. It is a fast-moving snake which feeds primarily on other snakes—killing and eating both venomous and non-venomous snakes.

The venom of King Cobra is less toxic than that of the Spectacled Cobra, however King Cobra can inject a larger amount of venom (7 ml) in a bite. The venom is toxic to the nervous system and causes death due to paralysis of muscles involved in breathing. It can live over 22 years in captivity.

PC: DR

PC: DR

SPECTACLED COBRA (H: NAG) ▼

Naja naja

Maximum length: 2.2 m; venomous; the word 'cobra' is derived from Portuguese '*cobra de capello*', meaning 'snake with a hood' and Latin, '*colubra*': snake. Body colouration can be yellowish, grey-brown, brown-black or black; hood mark is visible on spread hood, and may be absent in some individuals; the hood is a flap of skin supported by ribs which at rest, lie along the length of the body.

When disturbed, it raises its fore-body and spreads the hood, and in extreme cases the snake can strike with a hissing sound. Its venom is toxic to the nervous system, and paralyses muscles including those involved in breathing. It is found in forest, open areas and close to human habitations. It can live over 20 years in captivity.

PC: SD

PC: MS

PC: SM

RUSSELL'S VIPER

(H: DABOIA)

Daboia russelii

Maximum length:1.8 m; venomous; has a triangular head, very large nostrils and vertical pupil; upperside is brownish with three chains of oval spots—one chain in the middle of upperside and two on either side; found in grassy areas, scrubs and fringes of forest; usually active at night. It does not lay eggs, instead gives birth to young ones. The venom of vipers causes blood clotting, internal bleeding, bleeding from gums and skin, damage to red blood cells, and difficulty in breathing, etc.

HIMALAYAN WHITE-LIPPED PIT VIPER

Trimeresurus septentrionalis

Maximum length: about 0.6 m; venomous; greenish snake with white or pale lips; remains camouflaged in thick vegetation; not common in this area.

Pit Organs—Night Vision Devices in Snakes

Snakes such as vipers, boas and pythons have heat sensitive (or infrared sensitive) pits on their snout—'Pit Organs'. These pits have sensors which can sense slightest variation in the outside temperature. When the body heat of prey, such as rat, hare or deer, hits these sensors, snakes get a thermal image of prey and launch an attack even when pitch dark. Thus, pit organs function as night vision cameras for snakes.

Interesting Facts

- **Longest poisonous snake in the world:** King Cobra (*Ophiophagus hannah*), average length 3–4 m.
- **Longest snake in the world:** The Reticulated Python (*Python reticulatus*) of South-east Asia, exceeds 6.25 m. A specimen of python attained a length of about 10 m in Indonesia.
- **Heaviest reptile:** Saltwater Crocodile (*Crocodylus porosus*), which can weigh up to 1,000–1,200 kg.
- **Largest turtle:** Leatherback Turtle (*Dermochelys coriacea*), a specimen weighed 961 kg.
- **Most venomous lizard:** Gila Monster (*Heloderma suspectum*), native to south-western USA and north-western Mexico.

LIZARDS

One can commonly sight Monitor Lizard, Garden Lizard, geckos and skinks in CTR. To sight smaller lizards such as skinks and geckos, one needs to thoroughly scan areas close to the ground, tree bark, crevices, etc.

COMMON INDIAN MONITOR (H: GOH)

Varanus bengalensis

Length: 1.75 m; adults grey or brownish on the upperside with dark dots, and yellowish on the underside; long tail is flattened sideways; forked pinkish tongue is flicked regularly to sense chemicals in the surroundings, similar to snakes; active during the day and lives in crevices and below rocks.

Monitor lizards can fix themselves firmly inside crevices and it is difficult to dislodge them. It is said that Maratha soldiers used this behaviour of lizards to climb steep cliffs and walls of enemy's forts. Using the monitor lizard with ropes tied around its body, Tanaji Malusare (a general of Chhatrapati Shivaji Maharaj) could climb steep cliffs. Monitor lizards can climb trees, swim, remain submerged for some time, and run at a reasonably fast speed. They feed on insects, birds, eggs, snakes, fishes, etc. Monitor lizard can be sighted in all the zones of CTR usually moving amongst dry leaves or basking on the ground or rocks. They can live over 17 years in captivity.

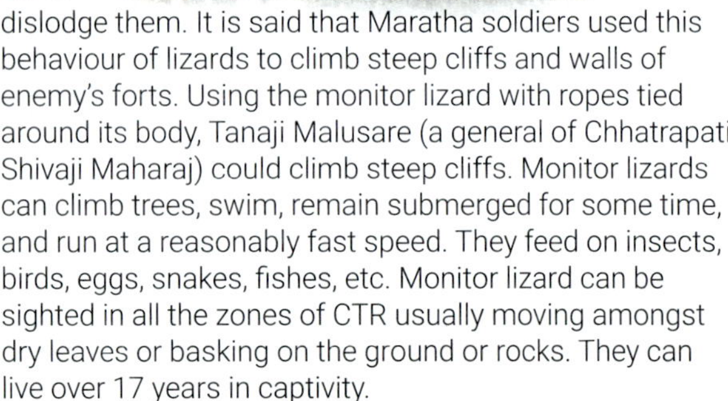

COMMON DOTTED GARDEN SKINK

(H: SANP KI MAUSI)

Lygosoma punctata

Length: about 8–9 cm; upperside bronze-brown with 4–6 rows of black spots and a wide pale or white line on both the sides; young animals have a bright red tail. It can be seen in gardens and fringes of forest moving swiftly among fallen leaves, grass, etc.

PC: RK

BRONZE GRASS SKINK

(H: SANP KI MAUSI)

Eutropis macularia

Length: about 7.5 cm; upperside is bronze-brown which may be spotted; flanks darker with white spots; breeding males have red lips and flanks; it prefers forested areas, and feeds on insects. It moves swiftly to take shelter under fallen leaves, grass, etc.

INDIAN GARDEN LIZARD

(H: GIRGIT)

Calotes versicolour

Length: about 14–15 cm; it has a sideways compressed body and rows of spines on the back; body colouration can be brown, greenish-brown or sandy-grey; body colouration is changeable—breeding or displaying males have a bright red head, shoulder and forelegs. There are black patches on the sides of the throat; males are larger than females and have swollen cheeks.

The commonly observed behaviour of performing 'push up' or 'press up' by garden lizards is indicative of their aggression or arousal. Females deposit eggs in loose soil and cover them with fallen leaves or flowers for camouflage. It mainly feeds on insects; longevity about 5 years in captivity; sighted in all the zones.

Checklist of Reptiles Seen In and Around CTR

Snakes and Lizards (*Squamata*)

Snakes

1	Slender Worm Snake	*Typhlops porrectus*
2	Brahminy Blind Snake	*Ramphotyphlops braminus*
3	Burmese Python	*Python bivittatus*
4	Common Sand Boa	*Eryx conicus*
5	Red Sand Boa	*Eryx johnii*
6	Himalayan Trinket Snake	*Orthriophis hodgsoni*
7	Copper-headed Trinket Snake	*Coelognathus radiatus*
8	Common Trinket Snake	*Coelognathus helena*
9	Indian Rat Snake	*Ptyas mucosa*
10	Glossy-bellied Racer	*Platyceps ventromaculatus*
11	Banded Racer	*Argyrogena fasciolatus*
12	Common Cliff Racer	*Platyceps rhodorachis*
13	Common Kukri Snake	*Oligodon arnensis*
14	Many-banded Tree Snake	*Boiga multifasciata*
15	Indian Egg-eating snake	*Boiga westermanni*
16	Common Bronzeback Tree Snake	*Dendrelaphis tristis*
17	Mackinnon's Wolf Snake	*Lycodon mackinnoni*
18	Common Wolf Snake	*Lycodon aulicus*
19	Barred Wolf Snake	*Lycodon striatus*
20	Twin-spotted Wolf Snake	*Lycodon jara*
21	Buff Striped Keelback	*Amphiesma stolatum*
22	Checkered Keelback	*Xenochrophis piscator*
23	Olive Oriental Slender Snake	*Trachischium laeve*
24	Common Cat Snake	*Boiga trigonata*
25	Forsten's Cat Snake	*Boiga forsteni*
26	Siebold's Smooth-scaled Water Snake	*Enhydris sieboldii*
27	Common Krait	*Bungarus caeruleus*
28	Banded Krait	*Bungarus fasciatus*
29	Spectacled Cobra	*Naja naja*
30	Monocled Cobra	*Naja kaouthia*
31	King Cobra	*Ophiophagus hannah*
32	Russell's Viper	*Daboia russelii*
33	Saw-scaled Viper	*Echis carinatus*
34	Himalayan White-lipped Pit Viper	*Trimeresurus septentrionalis*

Lizards

35	Spotted Indian House Gecko	*Hemidactylus brookii*
36	Yellow-bellied House Gecko	*Hemidactylus flaviviridis*
37	Bark Gecko	*Hemidactylus leschenaultii*
38	Banded Bent-toed Gecko	*Cyrtodactylus fasciolatus*
39	Kumaon Bent-toed Gecko	*Cyrtodactylus lawderanus*
40	Indian Garden Lizard	*Calotes versicolour*
41	Kashmir Rock Agama	*Laudakia tuberculata*
42	Kumaon Mountain Lizard	*Japalura kumaonensis*
43	Himalayan Skink	*Scincella himalayanum*
44	Bronze Grass Skink	*Eutropis macularia*
45	Common Dotted Garden Skink	*Lygosoma punctata*
46	Common Indian Monitor	*Varanus bengalensis*

Crocodiles and Gharial (*Crocodilia*)

47	Gharial	*Gavialis gangeticus*
48	Marsh Crocodile or Mugger	*Crocodylus palustris*

Turtles and Tortoises (*Testudines*)

49	Elongated Turtle	*Indotestudo elongata*
50	Tricarinate Hill Turtle	*Melanochelys tricarinata*
51	Indian Black Turtle	*Melanochelys trijuga*
52	Indian Roofed Turtle	*Pangshura tecta*
53	Three-striped Roofed Turtle	*Batagur dhongoka*
54	Indian Tent Turtle	*Pangshura tentoria*
55	Indian Flapshell Turtle	*Lissemys punctata*
56	Ganges Softshell Turtle	*Nilssonia gangetica*

Common Cat Snake

PC: DR

Amphibians

Amphibians include frogs and toads, lizard-like salamanders, and earthworm or snake-like limbless amphibians called 'Caecilians'. Amphibians were the first vertebrates which evolved the ability to live on land, and are thus, intermediate between fully aquatic animals (fishes) and fully land-dwelling animals (reptiles, birds and mammals). Amphibians evolved from certain fish-like animals which lived about 400–370 million years ago. These ancestors had limited capability to breathe in air, could walk underwater, and possibly wriggle on land. They gradually evolved a system of breathing in air, protection from being desiccated and powerful limbs to support the weight of their body to move on land—'Ancient Amphibians'.

Though modern amphibians (frogs and toads, etc.) are capable of living on land, they require water or moisture for survival: 1) their skin is moist and lacks scales, feathers or a thick horny layer that can prevent dessication of the body, 2) unlike reptiles and birds, their eggs are not covered with a shell to protect them from being dried up, and thus, they lay eggs near water, and 3) they spend a fish-like life when young (such as tadpoles). In fact, the word 'amphibia' (Greek, '*amphi*' meaning 'both'), denotes that these animals live a dual mode of life—in water and on land.

Over 8,400 species of amphibians are found worldwide, and close to 450 are known from India. About 15 species of amphibians have been reported from CTR and neighbouring areas, all of which are frogs and toads.

Role of Frogs and Toads in Nature

These are food for many animals, and they too eat several harmful insects. Amphibians are important indicators of the health of waterbodies and forests.

Frog or Toad

In general, frogs have smoother skin, longer hind limbs (enables long leaps) and heavily webbed or adhesive toes. Most frogs prefer living close to water (though some prefer living on plants). Toads, in contrast, have shorter hind limbs, usually lack webs between the toes, and have a stouter body. Their skin is drier and rough with prominent warts and patches.

Life of Frogs and Toads

These spend most of their time in or near water or damp places, and usually feed on insects. They have a good sense of hearing; however their sense of smell is poor. These are cold blooded animals and their skin rapidly loses water, thus they avoid hot and dry ambience. Camouflage, escape and hiding are their main modes of defence. Rainy season is the most conducive season for these animals. Male frogs and toads become quite noisy during the monsoon season. Their loud noise which demands a huge amount of energy is actually a mating call. Females lay eggs in thousands as a frothy or jelly-like mass near or in water. The Larva or 'Tadpole' emerging from the egg resembles a tiny fish and spends a fish-like life in water. The body of the tadpole gradually loses its tail and turns into a tiny frog or toad which can now begin its life on the land.

Where to Look for Frogs and Toads

These can be sighted near waterbodies and damp places. Since they camouflage perfectly with the background, a thorough scrutinization of the habitat is necessary. Some of these can also be seen foraging on insects near human habitations after sunset. The best season to sight frogs and toads is the rainy season.

COMMON INDIAN TOAD ▶

Duttaphrynus melanostictus

Size about 10 cm; has brownish, reddish or greyish body with dark markings and prominent warts; underside whitish.

INDIAN BULLFROG

Hoplobatrachus tigerinus

Size about 15 cm; upperside of adults ranges from yellow to olive-green or brownish with dark markings; upperside of juvenile frogs greenish with brown markings. ▼

SKITTERING FROG ▶

Euphlyctis cyanophlyctis

Size about 6 cm; body colouration olive or brownish marked with dark blotches; hind feet are completely webbed; usually seen floating on stagnant water.

COMMON INDIAN TREE FROG ▶

Polypedates maculatus

Size about 5–7 cm; its brownish body has dark blotches and a black band around the eyes; known to change colour for disguise; has long legs, tips of fingers with swollen discs help them stick to branches.

PC: NZ

PC: SC

Amphibians Do Not Drink Water!

Amphibians living on land do not drink, instead they acquire water by absorbing it through their skin. To absorb water, a frog presses its belly on the wet surface. Water absorbed through the skin fulfills most of the water demand of these animals.

Though amphibians have lungs, their skin is also a major breathing organ. They can absorb oxygen and flush out carbon dioxide through the skin.

PC: SC

▲

BURROWING FROG

Sphaerotheca sp.

Size about 5 cm; pale-brownish frog with dark area around the eyes.

Checklist of Amphibians Seen In and Around CTR

1	Common Indian Toad	*Duttaphrynus melanostictus*
2	Himalaya Toad	*Duttaphrynus himalayanus*
3	Marbled Toad	*Bufo stomaticus*
4	Ornate Narrow-mouthed Frog	*Microhyla ornata*
5	Marbled Balloon Frog	*Uperodon systoma*
6	Skittering Frog	*Euphlyctis cyanophlyctis*
7	Indian Cricket Frog	*Fejervarya limnocharis*
8	Small Cricket Frog	*Fejervarya syhadrensis*
9	Nepal Cricket Frog	*Fejervarya Nepalensis*
10	Terai Cricket Frog	*Fejervarya terraiensis*
11	Indian Bullfrog	*Hoplobatrachus tigerinus*
12	Jerdon's Bull Frog	*Hoplobatrachus crassus*
13	Nepal Paa Frog	*Nanorana minica*
14	Indian Burrowing Frog	*Sphaerotheca breviceps*
15	Common Indian Tree Frog	*Polypedates maculatus*

PC: VS

PC: VS

Frogs and Toads are common food items for several snakes

Butterflies

Butterflies are grouped together with moths under the order *'Lepidoptera'*, meaning 'scaly wings'. The name of the order is based on the fact that their two pairs of wings are covered with tiny scales. Butterflies are thought to have originated about 119 million years ago on the earth, and today about 18,000 species of butterflies are found worldwide. Of the over 1,300 species of butterflies found in India, close to 500 can be seen in Uttarakhand. CTR and its surroundings offer a blend of natural habitats and varieties of flora, which is home to over 150 species of butterflies. This section provides photographs of about 115 species of butterflies, which one is likely to see in and around CTR.

Butterfly or Moth

In general, most butterflies are day fliers and are sun-loving, whereas most moths come out after sunset. Moths have hairy bodies and usually rest with wings spread on the sides of the body; most butterflies, in contrast, rest with wings folded on their back. The antennae of butterflies are thread-like with clubbed or hooked tips; moths usually have feathery or comb-like or thread-like antennae, the tips of which are not clubbed (moths of family *Castniidae*, however have clubbed antennae). The forewing and hindwing of many moths are held together by a hook-like structure. Butterflies lack this feature, except for an Australian skipper butterfly.

Role of Butterflies in Nature

Butterflies pollinate flowers while looking for nectar (bees are known to be better pollinators than the butterflies!). Adult butterflies and larvae make up a part of the diet for many insect-eating animals. Loss of habitat including loss of host plants, exposure to pesticides and climate change are the major threats to butterflies.

Butterfly Watching—an Engaging Hobby

Watching butterflies in their natural habitat is sheer joy. Those who pursue butterfly watching as a hobby, walk through vegetation, observe behaviour and photograph various butterflies. The observations, which might serve as useful resources to lepidopterists, can be shared on various websites dedicated to butterflies.

Identifying Butterflies

Nearly all species of butterflies can be identified by features of wings such as size, shape, colour patterns and markings (spots, stripes, lines, bars and eyespots). A popular and scientifically acceptable way to identify butterflies is to take their photographs, clearly showing the upper and underside of wing features, and to match them with the reference image (such as those given in field guidebooks or authentic websites). In this way, most butterflies can be identified correctly. The identification of a few groups of butterflies (e.g. skippers and bushbrowns) up to species level requires consideration of additional criteria such as inspection of genitals, and marks concealed between the wings that are not evident from photographs.

The style of flying and the habitat in which a butterfly was observed may also sometimes serve as additional clues to its identification. Beginners must take precautions, especially in the following situations:
1) species wherein the appearance of male and female butterfly is radically different,
2) where the wing features of a particular species vary in different seasons 'seasonal forms' (e.g. Common Evening Brown, Spotless Grass Yellow), 3) where a butterfly species exists in various 'forms' with distinct appearance, in the same season (e.g. Common Mormon, Common Mime),
4) where one species mimics another, and
5) where different individuals of a given species have their own distinct markings on the wings (individual variation).

Watching Butterflies in CTR

One can enjoy butterfly-watching in the natural surroundings of CTR in a safari vehicle. Alighting from the safari vehicle is prohibited; nevertheless, one can observe and photograph the butterflies that have landed on tracks, on nearby bushes and surrounding trees. Another way to look for butterflies is to walk around within the premises of the Forest Rest House campuses, where one can conveniently list several butterfly species. Enthusiasts may also look for butterflies in villages around CTR.

Butterflies are best seen during the months of August–October (covering the rainy season) and March–April (spring). They are scarce during extreme cold and hot seasons. Most butterflies become active an hour after sunrise till sunset. The shade-loving butterflies such as evening browns and many skippers avoid sun and are active during dawn and dusk, and on overcast days.

Photographing Butterflies

Most butterflies can be photographed from a range of about 4–6 feet and if approached carefully, one can go even closer. While approaching a butterfly to photograph it, one should avoid making sudden body movements and refrain from casting one's own shadow on the resting butterfly.

Digital compact cameras with 50X zoom or more are the most suitable under all situations. One may also use cameras with interchangeable lenses (SLR and mirrorless cameras) if high quality pictures are desired. In this case, a macro lens would give stunning results; however, butterflies have to be approached very closely. Since opportunities to approach butterflies closely are limited in CTR, to capture the image of a distant butterfly from the safari vehicle, SLR/mirrorless camera users are advised to carry a telephoto lens, the focal length of which should not be less than 300 mm.

A Word of Caution

Though Forest Rest House campuses are safe, one must be cautious of snakes, monitor lizards, scorpions and other such creatures while walking near bushy areas. One must remember to cover bare arms and legs, and should wear high-ankled boots. One must also remember never to track butterflies beyond the boundary of the campus. It is advised not to crawl or lie down on the ground nor lean out of the safari vehicle in order to get impressive shots of butterflies.

Mating pair (Tiny Grass Blue, *Zizula hylax*)

Life Cycle of a Butterfly

A butterfly passes through four life stages—egg, larva, pupa and adult. These stages look strikingly different from one another. The familiar winged-form (adult) is the final stage of life.

Shortly after mating, the female butterfly begins to look for the right plant (larval host plant) to lay eggs, on which emerging larvae can feed. Butterflies are choosy about the larval host plants; usually a butterfly would lay eggs only on a few closely related plants. Butterfly eggs are superbly sculptured from outside and are as big as a regular paper pin head or slightly larger. Coating of gluey material keeps eggs in place on the leaves. It takes about a week for the eggs to hatch; thereafter, a worm-bodied creature, the 'caterpillar' or larva, emerges from each egg. Caterpillars voraciously feed on leaves and grow rapidly. In two to six weeks, the caterpillar anchors itself at a secure place and turns into a 'pupa'. Pupae of different butterflies display an amazing range of shapes and textures. Within a week or so, the pupa develops into a butterfly (adult) which cracks open the pupal covering and emerges. A butterfly is a completely formed individual and its size remains the same throughout its lifespan. Depending upon the species, butterflies can live for two weeks to about ten months.

Life cycle of Plain Tiger butterfly

Arrangement of Butterflies in the Section

Butterflies have been grouped according to their families: Swallowtails (*Papilionidae*), Skippers (*Hesperiidae*), Whites and Yellows (*Pieridae*), Punches and Judies (*Riodinidae*), Blues (*Lycaenidae*), and Brush-footed Butterflies (*Nymphalidae*).

Each species has been denoted with a 'Common English Name' and Scientific Name.

Size Guide: For easy visualization, the size ranges provided here represent the size of a butterfly from the tip of one forewing to another, when butterflies are in their fully open wings posture. The sizes provided are only an approximation of the actual size of butterflies. The size ranges are as follows:

XS (Extra Small):	1.5–2 cm
S (Small):	> 2–3 cm
M (Medium):	>3–4 cm
L (Large):	>4–6 cm
XL (Extra Large):	>6–8 cm
XXL (Extra Extra Large):	>8–10 cm

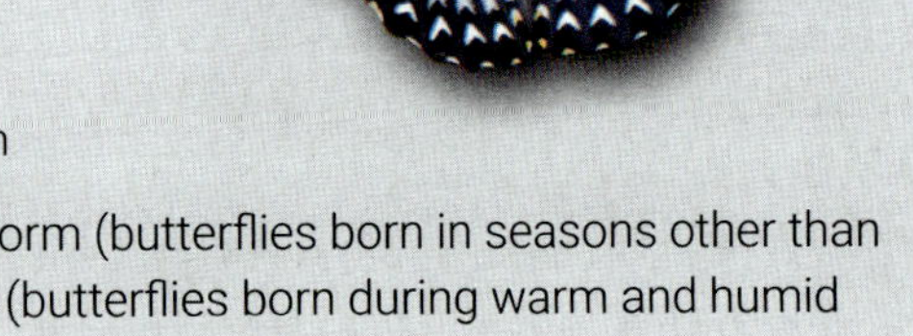

Abbreviations used: DSF= Dry Season Form (butterflies born in seasons other than rainy season), WSF= Wet Season Form (butterflies born during warm and humid conditions, i.e. rainy season).

Body Parts of the Butterfly

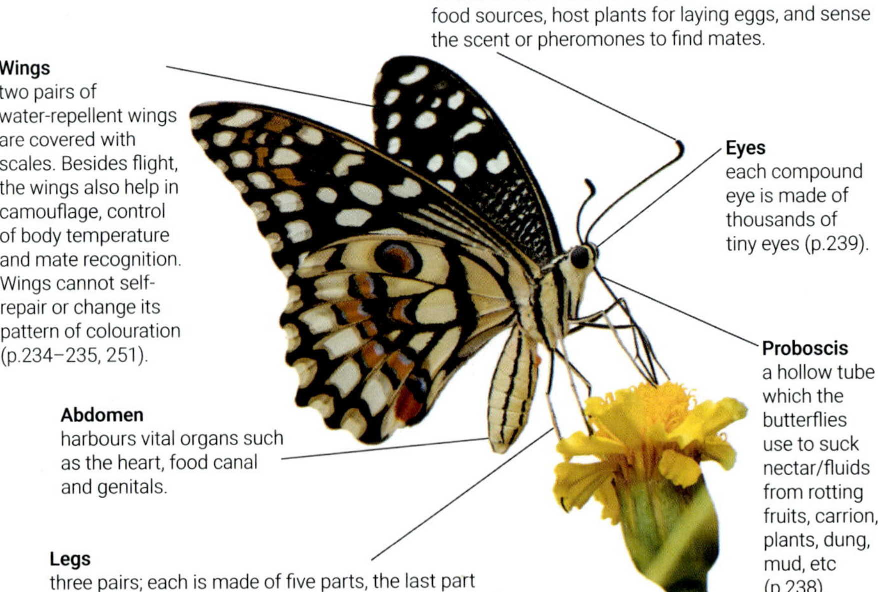

Swallowtails (*Papilionidae*)
A group of gorgeous and agile butterflies; wings of many of these are black and decorated with white, red, blue or yellow markings. Many members of this group have tailed hindwings, hence the name swallowtails. These butterflies have three pairs of well-developed legs, and in close wing posture, their hindwings cannot cover the abdomen.

Form: *romulus*

Form: *stichius*

Male

▲

COMMON MORMON

Papilio polytes

Size: XXL; seen hovering over bushes in thinly forested areas and near human habitations; females exist in three forms named as—'*cyrus*', '*romulus*' and '*stichius*'; wing markings of the form *cyrus* resemble that of males but with prominent red spots at the margins of hindwings; style of flying and wing colouration of forms *romulus* and *stichius* resemble that of poisonous butterflies Crimson Rose and Common Rose, respectively.

◀

COMMON ROSE

Pachliopta aristolochiae

Size: XXL; seen in thinly forested areas and fringes of forest; sexes similar. Distinguished from Common Mormon form *stichius*, which has a black thorax and abdomen.

Form: *dissimilis*

COMMON MIME

Papilio clytia

Size: XXL; seen along fringes of forest and areas close to the forest; sexes similar; two forms can be seen—*clytia* and *dissimilis*, these mimic Common Crow and Blue Tiger butterflies respectively. The shape of wings and series of yellow spots (arrow) at the margins of the underside of hindwings help in distinguishing Common Mime from these butterflies.

Form: *clytia*

P.C. PS

LIME BUTTERFLY

Papilio demoleus

Size: XXL; fast flier, seen along fringes of forest and open areas; sexes similar.

P.C. SC

SPOT SWORDTAIL

Graphium nomius

Size: XL–XXL; fast flier; seen along fringes of forest and open areas close to the forest; sexes similar; it has a long tail on its hindwings.

▲
TAILED JAY

Graphium agamemnon

Size: XXL; fast flier, seen along fringes of forest and open areas close to the forest; sexes similar.

▲
COMMON JAY

Graphium doson

Size: XL; seen along fringes of forest and near human habitations; sexes similar.

Puddling—Acquiring Food Supplements

Butterflies are sometimes seen probing damp sand, mud and animal excreta with their proboscis. This tendency, usually seen among male butterflies, is known as 'Mud Puddling' or simply 'Puddling'. Occasionally, hundreds of puddlers assemble at a spot, creating a spectacular sight. Puddling butterflies sip fluid rich in sodium and nitrogenous material, since their regular food (nectar and fluid from rotting fruits) does not provide them with adequate amounts of these nutrients. Sodium improves muscular activity in male butterflies during vigorous courtship display to impress potential mates. Also, in some butterflies, males transfer sodium along with sperm to females during copulation. Sodium, as a 'nuptial gift' from male butterflies to females, improves reproductive performance.

▲
COMMON BLUEBOTTLE

Graphium sarpedon

Size: XXL; a restless flier seen along the fringes of forest, near streams and thinly forested areas; sexes similar.

Skippers (*Hesperiidae*)

These are fast flying butterflies, their skipping manner of flight gives the group its name. Skippers can be confused with moths. Several of these become active at dusk and dawn. Skippers have hook-shaped antennae kept far apart from each other. In many cases to confirm the identity of butterflies of this group, the abdomen needs to be dissected and genitals examined.

▲

COMMON REDEYE

Matapa aria

Size: L; seen in forested areas and along fringes of forest; sexes similar; it has an unmarked pale brown upperside, and prominent red eyes.

◀

BANANA SKIPPER

Erionota torus

Size: L; seen in forested areas and fringes of forest; sexes similar; it can be distinguished from Common Redeye by its larger size, and paler undersides of the wings.

▲

WATER SNOW FLAT

Tagiades litigiosa

Size: S–M; seen in forest and along fringes of forest settled on foliage; sexes similar.

Bizarre Architecture of Butterfly Pupae

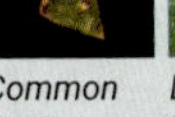

Common Castor

Lemon Pansy

Lime Butterfly

Common Palmfly

Common Grass Yellow

Red Pierrot

Plains Cupid

Pioneer

▲
BRANDED ORANGE AWLET

Burara oedipodea

Size: L–XL; fast flier, seen in forested areas and along fringes of forest. It can be identified by the presence of an orange patch in the middle of its hindwings.

▲
BROWN AWL

Badamia exclamationis

Size: L; seen in shady places and among dense vegetation. It can be identified by elongated narrow forewings, plain brown underside, and abdomen with alternating dark brown and pale rings.

▲
COMMON BANDED AWL

Hasora chromus

Size: L; fast flier, seen in shady places and among dense vegetation.

▲
GRASS DEMON

Udaspes folus

Size: L; seen among bushes in forested areas and fringes of forest; sexes similar.

▲
ANGLE

Caprona sp.

Size: M; seen on bushes in thinly forested areas and along fringes of forest.

▲
COMMON SMALL FLAT

Sarangesa dasahara

Size: S–M; seen in forested areas and along fringes of forest; sexes similar.

Whites and Yellows (*Pieridae*)

Wings of this group of butterflies have a yellow or white background with black, orange or red markings. Many of these butterflies prefer open scrubby areas for their habitat. Butterflies of this family have three pairs of well-developed legs, and hindwings cover the abdomen when wings are closed.

Male form: *pomona*

Female form: *catilla*

Female form: *crocale*

Female form: *pomona*

Male form: *crocale*

Congregation of emigrants

COMMON EMIGRANT

Catopsilia pomona

Size: L–XL; fast and erratic flier seen in scrubs, along fringes of forest and open areas; abundant during the rainy season. Three main forms of this butterfly can be seen namely; '*crocale*' (upperside of antennae blackish and no silvery spot in the centre of underside on hindwings), '*pomona*' (upperside of antennae reddish, and silvery spot in the centre of underside on hindwings), and female form '*catilla*' (with reddish-brown blotch on the underside of the wings).

MOTTLED EMIGRANT

Catopsilia pyranthe

Size: L–XL; habits and habitat similar to the Common Emigrant. The underside of the wings may have rings in the centre; the underside of wings are mottled with light green or brown which distinguishes it from Common Emigrant.

WSF

◀ SMALL GRASS YELLOW

Eurema brigitta

Size: M; seen in open areas along fringes of forest; flutters close to the ground; underside of DSF has thin pink edges to wings; WSF looks similar to the WSF of Spotless Grass Yellow, but the dark margin on upperside of forewings extends to the lower end (blue arrow), there is also a pair of spots (red arrow) on the underside of forewings (only one spot at the same place in Spotless Grass Yellow).

PC: PS

DSF

◀ SPOTLESS GRASS YELLOW

Eurema laeta

Size: M; habits and habitat similar to Small Grass Yellow; sexes similar. Cryptic DSF with angular apex of forewings.

PC: PS
WSF

PC: PS
DSF

WSF

◀ COMMON GRASS YELLOW

Eurema hecabe

Size: L; habits and habitat similar to Small Grass Yellow; sexes similar. DSF with prominent rusty markings on underside of wings and a dark patch at the top of the forewings.

DSF

▲

DARK CLOUDED YELLOW

Colias fieldii

Size: L; seen in open places and thinly forested areas; sexes similar, but the black borders of the upperside forewings of females have yellow spots.

▲

PSYCHE

Leptosia nina

Size: M–L; flutters lethargically close to the ground in forested areas and along fringes of forest; sexes similar.

▲

PIONEER

Belenois aurota

Size: L; seen flying rapidly in open areas, scrubs and thinly forested areas; sexes similar but females heavily marked with black on upperside. It can be easily identified by a 'J'-shaped mark on the upperside or underside of forewings (arrow).

▲

COMMON GULL

Cepora nerissa

Size: L; seen in open areas, scrubs and thinly forested areas; upperside of wings more heavily marked with black in females than in males; in underside of DSF, the black areas along the veins are faded.

◀ INDIAN CABBAGE WHITE

Pieris canidia

Size: L; seen flying in open areas, thinly forested areas and cultivated areas outside the reserve in winters. Females have two black spots on upperside of forewings, in males the lower spot is faded; likely to be confused with Large Cabbage White which is larger and males have no spot on upperside of forewings.

◀ LARGE CABBAGE WHITE

Pieris brassicae

Size: XL; habits and habitat similar to Indian Cabbage White; females have two spots and a mark, whereas males have no spot on the upperside of forewings.

▲ COMMON JEZEBEL

Delias eucharis

Size: XL; seen flying slowly at tree level and high bushes in forest and along fringes of forest. Females more heavily marked with black on upperside than males.

▲ BATH WHITE

Pontia daplidice

Size: L; seen in open areas and thinly forested areas; sexes similar.

▲

COMMON WANDERER

Pareronia valeria

Size: XL; fast flier, seen in thinly forested areas and along fringes of forest. Females resemble poisonous Blue Tiger butterfly, however the shape of wings and the details of wing markings can help in distinguishing the two.

Basking—Soaking Solar Heat to Warm up the Body

Butterflies are often seen resting or fluttering sluggishly on cool mornings or when the outside temperature is low. Unlike humans, the body temperature of butterflies varies with that of the surroundings; it goes down when the outside temperature is low, bringing down all their physiological processes and the activity of muscles used to flap wings for flight. For proper functioning, muscles of butterflies involved in flapping of wings need warm temperature close to 37°C. So, the butterflies expose their wings to the sun (bask) to harness the heat from sunlight and keep themselves warm. Some butterflies open their wings flat and expose their upperside to the sun, while others close their wings and present the undersides to the sun. Heat absorbed by the wings is conducted to the body. A dark colouration of wings improves the process; also, by changing the orientation of their wings relative to the sun, butterflies can adjust the rate of soaking in the solar heat. Many butterflies with white, blue or pale colouration on the upperside of wings expose their wings to the sun in a 'V-shaped' manner. In this case, the sunlight striking on the upperside of a wing at an angle bounces off and hits the next wing at a lower level. This way, the sunlight, after being volleyed a couple of times from one wing to another, finally hits the thorax/abdomen of the butterfly. When the outside temperature becomes too high, butterflies retire to the shade.

Basking postures

Magnified view of a part of butterfly wing

Butterfly Wings are Covered with Scales Arranged Like Roof Tiles

The wings of butterflies are composed of thin transparent films (membranes) supported by tubular veins, (not to be confused with our blood veins) much like ribs supporting the canopy of an umbrella. The membranes are covered by flat scales. The scales are as tiny as dust particles and arranged like overlapping tiles on a roof. Using scales of different colours, a range of patterns is created. The body of butterflies is also covered with hair, which are elongated scales.

How do Scales Get So Many Different Colours?

The colour of a scale (or other objects) seen by us is the 'colour' or 'wavelengths' of light it reflects. So, when white light (such as sunlight—a mixture of all the colours visible to humans) falls on the scale, it selectively reflects one or few colours, suppressing or removing many others. *How do the scales do this?* The butterfly scale is like an elongated flattened sac, fabricated of the material 'Chitin'—a long string of complex sugar molecules. The surface of scales is sculptured into regular nano-sized ridges and valleys, and cross ribs. This design can produce colours by 'structure-based colouration' mechanism. Usually, iridescent and bright non-iridescent blue-green or blue colours are produced by this mechanism. In addition to nano-structures, scales of many butterflies also contain various pigments which produce colour by 'pigment-based colouration'. Thus, butterfly scales loaded with pigments such as melanin, pterins, ommochromes and papiliochromes would appear black, yellow-orange, red-yellow, and reddish-brown, respectively. In the scales, structural and pigment-based colourations do not operate in isolation; therefore, the final colours we see are the outcome of complex interactions between light, nano-structures and pigments.

Breathing in Butterflies

Butterflies do not have lungs to soak up oxygen from air into the blood. Instead, their body has an extensive network of respiratory tubes which open to the outside via 'Spiracles'. Air from outside enters the spiracles and is carried to all the organs of the body via respiratory tubes.

Blues (*Lycaenidae*)

A large group of small-sized butterflies, many of these have a blue upperside of wings though some have red, orange or golden colourations marked with black. Several butterflies of this group have a thread-like tail on their hindwings. Blues have three pairs of well-developed legs.

ANGLED SUNBEAM ▶

Curetis acuta

Size: M–L; swift flier, seen in scrubs and open areas; its silvery-white underside of wings help in camouflage—when resting on green leaves, the silvery-white wings assume a greenish hue due to the illumination of wings by green light reflected from the leaf surface. This helps the butterfly blend with the background.

Male

Female

SORREL SAPPHIRE

Heliophorus sena

Size: S; seen along fringes of forest and thinly forested areas. In females, upperside of the wings have a prominent orange mark on the margins.

▼

Male

Female

▲

COMMON GEM

Poritia hewitsoni

Size: M; seen in forested areas on foliage and sometimes on the ground.

COMMON SILVERLINE

Spindasis vulcanus

Size: S–M; seen in thinly forested areas and along fringes of forest; sexes similar.

INDIAN OAKBLUE

Arhopala atrax

Size: M; seen in forested areas, settled among dry fallen leaves, perfectly merging with the surroundings. The upperside forewings of males are purplish-blue with thinner dark margins than that of the females.

LARGE OAKBLUE

Arhopala amantes

Size: L; habits and habitat similar to that of Indian Oakblue. Upperside of males shining blue with dark margins which is broader in females; distinguished from Indian Oakblue by its larger size and markings on underside of the wings.

SPANGLED PLUSHBLUE

Flos asoka

Size: M; seen in forested areas sometimes basking on bushes or on ground. Upperside of males shining blue with narrower margins; distinguished from Variegated Plushblue by presence of metallic green scales at the lower margin of hindwings (arrow).

VARIEGATED PLUSHBLUE

Flos adriana

Size: M; habits and habitat similar to that of Spangled Plushblue. Upperside of males bright blue with narrower black borders than that of the females.

COMMON APEFLY

Spalgis epius

Size: M; fast flier; can be seen among bushes in forested areas and fringes of forest. Its underside has wavy brownish lines.

Butterfly Proboscis—an Ingeniously Designed Straw

Adult butterflies can take food only in the form of liquid. They apply their straw-like 'Proboscis' to rotting fruits, plant sap, nectar, carrion, dung, etc., and suck the nutritious fluids. The trunk which remains coiled when not in use, is raised and extended with the help of muscles and by forcing blood in its wall just before the butterfly lands on a food source.

The basic architecture of the proboscis in all butterflies is similar—it is a sealed tube, having minute slits (drinking region) near the tip. Liquid food enters the proboscis through the slits and rises upwards, driven by the suction pressure created in the head to reach the gut. The proboscis is equipped with sensors which inform the butterflies about the nature and amount of food ingested, and also help in probing the flowers to locate nectar. With this basic plan, the design of the butterfly trunk is further fine-tuned to suit their specific feeding habits.

Those feeding from the wet surfaces of rotting fruits, carrion, dung, etc., have shorter probosces with a brush-like drinking region. The brush structure works like a sponge, rapidly soaking up a large amount of fluid when a feeding butterfly sweeps or places it on the wet surface. The soaked fluid is sucked into the trunk through the slits from where it is transferred to the gut.

The probosces of butterflies feeding on floral nectars are longer, more flexible and tapering, and lack complex brushy tips. This design is meant to ensure a thorough exploration of long tubular flowers and to suck even miniscule amounts of nectar droplets. Nectar-seeking butterflies prefer visiting the flowers producing dilute nectar, since a high suction pressure would be required to imbibe thick and syrupy nectar.

Butterflies which feed by piercing into soft fruits, dung or carrion and extracting nutritious fluid, possess a short and thick proboscis with pointed tips that help in poking through soft surfaces.

Ways of Protection in Caterpillars

Caterpillars are food for many animals including birds, lizards, wasps, ants and spiders. To protect themselves from being eaten and tackle predators, caterpillars have invented a range of strategies. Body coated with long bristles, bright warning colouration, disguise and release of foul smell when alarmed are some of the common defence strategies used by caterpillars to deter predators.

Protection by Killers—Ants Defending Butterfly Larvae

Ants are amongst the main enemies of butterfly larvae. However, for the larvae of many butterflies belonging to the family '*Lycaenidae*', ants perform the duty of babysitters. This is a case of mutual understanding: the larvae offer sugary nutritious secretions oozing from their body to the ants and in exchange, the ants protect them from other predators. Butterfly larvae are, however, far smarter—through their secretions, the larvae so modify the behaviour of the ants that the latter are compelled to behave gently towards the larvae and at the same time, drive off other predators with extreme aggression.

The Compound Eye of Butterflies

The eye of butterflies is an assembly of thousands of tiny eyes or 'Ommatidia', each of which has its own lens visible on the outside. And, the light-sensitive cells of Ommatidia lie deep inside the eye. Each tiny eye forms an image of the object in its field of view, and the final image seen by the butterfly is a mosaic formed by the adjacent tiny eyes. Another feature of the butterfly eyes, visible from outside, is the oval or spherical dark spots which give the impression of a pupil. These spots are, however, not equivalent to our pupil and are called 'False Pupil' or 'Pseudopupil'. These are formed because the light entering straight into the cluster of a few ommatidia is absorbed and not reflected, and hence that area of the eye looks darker.

Close-up of eyes showing thousands of 'Ommatidia'

Butterflies can also sense ultraviolet part of the spectrum (which we cannot see!) very well, and this helps them greatly in choosing nectar-bearing flowers and selecting mates. In fact, in some butterflies additional wing patterns are visible under ultraviolet light.

▲
YAMFLY

Loxura atymnus

Size: M; flies close to the ground along fringes of forest and nearby areas; sexes similar; upperside bright orange with broad black margins at the tip of forewings.

▲
PEACOCK ROYAL

Tajuria cippus

Size: M; seen in forested areas and along fringes of forest; upperside of females dull blue.

▲
INDIGO FLASH

Rapala varuna

Size: M; habits and habitat similar to Slate Flash; upperside of males dark shining blue.

▲
SLATE FLASH

Rapala manea

Size: M; seen along fringes of forest and thinly forested areas; upperside of males iridescent blue and females dull blue; distinguished from Indigo Flash by 'Equal Symbol' mark (arrow) away from the dark band running across the margins of wings.

◀
ORCHID TIT

Chliaria othona

Size: S; seen in forested areas and along fringes of forest; male bluish with dark borders and female brownish on upperside with some lighter area.

▲
COMMON RED FLASH

Rapala iarbus

Size: M; habits and habitat similar to that of Slate Flash; males bright whereas females are dull red on upperside.

▲
COMMON CILIATE BLUE

Anthene emolus

Size: S–M; seen in forest and along fringes of forest; upperside of males is bright purple-blue and of females, brownish; it has only one band in the middle of forewings (arrow), which distinguishes it from mentioned lineblues.

▲
TAILLESS LINEBLUE

Prosotas dubiosa

Size: S; habits and habitat similar to that of Common Ciliate Blue; upperside of males dull purplish and that of females, brownish with a bluish patch.

▲
COMMON LINEBLUE

Prosotas nora

Size: XS–S; habits and habitat similar to Common Ciliate Blue; upperside of females brownish. It can be confused with Tailless Lineblue from which it can be distinguished by having a tail on the hindwings.

COMMON CERULEAN

Jamides celeno

Size: M; seen in forest and along fringes of forest; upperside of males pale-blue; females have a broader black border on upperside of the forewings. On the underside the third white line from base extends across the wing (arrow). Underside of DSF with broad bands. In similar looking Dark Cerulean, the upperside of male is shining blue.

DARK CERULEAN

Jamides bochus

Size: S–M; seen along fringes of forest and thinly forested areas; male upperside shining blue, which is duller in females.

PEA BLUE

Lampides boeticus

Size: S–M; seen in thinly forested areas, along fringes of forest and open areas; the upperside of females is brownish with faint blue wash.

FORGET-ME-NOT

Catochrysops strabo

Size: S–M; fast flier, prefers thinly forested areas, scrubs and fringes of forest; upperside of females have dark borders.

ZEBRA BLUE

Leptotes plinius

Size: S; seen in thinly forested areas and fringes of forest.

◀ COMMON PIERROT

Castalius rosimon

Size: S; seen in thinly forested areas and scrubs; sexes similar; distinguished from similar-looking butterflies by absence of spots in the central part of the underside of hindwings (arrow) and black markings on white background on the upperside of the wings.

◀ BLACK SPOTTED PIERROT

Tarucus balkanicus

Size: S; seen in scrubs in close proximity with the host plant *Ziziphus* sp. (Hindi: *Ber*); upperside of females brownish-grey with black markings; similar to Striped Pierrot; males of the two (females of genus '*Tarucus*' are very similar, thus only males can be used for species identification) can be distinguished by number of spots on the upperside forewing, which in Black Spotted Pierrot is more than one (arrow).

▲ STRIPED PIERROT

Tarucus nara

Size: S; habits and habitat similar to that of Black Spotted Pierrot. Upperside of females is brownish-grey with black markings.

▲ RED PIERROT

Talicada nyseus

Size: M; seen fluttering slowly near its host plant, *Kalanchoe* sp.; sexes similar.

PALE GRASS BLUE

Pseudozizeeria maha

Size: S; seen in grassy patches in sunny areas, flying close to the ground; upperside of females dark brownish with pale-blue at the base.

DARK GRASS BLUE

Zizeeria karsandra

Size: XS; habits and habitat similar to that of Pale Grass Blue. Upperside of the females dark brownish; upperside of males dark blue with black margins (upperside of Pale Grass Blue is pale-blue in colouration).

LESSER GRASS BLUE

Zizina otis

Size: XS–S; habits and habitat similar to that of Pale Grass Blue. Upperside of males dark blue with black borders; upperside of females, brownish; on the underside absence of spot in the middle of the forewings (arrow) and pattern of spots on underside of hindwings (circle) distinguishes it from other mentioned grass blues.

TINY GRASS BLUE

Zizula hylax

Size: XS; habits and habitat similar to that of Pale Grass Blue. Upperside of males bluish with dark borders; females brownish; a sickle-shaped mark on the top of forewings (arrow) distinguishes it from all other mentioned grass blues.

INDIAN CUPID

Everes lacturnus

Size: S; seen in thinly forested areas and along fringes of forest. Upperside of males blue with thin dark borders, and that of females with broader borders; distinguished from Tailed Cupid by having most of the underside wing spots faded.

TAILED CUPID

Everes argiades

Size: S; seen in thinly forested areas and along fringes of forest. Upperside of males is bluish with black borders; females brownish; spots close to margin of hindwings (arrow) help in distinguishing it from Indian Cupid.

QUAKER

Neopithecops zalmora

Size: S; seen close to the ground on bushes, along fringes of forest and thinly forested areas; sexes similar. Marks on underside of wings faint or may be absent in DSF; wings are rounded.

MALAYAN

Megisba malaya

Size: S; seen close to bushes near fringes of forest and thinly forested areas. Upperside dark with a white patch. Presence of 4–6 spots at the margin of underside forewings (arrow) distinguish it from Common Hedge Blue.

COMMON HEDGE BLUE

Acytolepis puspa

Size: S–M; seen in thinly forested areas and along fringes of forest on bushes and the ground. Upperside forewings of females have a broad white patch with blackish-brown margins; in underside of DSF, wing markings are faded.

GRAM BLUE

Euchrysops cnejus

Size: S–M; fast flier; seen in thinly forested areas, scrubs and near human habitations. Upperside of males light blue; distance between the two marks at the bottom of hindwings (circle) is greater, distinguishing it from similar looking butterflies.

GRASS JEWEL

Freyeria trochylus

Size: XS; flies close to the ground in open grassy areas and scrubs; sexes similar. It can be distinguished from Lesser Grass Jewel in having three orange, crowned black spots at the margins of underside of hindwings (arrow), which span only half the margin of the wings.

LESSER GRASS JEWEL

Freyeria putli

Size: XS; flies close to the ground in sunny areas and scrubs; sexes similar. It has four black spots at the margins of hindwings (arrow).

▲
LIME BLUE

Chilades lajus

Size: S; seen along fringes of forest and nearby areas. Upperside of males bluish; females with broad black margins; DSF differs significantly from WSF.

▲
PLAINS CUPID

Chilades pandava

Size: S; seen in scrubs, and along fringes of forest. Upperside of males bluish; upperside of females with broader dark margins; marked difference in appearance between WSF and DSF.

To Deter Predators, Many Butterflies Store Poison in Their Body

Several butterflies are known to store deadly poisons or distasteful substances in their body. Such butterflies would often have bright and contrasting wing colouration. Predators, innately or based on previous bad experience, avoid attacking these butterflies (p.251).

Butterflies such as Plain Tiger store poisonous substances, collectively known as 'Cardenolides' (functions as heart poison in humans) in their body, which make them distasteful and poisonous to their predators. These butterflies store poison during their larval stage, while feeding on poisonous plants such as *Asclepias* sp. and *Calotropis* sp. (commonly known as milkweeds). Male, tiger and crow butterflies (p.249–250), in addition, store other distasteful substances collectively called 'Pyrrolizidine Alkaloids' which they acquire from plants such as *Ageratum* sp. *and Crotalaria* sp. (rattlepods). These alkaloids also serve as raw material for making pheromones (substances released to stimulate mates) in males; they spray these pheromones over the head and antennae of potential mates during courtship.

Butterflies such as Common Rose and Crimson Rose store plant-acquired poisons 'Aristolochic Acids' (functions as kidney poison in humans). Butterfly Indian Fritillary stores the substance 'Cyanogenic Glycoside' in its body. This compound gets converted into the highly poisonous 'Hydrogen Cyanide' in the gut of predators.

Punches and Judies (*Riodinidae*)

A small group of butterflies marked with prominent white or dark bands/spots on the wings. The planes of wings of the Judies are slightly curved, therefore they cannot close their wings on their back completely while resting in closed-wing posture. Males of this group of butterflies have undeveloped forelegs.

PLUM JUDY

Abisara bifasciata

Size: M–L; seen in forested areas and along fringes of forest; sexes similar.

PUNCHINELLO

Zemeros flegyas

Size: M; seen in forested areas close to the ground. It has rusty wings with black and white spots.

The Eggs of Butterflies are Superbly Sculptured

Large Cabbage White

Common Crow

Common Castor

Banana Skipper

Common Emigrant

Great Eggfly

Lime Butterfly

Peacock Pansy

Brush-footed Butterflies (*Nymphalidae*)

The largest family of butterflies in India. Their forelegs are smaller in size and appear like a brush. The wing colouration of butterflies of this group ranges from dull to elegantly ornamented. Many members of this group feed on fluids from rotting fruits, animal droppings and urine.

BLUE TIGER

Tirumala limniace

Size: XXL; seen in forest and along fringes of forest; flies slowly with gentle flapping of wings and gliding. Blue Tiger and many other mentioned tiger butterflies are known to be poisonous to predators. Their wing colouration is mimicked by many non-poisonous butterflies; males of these butterflies have a pouch or patch at the lower end of underside of the hindwings (arrow).

DARK BLUE TIGER

Tirumala septentrionis

Size: XXL; habits and habitat similar to Blue Tiger. It can be distinguished from Blue Tiger and Glassy Tiger by broader black streak in the 'V'-shaped mark at the base of hindwings (red arrow), and thinner marks on forewings (blue arrow).

GLASSY TIGER

Parantica aglea

Size: XL–XXL; habits and habitat similar to Blue Tiger. Longer streaks on the forewings (arrow) distinguish it from Blue Tiger and Dark Blue Tiger.

▲
CHESTNUT TIGER

Parantica sita

Size: XXL; seen along fringes of forest and thinly forested areas, sometimes flying at tree level; males have a small black patch at the lower end of hindwings.

▲
PLAIN TIGER

Danaus chrysippus

Size: XL; flies slowly in scrubs and along fringes of forest.

▲
STRIPED TIGER

Danaus genutia

Size: XL–XXL; habits and habitat similar to Plain Tiger. Distinguished from Plain Tiger by its prominent black striped wings.

▲
STRIPED BLUE CROW

Euploea mulciber

Size: XXL; seen gliding along fringes of forest and thinly forested areas. It is known to store poison in its body.

Warning, Imitation, Hide-and-Seek, Concealment and Deception—Defence Tactics of Butterflies Against Predators

Butterflies possess no special organs for defence, such as stings, or jaws to bite in order to retaliate when attacked by predators (lizards, birds, spiders, mantids, wasps and frogs). Butterflies, however, have devised several peaceful ways to safeguard themselves:

1. WARNING

A few butterflies such as crows and tigers store poisons and bitter substances in their body (p.247). Poisonous butterflies often have vivid wings with bright colourations adorned with contrasting stripes, spots and bars (warning colourations). They advertise their poisonous nature through warning colourations, and predators avoid feeding on such butterflies.

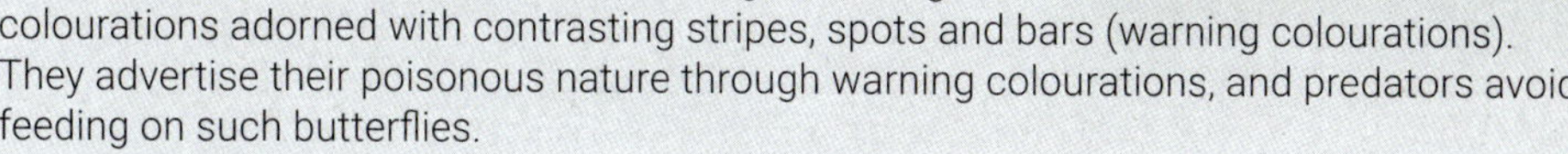

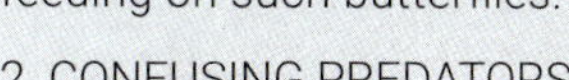

2. CONFUSING PREDATORS

Imitation: Certain non-poisonous butterflies copy warning colourations and behaviours of poisonous butterflies to keep the predators away. For instance, the non-poisonous female Common Wanderer mimics the colouration of the poisonous Blue Tiger butterfly, and the non-poisonous female Common Palmfly not only mimics the warning colouration of the poisonous Plain Tiger, but also imitates the flying style of the latter. Imitating colourations is not a conscious effort of butterflies, as an individual butterfly cannot change its colour pattern.

Concealment: On the other extreme are those butterflies which safeguard themselves by not being seen; they camouflage themselves amongst their surroundings. Their wing colouration helps them merge with the background. For instance, wing colouration of dry season form of Common Evening Brown enables them to merge so perfectly with the background of the shaded forest floor, that they tend to be overlooked (p.255).

Flash Colourations: The shape and underside wing colouration of the Orange Oakleaf butterfly (p.262) resemble dry leaves, while the upperside of the wing is brilliantly coloured. When a predator locates the butterfly by the bright upperside of its wings and approaches towards it, the butterfly quickly flies away and lands among dry foliage, closing its wings to merge with the background. Then the predator, with the image of the brightly coloured butterfly in its memory, often fails to find it.

Deception: Wings of many butterflies are decorated with bright concentric rings called eyespots. 'Solitary Large Eyespots' such as those found on the upperside wings of Peacock Pansy (p.261) are perceived by the predators as the real eyes of their own enemies/ predators, and therefore the predators of butterflies are scared away. For instance, a small bird or lizard may perceive the large eyespots as the eyes of its own predator such as an owl. 'Small Eyespots' are serially arranged at the margins of the wings, as in the Common Fourring and Common Evening Brown butterflies (p.254). These eyespots are perceived by the predator as the real eyes of their prey and the predator attacks on the margins of the wings. Therefore, by diverting the attack from the vital parts of the body, the butterfly escapes with partially torn wings, thereby saving its life (p.255).

Some butterflies such a silverlines (p.237) go even further to deceive their predators. They bear 'Small Solitary Eyespots' (false eye) and a long tail (false antennae) at the lower end of their hindwings. This arrangement mimics the head of a butterfly—'the false head'. To make their false head look more authentic, butterflies occasionally move their false antennae. Fooled predators attack the false head, and in this case too, the butterfly survives with slightly torn wing(s).

A portion of hindwings of Peacock Pansy butterfly. It might be perceived as head/eye of predatory birds such as an 'owl'.

The survivor—a Four/Fivering butterfly attacked at its marginal eyespots

Showing false head of Common Red Flash butterfly

A survivor—Common Red Flash butterfly attacked at its false head

COMMON CROW

Euploea core

Size: XXL; seen along fringes of forest and thinly forested areas; flight slow and gliding; sexes similar. It is known to be poisonous to predators; likely to be confused with female Great Eggfly (a mimic) due to similar upperside of wings (p.262).

PC: PS
Male

PC: PS
Female

COMMON PALMFLY

Elymnias hypermnestra

Size: XL; seen in thinly forested areas and along fringes of forest. Upperside wing pattern and style of flight of female Common Palmfly resembles poisonous Striped Tiger and Plain Tiger butterflies.

COMMON TREEBROWN

Lethe rohria

Size: L; shade loving, seen in forested area and fringes of forest; sexes similar. Likely to be confused with Common Evening Brown, which lacks a white band and thin pale or white wavy lines on the forewings.

COMMON EVENING BROWN

Melanitis leda

Size: XL; seen in bushes or on the forest floor; attracted to lamp light in the evenings; sexes similar. Marked difference between WSF and DSF; individuals of DSF vary considerably.

WSF

DSF

DSF

BUSHBROWN

Mycalesis sp.

Size: L; these butterflies are seen on bushes close to the ground in forested areas and fringes of forest. Camouflage with fallen dry leaves in dry season. Identification of bushbrowns upto species level requires comparison of markings of wings which are not visible in photographs.

COMMON FOURRING

Ypthima huebneri

Size: M; seen on ground or bushes, in forest and along fringes of forest; sexes similar. Eyespots reduced to dots in DSF; likely to be confused with Common Fivering which has five concentric rings on the margins of hindwings (lowest pair of spots counted as one) and not four.

COMMON FIVERING

Ypthima baldus

Size: M; habits and habitat similar to that of Common Fourring; sexes similar. Eyespots reduced to dots in DSF.

Dry and Wet Season Forms—Adaptation to Challenging Environs

In many butterflies, the wings of offspring emerging in the wet season (rainy season)—Wet Season Form or WSF, have a different wing pattern as compared to those that emerge in the dry season (other than rainy season)—Dry Season Form or DSF. This phenomenon is known to scientists as Polyphenism (*poly*: various; *phenism*: appearance). This allows butterflies to match their requirements (such as camouflage and thermoregulation) for survival in different seasonal conditions. For instance, the two seasonal forms of Common Evening Brown have striking differences in their appearance.

The WSF of Common Evening Brown has many concentric eyespots along the margins of the underside of the wings (p.253). The DSF lacks eyespots and has irregular dark blotches and stripes on a brown or chestnut-coloured background. During daytime, the butterfly remains inactive and spends most of its time resting on fallen dry leaves in the forest. It becomes active at dusk and at dawn.

Why and how does the Common Evening Brown change its appearance in different seasons? Wing colouration of DSF enables the butterfly resting on the forest floor to effectively camouflage with the dry leaves and evade predators such as a lizard. In this setting, bearing eyespots on wings would make butterfly noticeable. In the wet season, Common Evening Brown butterflies are more active and have to move in search of a mate and to lay eggs; here a background of green foliage makes them more visible. Also, there are new types of predators as well (grasshoppers, mantids and many other insects). To handle this situation, Common Evening Brown butterflies change their defence tactics–their WSFs bearing conspicuous eyespots at the margins of wings confuse predators. The latter when intending to capture the butterfly by its head mistake the eyespots for real eyes and attack the margins of the wings. Butterflies, by directing the attack to the margins of wings, protect their vital parts (head and abdomen) and escape with partially torn wings. The survivor now gets a new lease of life to reproduce.

Scientific investigations have revealed that seasonal variations in temperature and humidity, cause changes in the timing and levels of hormone secretion in early stages of butterflies (larva and pupa). This alters crucial in-time interactions between proteins and enzymes in the body of the larva responsible for the development of eyespots.

Cryptic DSF of Common Evening Brown resting on the forest floor

▲
ANOMALOUS NAWAB

Polyura agraria

Size: L–XL; seen in forested areas and along fringes of forest.

▲
COMMON NAWAB

Polyura athamas

Size: L–XL; seen in forested areas and along fringes of forest. Unlike Anomalous Nawab, it has one whitish spot (which may be absent) at the tip of forewings (arrow).

▲
LASCAR

Pantoporia sp.

Size: L; seen along fringes of forest and thinly forested areas; sexes similar; upperside markings resemble that of Common Jester, however, the two differ in shape of wings and details of markings.

▲
PAINTED COURTESAN

Euripus consimilis

Size: L; seen in forested areas and along fringes of forest.

COMMON SAILER

Neptis hylas

Size: L; seen along fringes of forest and thinly forested areas; flies with slow sailing flight; similar to Pallas's Sailer, however, its underside is pale-brownish and white marks on the underside are edged prominently with black.

PALLAS'S SAILER

Neptis sappho

Size: L; habits and habitat similar to that of Common Sailer.

COMMON SERGEANT

Athyma perius

Size: XL; seen in thinly forested areas and along fringes of forest; sexes similar; distinguished from mentioned sailers by black spots in white area on hindwings (arrow), and abdomen with black and white alternating rings.

PC: SC

INDIAN RED ADMIRAL

Vanessa indica

Size: L; seen in forest and along fringes of forest; sexes similar.

PAINTED LADY

Vanessa cardui

Size: L–XL; seen in thinly forested areas and along fringes of forest; sexes similar.

BLUE ADMIRAL

Kaniska canace

Size: XL; fast flier, seen in forest and along fringes of forest; sexes similar.

COMMANDER

Moduza procris

Size: XL; seen in thinly forested areas and along fringes of forest; sexes similar.

BARONET

Symphaedra nais

Size: XL; seen in thinly forested areas and along fringes of forest; sexes similar.

Female

COMMON BARON

Euthalia aconthea

Size: L–XL; seen in thinly forested areas and along fringes of forest, usually on the ground. Males darker than females.

GAUDY BARON

Euthalia lubentina

Size: XL; seen in forest and along fringes of forest. Males have less extensive white markings on forewings.

INDIAN FRITILLARY

Argynnis hyperbius

Size: XL; seen in scrubs and along fringes of forest.

VAGRANT

Vagrans egista

Size: L; seen in thinly forested areas and along fringes of forest; sexes similar.

COMMON LEOPARD

Phalanta phalantha

Size: L; seen along fringes of forest and thinly forested areas; sexes similar.

▲
COMMON CASTOR
Ariadne merione

Size: L; seen in open areas close to its host plant—'castor'; advances with combination of gliding and jerky wing flapping; sexes similar.

▲
RUSTIC
Cupha erymanthis

Size: L; seen in thinly forested areas and along fringes of forest; sexes similar.

▲
COMMON MAP
Cyrestis thyodamas

Size: L; seen in forested areas and along fringes of forest; sexes similar.

▲
COMMON JESTER
Symbrenthia lilaea

Size: L; seen on foliage, along fringes of forest, thinly forested areas and near small streams; sexes similar.

INDIAN TORTOISESHELL
Aglais caschmirensis

Size: L–XL; seen along fringes of forest and thinly forested areas; sexes similar.
▼

CHOCOLATE PANSY
Junonia iphita

Size: L–XL; seen in forest and along fringes of forest, obscured in dry foliage; sexes similar.
▼

▲
PEACOCK PANSY

Junonia almana

Size: L; seen in open areas and along fringes of forest; sexes similar. The shape and colouration of underside of wings of DSF resembles a dry leaf, which helps this butterfly conceal itself.

▲
YELLOW PANSY

Junonia hierta

Size: L; seen in open grassy and sunny places, flies close to the ground; sexes similar, but upperside of wings of females have small eyespots at the margins.

▲
BLUE PANSY

Junonia orithya

Size: L; swift flier, seen close to the ground in scrubs and grassy areas; sexes similar.

▲
GREY PANSY

Junonia atlites

Size: L; seen in open places close to marshy areas; keeps itself near the ground; sexes similar.

◀ **LEMON PANSY**

Junonia lemonias

Size: L; seen in open places, swift flier and keeps near the ground; sexes similar.

◀ **GREAT EGGFLY**

Hypolimnas bolina

Size: XL–XXL or larger; seen in thinly forested areas and along fringes of forest. Females mimic poisonous Common Crow butterfly, however, a careful examination of shape of wings and pattern of white markings on both the sides of wings help distinguish the two.

◀ **ORANGE OAKLEAF**

Kallima inachus

Size: XXL; seen in forested areas; sexes similar. The shape of wings and underside colouration resembles dried leaves which helps this butterfly to hide itself.

▲ **TAWNY COSTER**

Acraea terpsicore

Size: L; seen along fringes of forest and open areas; sexes similar.

▲ **CLUB BEAK**

Libythea myrrha

Size: L; seen in thinly forested areas and along fringes of forest; sexes similar but, upperside of the wings of females have more orange area.

Checklist of Butterflies Seen In and Around CTR

Swallowtails (*Papilionidae*)

1	Common Rose	*Pachliopta aristolochiae*
2	Common Peacock	*Papilio bianor*
3	Common Mime	*Papilio clytia*
4	Lime Butterfly	*Papilio demoleus*
5	Common Mormon	*Papilio polytes*
6	Spangle	*Papilio protenor*
7	Tailed Jay	*Graphium agamemnon*
8	Common Jay	*Graphium doson*
9	Spot Swordtail	*Graphium nomius*
10	Common Bluebottle	*Graphium sarpedon*
11	Glassy Bluebottle	*Graphium cloanthus*

Skippers (*Hesperiidae*)

12	Brown Awl	*Badamia exclamationis*
13	Orange-tailed Awl	*Bibasis sena*
14	Branded Orange Awlet	*Burara oedipodea*
15	Common Banded Awl	*Hasora chromus*
16	Angle	*Caprona* sp.
17	Spotted Snow Flat	*Tagiades menaka*
18	Water Snow Flat	*Tagiades litigiosa*
19	Fulvous Pied Flat	*Pseudocoladenia dan*
20	Spotted Small Flat	*Sarangesa purendra*
21	Common Small Flat	*Sarangesa dasahara*
22	Indian Grizzled Skipper	*Spialia galba*
23	Restricted Demon	*Notocrypta curvifascia*
24	Grass Demon	*Udaspes folus*
25	Tree Flitter	*Hyarotis adrastus*
26	Banana Skipper	*Erionota torus*
27	Common Redeye	*Matapa aria*
28	Common Straight Swift	*Parnara guttatus*
29	Beavan's Swift	*Borbo bevani*
30	Dark Palm Dart	*Telicota bambusae*
31	Paintbrush Swift	*Baoris farri*

Whites and Yellows (*Pieridae*)

32	Common Emigrant	*Catopsilia pomona*
33	Mottled Emigrant	*Catopsilia pyranthe*
34	Three-spot Grass Yellow	*Eurema blanda*
35	One-spot yellow grass	*Eurema andersoni*
36	Small Grass Yellow	*Eurema brigitta*
37	Common Grass Yellow	*Eurema hecabe*
38	Spotless Grass Yellow	*Eurema laeta*
39	Dark Clouded Yellow	*Colias fieldii*
40	Pale Clouded yellow	*Colias erate*
41	Psyche	*Leptosia nina*
42	Large Cabbage White	*Pieris brassicae*
43	Indian Cabbage White	*Pieris canidia*
44	Bath White	*Pontia daplidice*
45	Pioneer	*Belenois aurota*
46	Common Gull	*Cepora nerissa*
47	Common Jezebel	*Delias eucharis*
48	Common Wanderer	*Pareronia valeria*

Punches and Judies (*Riodinidae*)

49	Punchinello	*Zemeros flegyas*
50	Plum Judy	*Abisara bifasciata*

Blues (*Lycaenidae*)

51	Angled Sunbeam	*Curetis acuta*
52	Common Gem	*Poritia hewitsoni*
53	Apefly	*Spalgis epius*
54	Sorrel Sapphire	*Heliophorus sena*
55	Long-banded Silverline	*Spindasis lohita*
56	Common Silverline	*Spindasis vulcanus*
57	Common Shot Silverline	*Spindasis ictis*
58	Large Oakblue	*Arhopala amantes*
59	Indian Oakblue	*Arhopala atrax*
60	Variegated Plushblue	*Flos adriana*
61	Spangled Plushblue	*Flos asoka*
62	Yamfly	*Loxura atymnus*
63	Common Onyx	*Horaga onyx*
64	Peacock Royal	*Tajuria cippus*
65	Orchid Tit	*Chliaria othona*
66	Common Red flash	*Rapala iarbus*
67	Slate Flash	*Rapala manea*
68	Copper Flash	*Rapala pheretima*
69	Indigo Flash	*Rapala varuna*
70	Common Ciliate Blue	*Anthene emolus*
71	Tailless Lineblue	*Prosotas dubiosa*
72	Common Lineblue	*Prosotas nora*
73	Dark Cerulean	*Jamides bochus*
74	Common Cerulean	*Jamides celeno*
75	Forget-me-not	*Catochrysops strabo*
76	Pea Blue	*Lampides boeticus*
77	Zebra Blue	*Leptotes plinius*
78	Common Pierrot	*Castalius rosimon*
79	Black Spotted Pierrot	*Tarucus balkanicus*
80	Spotted Pierrot	*Tarucus callinara*
81	Transparent Pierrot	*Tarucus indica*
82	Striped Pierrot	*Tarucus nara*
83	Red Pierrot	*Tálicada nyseus*
84	Dark Grass Blue	*Zizeeria karsandra*
85	Pale Grass Blue	*Pseudozizeeria maha*
86	Lesser Grass Blue	*Zizina otis*
87	Tiny Grass Blue	*Zizula hylax*
88	Tailed Cupid	*Everes argiades*
89	Dusky Blue Cupid	*Everes huegelii*
90	Indian Cupid	*Everes lacturnus*
91	Quaker	*Neopithecops zalmora*

92	Malayan	*Megisba malaya*
93	Common Hedge Blue	*Acytolepis puspa*
94	Gram Blue	*Euchrysops cnejus*
95	Lesser Grass Jewel	*Freyeria putli*
96	Grass Jewel	*Freyeria trochylus*
97	Plains Cupid	*Chilades pandava*
98	Lime Blue	*Chilades lajus*
	Brush-footed Butterflies (*Nymphalidae*)	
99	Plain Tiger	*Danaus chrysippus*
100	Striped Tiger	*Danaus genutia*
101	Glassy Tiger	*Parantica aglea*
102	Chestnut Tiger	*Parantica sita*
103	Blue Tiger	*Tirumala limniace*
104	Dark Blue Tiger	*Tirumala septentrionis*
105	Common Crow	*Euploea core*
106	Striped Blue Crow	*Euploea mulciber*
107	Common Nawab	*Polyura athamas*
108	Anomalous Nawab	*Polyura agraria*
109	Common Palmfly	*Elymnias hypermnestra*
110	Common Evening Brown	*Melanitis leda*
111	Dark Evening Brown	*Melanitis phedima*
112	Banded Treebrown	*Lethe confusa*
113	Bamboo Treebrown	*Lethe europa*
114	Common Treebrown	*Lethe rohria*
115	Darkbrand Bushbrown	*Mycalesis mineus*
116	Common Bushbrown	*Mycalesis perseus*
117	Common Fivering	*Ypthima baldus*
118	Common Fourring	*Ypthima huebneri*
119	Himalayan Fivering	*Ypthima sacra*
120	Common Sailer	*Neptis hylas*
121	Broad-banded Sailer	*Neptis sankara*
122	Pallas's Sailer	*Neptis sappho*
123	Lascar	*Pantoporia* sp.

124	Colour Sergeant	*Athyma nefte*
125	Common Sergeant	*Athyma perius*
126	Staff Sergeant	*Athyma selenophora*
127	Small Staff Sergeant	*Athyma zeroca*
128	Commander	*Moduza procris*
129	Common Baron	*Euthalia aconthea*
130	Gaudy Baron	*Euthalia lubentina*
131	Baronet	*Symphaedra nais*
132	Indian Fritillary	*Argynnis hyperbius*
133	Common Leopard	*Phalanta phalantha*
134	Rustic	*Cupha erymanthis*
135	Vagrant	*Vagrans egista*
136	Common Castor	*Ariadne merione*
137	Painted Courtesan	*Euripus consimilis*
138	Circe	*Hestinalis nama*
139	Common Map	*Cyrestis thyodamas*
140	Common Jester	*Symbrenthia lilaea*
141	Indian Tortoiseshell	*Aglais caschmirensis*
142	Blue Admiral	*Kaniska canace*
143	Painted Lady	*Vanessa cardui*
144	Indian Red Admiral	*Vanessa indica*
145	Peacock Pansy	*Junonia almana*
146	Grey Pansy	*Junonia atlites*
147	Yellow Pansy	*Junonia hierta*
148	Chocolate Pansy	*Junonia iphita*
149	Lemon Pansy	*Junonia lemonias*
150	Blue Pansy	*Junonia orithya*
151	Great Eggfly	*Hypolimnas bolina*
152	Orange Oakleaf	*Kallima inachus*
153	Yellow Coster	*Acraea issoria*
154	Tawny Coster	*Acraea terpsicore*
155	Common Beak	*Libythea lepita*
156	Club Beak	*Libythea myrrha*

Baronet butterflies feeding on rotten fruit

Some Facts About Butterflies

- Worldwide 18,000–20,000 species of butterflies have been discovered.
- Butterflies such as skippers can fly at a speed of nearly 60 km per hour.
- Butterflies have been recorded as high as 5,400 m above sea level in the Himalayas.
- Butterflies such as Monarch and Painted Lady are known to migrate for distances of more than 3,000 km.
- Some butterflies lay eggs singly while others can lay 100–150 eggs in one go.
- Butterflies spend the night under leaves, among bushes and grasses, and on the forest floor.
- Extreme weather conditions such as heavy rains and extreme cold can kill butterflies.
- Largest butterfly in the World: Queen Alexandra's Birdwing (*Ornithoptera alexandrae*) of Papua New Guinea.
- Largest butterfly in India: Golden Birdwing (*Troides aeacus*) found in the Himalayas.
- Smallest butterfly in India: Grass Jewel (*Freyeria trochylus*) with a wingspan of 1.5–2 cm. Other butterflies of India close to the size of Grass Jewel are: Lesser Grass Jewel (*Freyeria putli*) and Tiny Grass Blue (*Zizula hylax*).

Mature pupa of Mottled Emigrant

Wings of a freshly emerged butterfly are crumpled and moist. To dry and straighten the wings, the butterfly hangs upside down and occasionally flaps its wings. It takes about half an hour before a butterfly can take its first flight.

Strong toothed jaws of dragonflies and damselflies help them lead a predatory lifestyle

Dragonflies and Damselflies

These insects belong to the order *'Odonata'* (Greek, *'Odous'* meaning 'tooth'), referring to their serrated jaws. About 6,000 species of odonates have been recorded worldwide, and India is home to about 500 of them. Over 40 species of odonates have been recorded from CTR. This section provides images and identification features of 24 species of odonates which can be seen in and around CTR.

Where to Look for Dragonflies and Damselflies

These can be sighted in thinly forested areas, fringes of forest and near waterbodies with good sunlight.

Dragonfly or Damselfly

The general body plan of both dragonflies and damselflies is similar, with minor differences. Dragonflies are strong fliers with hindwings broader than forewings, and while at rest, the wings are held perpendicular to the body. Damselflies, in contrast, have both hind and forewings of equal size, wings are narrow at the base, and usually held closed over the body while at rest.

Life of Dragonflies and Damselflies

These lay eggs in or near water, or on aquatic vegetation. Several hundreds to thousands of eggs can be laid per batch. It may take 5–40 days for the eggs to hatch. Larva emerging from the egg lives in water, and is a perfect predator like its parents—feeding on larvae of other insects, tadpoles, small fishes, etc. When mature, the larva climbs up to a rock or emerging part of aquatic plants. Here, it moults into an 'adult' or winged form, which is now capable of flying. Being predators, both larvae and adults have a important role in controlling population of harmful insects, such as mosquitoes, flies and pest insects.

Males are generally more brightly coloured than females. In some cases immature males, however, are less brightly coloured and take a few days to develop adult colouration. Males have accessory or 'secondary genitalia' on the second abdominal segment.

Size Guide

The size categories (size represents length of the abdomen):

Extra Small (XS):	1–2 cm
Small (S):	> 2–3 cm
Medium (M):	> 3–4 cm
Large (L):	> 4 cm

Body parts of odonates

Wherever there is a difference in the appearance of males and females, the images of males have been used for representation (unless otherwise mentioned).

Dragonflies

▲

SCARLET SKIMMER

Crocothemis servilia

Size: S; seen near wet areas, ponds and streams; females have a yellowish body.

▲

SHIVA CLAWTAIL

Onychogomphus biforceps

Size: L; seen near streams and rivers; males and females similar.

▲

BLUE GROUND SKIMMER

Diplacodes trivialis

Size: XS; seen in open areas, and along fringes of forest; females greenish-yellow.

▲

FULVOUS FOREST SKIMMER

Neurothemis fulvia

Size: S; seen in wet forested areas and along fringes of forest; females paler than males.

DITCH JEWEL

Brachythemis contaminata

Size: XS; seen in open areas, fringes of forest and close to waterbodies. Females yellowish and lack an orange patch on wings.

CRIMSON-TAILED MARSH HAWK

Orthetrum pruinosum

Size: S; seen near streams and rivers; females yellowish.

BLUE MARSH HAWK

Orthetrum glaucum

Size: S–M; seen near streams; females yellowish.

BLUE-TAILED FOREST HAWK

Orthetrum triangulare

Size: S–M; seen near streams and rivers; females yellowish-green.

GREEN MARSH HAWK

Orthetrum sabina

Size: M; seen near ponds, tanks etc.; males and females similar.

WANDERING GLIDER

Pantala flavescens

Size: S–M; seen in thinly forested areas; abdomen of females lack red colouration.

COMMON PICTUREWING

Rhyothemis variegata

Size: S; seen close to marshy areas and ponds; female as shown; wings of males have fewer brown and yellow patches.

Female

PIGMY SKIMMER

Tetrathemis platyptera

Size: XS; seen near streams and ponds; males and females similar.

BLACK STREAM GLIDER

Trithemis festiva

Size: S; seen near streams and rivers; females yellowish.

CRIMSON MARSH GLIDER

Trithemis aurora

Size: S; seen near wetlands and springs; females olive-yellow.

LONG-LEGGED MARSH GLIDER

Trithemis pallidinervis

Size: S; seen near ponds and streams or close by areas; sexes similar.

Damselflies

GOLDEN DARTLET *Ischnura aurora* ▲

Size: XS; seen near streams or close-by areas; females duller than males.

PIXIE DARTLET *Rhodischnura nursei* ▲

Size: XS; seen near streams or close by areas; Females lack bright red colouration on abdomen; some females (as shown) resemble males in colouration.

COROMANDEL MARSH DART *Ceriagrion coromandelianum* ▲

Size: S; seen near streams, ponds and canals; sexes similar.

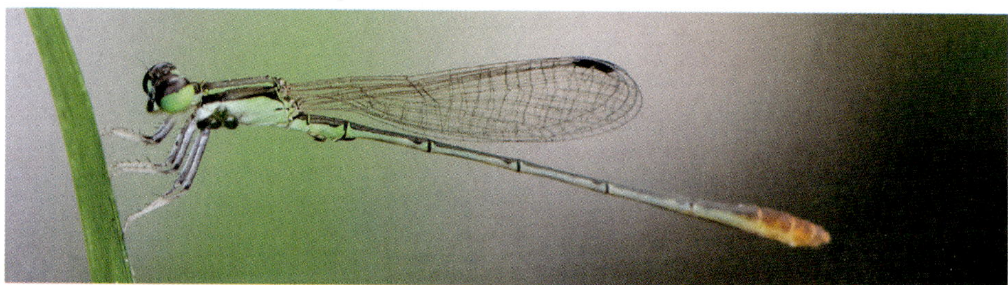

PYGMY DARTLET *Agriocnemis pygmaea* ▲

Size: XS; seen near streams; colouration of females variable, some reddish, others resemble males.

YELLOW BUSH DART *Copera marginipes* ▲

Size: S; seen near streams; females duller and less contrasting than males.

FORCIPATE DARTLET *Ischnura forcipata* ▲

Size: XS; seen near streams; some females duller than males, others reddish.

Male

STREAM GLORY ▲

Neurobasis chinensis

Size: L; seen near streams and rivers.

Female

BLACK EMPEROR

Rhinocypha quadrimaculata

Size: S; seen near streams and rivers; wings of females uniformly brownish.

PEACOCK JEWEL

Rhinocypha fenestrella

Size: XS–S; seen near streams and rivers; wings of females uniformly brownish.

Stream Glories are often sighted near forest streams. The hindwings of males produce blue-green iridescence by the phenomenon 'optical interference'. Males display their wings periodically to warn away competitors and woo mates.

Checklist of Dragonflies and Damselflies Seen In and Around CTR

Dragonflies

No.	Common name	Scientific name
1.	Shiva Clawtail	*Onychogomphus biforceps*
2.	Common Hooktail	*Paragomphus lineatus*
3.	Trumpet Tail	*Acisoma panorpoides*
4.	Ditch Jewel	*Brachythemis contaminata*
5.	Emerald-banded Skimmer	*Cratilla lineata*
6.	Scarlet Skimmer	*Crocothemis servilia*
7.	Black-tipped Ground Skimmer	*Diplacodes nebulosa*
8.	Blue Ground Skimmer	*Diplacodes trivialis*
9.	Fulvous Forest Skimmer	*Neurothemis fulvia*
10.	Blue-tailed Yellow Skimmer	*Palpopleura sexmaculata*
11.	Pigmy Skimmer	*Tetrathemis platyptera*
12.	Small Skimmer	*Orthetrum taeniolatum*
13.	Scarlet Marsh Hawk	*Aethriamanta brevipennis*
14.	Tricoloured Marsh Hawk	*Orthetrum luzonicum*
15.	Green Marsh Hawk	*Orthetrum sabina*
16.	Blue-tailed Forest Hawk	*Orthetrum triangulare*
17.	Not available	*Orthetrum japonicum*
18.	Blue Marsh Hawk	*Orthetrum glaucum*
19.	Crimson-tailed Marsh Hawk	*Orthetrum pruinosum*
20.	Common Picturewing	*Rhyothemis variegata*
21.	Coral-tailed Cloudwing	*Tholymis tillarga*
22.	Wandering Glider	*Pantala flavescens*
23.	Crimson Marsh Glider	*Trithemis aurora*
24.	Black Stream Glider	*Trithemis festiva*
25.	Long-legged Marsh Glider	*Trithemis pallidinervis*
26.	Not available	*Tramea virginia*
27.	Not available	*Sympetrum commixtum*

Damselflies

No.	Common name	Scientific name
28.	Pygmy Dartlet	*Agriocnemis pygmaea*
29.	Not available	*Agriocnemis clauseni*
30.	Coromandel Marsh Dart	*Ceriagrion coromandelianum*
31.	Forcipate Dartlet	*Ischnura forcipata*
32.	Golden Dartlet	*Ischnura aurora*
33.	Pixie Dartlet	*Rhodischnura nursei*
34.	Saffron-faced Blue Dart	*Pseudagrion rubriceps*
35.	Yellow Bush Dart	*Copera marginipes*
36.	Pale Slender Dartlet	*Aciagrion pallidum*
37.	Black Threadtail	*Prodasineura autumnalis*
38.	Emerald-striped Spreadwing	*Lestes viridula*
39.	Stream Glory	*Neurobasis chinensis*
40.	River Heliodor	*Libellago lineata*
41.	Peacock Jewel	*Rhinocypha fenestrella*
42.	Black Emperor	*Rhinocypha quadrimaculata*
43	Not available	*Rhinocypha bifasciata*

Odonate can prey upon another odonate

Other Animals

PC: AGA (fish)

DUNG BEETLES

(H: GOBAR BHRING)

Dung beetles are insects belonging to the order '*Coleoptera*' and superfamily '*Scarabaeoidea*'. Worldwide, about 7,000 species of dung beetles are known.

Living on Animal Waste

Dung beetles fly to fresh dung droppings, which they feed on and bury as food for their young ones. Some dung beetle species live and lay eggs in the dung itself, others make tunnels in the ground below the pile of dung, while the rest take away a piece of dung by rolling and store in tunnels at a distance. Dung beetles perform several useful tasks in nature:

- Prevent dung pollution.
- Suppress parasites present in dung by crushing their eggs.
- Promote release of nutrients from dung into the environment by burying and grinding dung.
- Improve fertility of soil by burying dung.
- Improve aeration and water-absorption capacity of soil by digging tunnels.
- Disperse seeds present in the dung.

GIANT HONEYBEE

(H: MADHU MAKKHI)

Apis dorsata

PC: MS

Large half-moon shaped combs hanging high on trees, cliffs and buildings are usually built by the Giant Honeybees or Rock Bees. The comb is a huge reservoir of pristine honey and pollen, and houses the growing brood. The comb is covered with three to six layers of aggressive bees which shield the honey and brood from robbers including wasps, birds, monkeys, bears, snakes, honey-hunting humans, and harsh environment (rain and solar heat).

To tackle enemies, bees have other strategies too: they make a loud buzzing noise with their wings to display aggression, and disperse suddenly in a big mass from the comb to chase invaders for a long distance. In a peculiar defensive behaviour, bees flip their abdomen upwards in a sequential manner that produces a 'Mexican Wave-like' pattern which propagates over the entire comb within a few seconds. The wave which is initiated by a few leader bees in response to the hovering of intruders close to the comb, alarms all the members of the hive and confuses the approaching predator.

Giant Honeybees tend to abscond to their seasonal alternative sites when forage becomes scarce. When conditions are favourable, they return to the same tree for nesting, or renovate the older nests. These are known to be important pollinators for trees and other plants.

Without Bees There is a Crisis

About one-third of all plant products consumed by humans are dependent on animals for pollination. Imagine acres of orchards where trees bear gorgeous flowers that never turn into fruits. This scenario can be a real one in the times to come if bees are not protected, as they are the most important pollinators (others being flies, butterflies, wasps, ants, etc.).

Bee-pollinated plants supply most of the fruits, nuts and seeds that are the main source of dietary vitamins, antioxidants, minerals and oils. Bees also have an important role in pollinating wild flora, thereby contributing largely to the maintenance of a healthy natural ecosystem on the planet. Shrinkage of natural vegetation and exposure to the cocktail of insecticides sprayed on crops has brought about a decline in the population of these hardworking creatures.

Farmers in many parts of the world these days rely on 'domesticated' or 'managed bee' services, particularly honeybees, for pollination. The pollination service, which otherwise was provided by wild bees absolutely free of cost, now costs millions of dollars per year. Expanding demand, susceptibility to disease and threat from pesticides has affected managed bees too. Therefore, to avail free pollination services for agriculture and forest flora worldwide, wild bee populations must be conserved by promotion of pesticide-free farming and restoration of lost habitats.

Life of Honeybees

There are about 25,000 species of bees known all over the world. Honeybees, bumblebees and carpenter bees are some of the commonly sighted bees. The honey-producing bees or honeybees live in a colony of thousands of nestmates. Their nests have thousands of hexagonal cells (honeycomb) made of beeswax. The cells are used to store nectar, honey and pollen, and also as a cradle for their young ones. The colony of honeybees has three main types of bees whose jobs are well defined:

Worker bee

Workers are caretakers of the colony and perform all the outdoor and indoor tasks, such as bringing nectar and pollen into the nest, nursing broods and attending to the queen.

Drones (male bees) mate with the queen and die shortly thereafter.

Queen increases the number of colony members by reproduction.

Both workers and queen bee possess a sting, which the former use for defending the colony from predators, and the latter against any rival queen.

Common honeybees found in India include Little Bee (*Apis florea*), Indian Honeybee (*Apis cerana*), European Bee (*Apis mellifera*) and Rock Bee (*Apis dorsata*). The latter three species are responsible for producing most of the table honey.

From Nectar to Honey

Honey is a kind of concentrated sugar, made from nectar by honeybees.

To convert nectar into honey, bees concentrate the nectar and modify its chemical constituents. Worker bees after taking sips of nectar from flowers return to the nest, and handover nectar to the storer bees. The latter distribute it to the hungry nest-mates and store the surplus in comb cells. As the nectar ripens, it loses its water content through evaporation, which is facilitated by the constant fanning of wings by bees. The salivary enzymes, mixed into nectar by bees, bring about a change in its chemical composition—breaking down most of the sucrose into glucose and fructose. Once the concentration of sugar is nearly 80 percent, the cell containing nectar is sealed till further use.

Licking floral nectar

To produce 1 kg of honey, bees need to visit about 20 million flowers and make about 50 thousand trips to flowers from their nest!

It takes about around one to ten days to ripen the honey, depending on humidity and nest ventilation. Mature honey contains about 200 substances including minerals, vitamins and amino acids. The flavour of honey depends on the flora where bees forage.

Bee Senses

Bees have a good sense of colour vision—though they are not good at sensing the colour red, they can see ultraviolet light. Thus, to them, the flower colours appear different from what we humans see. Bees are known to have a better sense of smell than humans.

Gift From Bees

Not just honey, bees also provide us 'Bee bread', 'Propolis', and 'Beeswax'.

Bee bread is a mass of processed pollen grains. After collecting the pollen grains from flowers, bees moisten it with saliva and fix it on the pollen basket on hind legs as a compact ball. They carry it to the hive, where it is mixed with honey and saliva, and sealed in the cells of the honeycomb. The reactions happening therein break down complex nutrients of pollen into simple and easily digestible mass—bee bread. Bees use bee bread as food, and it is valued by humans also as food.

Propolis or 'bee-glue' is produced from gum collected by bees from floral buds, which they mix with saliva and wax. Bees use propolis to seal cracks and smoothing of cells in the honeycomb. It is valued for its medicinal properties.

Beeswax is the building material of a honeycomb, secreted by worker bees from a special gland located in their abdomen. Beeswax is used as a constituent of creams and lotions, and as food additive.

An empty comb

Pollen deposited in pollen basket

Bee Dance—a Remarkable Method of Communication

A honeybee, after finding a site with plenty of food, returns to the hive and informs its nestmates about the location of the site by 'dance language'—they move in close circles on the hive when the food source is nearby. This is called 'round dance'. However when the food site is located at a distance, they give a clue about direction and distance by performing another kind of dance—'waggle dance'. In this type of dance, a bee moves about in the pattern of figure '8'—waggling its abdomen from side to side. To perform waggle dance the bee moves in a 'straight line', takes a right turn, makes 'half circle' and returns to the starting point. She repeats the entire step but this time takes a left turn and returns to the starting point. The angle, at which a bee performs the straight-line move with respect to the vertical axis of the hive, communicates the angle at which food is located with respect to the sun's azimuth. And, the duration of the waggle run is indicative of the distance of food site from the hive.

Bee Venom—a Medicine

Stabbing and pumping venom in the skin of the enemies is the ultimate defence tactic of honeybees. Injected venom induces local pain and redness, with gradual swelling. A bee may lose its life after stinging the enemy since a part of its abdominal tissue is torn off together with the sting while trying to withdraw the sting from a tough-skinned victim. Bee venom is a clear, bitter-tasting liquid with a complex mixture of enzymes, peptides and other substances. Venom from bees has traditionally been used as a medicine to relieve pain and for arthritis, and is an active ingredient in 'Bee Venom Acupuncture'.

TERMITE (H: DEEMAK)

Termite mound—a strong structure

Termite Mound—a Marvel of Nature

Termite mound or 'termitarium', houses a colony of thousands to millions of ant-sized creatures—termites or white ants. In this area of Himalayan foothills, tall mounds are known to be constructed by the termite *Odontotermes* sp.

A mound has an intricate internal structure with a central hollow space called 'chimney' surrounded by a thick mud wall. The termite colony lives in the 'nest', which is located at the base of the chimney and the remaining vast expanse of the mound is entered by residents only for patrolling or repair work. Termites, working as a team, ingeniously craft the mound in a duration of a few years.

Workers and soldiers

As a whole, the mound is a sturdy structure; however, a powerful hit or heavy rainfall can break or significantly erode its walls. The damaged portion of the mound is quickly sealed by termites. Mounds as old as four thousand years discovered by scientists in Brazil are an evidence of their resilient nature.

Life of Termites

Termites are social insects and there exists a caste system in the colony. The bodies of members of each caste are specialized to perform only limited types of tasks; therefore, different castes are interdependent on each other for survival:

Workers are caretakers of the colony; they feed other castes, build and repair mounds, and look after eggs and young ones.

Termites on repair work

Soldiers protect the colony from enemies (such as ants).

Royal pair (King and Queen) increase numbers of other members by reproduction. Queen is an egg-laying machine; she produces an egg every 2–3 seconds throughout her lifespan of 10–20 years, and keeps supplying new individuals to the colony. She has a large body and resides inside the royal chamber with the king who is much smaller in size.

Termites are Choosy About Construction Material

Termites pick finer clay particles from the nearby soil, blend them with saliva and knead it into tiny balls before fixing at an appropriate place. Use of proper size of clay balls and cementation effect of saliva makes walls of the mound stronger and water resistant.

Mound Protects and Serves as Lungs for the Termite Colony

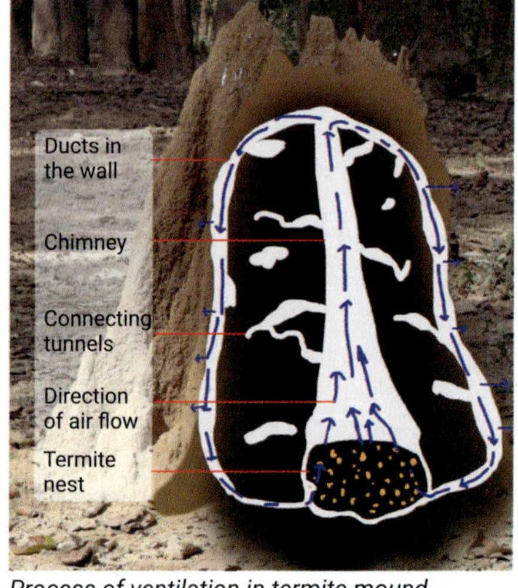

Process of ventilation in termite mound

Sealed from all sides, the mound protects termites from fluctuating climatic conditions, fire and enemies. However, inside such a tightly sealed structure, there arises an urgent need of ventilation—removal of metabolic waste gases generated by the inhabitants. The ingeniously engineered structure of the mound is equipped to handle this situation.

The design of the mound: in the center of the mound, there stands a long-hollow space above the nest called 'chimney'. The wall of the mound has a system of upright oriented 'ducts' interconnected by 'tunnels'. These ducts open in the chimney at the top of the mound. The surface wall of the mound has several micron-sized pores which are just large enough to allow passage of gases.

The process of ventilation: the waste gases produced by inhabitants of mounds accumulate in the chimney. It is brought to the surface walls via ducts for exchange with the cleaner outside air through micropores in the following manner:

At night, when surroundings of the mound are cooler, air filling the ducts in the wall of the mound cools faster than air in the chimney. The warmer (thus lighter) air (containing foul gases) in the chimney begins to rise and enter the ducts from the top of mound. Air entering the ducts pushes the duct's cooler (and cleaner) air downwards towards the nest, thereby ventilating the latter. In day time, air filling the ducts in the walls of the mound heats up quickly due to outside heat and the direction of flow of air inside the mound is reversed.

A broken mound exposing connecting tunnels

The process of ventilation in termite mounds has inspired 'building architects' to design self-cooling environmentally-friendly buildings.

Termites are Beneficial in Many Ways!

Termites have a bad reputation because of those varieties that eat and live in wood. However, there are several other kinds that live in soil and alter their surroundings in such a way that it creates a habitat for other creatures too. Ecologists use the term 'ecosystem engineers' for such generous organisms.

Tunnelling actions of termites in the soil improve water penetration that can significantly improve crop production in dry climate. Termites can variously modify properties of soil, and by feeding on litter, they decompose complex natural polymers such as cellulose and lignin. By breaking down these hard-to-degrade plant polymers, termites facilitate recycling of nutrients. Abundance of termites at a place is often indicative of a healthy ecosystem.

Termite mounds are indicators of presence of underground water and ore deposits, including gold. Mound soil can be used as fertilizer and for making bricks. Mounds are used as a refuge and nesting site for a variety of animals such as snakes, lizards, birds, frogs, etc.

GOLDEN MAHSEER

(H: MAHSEER)
Tor putitora

A gorgeous cold-water fish and an object of pride for local people. It belongs to the carp family of fishes, which also includes some of the well-known food fishes such as Catla, Rohu, Silver Carp, Grass carp, Mrigla, etc.

PC: GK

The body of Golden Mahseer is covered with large scales which have traditionally been used as playing cards in some parts of India. The flanks of adult fishes are golden-orange and the fins are yellow. It has fleshy lips, and there are two pairs of short barbels at the corner of the mouth. It prefers staying in rocky pools and flowing water where it feeds on small insects, fishes, worms and algae. It can grow over 2.7 m in length, and live over 17 years.

One might sight these shining golden fishes in clear waters of all major rivers of CTR. Over time, their population has declined due to hunting and loss of habitat. Golden Mahseer is amongst one of the world famous game-fishes.

GIANT DEVIL CATFISH

(H: GOONCH)
Bagarius yarrelli

PC: GK

Goonch is one of the largest catfish in India. Its greenish body can grow up to about 2 m in length, and weigh upto 135 kg. It feeds on small fishes, aquatic insects, prawns, etc.

Catfish

Catfish is a group of fishes named after their prominent barbels which resemble cat's whiskers. Catfishes are often naked and do not have scales on their bodies. Their barbels have several functions; they help in locating food, work as sensors for navigation in muddy water, holes and crevices, and are the displayer of aggression and defence. Most catfishes have bony spine-like extensions on upper and lower fins which are used as a weapon. Some catfishes can also introduce poison through these spines in the body of their enemies.

SIGNATURE SPIDERS

Argiope sp.

Size: females about 10 mm; males 5–6 mm; seen in bushy vegetation; web is decorated with an 'X'-shaped band made of zig-zag arranged silk.

Role of web decoration: 1) it makes the web more visible, thereby preventing damage by flying creatures and 2) makes spiders less noticeable to predators by acting as a bright background with which spiders can camouflage.

GIANT WOOD SPIDER

Nephila pilipes

Size: females about 40 mm; males 2–4 mm. Seen in forested areas and fringes of forest; makes large metre-sized webs often spanning across the gaps in foliage.

Spiders

Spiders belong to the group of animals called '*Arachnida*' (Greek, '*arakhnē*': Spider). Arachnids differ from insects in having eight legs (and not six legs as in insects). Scorpions, ticks and mites, are also arachnids. The body of a spider is divided into two parts: cephalothorax—head and thorax fused as a single unit, and abdomen—largest part of the spider's body. The abdomen encases organs for digestion, respiration, blood circulation, and silk production—building material for the spider web.

All spiders are predators and bulk of their diet constitutes insects. Some spiders use search, follow and attack on prey as their hunting strategy. Majority of others spin a web and wait on or near the web and attack the trapped insect. Spiders kill their prey by injecting venom through fangs located in the cephalothorax. Male spider usually dies after mating.

Spider Silk

The building material of spider silk is the protein 'fibroin'. The material is secreted as a liquid by the silk gland of spiders, and while it is being used by spiders for making the web, it solidifies as threads. Spiders not only use silk for making webs, but also use it for protection of young ones and to wrap prey. The tensile strength of spider silk is comparable to that of steel.

THREE-HUMPED LEUCAUGE SPIDER ▶
Leucauge decorata

Size: 8–10 mm; seen on bushes in the forested areas.

▲
CYRTARACHNE SPIDER
Cyrtarachne sp.

Size: 0.5–1 cm; seen among bushes.

NEOSCONA SPIDER
Neoscona sp.

Size: 0.5–1 cm; seen among bushes.
▼

▲
NILUS SPIDER
Nilus sp.

Size: 1.5–2 cm; seen near streams.

Ramganga river in Dhikala

Plants nurture our daily life by providing oxygen, food, water, clothes, medicines, and many more. It can thus be said that human and animal life cannot sustain on earth without plants. Estimates indicate that about 21% of global plant species are currently at the risk of extinction due to various threats; with habitat loss, overexploitation, invasive plant species, and climate change being the major ones.

The type of vegetation (plant life) in a geographical area depends on several interacting factors including climate, soil and natural events having occurred in the past. The vegetation of CTR and neighbouring areas is characteristic of northwest Himalayan foothills.

Of about 400,000 plant species known worldwide, nearly 47,000 species are found in India. Over 600 species of plants are known from CTR. The following section introduces about 155 species of plants including trees, shrubs and herbs that can be seen in CTR and surrounding areas.

Identifying Plants

To identify plants, one is recommended to take images of various parts of plants and compare with standard images provided in field guidebooks or reference websites created by experts and plant enthusiasts.

From images, plants are identified based on a combination of various features of leaves, flowers, stem, bark, and fruits (sometimes roots as well). The noteworthy features of plants include:

- *Habit of plant:* herb, shrub, tree, etc., and the overall look of plants.
- *Leaves:* types of leaves (simple or compound), shape and size, arrangement of veins, type of margin (plain, serrated, lobed, wavy, etc.), texture of upper and lower surface (glossy, hairy, rough, etc.), length of leaf stalk, arrangement of leaves (opposite or alternate), and the way leaves are arranged on twigs (e.g. clustered at the end or spread along the length of a twig).
- *Flowers:* colour, shape and size.

Arrangement, shape and numbers of various parts of flowers (petals, sepals, stamens and pistil), and arrangement of flowers on the twig (solo or in bunches).

- *Bark:* colour and texture of bark sometimes gives important clues about identification of trees. The texture of bark can be smooth (or more or less so), flaky, rough with thick chips, deeply or lightly cracked, tiled, with lumps, and spiny or thorny.
- *Fruits:* shape, texture and colour.

Photographing Plants

To take images of plants, a digital compact camera with not less than 50X zooming capability would be most suitable under all the situations (whether from safari vehicle or walking). For cameras with interchangeable lenses, one is recommended to carry the following lenses: a telephoto lens with focal length not less than 300 mm; and wide-angle lens with focal length 50 mm (or similar). In order to photograph minute details of plants, one may also carry a macro lens. It is however, advisable not to enter bushes in an attempt to take an impressive image.

Caution!

The medicinal uses of plants provided are only to introduce the reader to their medicinal importance. Treatment or therapy using plants or their parts depends on accurate identification of the plants, preparation or formulation of medicine, working out the correct dosage and method of application. In case of herbal therapy, one is advised to refrain from self-medication, and to visit/consult Ayurvedic practitioners for clinical advice.

Leaf types

Simple leaves: these are made of a single leaf blade, which is attached to the twig or stem with leaf stalk or petiole.

Compound leaves: the leaf blade is split into two or more independent leaflets. A compound leaf can be 'feathered type' or 'palmate type'. In the feathered type, a leaf is split into several leaflets along the central vein or midrib of leaf—'1-Pinnate Leaves'. Each leaflet may be further split into smaller leaflets—'2-Pinnate Leaves' or split one more time—'3-Pinnate Leaves'. In the palmate type, two or more leaflets radiate from a common point (resemble radiating fingers).

In the field, one might get confused if they are looking at a complete leaf or a leaflet. The two however can be easily differentiated as—a leaf has a tiny bud (axillary bud) at its base (point at which the leaf stalk is attached to the twig or stem) whereas a leaflet lacks it.

The margins of simple leaves and of leaflets of compound leaves may be smooth or serrated (toothed).

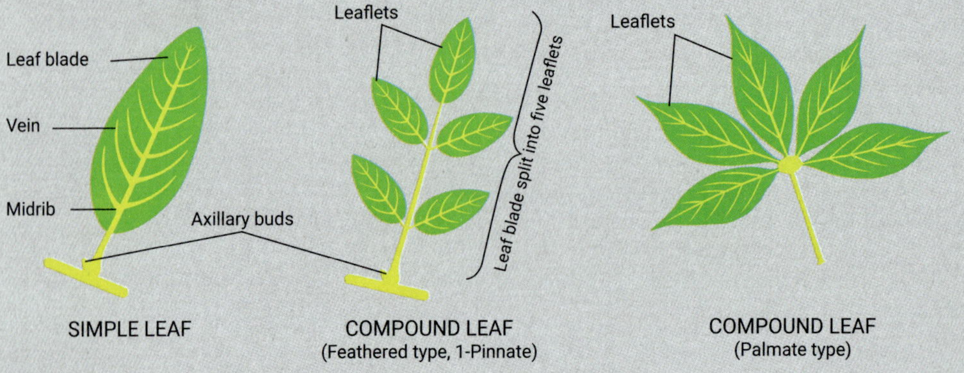

Arrangement of Plants in the Section

Plants section has been divided into two subsections—1) Trees, 2) Shrubs and Herbs. These have been defined as follows:

Trees: plants attached to the ground with a single, hard and woody trunk, growing twice to several times the height of an adult human.* The trunk divides into several woody branches and forms a crown.

Shrubs: plants with hard (but not woody) main stem which begins to divide into several branches just above, or right from ground level, and grow approximately as high as the height or upto twice the height of an adult human. Tall grasses have been included under shrubs.

Herbs: plants usually attached to the ground with one soft main stem and are either erect or running sideways (creepers) on the ground or with a climbing habit. Those which have erect habit, grow approximately to the waist level of an adult human. Short grasses have been included under herbs. Except for few, climbers and grasses have not been included in the book.

(*considering a height of 5.5–6 ft.)

Various trees have been arranged according to the types of leaves

a) Simple leaves (smooth margins) and lobed leaves

Lobed

Lobed

b) Simple leaves (serrated margins)

c) Compound feathered leaves

1-Pinnate

2-Pinnate

3-Pinnate

d) Palmate leaves and compound leaves with three leaflets

e) Other leaf shapes

Height of trees has been compared with the height of adult humans (5.5–6 ft).

Small (S):	about 2–4 times the height of adult human
Medium (M):	about 4–6 times the height of adult human
Large (L):	more than 6 times the height of adult human

Shrubs and herbs have been arranged according to the colour of their flowers

a) White-Cream

b) Orange-Yellow

c) Pink-Red

d) Blue-Violet

Naming of plants in the section

Each plant species has been denoted by common English name as primary name, and scientific name. Hindi or local names, wherever available, have also been provided. In cases where common English names of plants were not available, Hindi or local names have been used as primary names.

TREES

Over 100 species of trees are known from CTR, Sal being the most common amongst them...

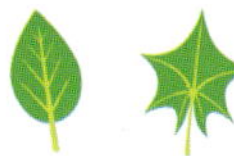

INDIAN ELM

(H: CHILBIL)

Holoptelea integrifolia

Size: L; *Leaves:* 8–15 cm long, arranged alternately on the branches. A tree with broad crown; acquires new leaves during months of April–May; seeds residing in the centre of flat disc are pressed to extract oil.

CLUSTER FIG

(H: GOOLAR)

Ficus racemosa

Size: M; *Leaves:* 10–20 cm long, arranged alternately on the branches. Its edible hairy fruits are clustered on the trunk and turn red when ripe; leaves are used as fodder for cattle and elephants.

HUMPED FIG

(H: CHHANCHRI)
Ficus tinctoria

Size: S–M; *Leaves:* 12–15 cm long, arranged alternately on the branches. It grows on other trees during early life; fruits turn bright yellow when ripe; leaves are good as cattle fodder and said to increase flow of milk in cows.

Other Figs

One may also find fig trees such as *Ficus arnottiana* (Rock Fig or H: Paras Pipal), and *Ficus rumphii;* the leaf of these resemble 'Peepal' (*Ficus religiosa*) but with shorter tips. The two grow on other trees during the early stage of life. The familiar *Ficus benghalensis* (Banyan Tree or H: Bargad) is also seen at places and attracts varieties of birds.

SPINOUS KINO TREE

(H: KASSI)
Bridelia retusa

Size: M–L; *Leaves:* 8–15 cm long, arranged alternately on the branches. Its spherical fruits are avidly consumed by birds.

INDIAN GOOSEBERRY

(H: AMLA)
Phyllanthus emblica

Size: M; *Leaves:* about 10–15 mm long, arranged alternately on the branches. The arrangement of its leaves (which are not leaflets) along twigs resembles feathered compound leaves.

Male flowers

Female flowers

MONKEY-FACE TREE
(H: ROHINI)
Mallotus philippensis

Size: S–M; *Leaves:* 8–23 cm long, arranged alternately on the branches. A small tree that appears dense when clothed with new leaves; young leaves are pretty violet in colour; crimson powdery dust covering ripe fruits is used for dyeing silk, in Hindu religious ceremonies, and as medicine; common throughout CTR and favourite food for elephants.

Fruits

Papery jacket over fruits

TEAK (H: SAGON) *Tectona grandis*

Size: L; *Leaves:* 30–60 cm long, arranged in opposite pairs. One can find pure stretches of teak at the boundaries of CTR, such as near Amdanda gate; an important Indian timber tree.

KEKARA (L: KEKRA) *Phoebe lanceolata*

Size: S; *Leaves:* 12–20 cm long, arranged alternately and crowded at the ends of branches. It is seen in forested areas in shady and damp places.

MEDA (H: MEDA) *Litsea monopetala*

Size: M; *Leaves:* 10–25 cm long, arranged alternately and crowded at the ends of branches. It gets a flush of flowers on bare twigs in March–April; sighted in thinly forested areas and along fringes of forest.

WHITE TEAK (H: GAMHAR)
Gmelina arborea

Size: M; *Leaves:* 10–20 cm long, arranged in opposite pairs. The heart-shaped leaves are darker above and lighter below; bears ovoid fruits; the fruit, bark and root of this tree are used as medicine; its strong and durable wood is used for making boats, plywood, toys, etc.

CHAMROR (H: CHAMROR)
Ehretia laevis

Size: S; *Leaves:* 8–15 cm long, arranged alternately on branches. It is seen in thinly forested areas; bears a bunch of tiny white flowers and bright orange fruits during the months of March–May.

BITTER OLEANDER (H: KURCHI)
Holarrhena pubescens

Size: S; *Leaves:* 15–30 cm long, arranged in opposite pairs. It is seen along fringes of forests and thinly forested areas; bears bunches of white mildly fragrant flowers in May–June; leaves, bark and fruits have traditionally been used to treat dysentery, constipation, piles and urinary disorders.

DUDHI (H: DUDHI)
Wrightia arborea

Size: S; *Leaves:* 8–15 cm long, slightly velvety arranged in opposite pairs. It is seen along fringes of forests and thinly forested areas; bark and roots are given as antidote to snake and scorpion bite.

EAST INDIAN EBONY

(H: TENDU)

Diospyros melanoxylon

Size: M–L; *Leaves:* 8–15 cm long, arranged alternately or nearly-opposite pairs. It is seen in thinly forested areas; has grey or blackish bark which is cracked into rectangular pieces; fruits are eaten by birds and bats, and wood has been used for making boxes, beams, carriage shafts, ploughs, etc. (p.299).

▲

INDIAN BUTTER TREE

(H: MAHUA)

Madhuca longifolia

Size: M–L; *Leaves:* 12–18 cm long, clustered at the tip of branches. It is seen in thinly forested areas. Mahua is a very useful tree—wood is durable and used for making doors, frames and furniture; sugar rich sweet smelling flowers are eaten raw or after drying in the sun, and used to make strong smelling country liquor 'mahua wine'; oil from seeds is used in oil-lamps, cooking and to cure skin disease.

▼

SAGE LEAVED ALANGIUM (H: AKOAL)

Alangium salviifolium

Size: S; *Leaves:* 8–15 cm long, arranged alternately on the branches. It is seen in thinly forested areas; bears fragrant white flowers in March–April; spherical fruits which turn blackish are edible.

HALDU (H: HALDU)
Haldina cordifolia

Size: L; *Leaves:* 10–22 cm long, heart-shaped leaves are arranged in opposite pairs. The flowers of Haldu are crowded together as a ball; wood is suitable for making furniture, boards, ornamental objects, toys, etc.

KAIM (L: PHALDU) *Mitragyna parvifolia* ▶

Size: M–L; *Leaves:* 5–15 cm long arranged in opposite pairs. It is seen in thinly forested areas and along fringes of forest; flowers are arranged in a ball; wood is suitable for making toys, ornamental objects, etc.

Cluster of flowers

Fruit capsules

BRIDAL COUCH TREE (H: BHAULAN)
Hymenodictyon orixense

Size: M–L; *Leaves:* 10–25 cm long, arranged in opposite pairs. It is seen in thinly forested areas and along fringes of forest; leaves turn bright yellowish before falling in early winter; wood is used for making agricultural implements, toys and other small items.

TILA
(H: TILA)
Wendlandia heynei

Size: S; *Leaves:* 10–23 cm long, narrow-long, leaves are arranged in opposite pairs. It is seen along seasonal water channels and landslips; the reddish-brown wood is used for making agricultural implements.

SMALL FLOWERED CRAPE MYRTLE (H: DHAURI) *Lagerstroemia parviflora*

Size: M–L; *Leaves:* 6–10 cm long; narrow leaves with short stalk are arranged in opposite pairs. A common tree seen in forest, and dots grasslands close to the forested areas; bears small sweet smelling flowers and new leaves in May–June; leaves turn purplish-brown before falling in late winters, adding beauty to the landscape; wood is durable and used for making agricultural implements.

Dotting grassland

INDIAN BLACKBERRY (H: JAMUN) *Syzygium cumini*

Size: M–L; *Leaves:* 8–15 cm long, arranged in opposite pairs. It is seen in low lying areas, swampy areas, and along streams and rivers; seeds are used to control blood sugar as some of the substances in the seeds prevent breakdown of starch into sugars; wood is suitable for use underwater.

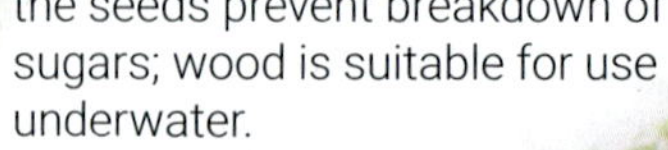

Fruits clustered as round heads

AXLE-WOOD TREE (H/L: BAKLI)
Anogeissus latifolia

Size: L; *Leaves:* 5–10 cm long, arranged alternately. It is seen on slopes, and alluvial banks; leaves turn into pretty purplish-brown or coppery before falling in winters; it is a source of resin 'gum-ghatti' which is tapped from its trunk and used in food, medicine and cosmetics as a stabilizer; its tough and elastic wood is used for making furniture, agricultural implements, carrying-poles, etc.

Triphala—a Herbal Preparation to Promote Healthy Life

It is a well known and highly effective Ayurvedic medicine. Triphala is made from fruits of Amala (*Phyllanthus emblica*), Bahera (*Terminalia bellirica*) and Harad (*Terminalia chebula*). The medicine has been used to maintain a healthy gut, and disease free longer life. The major chemical compounds identified in Triphala preparation include tannins, gallic acid, ellagic acid and chebulinic acid. These substances are responsible for various medicinal properties of Triphala.

Tendu Leaves—a Suitable Material for Making 'Bidis'

Tendu is a tree of high commercial importance as its leaves are used as wrapping material for *Bidis* (a kind of inexpensive cigarette), popular among rural Indians. To make *bidis,* tobacco is rolled within a dried leaf of Tendu and tied with a thin thread. Leaves of many trees such as Mango, Flame-of-the-Forest (Palash), Banana and Jackfruit have also been tried in the past to roll tobacco. Tendu leaf however, was found to be most suitable owing to its large size, pliability, smooth texture and capability of being rolled around tobacco without getting cracked. Upon lighting, its smoke goes well with the flavour of tobacco. Tendu is more common in central Indian dry deciduous forests.

BELLERIC MYROBALAN

(H: BAHERA)

Terminalia bellirica

Size: L; *Leaves:* 8–20 cm long, crowded at the end of branches. It is seen in the thinly forested areas; fruits are liked by monkeys and deer, and are used as one of the components of Ayurvedic preparation 'Triphala' (p.299).

BURMESE SILK ORCHID

(H: JHINJHORA)

Bauhinia racemosa

Size: S; *Leaves:* 2.5–5 cm long, broader than long, and split into two lobes at the tip. Leaves are arranged alternately. It is seen in thinly forested areas and drier parts of the forest; fibres obtained from the bark are used to make ropes.

ROXBURGH'S BAUHINIA
(H: SEMLA)
Bauhinia roxburghiana

Size: S–M; *Leaves:* 10–12 cm long, broader than long, and split into two lobes at the tip (which is shallower than in Jhinjhora). Leaves are arranged alternately. Gum collected by making cuts in bark is used in sweets and in medicine.

ORCHID TREE
(H: KACHNAR)
Bauhinia variegata

Size: M; *Leaves:* 12–15 cm long, split into two lobes at the tip. Leaves are arranged alternately. It bears fragrant flowers during March–April; gum obtained from the trunk of this tree is used as a substitute for 'gum-ghatti' (p.299).

CUDDAPAH ALMOND
(H: CHIRONJI)
Buchanania cochinchinensis

Size: M; *Leaves:* 15–25 cm long, arranged alternately at the tips of branches. Its roasted nuts are called 'Chironji' used in sweets, *khir*, etc.

MANGO (H: AAM)
Mangifera indica

Size: M; *Leaves:* 15–30 cm long, arranged alternately on the twigs. A familiar tree known for its fruits; dried kernels of fruits have been used as a substitute for wheat flour.

INDIAN MARKING NUT TREE

(H: BHILAWA)
Semecarpus anacardium

Size: M; *Leaves:* 22–60 cm long. Leaves are broader towards their tips and are clustered at the end of branches. It is seen in shady areas in Sal forest; fruits yield a substance which has been used as a substitute for marking-ink; fruits have several medicinal uses too.

HIMALAYAN MAPLE

(L: KIRMOLI)
Acer oblongum

Size: M–L; *Leaves:* 6–15 cm long with long stalk, arranged in opposite pairs. It can be seen along the northern boundary of CTR; wood is used in making agricultural implements and drinking cups.

Fruits

KYDIA (H: PULU) *Kydia calycina*

Size: S–M; *Leaves:* 10–15 cm in diameter, arranged alternately; bark has been used to clarify sugar.

SAL (H: SAKHU)
Shorea robusta

Size: L; *Leaves:* 10–20 cm long, arranged alternately at the tip of branches. It is the most abundant tree in CTR and well known for its strong and durable wood; resin from Sal is used as incense; leaves are used for making plates and as wraps; oil extracted from fruits is used for burning.

Winged fruits

Flowers

VELVETY MILIUSA (H: DOM SAL)
Miliusa velutina

Size: S; *Leaves:* 10–25 cm long, arranged alternately at the tips of branches.

SHOEBUTTON ARDISIA
Ardisia solanacea

Size: S; *Leaves:* 10–20 cm long, arranged alternately. It is seen in shady and damp places; bears pink flowers of 1.5–2 cm diameter.

SAND PAPER TREE (H: SIHORA)
Streblus asper

Size: S; *Leaves:* 5–10 cm long, with shallowly toothed margins are arranged alternately. Its twigs are used as a tooth brush, and rough leaves as a substitute for sandpaper.

ELEPHANT EAR FIG (H: TIRMALA)
Ficus auriculata

Size: S; *Leaves:* 15–40 cm long, arranged alternately. The broad leaves with long stalks are reminiscent of ears of elephants. The figs are edible and leaves are good fodder for cattle.

PAPER MULBERRY

(H: JANGALI TOOT)

Broussonetia papyrifera

Size: S; *Leaves:* 12–24 cm long, arranged alternately on the branches. Shape of leaves variable. It can be seen near villages outside CTR; female flowers are arranged in a ball; fruits are fleshy and bright red; bark provides fine fibres that can be made into paper.

GREWIA

Grewia sp.

Size: S–M; *Leaves:* about 8–10 cm long, slightly heart-shaped at base. Seen along fringes of forest, slopes and valleys.

◀ **DROOPING FIG** (H: KHAIN)
Ficus semicordata

Size: S; *Leaves:* 15–25 cm long. Leaves have an asymmetrical base and are arranged alternately. It can be seen along ravines and rivers; leaves are good fodder for cattle.

GENTHI (H: GENTHI) ▶
Boehmeria rugulosa

Size: S; *Leaves:* 8–15 cm long, arranged alternately on the branches. It is seen along the streams and ravines; wood is fairly hard and is used to make items such as utensils.

INDIAN WILLOW (H: JALMALA) ▼
Salix tetrasperma

Size: S–M; *Leaves:* 8–15 cm long, small narrow leaves are arranged alternately. It can be seen near gorges and streams; twigs are used to make baskets, and leaves as animal fodder.

PUTRANJIVA (H: PUTIJIA)
Putranjiva roxburghii

Size: S; *Leaves:* 5–10 cm long with finely serrated margins, are arranged alternately on the branches. It is a dense tree with drooping branches; necklaces of its seeds are tied around the necks of children to protect them from disease.

TIGER'S MILK SPRUCE
(H: KHINNA)
Falconeria insignis

Size: S–M; *Leaves:* 15–24 cm long, arranged alternately on the branches. Seen in thinly forested areas; milky juice from this tree is said to be poisonous.

KODA TREE

(H: PUNA)

Ehretia acuminata

Size: S–M; *Leaves:* 10–18 cm long, arranged alternately on the branches. It can be seen in thinly forested areas and fringes of forest.

INDIAN CHERRY

(H: LASURA)

Cordia dichotoma

Size: S–M; *Leaves:* 8–15 cm long, arranged alternately on the branches. It is seen in thinly forested areas; fruits are eaten and leaves are used as plates; sticky pulp of fruits has been used to trap birds.

WILD GUAVA
(H: KUMBHI)
Careya arborea

Size: M–L; *Leaves:* 15–30 cm long, clustered at the ends of branches. It can be seen in shady forested areas and sometimes along fringes of forest; leaves turn attractive reddish before falling in late winters; fruits of Kumbhi are eaten by animals.

CROCODILE-BARK TREE
(H: SAIN)
Terminalia elliptica

Size: L; *Leaves:* 12–22 cm long with finely serrated margins, are arranged alternately or in a nearly-opposite manner. This tall tree with bark exfoliating in thick rectangular pieces, can be seen in thinly forested areas and along fringes of forest; wood of Sain is very hard and used for making houses and agricultural implements; the tree has remarkable capacity to store water: about 4–6 litres of potable water can be collected by making a small hole in the stem.

Fruits

TOOTHED LEAF CHILLA

(H: CHILLA)

Casearia tomentosa

Size: S; *Leaves:* 10–15 cm long, arranged alternately on the branches. The margins of long-narrow leaves are finely serrated. It is seen in thinly forested areas and fringes of forest; pounded fruits or fruit juice is used as fish poison.

Leaf Fall—an Altruistic Death

Like animals, plants also age and die or show signs of 'senescence'. In annual plants (wheat, rice, etc.), senescence leads to death of whole plants leaving behind grains full of nutrition. For longer living plants such as trees, senescence comes to leaves which is observed in the form of splendid colours of fall. Leaf (or whole plant) senescence is a programmed and well-regulated process wherein ordered changes occur in the functioning of cells. The aim of these sequential changes is to breakdown the contents of leaves and relocate the nutrients to other parts of the plant. This nutrient management process maximizes the fitness of plants. For example, the earliest and most evident cellular change during leaf senescence is breakdown of plant chloroplasts (responsible for colour change of leaves) that holds up to 70% of plant protein.

The last step in senescence of a leaf is leaf fall. Before falling, leaves (also fruits and flowers) develop a fracture line (Abscission zones) at the point where it is attached to the branch. Degradation of cells along this line weakens the link between branch and leaf stalk. The loosely attached leaf finally falls under the force of gravity, action of wind, or due to shaking by animals.

INDIAN PLUM
(H: BER)
Ziziphus mauritiana

Size: S–M; *Leaves:* 2.5–8 cm long (usually 3–4 cm), alternately arranged on thorny branches. The upper surface of leaves is glossy whereas underside is hairy; edible fruits are round, oval or ellipsoid.

KATH BER
(H: KATH BER)
Ziziphus xylopyrus

Size: S; *Leaves:* 2–8 cm long, arranged alternately. It is seen in thinly forested areas.

CEYLON ROSEWOOD (H: KALA SIRIS)
Albizia odoratissima

Size: L; *Leaves:* the leaf is split into 3–8 pairs of side stalks, each of which bears 8–20 pairs of small leaflets of about 2 cm length. Its wood is suitable for making furniture, agricultural implements and house-building.

WHITE SIRIS
(H: SAFED SIRIS)
Albizia procera

Size: L; *Leaves:* the leaf is split into 3–5 pairs of side stalks, each of which bears 6–12 pairs of leaflets of about 2–5 cm length. It can be seen near ravines, streams and other similar localities; wood has been used for making sugarcane crushers, wheels and agricultural implements.

BLACK CATECHU
(H: KHAIR)
Acacia catechu

Size: S; *Leaves:* the leaf is split into 10–30 pairs of side stalks each of which bears 30–50 pairs of tiny leaflets of about 4–5 mm length. It can be seen along rivers and streams together with companion Sheesham, forming 'Khair-Sisso' stretch; it is source of Catechu (H: Kattha), which is obtained by boiling chips of heartwood with water.

FRAGRANT PADRI TREE (H: PADAL)
Stereospermum chelonoides

Size: M–L; *Leaves:* the leaf is split into 3–4 pairs of oppositely arranged leaflets, plus a leaflet at the terminus; leaflets are 8–15 cm long, velvety with short stalk. It can be seen along the fringes of forest and thinly forested areas; provides useful wood, and bark has medicinal uses.

CHINABERRY TREE
(H: BAKAIN)
Melia azedarach

Size: S–M; *Leaves:* the leaf is split into side stalks, each of which bears 1–4 cm long leaflets with serrated margins. Its leaves and bark have been used to relieve fever, pain, skin diseases and stomach disorders.

INDIAN ROSEWOOD (H: SHEESHAM)
Dalbergia sissoo

Size: M–L; *Leaves:* the leaf is split into 3–5 leaflets of about 2–5 cm length and are arranged alternately. Pure Sheesham stretch can be seen along streams and river beds; wood is strong and elastic, and used for several purposes; leaves are good fodder for cattle.

GOLDEN SHOWER
(H: AMALTASH)
Cassia fistula

Size: M; *Leaves:* the leaf is split into 4–8 pairs of 8–15 cm long leaflets. It bears long hanging bunches of bright yellow flowers during April–June. Amaltash has been widely used in Ayurveda, Unani and Chinese traditional medicines.

INDIAN ASH TREE
(H/L: JHINGHAN)
Lannea coromandelica

Size: M–L; *Leaves:* the leaf is split into 3–6 pairs of leaflets, and a solo leaflet at the terminus. The 8–15 cm long leaflets are arranged in opposite pairs. It is seen in thinly forested areas and remains leafless during late winters; gets new leaves, flowers and fruits during spring and early summers; wounded bark provides 'Jhinghan Gum' which is used in calico printing and confectionery.

CEYLON OAK

(H: KUSUM)

Schleichera oleosa

Size: M–L; *Leaves:* the leaf is split into 2-4 pairs of about 5–23 cm long stalk-less leaflets, arranged in opposite pairs. The tree bears young red leaves in March–April presenting a stunning sight; shelters the Lac insect which produces a fine quality of commercial 'Lac' (a resinous secretion).

KHARPAT

(H: KHARPAT)

Garuga pinnata

Size: M–L; *Leaves:* the leaf is split into 6-9 pairs of about 5–10 cm long leaflets arranged in opposite pairs, and a solo leaflet at the terminus. Leaflets have serrated margins. It can be seen in thinly forested areas; remains leafless for several months and gets a new flush of leaves, and flowers in the month of April–May.

Nascent Red Spring Leaves—a Protective Strategy of Plants

In many trees, younger or nascent leaves display a range of reddish-orange colouration; also in several other trees older leaves turn yellow, red or magenta before fall. Leaf colour is due to predominance of one or more pigments.

> Three main groups of pigments impart colour to leaves—chlorophyll (green), carotenoids (yellow, orange and red) and flavonoids (yellow, red, blue and magenta). Tempting colours of many fruits and flowers are primarily due to carotenoids and flavonoids (p.351).

A leaf appears green if it has chlorophyll as the predominant pigment, which masks the colour of other pigments. In senescent leaves (nearing fall), chlorophyll is broken down into colourless constituents; this unmasks the other two groups of pigments, i.e. carotenoids and flavonoids, which degrade rather slowly. Before fall, a leaf would appear yellow if carotenoids are left behind, and with hues of red if 'anthocyanins' (a flavonoid) are accumulated. Young leaves in contrast, lack chlorophyll and have a higher amount of flavonoids, which gives them various spectacular shades of red. And, as leaves mature, the production and accumulation of chlorophyll turns them green.

What do trees achieve by shifting colouration of their young leaves and senescent leaves to various shades of red, or why do they put more anthocyanins in the leaves? Many scientific explanations have been put forward to rationalize this puzzle of nature, but a unanimous acceptance is still lacking. Anthocyanins acts as a sunscreen to protect leaves from the damaging effect of bright light, and also work as an antioxidant. Thus, anthocyanins temporarily protect young leaves (wherein protective gears have not yet developed) and dying leaves (protective gears on decline) from harsh conditions.

Another set of explanations appreciate the role of redness of leaves as a defence tactic against leaf damaging insects. Red leaves look unattractive or invisible to certain insects blind to red colour. These insects thus are not attracted towards trees with red leaves for feeding or laying eggs.

Another explanation states that red colour is a signal for leaves being unpalatable, less nutritious or toxic to foragers. The latter thus avoid feeding on such leaves.

A Kusum tree in the month of April

INDIAN MAHOGANY

(H: TOON)

Toona ciliata

Size: M–L; *Leaves:* the leaf is split into 4–15 pairs of 5–15 cm long leaflets arranged in opposite pairs. It can be seen in thinly forested areas; a fast growing tree; provides useful reddish wood which is said to be resistant to attack by termites.

INDIAN BEECH (H: KARANJ)

Pongamia pinnata

Size: S–M; *Leaves:* the leaf is split into 3–4 pairs of leaflets arranged in opposite pairs, and a solo leaflet at the tip. The leaflets are 6–10 cm long. It can be seen in thinly forested areas and at the boundaries of CTR.

WOOD APPLE (H: BEL)

Aegle marmelos

Size: S–M; *Leaves:* the leaf is split into three 5–10 cm long leaflets. It is seen in thinly forested areas. Bel is known for its spherical hard shelled fruit with aromatic pulp, which is used as a laxative (substance used to loosen stool).

CORAL TREE (H: DHAUL DHAK)

Erythrina sp.

Size: S; *Leaves:* split into three leaflets. It bears bunches of bright red flowers during March–April which attract birds seeking nectar and insects.

FLAME-OF-THE-FOREST (H: PALASH) *Butea monosperma*

Size: S–M; *Leaves:* the leaf is split into three 15–20 cm long leaflets. It bears spectacular bright red flowers during March–April, which attract several species of birds seeking nectar and insects; flowers provide orange dye; leaves are used as plates and as wraps.

UJJAIN DESMODIUM TREE
(H: SANDAN)
Desmodium oojeinense

Size: S–M; *Leaves:* the leaf is split into three leaflets. The terminal leaflet is larger (8–15 cm) than others (6–10 cm). The tree looks outstanding in March–April when it bears bunches of pink flowers; the wood has been used for making agricultural appliances and furniture.

RED SILK-COTTON (H: SEMAL) *Bombax ceiba*

Size: L; *Leaves:* the leaf is split into 5–7 leaflets (15–24 cm long) radiating from a common point. It can be seen in open places and near grasslands; bark has prominent large conical prickles particularly in young trees; bears bright red flowers in February–March visited by several species of birds which feast on nectar; seeds are covered with white silken fibres which have been used to stuff pillows and cushions; wood is soft and suitable for making match sticks and match boxes; roots have been used to treat intestinal and heart disorders, and diabetes; extract of prickles is used for treatment of acne.

TREES WITH OTHER LEAF SHAPES

CHIR PINE (H: CHIR)
Pinus roxburghii

Size: L; *Leaves:* in the form of bundles of needle-like leaves. The tree provides good quality resin which is a source of Turpentine oil and Rosin. The former is used in preparation of paints, varnishes and polishes, and the latter in soaps, sealing wax, inks and disinfectants.

SHRUBS
AND
HERBS
About 500 species of
shrubs, herbs and grasses
are known from CTR...

◀ **INDIAN MILKWEED** (H: MADAR)
Calotropis procera

Shrub; *Leaves:* about 18–20 cm long; *Flowers:* about 2 cm dia. It is seen in open areas such as ravines, river banks, etc.; similar to *Calotropis gigantea,* however it differs in shape of flowers and leaves.

▲
WOODWORM
Artemisia sp.

Shrub or Herb; *Leaves:* 5–10 cm long segmented; *Flowers:* about 4–6 mm long. It is seen in open sunny areas; leaves and flowers have aromatic smell; essential oils from this plant have been used in folk and modern medicines.

FALSE DAISY (H: BHRINGRAJ) ▶
Eclipta prostrata

Herb; *Leaves:* about 3–7 cm long, narrow with serrated margins; *Flowers:* about 1 cm dia. Seen growing in moist areas; it is covered with minute hairs; has been traditionally used to prevent loss and greying of hair, treatment of asthma and skin diseases.

BIG EGGPLANT

Solanum erianthum

Shrub; *Leaves:* about 10–18 cm long and arranged alternately or nearly-opposite; *Flowers:* about 1.5–2 cm dia. It is seen in shady places and near human habitations; fruits and leaves are used to treat urinary disorders, leprosy, malaria and as a purgative.

WILD BERRY

Maesa sp.

Shrub; *Leaves:* about 8–12 cm long, serrated, arranged alternately; *Flowers:* about 5 mm dia. It is seen in shady forested areas.

CATWEED

Ageratina adenophora

Shrub; *Leaves:* about 5–12 cm long diamond shaped, margins serrated, arranged in opposite pairs; *Flowers*: heads about 5–10 mm dia. It is seen along the tracks in shady and moist areas; an aggressive colonizer and native to tropical America which has invaded several parts of India.

COATBUTTONS

Tridax procumbens

Herb; *Leaves:* about 3–6 cm long, slightly hairy with coarsely serrated margins; *Flowers:* heads about 1 cm dia. It is seen in open moist areas where it spreads at ground level; flowers stand 20–30 cm above ground; native to Central America and has invaded several parts of India; flowers are liked by butterflies seeking nectar.

SHOWY DESMODIUM

(H: JATSALPAN)

Phyllodium pulchellum

Shrub; *Leaves:* split into three leaflets of about 8–13 cm length; *Flowers:* about 5–8 mm long, and are covered with round leaf-like structures. It can be seen in shady forested areas.

CAMEL'S FOOT CLIMBER

(H/L: MALOOAN)

Bauhinia vahlii

Climber; *Leaves:* up to 45 cm long, split into two halves at the tip; *Flowers:* about 2–3 cm dia. Seen in the forested areas; leaves are stitched together to make plates, cups and rain caps.

ORANGE JASMINE
(H: KAMINI)
Murraya paniculata

Shrub or Small tree; *Leaves:* split into 8–10 leaflets with 3–8 cm length; *Flowers:* about 2–2.5 cm long. It can be seen in thinly forested areas; bears white fragrant flowers during spring and rainy season.

CURRY LEAF (H: KARI PATTA)
Murraya koenigii

Shrub; *Leaves:* split into 10–25 leaflets with nearly 2–5 cm length; *Flowers:* about 1 cm long. It is commonly seen along tracks in shaded or partly shaded areas; bears bunches of white fragrant flowers during April–May; leaves are used to flavour curries.

Floral Scent—Helps in Locating Flowers by Night

Many flowers emit a blend of volatile substances from petals, stamens and anthers, known as 'Floral Scent'. Scientists have identified over 1,700 compounds in the floral scents across flowering plants. Certain classes of chemical compounds such as terpenoids, benzenoids esters, ketones, etc., are the most common constituents of floral scents. The composition and relative abundance of chemical constituents impart uniqueness to each fragrance. Scent is meant to attract pollinators, therefore, emission of scent by many flowers peaks only during that period of the day when the potential pollinator is most active. Flowers pollinated by animals such as bats and moths active at night, emit strong scent during night time. The emitted scent reveals the location of flowers to the distant pollinators in pitch dark. Once pollinated, flowers generally cease to emit scent.

Plants' Strategies to Protect Themselves from Being Eaten

Many plant-eating animals (insects and other large animals) can consume a sizeable portion of plant body, posing a threat to the survival of the plant. To protect themselves, many plants have devised methods to limit damage caused by animals.

Thorns, spines, dense hair and toughened leaves borne by plants are meant to deter predators.

Many plants produce an arsenal of chemical weapons (such as alkaloids, phenolics and terpenes) which repel or even kill their predators. These chemicals have their unique ways to impart protection. *Alkaloids* such as pyrrolizidines, nicotine, caffeine and sanguinarine, to name a few, cause poisoning when plants containing them are consumed in significant quantities. *Terpenes* are repellents, and release of certain volatile terpenes when a plant is being consumed by insects might attract the predators of the insects. *Phenolics* such as tannins and lignin present in all the plants, interfere with digestion and reduce palatability of forage; tannins taste bitter and also have the ability to render digestive enzymes non-functional, and lignin acts as a barrier between digestive enzymes and digestible nutrients present in the consumed foliage.

Silica laden leaves of grasses make them abrasive and are less agreeable to foragers. *Latex* and *resins* (sticky substances) oozing when a plant is wounded by foraging insects can intoxicate or entrap the latter.

Blooms of Fire-Flame Bush (*Woodfordia fruticosa*) near the northern boundary of CTR

▲

ORANGEBERRY

(H: BAN NIMBU)

Glycosmis pentaphylla

Shrub; *Leaves:* split into 3–7 leaflets of about 10–15 cm in length; *Flowers:* 5–8 mm long. Seen commonly along tracks; cool shade under this plant provides refuge to animals from scorching heat.

▲

JACKAL JUJUBE

(H: MAKOH)

Ziziphus oenoplia

Shrub; *Leaves:* about 3 cm long, margins serrated, arranged alternately; *Flowers:* about 3 mm dia. This thorny plant can be seen along the fringes of forest, and thinly forested areas; spherical fruits turn black when fully ripe.

▲
CEYLON HOUND'S TONGUE
Cynoglossum zeylanicum

Herb; *Leaves:* about 3–8 cm long with faintly serrated margins; *Flowers:* about 5–7 mm dia. It can be seen in open areas and along fringes of forest. Plants similar to *Cynoglossum zeylanicum* but with more bluish or smaller flowers are also seen. These may represent different species of genus *Cynoglossum*.

▲
INDIAN BORAGE
Trichodesma indicum

Herb; *Leaves:* about 2.5–6 cm long, narrow and stalk-less leaves are arranged in opposite pairs; *Flowers:* about 1–1.5 cm dia. It is seen in open areas growing close to the ground; stem, buds and leaves have prominent hair.

CREPE GINGER
(H: KEU)
Cheilocostus speciosus

Herb; *Leaves:* about 15–20 cm long; *Flowers:* about 6–8 cm long. Seen blooming during late summer and rainy seasons; has been used for several medicinal purposes including treatment of asthma, constipation, skin diseases and snake bite.

MALABAR NUT (H: VASIKA)

Justicia adhatoda

Herb; *Leaves:* about 10–20 cm long; *Flowers:* about 2.5–3 cm long. Seen in thinly forested areas and near human habitations; valued as a medicinal plant for treatment of cough, asthma, skin diseases and joint pain.

HEAD LEUCAS (H: DRONAPUSHPI)

Leucas cephalotes

Herb; *Leaves:* about 5–8 cm long with serrated margins; *Flowers:* about 1–2 cm long. The plant is covered with dense hair; seen growing in open areas near human habitations and fringes of forest; syrup of flowers has been used as remedy for cough and cold.

INDIAN SQUIRREL TAIL (H: BINDA)
Colebrookea oppositifolia

Shrub; *Leaves:* about 10–15 cm long with serrated margins; *Flowers:* 3–4 mm long. Seen in thinly forested areas, along fringes of forest and ravines.

HILL GLORY BOWER (H: BHANT)
Clerodendrum infortunatum

Shrub; *Leaves:* about 5–20 cm long; *Flowers:* about 1.5–2 cm dia. Seen in forested areas, and along fringes of forest; sweet scent from flowers creates soothing environs in the forest during March–April.

BENGAL POGOSTEMON

Pogostemon benghalensis

Herb; *Leaves:* about 5–15 cm long; *Flowers:* about 5–7 mm long. Seen commonly in forested areas, and along fringes of forests.

SPINY LEPIDAGATHIS

Lepidagathis cuspidata

Herb; *Leaves:* about 5–10 cm long; *Flowers:* about 1–1.5 cm long. It is seen in open areas, ravines, sandy banks, etc.

FALSE STRAWBERRY

Duchesnea indica

Herb; *Leaves:* split into three, about 2–4 cm long leaflets; *Flowers:* about 1.5–2 cm dia. Grows close to the ground in moist places.

LANTANA

Lantana camara

Shrub; *Leaves:* about 3–9 cm long with serrated margins; *Flowers:* occur in clusters.

Seen along tracks in thinly forested areas, fringes of forest and grasslands, from where it is periodically removed by the Forest Department.

It bears flowers of many colours: reddish, orangish, whitish-yellow, pink and bluish.

Alien Invasive Plants—a Menace by Outsiders

Plants that are non-native to a country or continent (exotic or non-indigenous) are called alien plant species. These plants have been introduced outside their native habitat range by humans either purposely or accidentally. They have superior capability to adapt, grow and spread aggressively in the new environment, out-competing the local flora (they invade). Thus, by replacing native flora of an area, alien invasive plants not only cause a loss of plant diversity, but also affect animals which survive on native flora. Alien invasive plants are considered to be one of the major threats to global biodiversity.

What makes these exotic plants a successful competitor? The key winning factors are: long flowering, fruiting and seed dispersal period; production of large numbers of easily dispersible seeds; short regeneration time and short juvenile period. In addition, they resist being eaten by herbivores by releasing certain noxious chemicals. These chemicals also suppress the growth of nearby native plants.

A variety of climatic conditions and habitats in India offer a range of options to invading plants for flourishing successfully. About 170 alien invasive plants have been documented in the country; most of which are natives of tropical America.

Lantana—Beauty but at a Cost

Lantana is native to South America and was introduced in India, in 1809, by the East India Company as an ornamental hedge plant. Today, it has invaded and naturalized almost the entire country.

An expanse covered with Lantana in full bloom is visited by colourful butterflies and birds, presenting a mesmerizing sight. This picture however, does not please an ecologist. To them, Lantana is the most undesirable invasive weed which adversely affects the native ecosystem. A dense patch of Lantana attracts only few bird species (those enjoy its fruits, and take refuge under dense bushes) which would have been more if a variety of native weeds persisted. The invasive potential of Lantana is due to its fire tolerance, ability to spread sideways via roots, and dispersal of seeds, primarily by birds which feed on its berries.

YELLOW FLAX
(H: BASANTI)
Reinwardtia indica
Shrub; *Leaves:* 3-5 cm long; *Flowers:* about 3 cm dia. Seen in shady places.

WILLOW PRIMROSE
(H: BAN LOUNG)
Ludwigia octovalvis

Herb; *Leaves:* narrow about 8–15 cm long; *Flowers:* about 1.5–2 cm dia. It can be seen in wet and damp places along the fringes of forest and thinly forested areas. Plants with flowers similar to *Ludwigia octovalvis,* but broader leaves and narrower petals may also be seen. These may represent different species of genus *Ludwigia.*

CHINESE MULLEIN
(H: GIDAR TAMBAKHU)
Verbascum chinense

Herb; *Leaves:* those at the lower level of the plant are 5–10 cm long, and serrated; *Flowers:* about 1 cm dia. It is seen growing along rivers and sandy areas; has been used to treat stomach disorders, skin diseases and jaundice.

YELLOW SWAN FLOWER ▶

Globba sp.

Herb; *Leaves:* 10–20 cm long; *Flowers:* about 1.5–2 cm long. It can be seen in shady and moist places during the rainy season.

BONDUC NUT (H: KATH)

Caesalpinia bonducella

Shrub; *Leaves:* compound, with 6–10 pairs of 1–2 cm long leaflets; *Flowers:* about 1–1.5 cm long. A prickly plant, can be seen in shaded areas near human habitations; seeds are known to have several medicinal properties such as cure for skin diseases, malaria and stomach disorders.

▼

COMMON FANPETALS

(H: MAHABALA)
Sida acuta

Herb; *Leaves:* 4–6 cm long, narrow with serrated margins; *Flowers:* about 1 cm dia. Seen along roads and fringes of forest.

HEART-LEAF SIDA

(H: BHUINI)
Sida cordata

Herb; *Leaves:* about 2–5 cm long, heart-shaped with serrated margins; *Flowers:* about 1 cm dia. It is seen in thinly forested areas and scrubs, close to the ground level; closely resembles Country Mallow which has an erect appearance.

COUNTRY MALLOW

(H: NAGBALA)
Sida cordifolia

Shrub or Herb; *Leaves:* about 1–4 cm long heart-shaped with serrated margins; *Flowers:* about 1–1.5 cm dia. The plant is covered with minute hair; seen in scrubs, thinly forested areas and near human habitations.

Medicinal Values of *Sida* Plants

The plants belonging to genus *Sida* are well known in Sanskrit by name *'Bala'.* The name is however, commonly used for *Sida cordifolia.* In Ayurveda and Tibbi, *Bala* is a much-valued medicine. Its roots are useful in assisting digestion, in treatment of urinary disorders and nervous disorders and promoting wound healing. It has also been used as an aphrodisiac.

COFFEE SENNA

(H: KASAUNDA)

Senna occidentalis

Herb or shrub; *Leaves:* split into 3–5 pairs of 2–10 cm long leaflets; *Flowers:* 1–2.5 cm dia. It is seen in thinly forested areas, along fringes of forest and near human habitations; roasted seeds are used as a substitute for coffee.

STINKING CASSIA

(H: CHAKWAT)

Senna tora

Herb; *Leaves:* split into 3 pairs of 2–5 cm long leaflets; *Flowers:* 1–1.5 cm dia. It is commonly seen near human habitation and thinly forested areas; its seeds have several medicinal uses.

LANCE-LEAF INULA

Inula cuspidata

Shrub or Herb; *Leaves:* 6–12 cm long, margins serrated, arranged alternately; *Flowers:* heads about 1 cm dia. It can be seen along tracks in forested areas.

RATTLEPODS

Crotalaria spectabilis

Herb or Shrub; *Leaves:* about 5–10 cm long; *Flowers:* about 2–3 cm wide. Its common name is due to the fact that the loose seeds in the dry pod rattle when the pod is shaken; its close relative '*Crotalaria juncea*' (Sunn Hemp) is cultivated for high quality textile fibres. Plants with height and habitat similar to *Crotalaria spectabilis* but differing in shape of flowers, and shape and arrangement of leaves may also be sighted. These represent different species of genus *Crotalaria*.

CREEPING OXALIS

(H: KHATTI BUTI)

Oxalis corniculata

Herb; *Leaves:* split into 3 heart-shaped leaflets radiating from a common point; *Flowers:* about 1 cm dia. It is seen growing at ground level in moist areas; various parts of the plant taste sour due to the presence of 'oxalic acid'; used for making chutneys and added to salads.

The Response to Touch by the Touch-me-Not Plant

The leaflets of Touch-me-Not plant when touched, fold upwards and the entire leaf collapses. The same also happens under natural conditions when the leaves are hit by rain drops, shaken by wind and high temperature. The scientific term for such movement of plant parts in response to mechanical stimulation is known as 'Seismonasty'. This response is considered a defence tactic of plants against damage by animals feeding on them, drying effect of wind and damage by heavy rainfall.

What mechanism underlies such movements in the Touch-me-Not plant? Under normal conditions, cells arranged along the leaf stalk are tightly filled with water keeping them stretched and the leaves stay open and straight. Touching a leaf causes leakage of water and ions out of the cell. This results in shrinkage of cells and subsequent folding of leaflets and collapse of leaves.

TOUCH-ME-NOT

(H: CHUI-MUI)
Mimosa pudica

Herb; *Leaves:* compound with about 5–10 mm long leaflets; *Flowers:* heads about 1 cm dia. It is seen in open, sunny places.

HIMALAYAN MIMOSA

(H: ALAY)
Mimosa himalayana

Shrub; *Leaves:* split into 8–12 side stalks each of which bears 3–8 mm long, 16–20 leaflets; *Flowers:* 1–1.5 cm dia. This prickly shrub is seen in open areas, near streams, ravines and grasslands.

BIRDSVILLE INDIGO

(H: LEEL)
Indigofera linnaei

Herb; *Leaves:* split into 5–9 leaflets with about 8–12 mm length; *Flowers:* about 5–10 mm long. It grows close to ground level and can be seen in grassy open areas.

INDIAN LIQUORICE

(H: RATTI)

Abrus precatorius

Climber; *Leaves:* the leaf is split into 20–40 leaflets each about 1–2 cm in length; *Flowers:* about 1–1.5 cm long. The seeds are highly toxic and have been used by Indian jewellers as a minimum unit of weight for weighing gold and precious stones.

WILD INDIGO

(H: BAN-NIL)

Tephrosia purpurea

Herb; *Leaves:* leaf is split into 7–15 leaflets each of 1–2 cm length; *Flowers:* about 7–10 mm long. It can be seen in open grassy areas.

SAL-LEAVED DESMODIUM

(H: SHALPARNI)

Desmodium gangeticum

Herb; *Leaves:* 10–12 cm long; *Flowers:* 5–8 mm long. It is seen in shady areas.

▲

SCARLET SAGE

Salvia coccinea

Herb; *Leaves:* about 2–5 cm long with serrated margins; *Flowers:* about 1.5–3 cm long. It is seen in shady places.

▲

COMMON KNOTWEED

Polygonum plebeium

Herb; *Leaves:* about 1.5–3 cm long; *Flowers:* about 2–3 mm dia. Seen growing close to ground level among short grasses.

LION'S EAR (H: BARA)

Leonotis nepetifolia

Shrub; *Leaves:* 5–10 cm long with serrated margins; *Flowers:* about 2–3 cm long. It is seen in open forested areas and fringes of forest.

CHINESE HAT PLANT (H: KAPNI)
Holmskioldia sanguinea

Shrub; *Leaves:* 8–10 cm long; *Flowers:* about 1.5–2 cm dia. It is seen hanging in shady and moist places near springs, ravines and cliffs.

FIRE-FLAME BUSH (H: DHAWAI)
Woodfordia fruticosa

Shrub; *Leaves:* about 5–10 cm long, almost stalkless; *Flowers:* about 1–1.5 cm long. It is seen on slopes, cliffs and near streams; gets covered with bright crimson-red flowers during the months of March–April attracting birds seeking nectar; birds also pollinate and disperse seeds of this plant.

▲

JUSTICIA

Justicia diffusa

Herb; *Leaves:* about 1.5–2 cm long; *Flowers:* about 5–8 mm long. It is seen in open grassy areas, and thinly forested areas.

▲

LARGE-FLOWERED PINK SORREL

Oxalis debilis

Herb; *Leaves:* split into three 1.5–3 cm long leaflets radiating from a common point; *Flowers:* about 2 cm dia. It can be seen growing in shady places.

LALBASAK (H: LALBASAK)

Phlogacanthus thyrsiformis

Herb; *Leaves:* about 15–20 cm long; *Flowers:* 2–2.5 cm long. Seen in shady areas; bitter tasting leaves and flowers are used to relieve cough, stomach ache and rashes.

▲ **DEWFLOWER**
Murdannia sp.

Herb; *Leaves:* narrow; *Flowers:* 1–1.5 cm dia. It can be seen in grasslands and scrubs.

▲ **FOLDWING** *Dicliptera* sp.

Herb; *Leaves:* about 2–5 cm long. *Flowers:* 1–1.5 cm long. Seen growing close to ground level in moist places near human habitations and along fringes of forest.

RED HOGWEED (H: BISKHAPARA)
Boerhavia diffusa

Herb; *Leaves:* about 2–4 cm long, hairy with heart-shaped base; *Flowers:* about 5–8 mm dia. It is seen growing and spreading close to the ground in open areas; used for treating stomach disorders, jaundice, and keeping a healthy liver. ▼

CAESARWEED
(H: BACHITA)
Urena lobata

Shrub or Herb; *Leaves:* 4–10 cm long broad and shallowly lobed; *Flowers:* about 1–1.5 cm dia. It can be seen near fringes of forest, and human habitations; stem provides useful fibre. ▼

DEVIL'S CLAWS (H: BAGHNAKH)
Martynia annua

Herb; *Leaves:* 5–10 cm long, broad heart-shaped with shallowly lobed margins; *Flowers:* 3–5 cm long. It is seen along fringes of forest and open areas; has been used for treatment of epilepsy, sore throat, burns and skin infections.

EAST-INDIAN SCREW TREE
(H: MAROR-FALI)
Helicteres isora

Shrub; *Leaves:* about 8–15 cm long, broad and heart-shaped with serrated margins, arranged alternately; *Flowers:* about 2.5–3 cm long. It can be seen in thinly forested areas. It is more common in Jhirna and Dhela zones.

GLORY LILY

(H: KALHARI)
Gloriosa superba

Herb; *Leaves:* about 6–12 cm long, narrow and stalkless; *Flowers:* 5–8 cm long. It is seen near fringes of forest; bears flowers during rainy season; contains high amount of toxin 'Colchicine' which has been used to cure arthritis, gout, ulcers, piles and skin diseases.

SCARLET MILKWEED

(H: KAKATUNDI)
Asclepias curassavica

Herb; *Leaves:* about 10–12 cm long, narrow; *Flowers:* about 1–1.5 cm dia. It is seen near human habitations, fringes of forest and forest clearings.

CREEPING THISTLE

Cirsium arvense

Herb; *Leaves:* 15–20 cm long and prickly; *Flowers:* heads about 1–2.5 cm dia. It is seen in open areas, and along rivers and streams.

PAINTED LEAF BEGONIA

(H: PATTHARCHATTA)

Begonia picta

Herb; *Leaves:* about 5–10 cm long, broader at the base; *Flowers:* about 1–1.5 cm broad. Seen in shady and damp places.

Nature's Palette—Painting Flowers

Brilliant colouration of flowers is conferred by several natural colourants—'pigments'. Major classes of pigments include; *Flavonoids*: imparting orange-red to blue-violet (e.g. gives colour to red pomegranate and blue poppy), *Carotenoids:* yellow to red (giving shades of orange and yellow to *Calendula* and marigold) and *Betalains:* yellow to red colouration (give colour to beetroot). Their various combinations further increase the spectrum of colouration. Some of these pigments are also widely used as natural food colourants. Bright colouration of day blooming flowers are clues by which pollinators locate flowers of their interest (p.352). Colours also help flowers stand out against their background and make them conspicuous.

Aesthetic Properties of Flowers—Colour, Shape, Texture and Scent are Meant to Entice Pollinators

Animals feeding on nectar are choosy about concentration of sugars in nectar and its volume. To extract nectar efficiently from flowers, various groups of insects have appropriate mouth parts. For example, the straw-like proboscis of butterflies allows them to extract nectar from long tubular flowers, but limits intake to only diluted nectar. Bees on the other hand, can feed on concentrated nectar as they have different types of mouth parts.

How do these animals decide which of the several varieties of flowers have nectar of their choice? By instinct or experience, animals are well aware of the shape, colour pattern, and scent of flowers they should visit for nectar. Accordingly, butterflies would go to the flowers with red, orange, yellow or mauve colouration, emitting slight to moderately sweet odour and providing a flat platform to land. Bees have preference for yellow, pink, purple, blue and white, moderately sweet-scented flowers. Bats and moths feeding after sunset prefer flowers with dull white colouration and strong smell (including fruity and sweet fragrance, or foul smelling). A large funnel-shaped flower with strong perching site and bright colours such as red/orange attracts birds. Further, myriads of colourful markings such as spots, bars, streaks, etc., guide animals to locate nectar seated deep inside the flowers.

Nectar—a Sweet Energy Drink

Nectar is a blend of sugars, water, amino acids, ions, proteins, fats, antioxidants, etc. Sugars such as sucrose, glucose and fructose are the most abundant ingredients of nectar. The total sugar content in nectar in different flowers can range from 5–80%. Nectar is formed inside specialized structures—nectaries located in flowers (floral nectary) and other parts of plants such as leaf, leaf stalk and stipules (extra-floral nectary). The two types of nectaries lend different functions to plants. Nectar from floral nectaries attracts pollinators whereas extra-floral nectar attracts ants and wasps to the plant, which in addition to feeding on nectar, also eat up (or keep away) other insects that infest plants.

Accessing nectar

Pollination Services Offered to Plants by Animals

Pollination, a fascinating process of Mother Nature, is transfer of pollen grains (male component of flowers) from the anthers to the stigma (female organ of flowers) on the flower of the same plant or another plant. The mixing of male and female components leads to the formation of fruits and seeds. Pollination is therefore, a vital process for survival and perpetuation of plants. In more than 80% of flowering plants, the transfer of pollen grains is done by animals—bees, flies, beetles, butterflies and moths being the most common pollinators. Animals such as birds, bats, squirrels, etc., are also known to pollinate many plants.

Coffee Bee Hawk Moth
(Cephonodes hylas)

Carpenter Bee
(Xylocopa sp.)

Why do animals offer pollination services to plants? Most animals (including insects) visit flowers to seek nectar (food). In the process of collecting nectar, their bodies rub against the anthers and get coated with pollen grains. On their visit to the next flower, pollen carried by the animals may get shed on to the female stigma. Plant-pollinator interaction is a good example of mutual relationship wherein for providing pollination service, animals are rewarded with food by plants. A few animals feed on nectar but do not transfer pollen grains to female stigmas. They are called 'nectar robbers'. Such animals make holes in flowers to reach nectar rather than entering through the natural opening. Sometimes Carpenter Bees and some birds practice nectar robbing.

Bees are the most important pollinators as they not only pollinate wild plants but also several food-providing plants important to humans (p.276).

Some Plants Cheat Pollinators

Some plants are cheaters. Their flowers mimic something towards which pollinators (especially insects) have a natural tendency to get attracted. Such plants accomplish pollination without providing any apparent benefit to pollinators. In an interesting instance: the flower shape of certain orchids resembles female wasps and the scent produced by them arouses sexual behaviour of male wasps. The flower attracts male wasps which, misled by the flower shape, try to copulate with the flower and in the process, pick up pollen for pollination.

THORNY NIGHTSHADE

(H: KATELI)
Solanum virginianum

Herb; *Leaves:* about 5–10 cm long with prickles; *Flowers:* about 1.5–2 cm dia. Creeper or slightly erect plant seen in ravines and sandy banks.

FLOSS FLOWER

Ageratum houstonianum

Herb; *Leaves:* about 3–8 cm long, margins serrated, hairy; *Flowers:* about 5–10 mm dia. occurring in clusters. It is seen in open areas and wastelands; an aggressive colonizer and native to tropical America; it has invaded and naturalized several parts of India. Plants similar to *Ageratum houstonianum* but with less hairy parts, and less dense cluster of flowers may also be seen. Such plants may represent different species of genus *Ageratum*.

▼

▲

BLUE PIMPERNEL

Anagallis arvensis

Herb; *Leaves:* about 2–3 cm long; *Flowers:* about 1–1.5 cm dia. A small plant growing close to ground level; seen in wet open areas and near human habitations.

SIAM WEED

Chromolaena odorata

Shrub; *Leaves:* about 5–12 cm long, margins serrated, arranged in opposite pairs; *Flowers:* heads about 5 mm dia. It can be seen in open areas, along the fringes of forest; aggressive colonizer and native to tropical America; invaded and naturalized in several parts of India.

URARIA ▶

Uraria sp.

Herb; *Leaves:* split into three 3–6 cm long leaflets; *Flowers:* about 5–8 mm long. It can be seen in moist and shady places.

◀ LOOSE-FLOWERED DESMODIUM

Desmodium laxiflorum

Herb; *Leaves:* split into three about 8–15 cm long leaflets; *Flowers:* about 6–10 mm long. It is seen in moist and shady places.

LARKSPUR

(H: JADWAR)

Delphinium denudatum

Herb; *Leaves:* about 4–16 cm disc shaped, divided into 5–7 segments; *Flowers:* about 2–2.5 cm dia. with about 1.5 cm long tail. Seen on slopes along roads and tracks.

CATMINT

Nepeta sp.

Herb; *Leaves:* about 2–3 cm long, hairy; *Flowers:* about 8-10 mm long. It can be seen along roads in shady places.

BLUE SAGE

(H: GULSHAM)

Eranthemum pulchellum

Herb or Shrub; *Leaves:* about 10–20 cm long; *Flowers:* about 2–3 cm dia. It is seen in shady places in thinly forested areas.

BLUEBELL BARLERIA
(H: NILI JHINTI)
Barleria cristata

Herb; *Leaves:* about 5–10 cm long; *Flowers:* 3–4 cm dia. It is seen in shady places in forested areas and fringes of forest.

HEMIGRAPHIS
Hemigraphis latebrosa

Herb; *Leaves:* 4–8 cm long, hairy with serrated margins; *Flowers:* about 1–1.5 cm long. It is seen in moist open areas and fringes of forests.

BUSH MINT
Hyptis suaveolens

Herb or Shrub; *Leaves:* about 5–7 cm long with serrated margins; *Flowers:* about 1 cm long. It can be seen along fringes of forest and near human habitations.

INDIAN CATMINT

(H: KALA BHANGRA)

Anisomeles indica

Herb; *Leaves:* about 5–10 cm long, woolly, with serrated margins; *Flowers:* about 1–1.5 cm long. It is seen growing in open areas close to the fringes of forest and human habitations; has been used to relieve pain, fever and skin problems, and applied to treat snake bite. Certain related plants to it contain substances that attract cats and are known to cause euphoria and sedation in cats.

▲

GIANT MILKWEED

(H: SAFED ARKA)

Calotropis gigantea

Shrub; *Leaves:* about 10–20 cm long, broad, and light green with cottony lower surface; *Flowers:* about 2–4 cm dia; plants with white flowers are also seen. It is seen in open areas such as ravines, river banks, etc. Silky fibres coated over seeds are mixed with a small amount of cotton and used to fill pillows; milky juice is used as medicine.

▲

LARGE-LEAF BEAUTY BERRY

(H: BASTARA)

Callicarpa macrophylla

Shrub; *Leaves:* 10–25 cm long, woolly; *Flowers:* about 4–6 mm dia. It can be seen in thinly forested areas and fringes of forest.

CHASTE TREE (H: INDRANI)
Vitex negundo

Shrub; *Leaves:* split into 3–5 leaflets with 3–10 cm length; *Flowers:* about 5–8 mm dia. It can be seen along fringes of forests; used for treatment of pain, fever, and has liver protective and anti-inflammatory properties.

BLUEBEARD
(H: Kauri)
Pseudocaryopteris bicolour

Shrub; *Leaves:* about 5–12 cm long with serrated margins; *Flowers:* 1–1.5 cm dia. A shrub seen along ravines and open areas.

COMMON SPURGE ▶
(H: BARA-DUDHI)
Euphorbia hirta

Herb; *Leaves:* 1–3 cm long with serrated margins.

◀ **CASTOR OIL PLANT**
(H: ARANDI)
Ricinus communis

Shrub; *Leaves:* broad palm shaped with 6–11 lobes; *Flowers:* the twig bearing flowers have female flowers at higher level and male at lower. Seen near human habitations; oil extracted by pressing seeds have several industrial uses such as in cosmetics, medicine, lubricants, greases, fuel, etc.

Grasses belonging to the family of plants '*Poaceae*'. These have a non-woody and unbranched stem. Their leaves are long and narrow, and have parallel veins. Cereal plants, bamboos, etc., are examples of grasses. More than 70 species of wild grasses have been reported from CTR. The flowers of grasses become noticeable when in full bloom during the rainy season.

▲
REED GRASS (H: NAL)
Phragmites sp.

A tall grass growing upto 3–4 mtr. Stem is suitable for making mattings.

▲
TIGER GRASS
Thysanolaena maxima

A tall grass growing up to 2–3 mtr. It is used for making brooms *(Phul jharu)*.

PRICKLY PEAR
(H: NAGFANI)
Opuntia sp.

Shrub; *Leaves:* leaf-like flat structures are actually a modified form of stem. It is seen in open areas, scrubs and dry localities.
▼

STINGING NETTLE
Urtica sp.

Herb; *Leaves:* prickly with serrated margins. Its leaves and stem are covered with prickles. On contact with skin causes burning sensation.
▼

FLOURY CLOAK FERN
Cheilanthes farinosa

RIVERINE SCRAMBLER FERN
Ampelopteris prolifera

Pteridophytes (*Petron*: Feather; *Phyton*: Plant)

Most plants of this group grow in moist, shady and cool places. These plants do not bear flowers or seeds; instead they reproduce by producing spores—reproductive cells, which can produce a new plant under suitable environmental conditions. Ferns and spikemosses are examples of pteridophytes.

TAILED MAIDENHAIR FERN
Adiantum caudatum

SPIKEMOSS
Selaginella chrysocaulos

Checklist of Trees Seen In and Around CTR

No.	Common Name	Scientific Name
1	Sage Leaved Alangium	*Alangium salviifolium*
2	Black Catechu	*Acacia catechu*
3	Shoebutton Ardisia	*Ardisia solanacea*
4	Himalayan Maple	*Acer oblongum*
5	Wood Apple	*Aegle marmelos*
6	Ceylon Rosewood	*Albizia odoratissima*
7	Siris Tree	*Albizia lebbeck*
8	White Siris	*Albizia procera*
9	Axle-wood Tree	*Anogeissus latifolia*
10	Burmese Silk Orchid	*Bauhinia racemosa*
11	Roxburgh's Bauhinia	*Bauhinia roxburghiana*
12	Orchid Tree	*Bauhinia variegata*
13	Malabar Bauhinia	*Bauhinia malabarica*
14	Genthi	*Boehmeria rugulosa*
15	Red Silk-cotton	*Bombax ceiba*
16	Spinous Kino Tree	*Bridelia retusa*
17	Gondani	*Bridelia verrucosa*
18	Paper Mulberry	*Broussonetia papyrifera*
19	Cuddapah Almond	*Buchanania cochinchinensis*
20	Flame-of-the-Forest	*Butea monosperma*
21	Toothed Leaf Chilla	*Casearia tomentosa*
22	Wild Guava	*Careya arborea*
23	Golden Shower	*Cassia fistula*
24	Ceylon Tea	*Cassine glauca*
25	False Guava	*Catunaregam spinosa*
26	Indian Cherry	*Cordia dichotoma*
27	Bairola	*Cordia vestita*
28	Garlic Pear Tree	*Crateva adansonii*
29	Thanela	*Ceriscoides turgida*
30	Indian Rosewood	*Dalbergia sissoo*
31	Ujjain Desmodium Tree	*Desmodium oojeinense*
32	East Indian Ebony	*Diospyros melanoxylon*
33	Koda Tree	*Ehretia acuminata*
34	Chamror	*Ehretia laevis*
35	Indian Coral Tree	*Erythrina suberosa*
36	Tiger's Milk Spruce	*Falconeria insignis*
37	Indian Rock Fig	*Ficus arnottiana*
38	Elephant Ear Fig	*Ficus auriculata*
39	Banyan Tree	*Ficus benghalensis*
40	Hairy Fig	*Ficus hispida*
41	White Fig	*Ficus infectoria*
42	Cluster Fig	*Ficus racemosa*
43	Golden Rumph's Fig	*Ficus rumphii*
44	Drooping Fig.	*Ficus semicordata*
45	Humped Fig	*Ficus tinctoria*
46	Laurel Fig	*Ficus microcarpa*
47	Batoka Plum	*Flacourtia indica*
48	Kharpat	*Garuga pinnata*
49	White Teak	*Gmelina arborea*

No.	Common Name	Scientific Name
50	Dhaman	*Grewia eriocarpa*
51	Bhemal	*Grewia multiflora*
52	Bistu	*Grewia sapida*
53	Haldu	*Haldina cordifolia*
54	Bitter Oleander	*Holarrhena pubescens*
55	Indian Elm	*Holoptelea integrifolia*
56	Bridal Couch Tree	*Hymenodictyon orixense*
57	Kydia	*Kydia calycina*
58	Small Flowered Crape Myrtle	*Lagerstroemia parviflora*
59	Indian Ash Tree	*Lannea coromandelica*
60	Maidalakri	*Litsea glutinosa*
61	Meda	*Litsea monopetala*
62	Indian Butter Tree	*Madhuca longifolia*
63	Monkey-face Tree	*Mallotus philippensis*
64	Mango	*Mangifera indica*
65	Chinaberry Tree	*Melia azedarach*
66	Velvety Miliusa	*Miliusa velutina*
67	Kaim	*Mitragyna parvifolia*
68	White Mulberry	*Morus alba*
69	Coral Jasmine	*Nyctanthes arbor-tristis*
70	Gair	*Olea glandulifera*
71	Kekara	*Phoebe lanceolata*
72	Indian Gooseberry	*Phyllanthus emblica*
73	Indian Beech	*Pongamia pinnata*
74	Bakar	*Premna barbata*
75	Bharkhar	*Premna mollissima*
76	Chir Pine	*Pinus roxburghii*
77	Putranjiva	*Putranjiva roxburghii*
78	Ban Oak	*Quercus oblongata*
79	Indian Willow	*Salix tetrasperma*
80	Ceylon Oak	*Schleichera oleosa*
81	Indian Marking Nut Tree	*Semecarpus anacardium*
82	Sal	*Shorea robusta*
83	Fragrant Padri Tree	*Stereospermum chelonoides*
84	Sand Paper Tree	*Streblus asper*
85	Indian Blackberry	*Syzygium cumini*
86	Paiman	*Syzygium nervosum*
87	Teak	*Tectona grandis*
88	Belleric Myrobalan	*Terminalia bellirica*
89	Yellow Myrobalan	*Terminalia chebula*
90	Crocodile-bark Tree	*Terminalia elliptica*
91	Indian Mahogany	*Toona ciliata*
92	Khagshi	*Trema politoria*
93	Tila	*Wendlandia heynei*
94	Dudhi	*Wrightia arborea*
95	Kath Ber	*Ziziphus xylopyrus*
96	Indian Plum	*Ziziphus mauritiana*

For exhaustive list of plants see reference: Pant, P.C. 1986, BSI

CORBETT NATIONAL PARK

Visiting CTR

Ecotourism Zones and Route Maps

CTR is located in the Himalayan foothills of the state of Uttarakhand. The nearest towns or the gateways to CTR are 'Ramnagar' and 'Kotdwar' which are well connected with the major cities of northern India via road and railway.

Getting into CTR*

Currently, the section of CTR open for tourists is divided into 7 ecotourism zones:

Ecotourism Zones	*Entry Gates*
Dhela	Dhela
Jhirna	Dhela
Bijrani	Amdanda
Garjia	Ringora/Garjia/Amdanda
Dhikala	Dhangarhi
Durgadevi (Lohachaur)	Durgadevi/Maidavan
Sonanadi	Vatanvasa Gate (for visiting Halduparao area), and Pakhro Gate (for visiting Pakhro area)

Safariing in 'Sitabani' and 'Phanto' Jungles

The forest on the eastern bank of Kosi river is administratively known as Ramnagar Forest Division, within which, a section of forest is popularly known as 'Sitabani Jungle'. Mythologically, this jungle harboured the hermitage of Maharishi Balmiki, and Goddess Sita stayed here during her exile. Presently, there is an ancient temple with few antique sculptures. Phanto jungle lies south of CTR.

Sitabani and Phanto jungles are frequented by numerous wildlife enthusiasts. The wealth of flora and fauna and the landscape in both the jungles are similar to the CTR.

Presently there are two ways to visit or enter CTR:

1) taking a day-visit safari (jungle safari), and 2) booking a night stay in the Forest Rest Houses (FRHs) inside CTR.

In the former case, tourists are allowed to visit or enter CTR for a limited period of time (about 3–4 hrs) during the 'Morning Safari'/'Evening Safari' after which, they exit CTR and spend the night in a hotel or resort (outside CTR). In the latter case, the visitors spend the night in FRHs located within CTR and go on safari rides in the morning and evening. A night stay inside CTR is recommended to get a thrilling experience in the middle of the jungle. In both the cases, one needs to obtain a permit from the Forest Department.

The following steps may be taken, to visit CTR:

1. Choose the zone you wish to visit—one may consult guidebooks such as this one or discuss with local guides/travel agents, or visit various websites providing a review of each zone,

2.obtain the appropriate permit i.e., for a day-visit safari or night stay; visitors may get the permit online from the Forest Department website or seek assistance from authorised travel agents,

3. check the town nearest to the entry gate of the zone of visit: Pakhro, Vatanvasa and Maidavan entry gates lie close to the town of Kotdwar in Pauri Garhwal, whereas the

* Information under this section is liable to change. Visitors are advised to consult Forest Department website for updates.

remaining gates are closer to Ramnagar; ensure accommodation in or near these towns if you have planned a day-visit safari; check online for the exact timing of entry and exit from entry gates, as the timings are subject to change depending on the season.

> *Only a limited number of vehicles/permits are allowed during the morning and evening safari (for day visits), and there is a limited number of rooms for night stay inside the CTR, therefore, one needs to finish all the visit-related formalities as early as possible.*

Choosing the Desired Season for a Visit

There are four well-marked seasons in CTR: summer, rains, winter and spring. The ambience of the forest varies with seasonally changing temperatures, moisture and day length. The suggestions below may help visitors to choose their preferred season of visit:

Summer: It stretches from the end of April till the arrival of monsoon in late June or early July. The weather conditions are warm in April to moderately hot and dry during May and June. The temperature may soar above 40°C in the afternoon. Forested, well-shaded areas and nights, however, are cooler and pleasant. It is the most appropriate season to witness trees with renewed green leaves, flowers of late flowering tree species and trees with fruits (though many species have immature fruits in summer). Expanses of tall Sal trees covered with nascent fluorescent green leaves, and the forest floor coated with a layer of reddish-brown fallen leaves, offer a spectacular view. This is the right time of the year to observe nesting behaviour of many birds, and a chance to witness large herds of deer and elephants in lush green grasslands, particularly in the early mornings and evenings.

Rainy Season: Arrival of monsoon in late June or early July changes the weather conditions to warm and humid, which continue till the retreat of monsoon by late September. A part of the reserve is inaccessible during the rainy season. Spells of heavy rains locally or in the higher reaches of the Himalayas cause excessive flooding of rivers and streams, causing damage to the safari tracks. The vegetation is uniformly

green all over, and short-lived ground herbs, ferns and mosses are at their best. It is the best time to look for butterflies, particularly from September to mid October.

Winter: Monsoon rains vanish by October (there may be spells of rain in winters too), and day and night are pleasant. The effect of rains, however, is still visible; there is greenery and overgrown plants all over. It is a good time to look for butterflies, particularly till mid-October, after which the butterfly population begins to decline. Nights are moderately cold in November; days are pleasant, and sky is clear with plenty of sunshine. It is a good time for tourist activities. Days and nights are cold to very cold during December to mid-February, and the temperature may drop to 3–4°C. Mornings are foggy and chilly, but the rising sun brings about warmth and the fog fades out. Vegetation shows signs of decline. It is a good time to look for migratory birds and observe other wildlife activities.

Spring: It arrives by the end of February and continues throughout March till early April. Pleasant weather, clear sky, floral aroma and various shades of nature are at their best. It is the best season for bird watching, particularly early spring, and for observing breeding related activities of birds (songs, calls, courtship and male aggressiveness). Spring is also a good time to look for butterflies, flowering trees and herbs, and other wildlife and tourist activities. Spring is the most recommended season for a CTR visit.

Tune Your Affection and Enjoy the Wild Milieu

The thrill of exploring wildlife, pleasure of being in the ambience of nature and observing various ways of its functioning drive many towards the jungles. One must leave behind all tension as well as urban gadgets of entertainment, and spend a few rejuvenating moments in the lap of Mother Nature. Maintain silence, listen to the sounds of the jungle, look around with expectation and imbibe your surroundings. Avoid spending time in capturing the moment with your camera unless you have a reason to do that. Your brain is the best hard disc drive to record special moments, and there is nothing equivalent to it in the world. Camera gives you recallable visuals, however, images stored in the brain can be recalled with associated feelings that cause enough of a 'dopamine rush' in the body to take you back into the pleasurable past.

Choosing the Desired Ecotourism Zone for Your Visit

The map of CTR, safari route maps and visuals for ecotourism zones provided, will help visitors in selecting the zones they wish to visit.

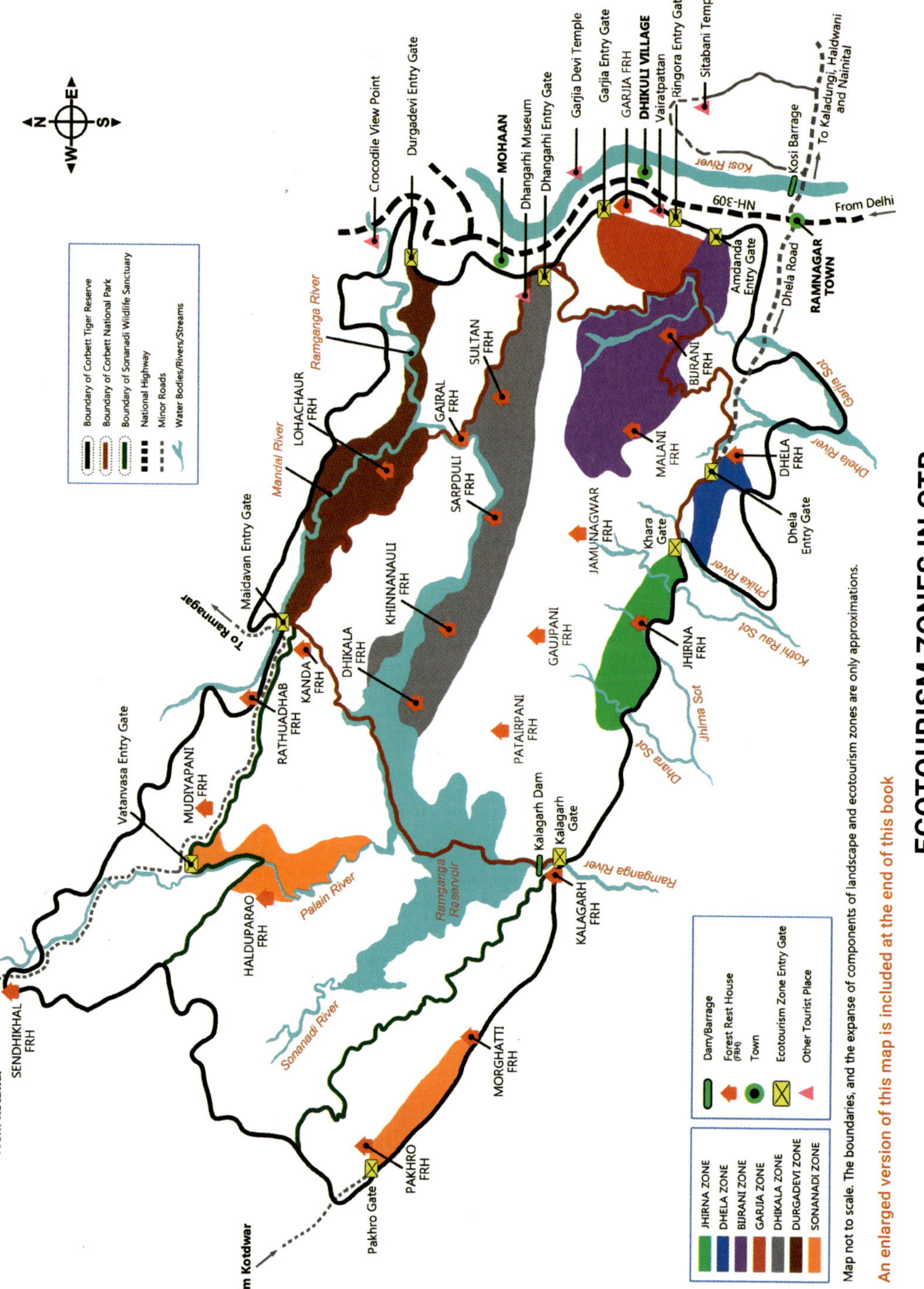

Dhela Zone

Entry gate: Dhela
Ambience: Flat terrain with streams and rivers; the surroundings are drier than the other zones; vegetation consists of thick to thin forest with mixed trees, scrub and grasslands; good for birdwatching and besides other mammals, one may also sight Sloth Bear and Nilgai.

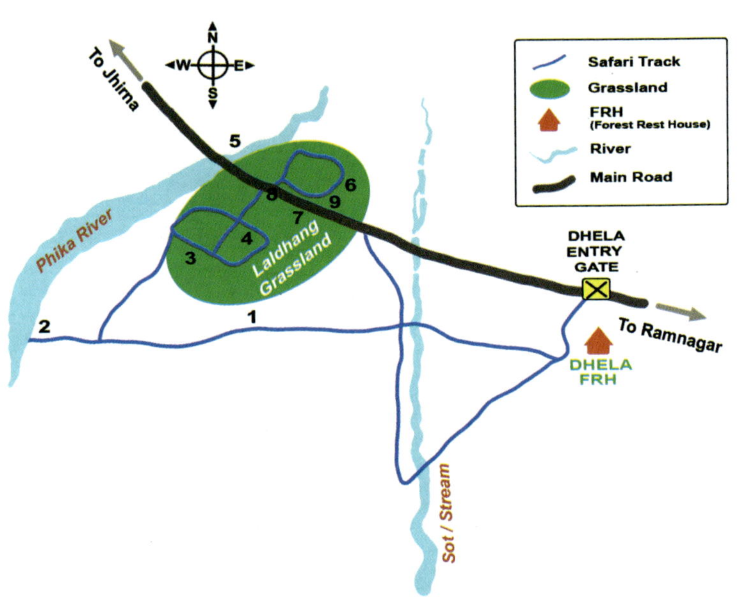

Jhirna Zone

Entry gate: Dhela

Ambience: Flat to undulating terrain criss-crossed by gorges and streams; the surroundings are drier at most places; vegetation consists of thick to thin forest with mixed trees, scrubs and grasslands; Jhirna zone is good for birdwatching, and besides other mammals, there is a chance to sight Sloth Bear and Nilgai.

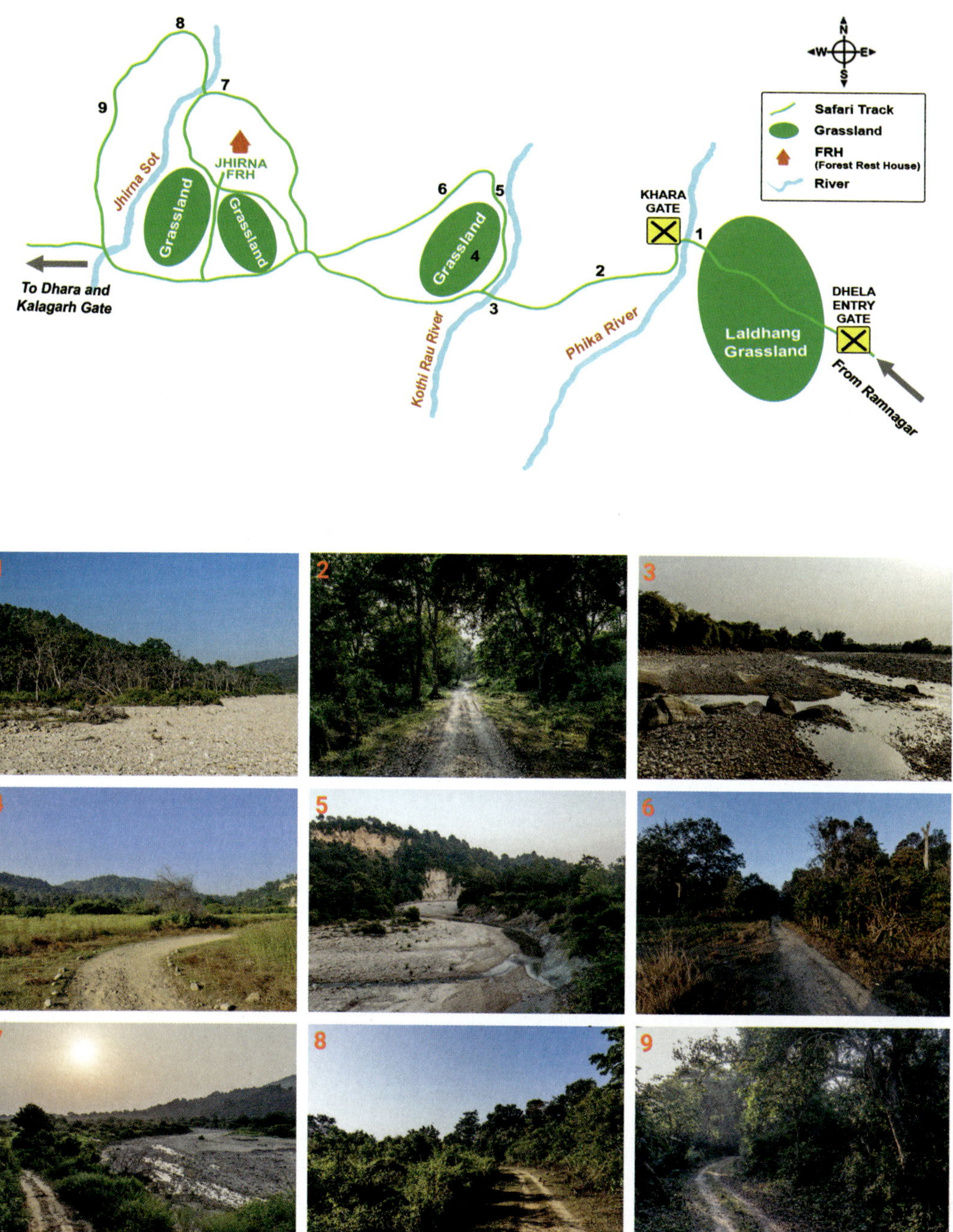

Bijrani Zone

Entry gate: Amdanda

Ambience: Flat to undulating terrain criss-crossed by numerous streams and deep gorges; steep to gentle sloping hills and cliffs; good for landscape photography; the surroundings are mostly moist-shady, dry-shady and dry; vegetation consists of dense Sal forest, thin forest with mixed trees, grasslands and scrubs; Bijrani zone is good for birdwatching and for sighting animals such as deer and other mammals.

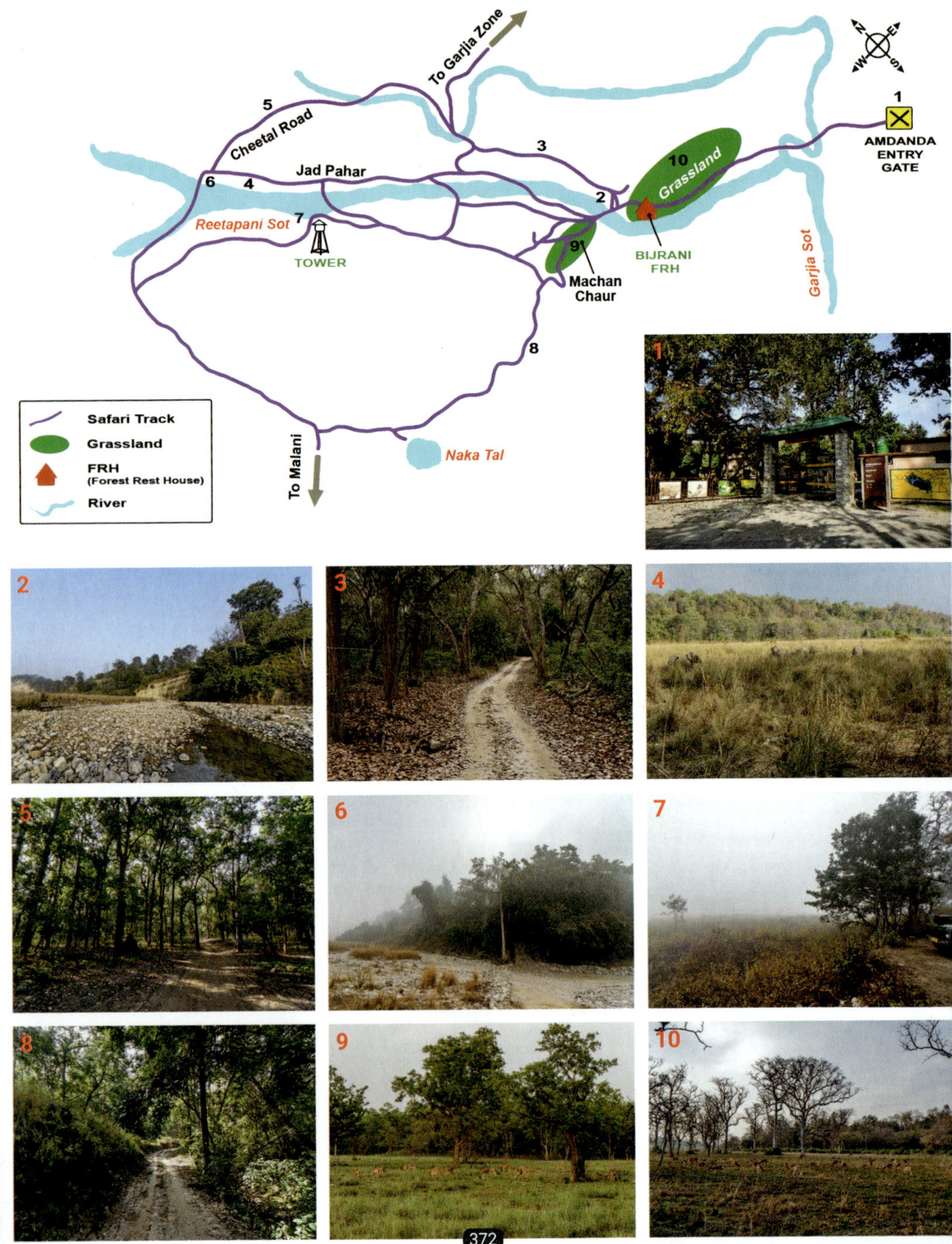

Garjia Zone

Entry gate: Ringora/Garjia/Amdanda

Ambience: Flat to undulating terrain criss-crossed by streams and gorges; gently sloping hills, hill tops and cliffs; good for landscape photography; the surroundings are moist-shady to open-dry; vegetation consists of dense Sal forest, thin Sal forest mixed with other trees, scrubs and grasslands (Phool Tal and Ringora grasslands); good place for birdwatching; one can see large herds of Spotted Deer in Phool Tal grasslands, and spot groups of Elephants.

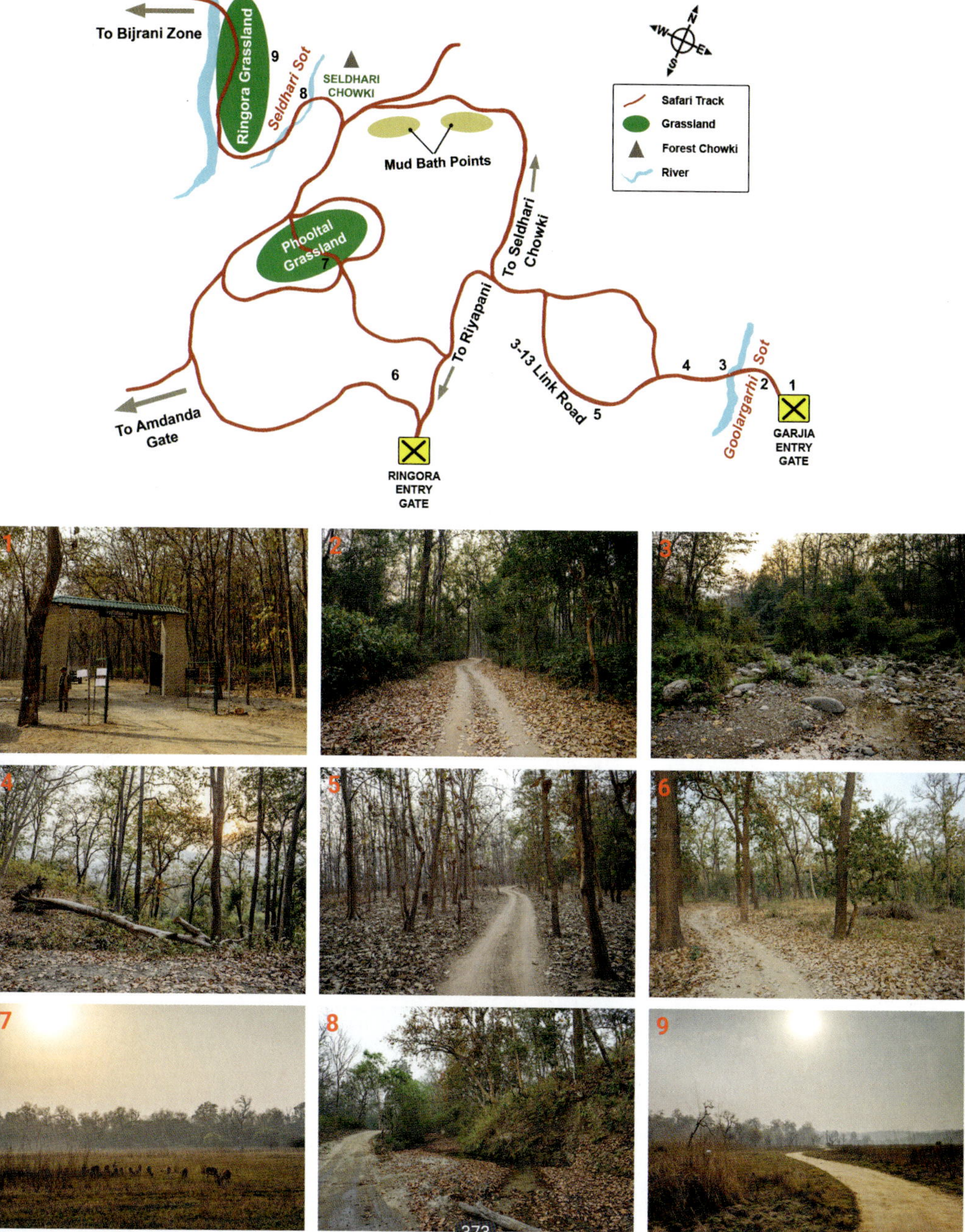

Dhikala Zone

Entry gate: Dhangarhi

Ambience: Terrain undulating to flat, criss-crossed by small streams and gorges; the magnificent view of Ramganga river is a plus; paradise for landscape photographers; the surroundings are moist-shady to open-dry; vegetation consists of pure Sal forest, mixed Sal forest, vast grasslands and scrubs; best place for birdwatching in CTR, particularly raptors; glimpse of large herds of Elephants and Spotted Deer; best place to sight Hog Deer, Smooth Coated Otter, Crocodile and Gharial.

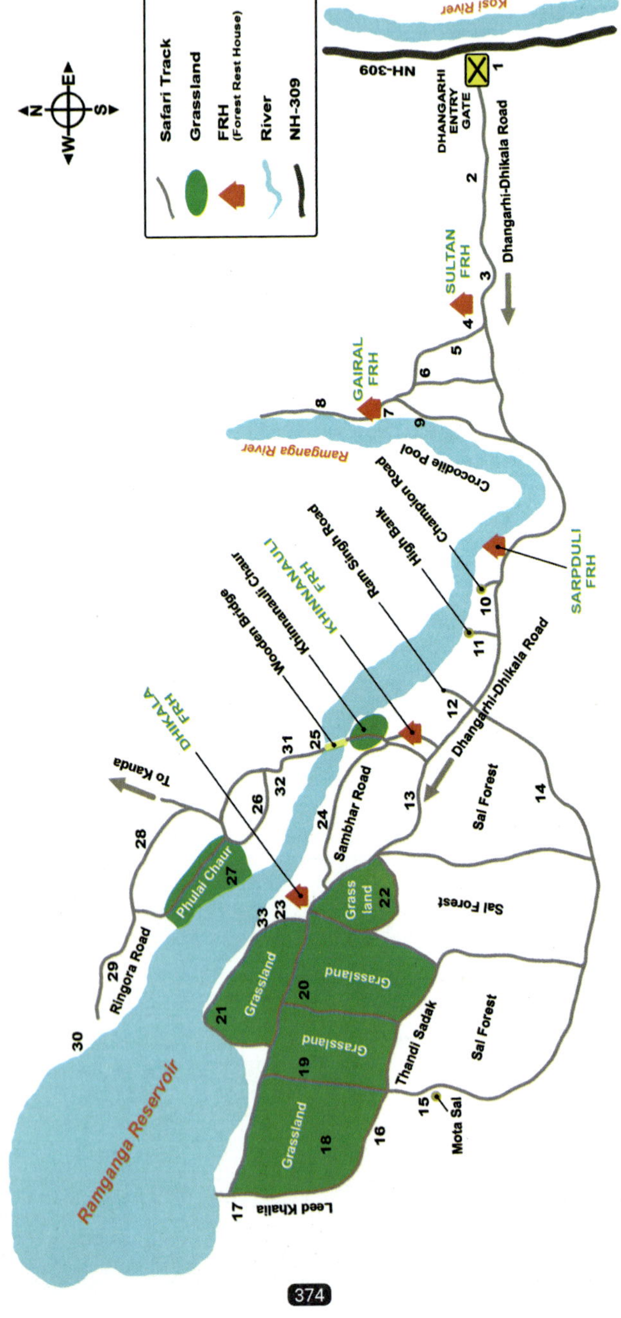

1
2
3
4
5
6
7
8
9
10
11
12
13
14
15
16
17
18
19
20
21

22

23

24

25

26

27

28

29

30

31

32

33

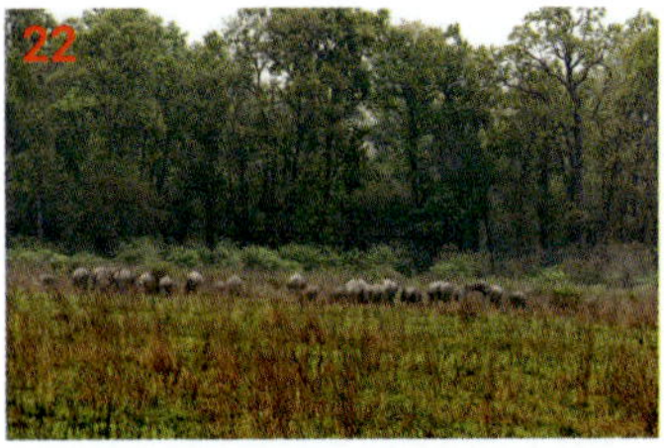

A Few Tips for Landscape Photography

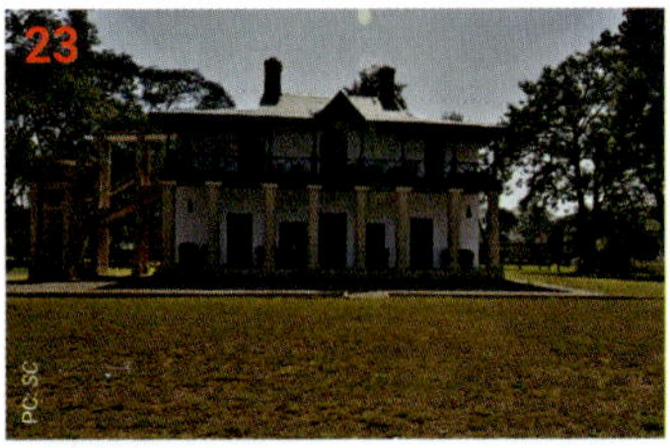

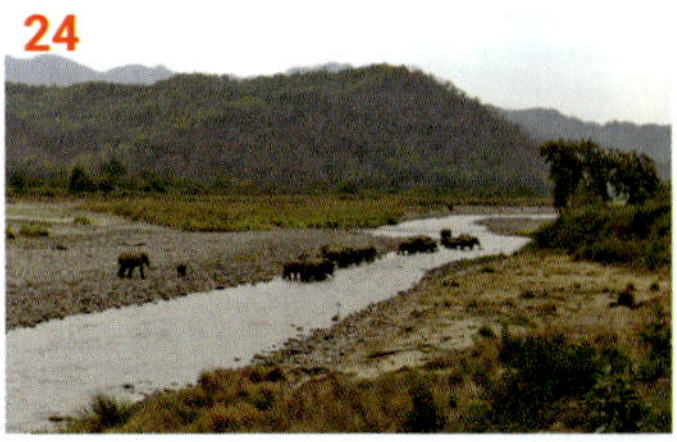

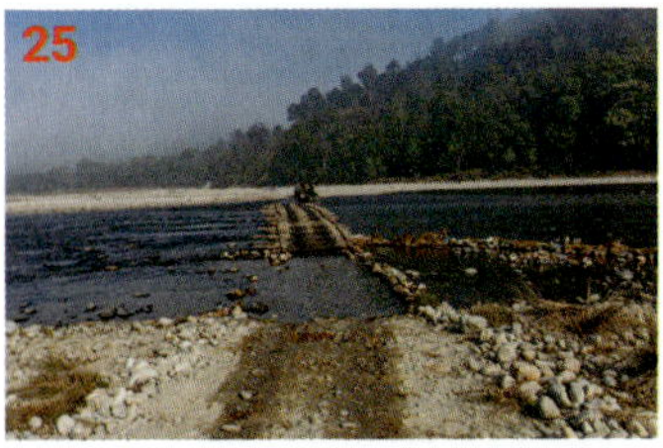

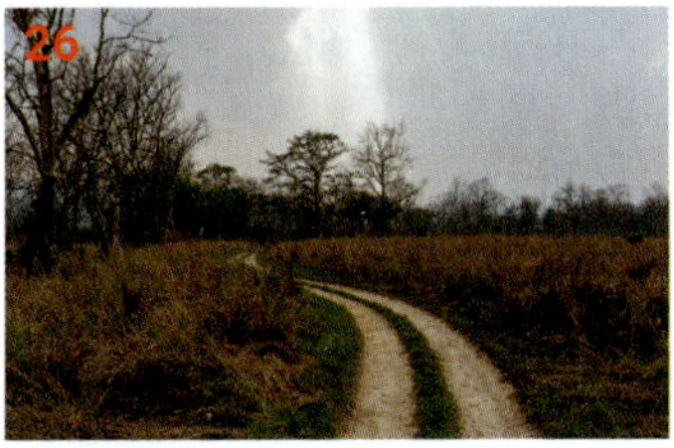

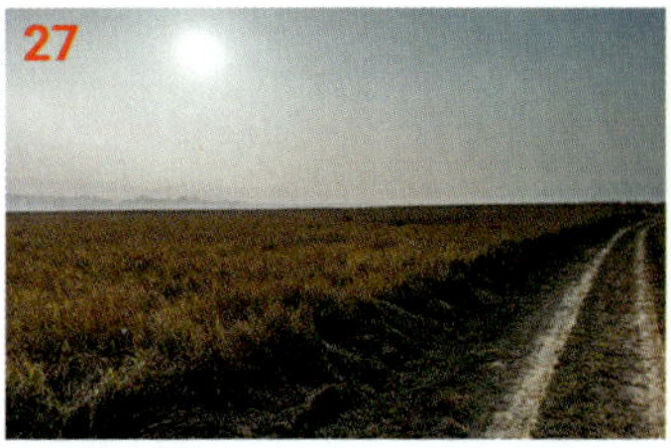

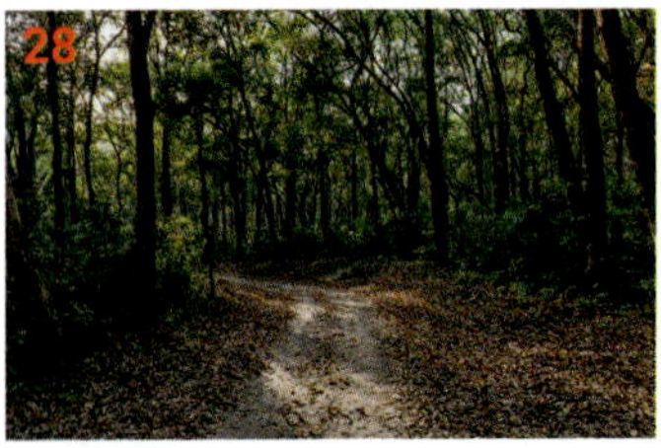

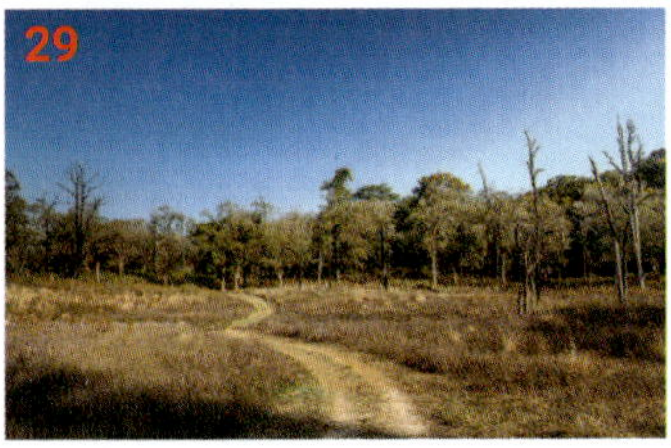

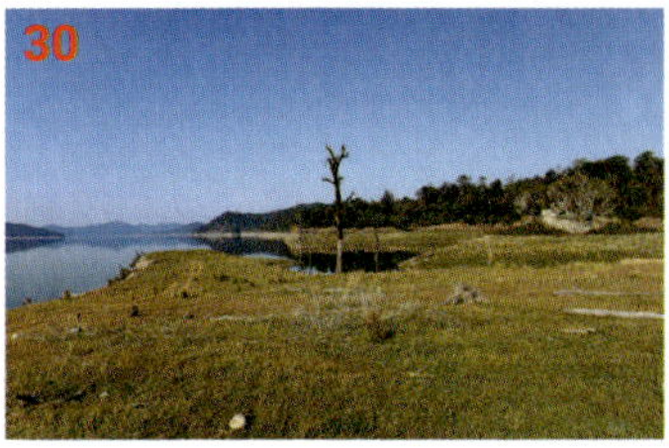

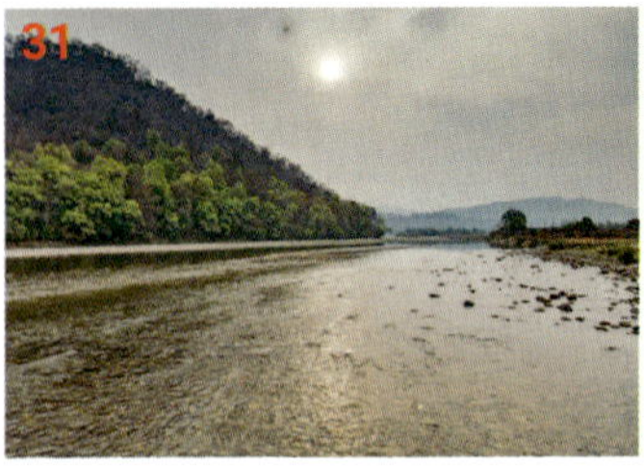

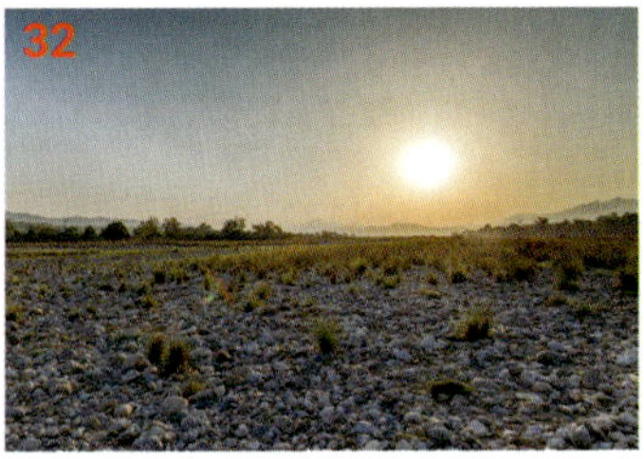

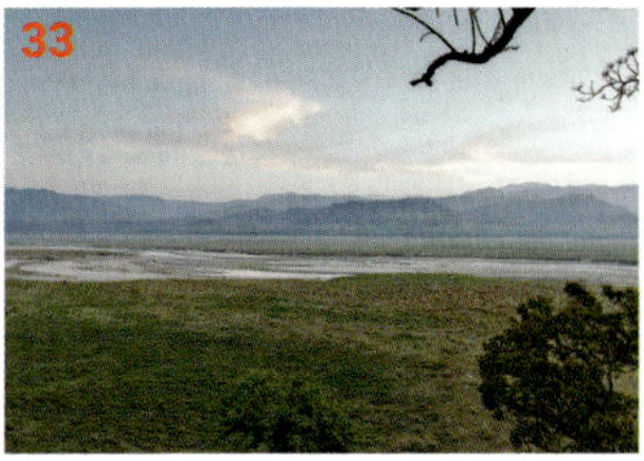

Visitors must not miss the first and last few minutes of the day to capture the dramatic sunrise and sunset. Keep an interesting foreground such as animals, water bodies, fallen trees and dried trunks, tall grass, etc. while framing a scene. Patterns of clouds often add a splendid effect to the landscape. While inside the forest, look for the area with various shades of leaves, flowers, fallen leaves and tree trunks, disintegrating tree trunks coated with mosses, pattern of bushes, etc.

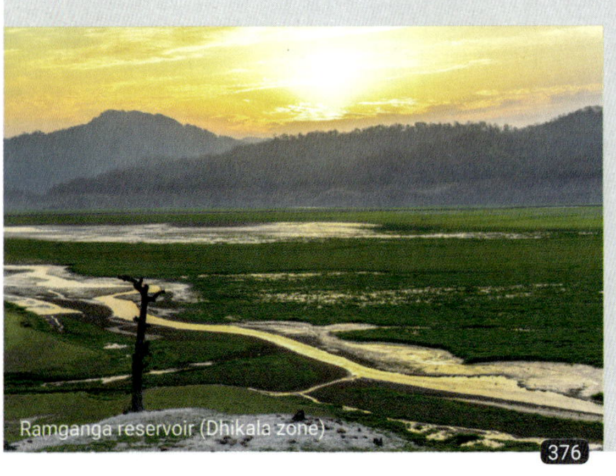

Ramganga reservoir (Dhikala zone)

A wide angle lens is a must for landscape photography; lenses with a focal length between16–50 mm are the most suitable. A two stop, soft edge 'Graduated Neutral Density Filter' would be of good use for shooting against the bright sky and a darker foreground, such as during sunset and sunrise. Also, a Polarizing Filter may be helpful in cutting down the unwanted reflection from foliage, water bodies, etc., and in capturing vibrant colours.

Durgadevi Zone (Lohachaur Zone)

Entry gate: Durgadevi/Maidavan

Ambience: Undulating terrain incised by Mandal river; steep slopes, gorges, cliffs; confluence of Ramganga and Mandal rivers; opportunity to drive along Mandal river; the surroundings are moist-shady and open riverine; vegetation includes dense mixed Sal forest, thin forest and scrubs; good place for birdwatching; opportunity to spot the Himalayan Goral, Golden Mahseer, and a possibility of sighting the Serow.

Sonanadi Zone

Entry gates: Vatanvasa gate at the Northern boundary (for Halduparao area), and Pakhro gate at the Southern boundary (for Pakhro area) of CTR.

Ambience (Halduparao area): Undulating terrain incised by Palain river and small streams; deep gorges, cliffs, and riverine landscape; opportunity to drive through high cliffs and bed of Palain river; the surroundings are a combination of shady-moist, open-dry, and riverine areas; vegetation is composed of mixed Sal forest, scrubs and grasslands; this zone and its nearby areas are an excellent place for birdwatching; besides other mammals, there is also a possibility to spot the Serow in this zone.

Ambience (Pakhro area): Similar to Jhirna and Dhela zones.

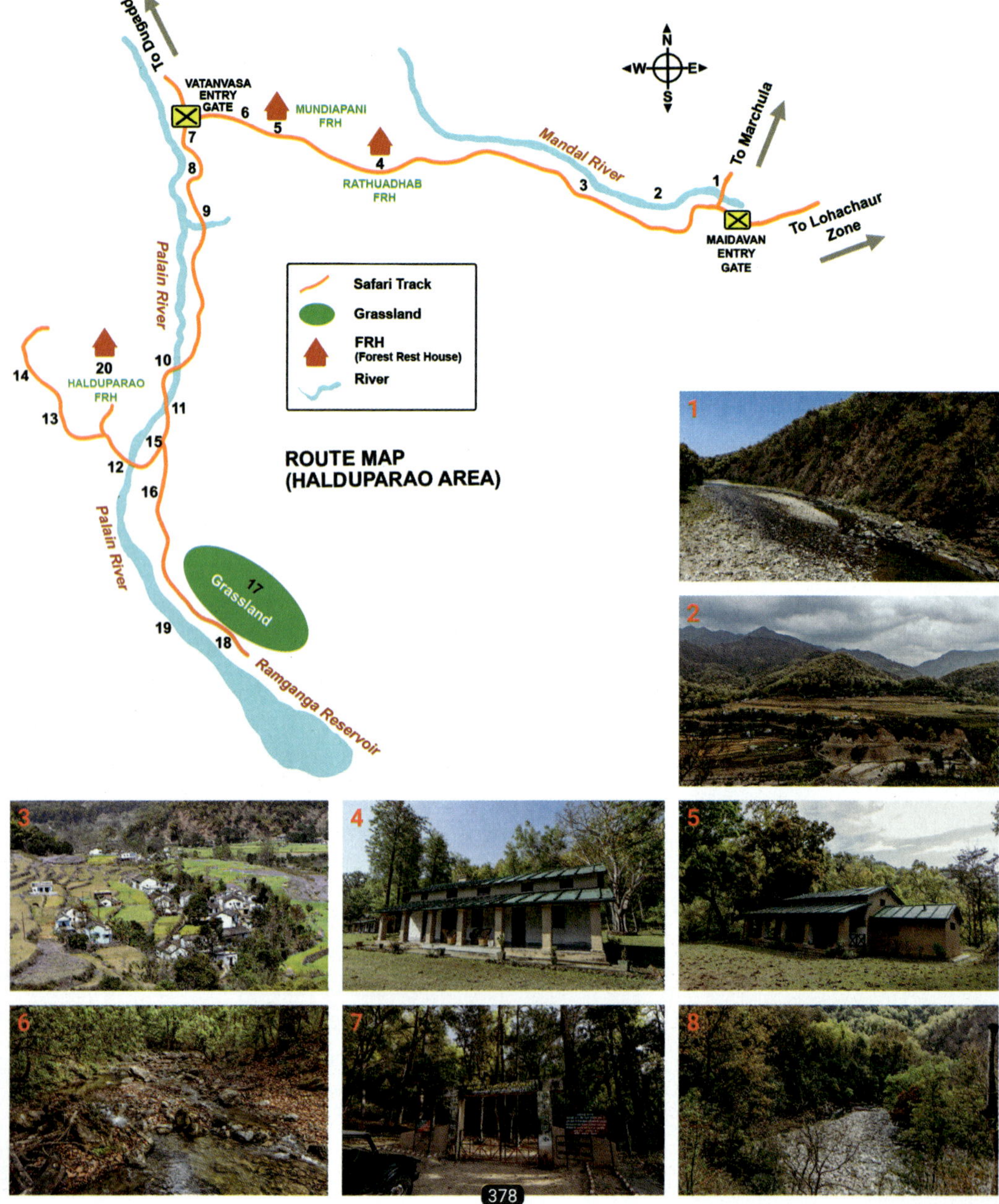

9

10

11

12

13

14

15

16

17

18

19

20

Green Lynx Spiders
(*Peucetia* sp.)

Lynx Spiders
(*Oxyopes* sp.)

Jumping Spiders
(*Telamonia* sp.)

Lynx Spiders
(*Hamadruas* sp.)

Dos and Don'ts and a Few Suggestions

- Choose a colour of clothing that merges with the background of the forest; dull browns, dull green and camouflage prints are the most suitable.
- Avoid using perfumes, deodorants or other fragrances as the scent may attract harmful insects or other animals.
- Sit and hold firmly inside the vehicle as the tracks are bumpy at many places. Avoid touching and plucking fruits and leaves in the forest.
- Always keep a safe distance from the wild animals, and do not tease and feed them.
- Do not litter inside the reserve; if you find any such trash/waste material lying inside the forest, inform your guide, driver or the forest staff about it.
- Refrain from using harsh flashlights to take photographs.
- Getting down from the vehicle and walking on the safari tracks is strictly prohibited inside CTR. Always wear high-ankle shoes even when walking within the premises of the Forest Rest Houses (FRHs).
- Do not cross the boundaries of FRHs as this might lead to life-threatening encounters with wild animals.
- As fire is destructive to forests, do not smoke or light fire inside the forest.
- Please remember that you are in a forest and do not expect high-end facilities. All Forest Rest Houses are well-equipped with basic amenities to have a comfortable stay. Do not put forest staff under pressure by making never-ending demands, as they are the caretakers of the forest too.
- Bringing fire-arms, alcoholic beverages, non-vegetarian food, narcotics and pets is prohibited in the CTR.
- Always book an experienced guide in case you wish to explore some areas outside the CTR. Do not enter the forested areas as there are wild animals everywhere, which may not be initially visible to you due to excellent camouflage.
- Do not get disappointed if you are not able to sight a tiger. CTR has many other appealing creatures seeking the attention of visitors.

Understanding Jungle Clues and Pugmarks

A safari ride can be more thrilling and informative if one has the ability to seek and decipher 'clues hidden in the jungle'. One may ask questions like "who has torn away a piece of tree bark?", or "who has dropped the leaves and fruits beneath the tree and why?", or "whose footprint and excreta is that?", or "whose call is it and what does it convey?", or "which flower or fruit attracts these birds or animals?", etc. Correct interpretation of clues gives us a 'Jungle Sense' or the skill to talk to the wild-folks.

▲ A large section of the bark stripped from the tree trunk–the handiwork of tuskers in order to get fibre and minerals from bark.

Vertical scratch marks on tree trunk—the handiwork of a Tiger (territory marking behaviour). ▲

Pugmarks on tyre impression, indicates that the animal used the path after the vehicle passed. ▲

Long segmented droppings tapered at one end and often with animal hair are indicative of excreta of Tiger or Leopard. ▲

Elephant footprint ▲

White patches on boulders, tree branches or beneath the trees—a perch regularly used by birds. ▲

▲ Large pile of dung with long fibres—excreta of an Elephant.

◀ Sloth Bear footprint (hind foot)

Sloth Bear footprint (front foot) ▶

Holes in dead tree trunks—handiwork of woodpeckers. ▶

▲ Mud pool with mashed up mud—wallowing place for animals such as Elephant, Sambar, Tiger, Wild Boar, etc.

Long trailing groove with foot marks on sandy banks of rivers—track of a crocodile. ▲

Pugmarks of a hyaena ▲

▲ Pugmark of a Tiger

Small pellet droppings—excreta of deer. ▲

Excreta of a flesh-eating animal packed with hair of prey. ▲

Large basket shaped nest of twigs placed high on the trees—nest of a raptor such as eagle. ◀

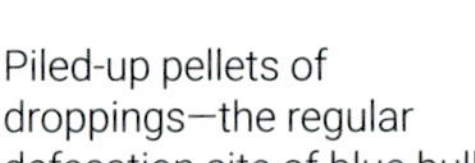

Piled-up pellets of droppings—the regular defecation site of blue bulls. ▶

- Dislodged branches and ruined vegetation, or the sound of cracking of a tree branch or trunk indicates the feeding activity of elephants.
- Smell of decomposing flesh can be an indicator of the presence of Tiger or Leopard kill.
- Alarm calls by deer and monkeys indicate the presence of predators such as tigers or leopards nearby.
- Sound resembling the barking of a dog in the jungle can be the call of a Barking Deer.

An experienced nature guide can help in locating and interpreting these and many other clues.

Scanning Pugmarks

Pugmarks or footprints that animals leave behind on the ground are amongst the key evidences of presence of animals in an area.

1. Differentiating pugmarks of animals of cat family (Leopard, Tiger, etc.) from those of dog family (jackal, hyaena, etc.)

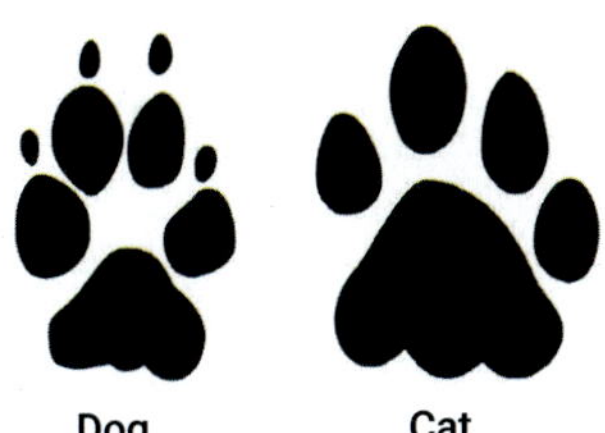

Dog Cat

Pugmarks of dogs and cats show the impression of a broad pad and four toes. The pugmark of dogs show claw marks at the tip of toes, and there is a wide gap between the tip of triangular pad and the base of middle two toes (except hyaena). Under most walking conditions pugmarks of cats do not show the impression of claws.

2. Differentiating pugmarks of a male and a female Tiger

Male

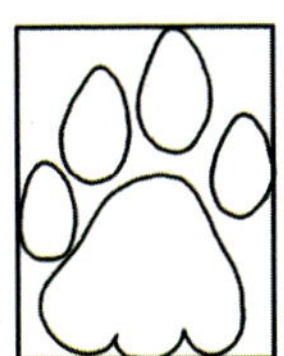

Female

The hind pugmark of a male Tiger fits into a square whereas that of female into a rectangle, and the shape of toes is more rounded in males than females. The front pugs of tigers are larger than hind pugs.

3. Differentiating pugmarks of a Tiger from that of a Leopard

Tiger cub

Leopard

Pugmarks of adult tigers are larger than that of leopards, however there may be a confusion between pugmarks of Tiger cubs and leopards. The pugmarks of leopards are compact; toes and pads are close to each other. The toes of Tiger cubs are more spread out.

4. Pugmark of hyaena

5. Footprints of Sloth Bear

Daylong Excursions Around CTR

There are many places of natural and historical significance near CTR which are worth visiting. Tourists can cover several of these in daylong trips.

Corbett Fall and Barati Rau Fall

These two small yet picturesque waterfalls are sitting in the midst of a dense jungle, within 30 km from Ramnagar. A short walk of a few hundred metres is all that is needed to reach the waterfalls from the place where you leave your vehicle. This walk offers a visual treat of beautiful birds and insects. Visitors are requested not to litter around in these pristine places.

Barati Rau Fall

Corbett Fall

Kaladhungi

Kaladhungi (Local, '*Kala*': black+'*Dhungi*': stone or rock) is a small Bhabar town about 32 km from Ramnagar, on the Nainital road. It was chosen by Jim Corbett as his place of residence. Moreover, it is in the jungles near Kaladhungi that young Jim learnt the basics of jungle sense and hunting.
At Kaladhungi, visitors have several things to do:

Visit to Chhoti Haldwani Village: this small hamlet was established by Jim Corbett in 1915, close to his childhood winter resort 'Arundel'. One can spend a memorable couple of days in Corbett's village at the home-stays offered by the villagers, and enjoy various guided trails. In 1922, Jim Corbett built a new house in this village, which is presently the 'Jim Corbett Museum' housing many of his belongings.

Jim Corbett Museum

Nature trails: Kaladhungi lies next to the forested areas and is endowed with ample natural beauty. One can go for guided birding and nature trails around Kaladhungi.

Trail along the old water canal: the refreshing walk along the old canal will also take you to places such as the 'jungle studio' (where Jim Corbett used to make films), 'the farmyard', the *Panchakki* (water mill), the old Forest Rest House, the place where Arundel was located, and the old iron foundry (that is over a hundred years old). For various trails, visits, stay in Chhoti Haldwani village and other activities, visitors can get detailed information online.

Nainital Town

This beautiful historical town is about 70 km from Ramnagar via Kaladhungi and Khurpatal. One may also take an extra effort to visit places near Nainital such as Bhimtal (about 24 km from Nainital), Naukuchiatal (about 28 km from Nainital via Bhimtal) and Sattal (about 24 km from Nainital).

Nainital Town

Remains of 'Vairatpattan' near Dhikuli

There is an archaeological site near Dhikuli village (about 8 km from Ramnagar), which is considered a remnant of the ancient town of Vairatpattan. It was the capital of the old kingdom of *Govisana*. It is said that the *Pandavas* spent one year of *Agyatvasa* (incognito period) here. The remains of Vairatpattan—sculptured stones, pillars and platforms can be seen near the modern temple.

Garjia Temple

The temple is located at a distance of about 10 km from Ramnagar. It is situated on a slim hillock in the midst of Kosi river. Besides holy *darshan*, one can enjoy birdwatching and walking along the banks of the river.

Dhangarhi Gate Museum

It is a must-visit place situated at the Dhangarhi gate of Dhikala zone, about 14 km from Ramnagar. The museum showcases the history and models of habitats found in CTR, Light and Sound show, along with real looking stuffed bodies (taxidermy) and skeletons of wild animals such as Tiger, Leopard, deer, etc.

Himalaya View Point

It is located about 35 km from Ramnagar near Bhaunkhal. This high point provides a breathtaking panoramic view of snow-clad peaks of Greater Himalayas.

Remains of 'Vairatpattan'

PC:SC

Garjia Temple

A view of Greater Himalayas

PC:SC

Biography of Jim Corbett

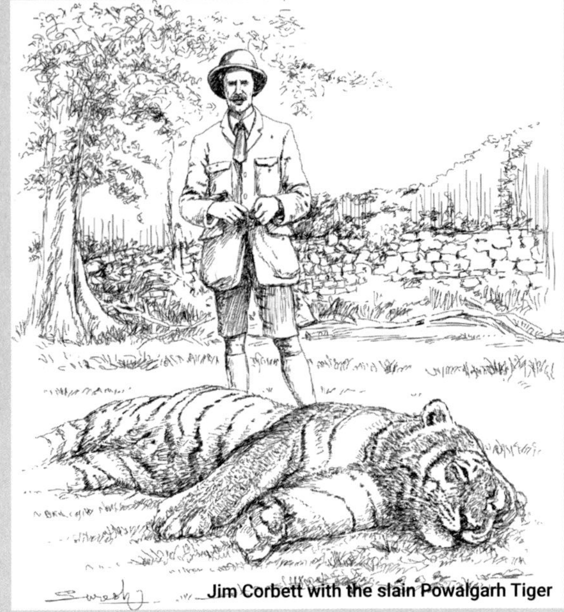
Jim Corbett with the slain Powalgarh Tiger

Lieutenant-Colonel Edward James Corbett, or 'Jim' to his near & dear ones and 'Carpet Sahib' to the local people, was born on 25 July 1875, in Nainital to Christopher William Corbett, a postmaster, and his wife Mary Jane. His mother, a courageous and determined lady had lost her first husband Charles James Doyle during the uprising in 1858 while he was confronting the Indian rebels.

Jim grew up in a family comprising several elder brothers, sisters and servants. The servants enlightened him on the local life and beliefs, and also taught him the local tongue. European conduct was taught to him by his mother and sister. The family used to spend the summers mostly in Nainital and move to their winter house 'Arundel' in Kaladhungi. Little Jim had an initial brush with wildlife in the immediate surroundings of his homes in Nainital and Kaladhungi. Unlike the present times, back then the forests in these areas were replete with various wild animals. Kaladhungi, located at the foothills, was covered with thick impenetrable forest; a stretch of forest behind Arundel was named 'Farmyard' by the Corbetts.

It is in the farmyard, that young Jim had his first experience of the forest, overcame the fear of wild animals, got the first glimpse of a Tiger and shot his last one in his seventies. His elder brother Tom, local friend Kunwar Singh and the animals themselves were his jungle teachers. Accompanying them for shoots, Jim learnt his basic lessons about the forest and the ethics involved in hunting animals. He could accurately read the forest signs and understand calls and behaviour of animals, could move without being noticed by animals and use cover while following his game. All these qualities made him an expert, who in the near future would venture into the jungles declared infested with man-eating tigers to eliminate them.

Jim received his formal education in Nainital and wanted to become an engineer. But the financial conditions of his family were not favourable to support his dream. At the age of eighteen, Jim joined 'Bengal and North-Western Railway' in Bihar, as a temporary fuel inspector, earning a wage of Rs 100. Soon he was transferred to a nearby place called Mokameh Ghat, with a salary hike of Rs 50 per month. At Mokameh, his responsibilities were challenging and tough, which he carried out successfully. Here he had to interact with a subset of people from India, who were working under him and with him. He loved, took care of and was generous to the people around him. The boy learnt management and leadership. When World War I broke out, Jim wanted to offer his services to the army but got rejected on the ground of his age which was then 38. He, however, got the opportunity to command. Captain Corbett recruited 500 Kumaoni people and sailed towards Europe after giving an assurance to Railways that the work would go on even in his absence.

After serving for over two decades, he quit his job and left Mokameh Ghat forever and returned to Nainital to take care of his previously acquired business. In 1915, Jim had purchased a village "Chhoti Haldwani" in Kaladhungi, close to Arundel. The village had ruined houses with a few dwellers, fields were covered with weeds and there was not much scope to grow anything. The fields were cleared of all the unwanted growth, irrigation was improved and stone fencing of the village was raised to protect the crops from wild pigs. Jim encouraged his villagers to grow new types of crops and provided improved varieties of seeds. Soon more people arrived in the village and the population grew. It is at one side of this village that Jim constructed his house in 1922. The bungalow is situated at the tri-junction of roads coming in from Haldwani, Ramnagar and Nainital.

In the later part of his life, Jim got motivated towards photography after looking at the photographs of tigers taken by F.W. Champion, a Forest Officer, known for photographing wildlife in India at night using tripwire. Jim decided to do this with cine camera in daylight. After some initial failures, he could capture interesting moments of a tiger's life.

After the death of his mother, Jim lived with his sister Margaret Winfred Corbett a.k.a. 'Maggie'. Both of them shared a deep bond since childhood; they lived together as great buddies till death.

In the year 1944, Jim was commissioned as a Lieutenant Colonel and trained troops in jungle-survival strategies. After India's Independence in 1947, the Corbetts (Jim and Maggie), facing the dilemma of their fate in free India, left for Kenya. He loved India and its people from the bottom of his heart and empathised with them.

Jim, a hunter, naturalist, conservationist and philanthrope, died a bachelor in 1955 due to a heart attack. He is buried in Nyeri, Kenya.

Jim was a hunter, but not a reckless killer. He hunted down those big cats in his surrounding areas, which were notorious for killing humans.

'I have not seen a case where a tiger has been deliberately cruel or where it has been bloodthirsty to the extent that it has killed, without provocation, more than it has needed to satisfy its hunger or the hunger of its cubs'

(From 'My Kumaon: Uncollected Writings')

When leaving India, Jim sold his Kaladhungi Bungalow to one Chiranji Lal. It was later acquired by the Forest Department to be converted into a museum, in the memory of Jim Corbett.

ACKNOWLEDGEMENTS

We are fortunate to have received the 'Foreword' to this book from Shri Samir Sinha, IFS, Principal Chief Conservator of Forests (Wildlife) & Chief Wildlife Warden, Uttarakhand.

Thank you Sir, for your suggestions which helped us refine the content.

Rajesh Chaudhary
I would like to express my deepest gratitude to Saket Badola Ji (Presently, Field Director, Rajaji Tiger Reserve) for sharing his experience about CTR, informative discussions and much required 'encouragement', at the initial stages of our work on this book.

The journey would have been incomplete without the invaluable and continued support from A.G. Ansari (Member Tiger Conservation Foundation, CTR)—a connoisseur on environs of CTR. My sincere gratitude to you, Ansari Ji, for educating me with the basics of the jungle and for being the one-stop solution to all my problems. You always lent a patient ear to my unending questions.

When Ansari Ji suggested the name of Manoj Sharma (Senior Naturalist at Jim's Jungle Retreat) for discussion on birds in CTR, I had no idea that he is another repository of knowledge on the natural world and I would add him to my list of friends. Thanks, Manoj Ji, for helping and listening to me throughout, even under unfavourable conditions.

I thank Shantanu for urging me to keep going and complete the project. You always gave me the much needed impetus. Thanks to my neighbour, Sandeep Deswal Ji, for your positive words. Gratitude to Abhinav Malhotra—without your help, we could not have been able to present to the readers several images taken in CTR landscape. Thanks to you and your friends for the invaluable contribution.

Shashi, I acknowledge your expertise in book designing software, which really made designing easier. Thanks, Priyamvada, for the crucial fine-tuning of the book's content.

I must acknowledge you too here, Vinesh! You have been much more than a travel companion and co-author. Only you know the ups and downs the project went through, and each time, it is your determination that gave me the strength not to give up! Hope to work together on many more....

Rajesh Chaudhary and Vinesh Kumar
Several people have enriched the content by providing images clicked in CTR: Mr Sanjay Chhimwal (Pugmark Safari)—we would title him a 'keen wildlife observer'. Thanks Sanjay for sharing your experience on butterflies of CTR, and keeping us updated with the latest happenings in the wild. We would also like to acknowledge image contributors, particularly: Abhinav Chaudhary, Deep Rajwar, Hardik Pala, Rajiv Bisht, Puran Singh, Sheri Chander, Sohail Madan, Surya Ramachandran, Sumantha Ghosh, Vivek Sharma, and all those who agreed to provide photographs on a single request.

Amit Thakur is thanked for his insights on readers' likes and preferences.

We are thankful to James Champion for providing the iconic image of the tiger taken by his grandfather, F.W. Champion.

Our sincere gratitude to several experts for their guidance in correct identification of flora and fauna: Abhinav Tyagi and Rupsee, Aparajita Datta, Devi Priyadarshini, Dr Shashank P.R., Dr K.A. Subramanian, Peter Smetacek, Pradip Krishen, Sanjay Sondhi, Surya Ramachandran, Vijay Dhasmana and Vivek Sharma. Thanks, Dr Varunendra Singh Rawat and Shilpi Chakravarty for improving the manuscript.

We must mention those who always encouraged us: Principal Acharya Narendra Dev College, Savithri madam, Amit sir, Arijit sir, Rajeshwari madam, Urmi madam, Jatin Lamba, Yash Mangla, Abhishek Mehta and others at our workplace.

We would like to thank Nizam for steering us through each nook and corner of CTR, and providing his extremely caring companionship. Babbu, Mahfuz, Shibu (Kotdwar), Mohan (Kaladhungi)—thanks for your services. We acknowledge all the guides accompanying us during safaris. Delectable food and hospitality will always remind us of Rawat Ji (Bijrani Jungle Camp). We acknowledge Nitesh, Mukesh and Durga Bhai Saheb for being our companions during trips to CTR.

Due to space constraints, we are unable to list the names of many others whose contributions were no less. The acknowledgements would be incomplete without mention of the untiring contribution of 'the lifeline of CTR'—the on-field CTR Staff, and entire Forest Department of Uttarakhand.

PHOTO CREDITS

All the photographs without credits are copyright of the authors. For other images, Photo Credit (PC) has been given alongside the images. The name of the photo-contributors, have been abbreviated as follows:

A.G. Ansari (AGA)
Abhinav Chaudhary (AC)
Abhinav Malhotra (AM)
Adesh Shivkar (AS)
Anil Goyal (AG)
Chandra Bhusan (CB)
Dattatreya MS (DMS)
Deep Rajwar (DR)
Devendra Singh (DS)
Gaurav Kataria (GK)
Gauri Rana (GR)
Hardik Pala (HP)
Kalyan Singh Sajwan (KSS)
Kshitij Sharma (KS)
Mandar Khadilkar (MK)
Manoj Negi (MN)
Manoj Sharma (MS)
Mukesh Verma (MV)
Naseer Ahmad (NA)
Niraj Pathak (NP)
Nizam (NZ)
Nabnita Sen (NS)
Peter Smetacek (PS)
Prashant Kumar (PK)
Rajesh Panwar (RP)
Rajiv Bisht Puran Singh (RBP)
Rakesh (RK)
Richard Baines (RB)
Saket Badola (SB)
Sanjay Chimwal (SC)
Saikat Banerjee (SBJ)
Sanjay Sondhi (SSD)
Savithri Singh (SS)
Shantanu Dey (SD)
Sheri Chander (SCH)
Shubham Mohanty (SHM)
Sohail Madan (SM)
Subramanya Chandrashekar (SCS)
Sumanta Pramanick (SP)
Surya Ramachandran (SR)
Varunendra. S. Rawat (VSR)
Vikramsinh Sodha (VSS)
Vishal Bhasin (VB)
Vivek Sharma (VS)

Ladybird Beetle
(*Harmonia* sp.)

Leaf Beetle
(*Zygogramma* sp.)

Blister Beetle
(*Mylabris pustulata*)

Of nearly 1.5 million animals catalogued so far, about 70 percent are insects. Coleoptera (Beetles) is the most abundant group of insects (about 0.32 million species). According to year 2006 estimate, in United States alone, the value of ecosystem services (p.24) provided by insects was around 57 billion dollars/year.

BIBLIOGRAPHY

Bees, Termites

Allsopp M. H. 2008, *PLOS ONE*. doi:10.1371/ journal.pone.0003128; **Avitabile S.C. et al.** 2015, *PLOS ONE*, doi:10.1371/journal.pone.0140114; **Ball D.W.** 2007, *Journal of Chemical Education*, 84: 1643; **Charles D. Michener**, 2007, The Johns Hopkins University Press, ISBN: 9780801885730; **Chittka L.** 2004, *PLoS Biol.*, 2(7): e216. https://doi.org/10.1371/journal.pbio.0020216; **Evans T. A. et al.** 2013, *Annu. Rev. Entomol.*, 58: 455; **Eyer M. et al.** 2016, *PLOS ONE*, doi:10.1371/journal.pone.0161059; **Goulson et al.** 2015, *Science*, 347: 1435; **Joan E. et al.** 2000, *Ecology*, 81, 2651; **Jouquet P. et al.** 2011, *Eur. J. Soil. Biol.*, 47: 215; **King H. et al.** 2015, *Proc. Natl. Acad. Sci. (USA)*, 112: 11589; **Klatt B. K. et al.** 2013, *Proc. R. Soc. B.*, http://dx.doi.org/10.1098/rspb.2013.2440; **Klei A. M.** 2007, *Proc. R. Soc. B*, 274: 303; **Kremen C.** 2002, *Proc. Natl. Acad. Sci. (USA)*, 99: 16812; **L. A. Lobry de Bruyn et al.** 1990, *Aust. J. Soil Res.*, 28: 55; **Li H. et al.** 2017, *Proc. Natl. Acad. Sci. (USA)*, 114: 4709; **Mark L. Winston,** 1991, Publisher: Harvard University Press, ISBN: 9780674074095; **Martin S. J. et al.** 2018, *Curr. Biol.*, doi: https://doi.org/10.1016/j.cub.2018.09.061; **Nicolson S.W. et al.** 2008, *Biol. Lett.*, 4: 299; **Nicolson S.W. et al**. 2007, Publisher: Springer, ISBN: 9781402059377.; **Oldroyd B. P. et al.** 2015, *Advances in Insect Physiology*, 49: 101; **Paar J. et al.** 2000, *Nature*, 406, 475; **Paul Eggleton.** 2011, Publisher: Springer, ISBN 9789048139767; **Pettis J. S. et al.** 2012, *PLOS ONE*, doi:10.1371/journal.pone.0070182; **Seeley T.D. et al.** 1982, *Ecol. Monogr.*, DOI: 10.2307/2937344; **Silva P. M. et al.** 2016, *Food Chemistry*, 196: 309; **Susan W. Nicolson et al.** (Eds), 2007, Publisher: Springer Science & Business Media, ISBN: 9781402059377; **Turner J. S.** 2005, *American Entomologist*, 51: 36; **Vanbergen A. J. et al.** 2013, *Front Ecol. Environ.*, doi:10.1890/120126.

Birds

Caro M.S. et al. 2016, *Nat. Commun.*, 10985 doi: 10.1038/ncomms10985(2016); **Chen F.C. et al.** 2015, *Annu. Rev. Anim. Biosci.*, 3: 169; **Berger C.** 2005, Publisher: Stackpole Books, ISBN: 9780811732130; **Dawson A.** 2008, *Phil. Trans. R. Soc. B*, 363: 1621, doi:10.1098/rstb.2007.0004; **Dhawan S.** 1991, *Sadhana*, 16: 275; **Field D. J. et al.** 2018, *Curr. Biol.*, 28, 1825; **Gil D. et al.** 2014, *Behavioral Ecology*, doi:10.1093/beheco/aru207; **Goodale E. et al.** 2006, *Animal Behaviour*, doi:10.1016/j.anbehav.2006.02.004; **Griffith S.C. et al.** 2002, *Molecular Ecology*, 11: 2195; **Grimmett R. et al.** 1999, Publisher: Oxford University Press, ISBN: 9780195649079; **Grimmett R. et al.** 2011, Publisher: Christopher Helm, ISBN: 978019807722; **Heppner F.H.** 1974, *Bird-Banding*, 45: 160; **Irby J. Lovette et al.** 2016, Publisher: Wiley-Blackwell, ISBN: 9781118291054; **Kempenaers B. et. al.** 2010, *Curr. Biol.*, 20: 1735; **Kennedy G.Y. et al.** 1976, *Comp. Biochem. Physiol. B.*, 55: 117; **Kilner R. M.** 2006, *Biol. Rev.*, 81: 383; **King D. I. et al.** 2001, *Forktail*, 17: 121; **Krys Kazmierczak,** 2017, Publisher: Bloomsbury Natural History; EPZ edition, ISBN: 9781472915184; **Michael L. Morrison et al.** 2018, Publisher: JHU press, ISBN: 9781421424712; **Miller M. W.** 2006, *The Condor*, 108: 130; **Oaks J. L. et al.** 2004, *Nature*, 427: 630; **Pena J. L. et al.** 2010, Institute for Laboratory Animal Research, 51: 338; **Pesendorfer M. B. et al.** 2016, *The Condor*, 118: 215, doi: 10.1650/CONDOR-15-125.1; **Praveen J. et al.** *Indian Birds*, 2016, 11:113; **Rattenborg N.C. et al.** 2016, *Nat. Commun.*, 7, DOI: 10.1038/ncomms12468; **Salim Ali,** 2002, Publisher: BNHS Oxford University Press, ISBN:0195665236; **Schulte P. et al.** 2010, *Science*, 327: 1214; **Sharma et al.** 2011, http://www.kolkatabirds.com/corbett.html; **Smith M.** 2009, *Nature*, https://doi.org/10.1038/457027a; **Sridhar H. et al.** 2009, *Animal Behaviour*, 78: 337; **Stevens M.** 2013, *Curr. Biol.*, 23, R909-R913; **Swan G.E. et al.** 2006, *Biol. Lett.*, 2: 279; **Van Doren M. B. et al.** 2017, *Proc. Natl. Acad. Sci. (USA)*, 114: 11177.

Butterflies

Bhakare, M. et al. 2018, Publisher: Milind Bhakare, ISBN: 9789353115425; **Brakefield P. M. et al.** 1999, *BioEssays*, 21: 391; **Brakefield P. M.** 1987, *Biol. J. Linnean. Soc. B*, 31: 175; **Chaudhary R. et al.** 2020, *Bionotes*, 22: 167; **De Bona S. et al.** 2015, *Proc. Biol. Sci. B*, 282, http://doi.org/10.1098/rspb.2015.0202; **Dellaglio D.D. et al.** 2016, *Ecological Entomology*, 41: 627; **Greeney H. et al.** 2012, *Invertebr. Surviv. J.*, 9: 7; **Hojo M. K. et al.** 2015, *Curr. Biol.*, 25: 2260; **Kehimkar I.** 2016, Publisher: BNHS, ISBN: 978-9384678012; **Krenn H.W.** 2010, *Annu. Rev. Entomol.*, 55: 307; **Lehnert et al.** 2016, *J. Morphol.*, 277: 167; **Lewis S. et al.** 2011, *Curr. Biol.*, 21: R644; **Nishida R.** 2005, *Chem. Senses*, 30 (suppl 1), i293; **Pierce N.E. et al.** 2002, *Annu. Rev. Entomol.*, 47: 733; **Renwick J.** 1994, *Ann. Rev. Entomol.*, 39: 377; **Sekimura T. et al.** 2017, Publisher: Springer, ISBN: 9789811049552; **Simpson et al.** 2011, *Curr. Biol.*, 21: R738; **Smetacek P.** 2000, *Resonance*, 5: 4; **Smetacek P.** 2001, *Resonance*, 6: 8; **Smetacek P.** 2016, John Beaufoy Publishing Ltd, ISBN: 9781909612792; **Sondhi S. et al.** 2018, Publisher: M/s Bishen Singh Mahendra Pal Singh; First edition, ISBN: 978-8121109185; **Varshney R. K. et al.** (Eds), 2015, Publisher: Butterfly Research Centre, Bhimtal & Indinov Publishing, New Delhi, ISBN: 9788192982649; **Vukusic P. et al.** 2003, *Nature*, 424: 852.

Mammals

A.J.T. Johnsingh et al. (Eds) Vol. 1 and 2. 2015, Publisher: University Press, ISBN- 9788173715907 and 9788173715891; **Baskaran N. et al.** 2011, *Gajah*, 35: 47; **Bates L. A. et al.** 2008, *Curr. Biol.*, 18: R544-R556; **Brandon-Jones D.** 2004, *Zoos' Print Journal*, 19:1552; **Dudley J.P.** 1993, *Gajah*, 10: 4; **Editor-Director,** 2010, Fauna of Uttarakhand, 18 (Part-I) 1-621 Publisher ZSI; **Editor-Director.** 2008, Fauna of Corbett Tiger Reserve, Conservation Area Series, 35: 1-230 ZSI Kolkata; **Garstang M.** 2009, *The Open Conservation Biology Journal*, 3: 1; **Gerhard Neuweiler.** 2000, Publisher: Oxford University Press, ISBN: 9780195099508; **Irsha N. et al.** 2015, *Animal Biology*, 65: 57; **Jhala Y. V. et al.** (Eds). 2019, National Tiger Conservation Authority, Government of India, New Delhi & Wildlife Institute of India, Dehradun,

TR No./2019/05; **Johnsingh A. J.T.** 2007, *Pachyderm*, 43: 108; **Johnsingh A. J. T. et al.** 2006, *Gajah*, 25: 61; **Jones G. et al.** 2006, *Trends Ecol. Evol.*, 21: 149; **Karanth U.K.** 2006, University Press, India, ISBN: 9788173715563; **Kundu et al.** 2018, *Indian Forester*, 144:992; **Kurtz F. et al.** 2006, Foundation Books, ISBN: 9788175963580; **Lamba B. S.** 1987, Fauna Of Corbett National Park, ZSI; **Lee P. F. et al.** 1993, *J. Mammal.*, 74: 982; **Mahmood T. et al.** 2015, *Mammalia*, DOI 10.1515/mammalia-2014-0153; **Menon V. et al.** Right of Passage: Elephant Corridors of India (2nd Edition), 2017, Conservation Reference Series No. 3, WTI, New Delhi; **Menon V.** 2014, Publisher: Hachette India, ISBN: 9789350097601; **Miththapala S. et al.** 1989, *J. Zool.*, 218: 527; **Napier J.R. et al.** 1967, Academic Press, SBN: 12-5138504; **O'Connell-Rodwell C.E.** 2007, *Physiology*, 22: 287; **Poole J.H.** 1999, *Animal Behaviour*, 58: 185; **Prater S.H.** 1997, Bombay Natural History Society, Oxford University Press, ISBN: 0195621697; **Raghuram H. et al.** 2011, in: Bats: Biology, Behavior and Conservation, Publisher: Nova Science, ISBN: 9781612097497; **Rasmussen L.E.L.** 2003, *Chem. Senses*, 28: 433; **Schaller G. B.** 1998, Natraj Publication, Dehradun, India. ISBN: 8185019746; **Shoshani J. et al.** 1982, *Mammalian Species*, 182: 1. https://doi.org/10.2307/3504045; **Shoshani J.** 2006, in: Biology, Medicine, and Surgery of Elephants, Blackwell Publisher 2006, ISBN: 9780813806761; **Sukumar R.** 2011, Publisher: Marg Publications, ISBN: 9789380581101; **Tak P. G. et al.** 1984, Zoological Survey of India; **Vidya T.N.C. et al.** 2005, *Curr. Sci.*, 89: 1200; **Walker's** The carnivores of the world, 2005, Johns Hopkins University Press, ISBN: 9780801880339; **Wiliams A.C.** 2008, *J. Bombay Nat. Hist. Soc.*, 105: 145; **Xu X. et al.** 2013, *Curr. Biol.*, 23: 1031.

Reptiles, Amphibians, Fishes

Alirol E. et al. 2010, *PLOS Neglected Tropical Disease*, https://doi.org/10.1371/journal.pntd.0000603; **Bahuguna et al.** 2017, *Flora and Fauna*; 23: 391; **Captain A. et al.** 2016, ISBN: 9789385724237; **Colbert E.H.** 2001, 5 edition, Publisher: Wiley-Liss, ISBN: 9780471384618; **Cordero G. A.** 2017, *Curr. Biol.*, 27: R163; **Das I.** 2008, Om Books International, ISBN: 8187108355; **Das I.** 2017, Publisher: JB Publishing, ISBN: 9781909612815; **Duellman W. E.** 1994, Publisher: Johns Hopkins University Press, ISBN: 9780801847806; **Fang J.** 2010, *Nature*, doi:10.1038/news.2010.122; **Grigg G.** 2015, Publisher: Csiro Publishing, ISBN: 9781486300679; **Haneef F.** 1999, A WWF-India field guide to Freshwater Turtles and Tortoises of India, Publisher: TRAFFIC-India/WWF-India; **J. A. Johnson** (Fish), 2012, Publisher: Uttarakhand Forest Department and Bishen Singh Mahendra Pal Singh, ISBN: 9788121108508; **J.C. Daniel,** 2002, BNHS-Oxford University Press, ISBN: 0195660994; **Jaden Howard,** 2019, Publisher: Scientific e-Resources, ISBN: 9781839474484; **Johnsingh A.J.T. et al.** 2006, *Cheetah*, 43: 9; **Khaire N.** 2015, Publisher: Jyotsna Prakashan, ISBN: 9788179253892; **Krishna N.** 2010, Publisher; Pienguin Books India, ISBN: 9780143066194; **Lillywhite H. B.** 2014, Publisher: OUP, USA, ISBN: 9780195380378.; **Nautyal P.** 2014, *Proc. Natl. Acad. Sci., India, Sect. B Biol. Sci.*, 84: 215; **Peter Uetz.** http://www.reptile-database.org/db-info/SpeciesStat.html; **Vasudevan K et al.** 2010, Amphibians and Reptiles of Uttarakhand, India, Publisher: Wildlife Institute of India Dehradun, Uttarakhand.

Plants

C. Sudhakar Reddy et al. 2008, Publisher: National Biological Information Infrastructure, US Geological Survey, USA; **Dominy J. N. et al.** 2002, *Oikos*, 98: 163; **Dudareva N et al.** 2006, CRC Press, ISBN: 9781420004007; **Fürstenberg-Hägg J. et al.** 2013, *Int. J .Mol. Sci.*, 14: 10242; **Gould et al.** 2004, *J. Biomed. Biotechnol.*, 5: 314; **Gurevitch J. et al.** 2006, Publisher: Sinauer Associates, ISBN: 9780878932948; **Kanjilal U.N.** 2004, Publisher: Natraj, ISBN: 8181580060; **Krishen P.** 2014, Publisher: Penguin India, ISBN: 9780143420743; **Lim P.O. et al.** 2007, *Annu. Rev. Plant. Biol.*, 58: 115; **Pant P. C. et al.** 1986, Flora of Corbett National Park, Botanical Survey of India, Publisher: The Director BSI, Howrah; **Rathore J. S.** 1972, *Economic Botany*, 26: 333; **Royal Botanic Gardens, Kew,** 2016, ISBN: 9781842466285; **Willmer P.** 2011, publisher: Princeton University Press, ISBN: 9780691128610.

Dragonflies and Damselflies, Spiders

Subramanian K. A. 2009, Publisher: Vigyan Prasar, ISBN: 9788174801920; **Dayakrishna et al.** 2015, *Journal of Entomology and Zoology Studies*, 3: 467; **Sebastian P. A. et al.** 2009, Publisher: Universities Press (India) Pvt. Ltd, ISBN: 9788173716416.

Miscellaneous

Badola R. et al. 2010, *The Environmentalist*, doi 10.1007/s10669-010-9278-5; **Ceballos G. et al.** 2017, *Proc. Natl. Acad. Sci. (USA)*, https://doi.org/10.1073/pnas.1704949114; **Champion F.W.** 2012, Rainfed Books, Chennai, ISBN: 9788192326900; **Champion H.G. et al.** 2005, Publisher: Natraj Publishers, Dehradun, ISBN: 8181580613; **Dangwal D. D.** 2005, *Conservation and Society*, 3: 110; **Handa O. C.** 2002, Indus Publishing, ISBN: 9788173871344; **Mittal A. K.** 1986, Publisher: Mittal Publication; **Mora C. et al.** 2011, *PLoS Biol.* doi:10.1371/journal.pbio.1001127; **Nanda A.C.** 2013, *J. Palaeontol. Soc. India*, 58: 75; **Nevill H. R.** 2016 (reprint), Natraj Publisher, ISBN:9788181582683; **Pandey B. D.** 2011, Publisher: Shyam Prakashan, Almora Book Depot, Uttarakhand ISBN: 819000865X; **Pimm S. L. et al.** 2000, *Nature*, 403, 843-845; **Rawat J.S.** 2014, Workshop on rejuvenation of non-glacial rain- fed rivers of the Kumaun region, http://coenrdmsalmora.org/downloads/Regeneration.pdf; **Semwal R. L.** 2005, The Terai Arc Landscape in India, Securing Protected Areas in the Face of Global Change, WWF-India, New Delhi; **Strahorn E. A. et al.** 2009, Publisher: Peter Lang, ISBN: 9781433105807; **Valdiya K. S.** 2017, Publisher Elsevier, ISBN: 9780444639721; **Valdiya K.S.** 2010, Publisher Macmillan, ISBN: 9780230328334; **Walton H.G.** 2016 (reprint), Natraj Publisher, ISBN: 9788181582669; **Wetlands of Uttarakhand,** 2012, Report jointly published by the Uttarakhand Forest Department and WWF India.

INDEX

My Field Notes

Corbett Ti

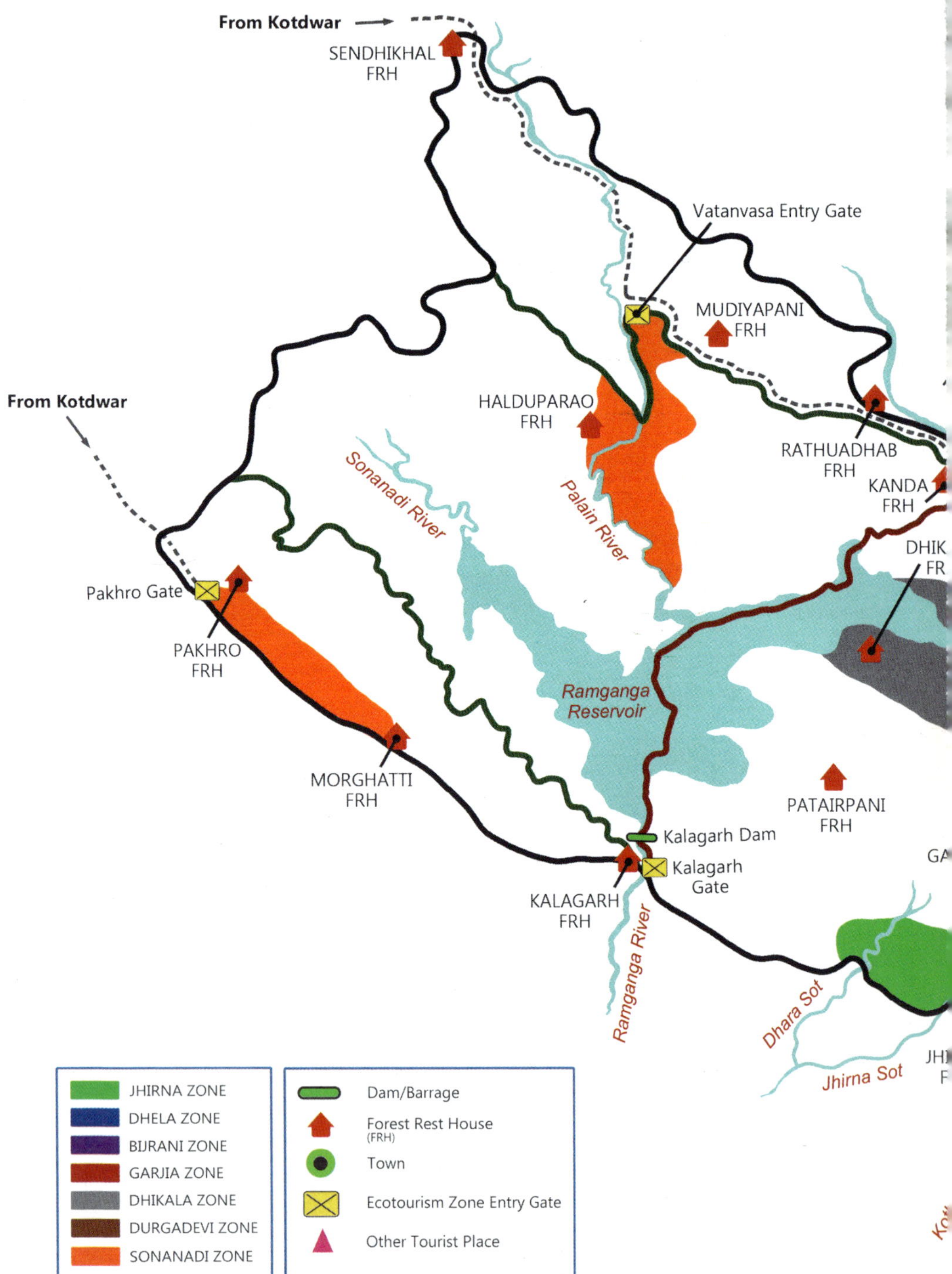

Map not to scale. The boundaries, and the expanse of components of landscape and ecotourism zones are only

Wildlife In and Around Corbett Tiger Reserve, Publisher Niyogi Books; Map © Rajesh Chaudhary & Vinesh Kumar

ger Reserve

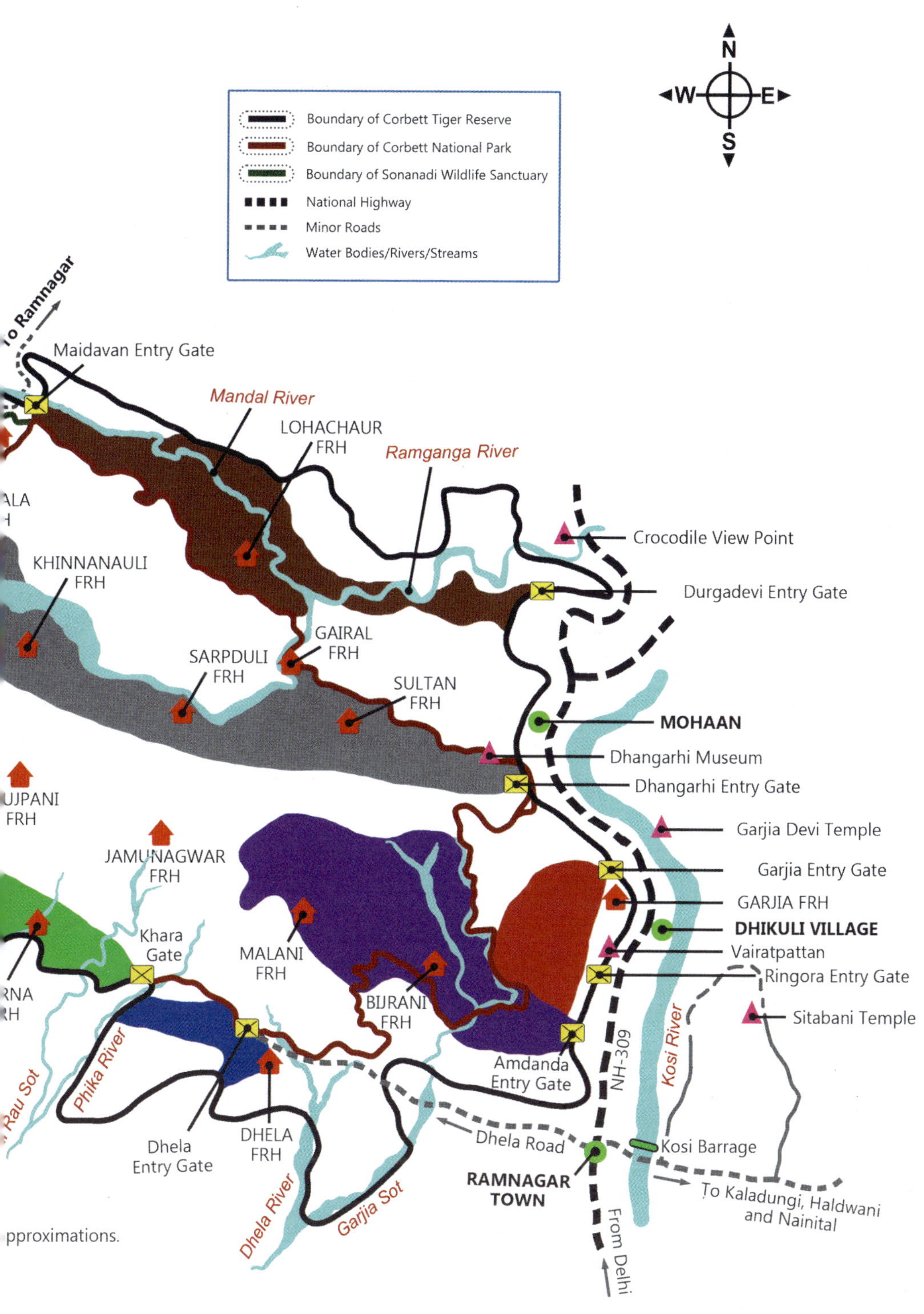

pproximations.